International Series in Operations Research & Management Science

Series Editor:
Fredrick S. Hillier
Stanford University

Special Editorial Consultant:
Camille C. Price
Stephen F. Austin State University

For further volumes:
http://www.springer.com/series/6161

Evangelos Grigoroudis • Yannis Siskos

Customer Satisfaction Evaluation

Methods for Measuring and Implementing Service Quality

 Springer

Evangelos Grigoroudis
Technical University of Crete
Dept. of Production Engineering & Management
University Campus, Kounoupidiana
73100 Chania, Greece
vangelis@ergasya.tuc.gr

Yannis Siskos
University of Piraeus
Dept. of Informatics
80, Karaoli & Dimitriou str.
18534 Pireaus, Greece
ysiskos@unipi.gr

ISSN 0884-8289
ISBN 978-1-4419-1639-6   e-ISBN 978-1-4419-1640-2
DOI 10.1007/978-1-4419-1640-2
Springer New York Dordrecht Heidelberg London

Library of Congress Control Number: 2009939837

Printed on acid-free paper

Springer is part of Springer Science+Business Media (www.springer.com)

Preface

The customer orientation philosophy of modern business organizations and the implementation of the main principles of continuous improvement, justifies the importance of evaluating and analyzing customer satisfaction. In fact, customer satisfaction is considered today as a baseline standard of performance and a possible standard of excellence for any business organization.

Extensive research has defined several alternative approaches, which examine the customer satisfaction evaluation problem from very different perspectives. These approaches include simple quantitative tools, statistical and data analysis techniques, consumer behavioral models, etc. and adopt the following main principles:

- The data of the problem are based on the customers' judgments and are directly collected from them.
- This is a multivariate evaluation problem given that customer's overall satisfaction depends on a set of variables representing product/service characteristic dimensions.
- Usually, an additive formula is used in order to aggregate partial evaluations in an overall satisfaction measure.

Many of the aforementioned approaches do not consider the qualitative form of customers' judgments, although this information constitutes the main satisfaction input data. Furthermore, in several cases, the measurements are not sufficient enough to analyze in detail customer satisfaction because models' results are mainly focused on a simple descriptive analysis.

Taking into account all the above, the aim of this book is to provide a comprehensive discussion of the customer satisfaction evaluation problem, by presenting an overview of the existing methodologies, as well as the development and implementation of an original multicriteria method in the context of this particular problem. The main objective of the proposed multicriteria method is the development of a model able to evaluate the level of customer satisfaction both globally and partially for each of the characteristics/attributes of the offered product/service. Moreover, the method aims at providing an integrated set of results capable to analyze customer needs and expectations and to justify their satisfaction level. Finally, the development of a decision support tool emphasizing the understanding and applicability of the results is also examined.

The book is organized in nine chapters aiming to comprehensively present the alternative methodological approaches and the different perspectives of the customer satisfaction evaluation problem.

Chapter 1 is devoted to the presentation of the customer satisfaction measurement problem. Based on the literature, the definitions of "satisfaction" and "customer" are given in detail, while a short historical review and reporting of relevant efforts are discussed.

The problem of measuring customer satisfaction is approached by several different scientific fields. Chapter 2 describes such alternative methodologies, including the most important quantitative techniques, as well as the related consumer behavioral models.

Chapter 3 presents additional quality-based approaches that may be used in the satisfaction measurement and analysis problem. In this context, service quality models are presented and the linkage between customer/employee satisfaction and Total Quality Management is discussed.

Chapter 4 is devoted to the development of the multicriteria method MUSA (MUlticriteria Satisfaction Analysis) aiming at measuring and analyzing customer satisfaction. The MUSA method is a preference disaggregation model following the principles of ordinal regression analysis (inference procedure). The results of the method are able to provide a decision-aid tool and assess an integrated benchmarking system.

Several extensions of the MUSA method are discussed in Chapter 5. These include different formulations of value functions, multiple satisfaction criteria levels, additional constraints, different types of input data, and alternative optimality criteria. Moreover the problem of modeling preference on criteria importance is discussed, and a satisfaction barometer model is described.

Chapter 6 refers to advanced topics on the MUSA method. In this context, computational issues of the method and the selection of appropriate values of model parameters are discussed, while several reliability indicators are proposed. In addition, an experimental simulation process is used in order to compare alternative satisfaction measurement methods.

Chapter 7 is devoted to customer satisfaction surveys and barometers. More specifically, several issues for designing and conducting satisfaction surveys are discussed and the most important national customer satisfaction barometers are presented.

The main aim of Chapter 8 is to present applications of the MUSA method in real-world customer satisfaction surveys. These applications refer to business organizations of several types and demonstrate the implementation process of the method.

Finally, Chapter 9 presents different information technology approaches related to customer satisfaction. These approaches not only focus on measuring and analyzing customer satisfaction, but also refer to the management of relations/transactions between companies and customers. In this context several customer service information systems are discussed, along with the MUSA software.

As authors of this book, we would like to thank the management of the business organizations that assigned us the presented customer satisfaction measurement projects, and kindly permitted the publication of parts of these studies. Moreover, we thank the researchers Andreas Samaras and Yannis Politis for their help in several parts of the book, as well as all the members of the Decision Support Systems Design and Development Laboratory (ERGASYA) of Technical University of Crete, Greece. Especially, we would like to thank Dr. Christina Diakaki for her valuable comments and edits of the whole manuscript; without her help and encouragement, this book may have not been achieved. Finally, we would like to extend our sincere thanks to Springer publishing editor, Fred S. Hillier, for his patience and encouragement during the preparation of this book.

Evangelos Grigoroudis
Yannis Siskos

Contents

Chapter 1

Introduction

1.1 Importance of Customer Satisfaction

Customer satisfaction measurement is one of the most important issues concerning business organizations of all types, which is justified by the customer-orientation philosophy and the main principles of continuous improvement of modern enterprises. In fact, measurement constitutes one of the five main functions of the management science allowing for the understanding, the analysis, and the improvement (Massnick, 1997). As it is rumored, Lord Kelvin (19th century) said that *"...if you cannot measure something, you cannot understand it..."*

For these reasons, customer satisfaction should be measured and translated into a number of measurable parameters. In the recent decades, the importance of customer satisfaction for business organizations has been increased. Thus, customer satisfaction measurement is now considered as the most reliable feedback, taking into account that it provides in an effective, direct, meaningful and objective way the customers' preferences and expectations. In this way, customer satisfaction is a baseline standard of performance and a possible standard of excellence for any business organization (Gerson, 1993).

To reinforce customer orientation on a day-to-day basis, a growing number of companies choose customer satisfaction as their main performance indicator. It is almost impossible, however, to keep an entire company permanently motivated by a notion as abstract and intangible as customer satisfaction. Therefore, customer satisfaction must be translated into a number of measurable parameters directly linked to people's job, i.e. factors that people can understand and influence (Deschamps and Nayak, 1995). Moreover, customer satisfaction measurement provides a sense of achievement and accomplishment for all employees involved in any stage of the customer service process. In this way, satisfaction measurement motivates people to perform and achieve higher levels of productivity (Wild, 1980; Hill, 1996).

E. Grigoroudis and Y. Siskos, *Customer Satisfaction Evaluation*, International Series in Operations Research & Management Science 139, DOI 10.1007/978-1-4419-1640-2_1, © Springer Science + Business Media, LLC 2010

The importance of customer satisfaction measurement is also justified by the fact that the field of Consumer Behavioral Analysis has centered its interest in the post-purchase customer behavior (Kotler, 1994; Hill, 1996). More specifically, research is focused on the evaluation of the usage results of a product/service, and the way that this usage affects customer's post-purchase actions, as displayed in Figure 1.1.

Generally, the main reasons for measuring customer satisfaction are summarized in the following (Motorola, 1995; Dutka, 1995):

- Customer satisfaction constitutes the most reliable market information. This way, a business organization is able to evaluate its current position against competition, and accordingly design its future plans.
- A large number of customers avoid expressing their complaints or their dissatisfaction from the product or service provided, either due to a particular attitude or because they are not sure that the company will perform any corrective action (Figure 1.2).
- Customer satisfaction measurement is able to identify potential market opportunities.
- The main principles of continuous improvement require the development of a specific customer satisfaction measurement process. This way, any improvement action is based on standards that take into account customer expectations and needs.
- Customer satisfaction measurement may help business organizations to understand customer behavior, and particularly to identify and analyze customer expectations, needs, and desires.
- The application of a customer satisfaction measurement program (see section 1.4) may reveal potential differences in the service quality perceptions between the customer and the management of the business organization.

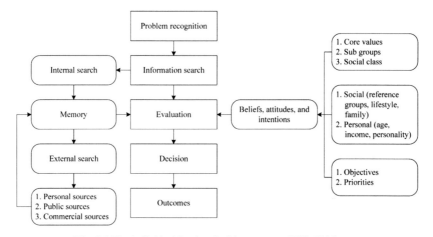

Fig. 1.1 The individual buying decision process (Hill, 1996)

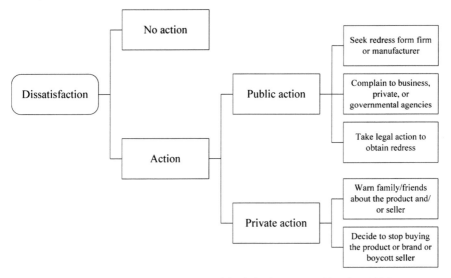

Fig. 1.2 Dissatisfied customers complaint behavior (Day and Landon, 1977)

Market-driven business organizations place special emphasis on customer satisfaction. Edosomwan (1993) defines these organizations as follows:

"...A customer- and market-driven enterprise is one that is committed to providing excellent quality and competitive products and services to satisfy the needs and wants of customers in a well-defined market segment...Such an enterprise analyzes its market capabilities and provides products and services to satisfy market needs. It considers its customers as the final judges who determine product and service satisfaction level, delivery, price, and performance..."

The most important advantages of a customer satisfaction measurement survey may be summarized in the following (Dutka, 1995; Naumann and Giel, 1995; Czarnecki, 1999):

- Customer satisfaction measurement programs improve the communication with the total clientele, provided that they constitute continuous and systematic efforts of the business organization.
- Business organizations may examine whether the provided services fulfill customer expectations. Furthermore, it is possible to examine whether new actions, efforts, and programs have any impact on the organizations' clientele.
- The critical satisfaction dimensions that should be improved are identified, as well as the ways through which this improvement may be achieved.
- The most important strengths and weakness of the business organization against competition are determined, based on customer perceptions and judgments.
- The personnel of the business organization is motivated to increase its productivity given that all improvement efforts, regarding the offered services, are evaluated by the customers themselves.

Finally, it should be mentioned that although customer satisfaction is a necessary but not a sufficient condition for the financial viability, several researches have shown that there is a significant correlation among satisfaction level, customer loyalty, and profitability (Dutka, 1995; Naumann and Giel, 1995).

1.2 Main Definitions

1.2.1 Definition of Satisfaction

The different aspects of satisfaction make definition difficult, mainly because it is related to the complete consumption experience (Oliver, 1997):

- Satisfaction with events that happen during consumption.
- Satisfaction with final outcome.
- Satisfaction with level of satisfaction received.

In this context, satisfaction is viewed in terms of singular events leading to up to a consumption outcome (collective impression of these events), and finally to the entire experience judgment.

A comprehensive definition of customer satisfaction in terms of pleasurable fulfillment is given by Oliver (1997):

> *"...Satisfaction is the consumer's fulfillment response. It is a judgment that a product or service feature, or the product or service itself, provided (or is providing) a pleasurable level of consumption-related fulfillment, including levels of under- or overfulfillment..."*

According to an exhaustive review of Yi (1991), customer satisfaction may be defined in two basic ways: either as an outcome, or as a process (Table 1.1):

1. The first approach defines satisfaction as a final situation or as an end-state resulting from the consumption experience.
2. The second approach emphasizes the perceptual, evaluative and psychological process that contributes to satisfaction.

Although different approaches of defining customer satisfaction may be found in the literature, the most popular of them are based on the fulfillment of customer expectations. As, Gerson (1993), Hill (1996), Oliver (1997), and Vavra (1997), mention, satisfaction is a standard of how the offered "total" product or service fulfils customer expectations.

The criticism of the previous approach is focused on the cases where the comparison with the expectations, especially when they are not too high, may create inconsistencies in the analysis of customer behavior (Dutka, 1995). Moreover, as mentioned by Zifko-Baliga (1998), satisfaction according to this particular approach is a standard for how well the customers can predict the performance level at which a product or a service will satisfy them.

Table 1.1 Definitions of customer satisfaction (Yi, 1991)

Approach	Definition	Author
Satisfaction as an outcome	The buyer's cognitive state of being adequately or inadequately rewarded for the sacrifices he has undergone	Howard and Sheth (1969)
	An emotional response to the experience provided by, (or associated with) particular products or services purchased, retail outlets, or even molar patterns of behavior, as well as the overall marketplace	Westbrook and Reilly (1983)
	An outcome of purchase and use resulting from the buyer's comparison of the rewards and the costs of the purchase in relation to the anticipated consequences	Churchill and Suprenant (1982)
Satisfaction as a process	An evaluation rendered that the experience was at least as good as it was supposed to be	Hunt (1977)
	An evaluation that the chosen alternative is consistent with prior beliefs with respect to that alternative	Engel and Blackwell (1982)
	The consumer's response to the evaluation of the perceived discrepancy between prior expectations and the actual performance of the product as perceived after its consumption	Tse and Wilton (1988)

Several researchers (Parasuraman et al., 1985, 1988; Hill, 1996) place emphasis on the fact that customer satisfaction is a perception, and thus, this particular information is not readily available, but instead additional effort is required in order to collect, measure, analyze, and explain it.

Moreover, customer perceptions play a key role in the theory of "service gaps", which tries to study the differences between expectations and experience. As shown in Figure 1.3, the overall gap that results in a dissatisfied customer is caused by one (or more) of the following earlier gaps (Hill, 1996):

1. *Promotional gap*: the inability of the business organization to fulfill expectations created in the minds of customers mainly by marketing communications.
2. *Understanding gap*: the gap occurred due to the inaccurate understanding of customer needs and priorities by the managers of the organization.
3. *Procedural gap*: the gap occurred due to the translation of customer expectations into appropriate operating procedures and systems with the business organization.
4. *Behavioral gap*: the difference between customer expectations and organization's performance, focusing on how procedures adequately cover service delivery requirements.
5. *Perception gap*: the difference between customer performance perceptions and reality.

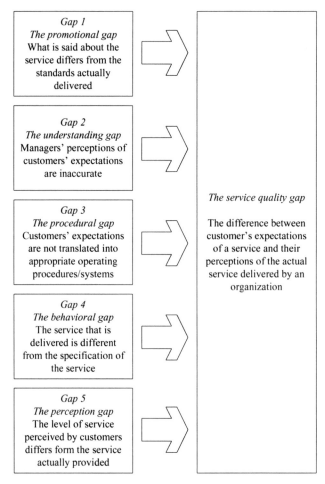

Fig. 1.3 Service gaps (Hill, 1996)

The "service gaps" theory is able to explain different service quality perceptions between the customer and it is the core concept of the Servqual model (see section 3.2.2).

Further to expectations, several alternative comparison standards have been proposed for defining customer satisfaction:

- Spreng and Olshavsky (1992) argue that customer desires instead of expectations should be used when comparing the performance of a product or a service.
- The research study of Churchill and Suprenant (1982) shows that the performance of the partial characteristics of a product is a very important customer satisfaction index, especially in the case of durable goods.
- Similarly, Woodruff et al. (1991) claim that the comparison should be based on particular performance standards instead of customer expectations. Their ap-

proach focuses on the formulation of performance standards, based on the experience from the use (experience-based norms) of not only the particular product, but also other competitive products. This way, the examined product does not necessarily constitutes a reference standard for the comparison process.

Based on the aforementioned definitions, it is clear that different viewpoints may emphasize different aspects of customer satisfaction. Additionally, other conceptual distinctions at different vertical (micro/individual and macro/aggregate dimension) and horizontal (antecedents and consequences) levels may be reveal the complexity of the meaning of satisfaction, as shown in Table 1.2 (Oliver, 1997).

Consequently, alternative definitions of customer satisfaction vary with regard to the object focus and the level of specificity. These levels include mainly the following (Yi, 1991):

- Satisfaction with a product or service.
- Satisfaction with a purchase decision experience.
- Satisfaction with a performance attribute.
- Satisfaction from a consumption-use experience.
- Satisfaction with a department or store of the business organization.
- Satisfaction with a pre-purchasing experience.

Table 1.2 Vertical and horizontal views of satisfaction (Oliver, 1997)

Viewpoint	Antecedents	Core concept	Consequences
Individual (single transaction)	Performance or service encounter	Transaction-specific satisfaction	Complimenting Complaining Word of mouth
Individual (time-accumulated)	Accumulated performance history	Summary classification	Attitude Loyalty Switching
Firm's customers in the aggregate	Reputation Product quality Promotion	Average satisfaction Repurchase rates Competitive ranking	Share Profits
Industry or commercial sector	Average quality Monopoly power	Consumer sentiment	Regulation Taxation
Society	Product or service variety Average quality	Psychological well-being	Tranquility Productivity Social progress Alienation Consumerism

Finally, it should be mentioned that in several cases the definition of customer satisfaction is examined in parallel to other related terms like quality, customer value, service, etc. (Burns and Woodruff, 1991; Sheth et al., 1991; Gerson, 1993; Edosomwan, 1993; Woodruff et al., 1993; Dutka, 1995; Naumann, 1995;

Naumann and Giel, 1995; Woodruff and Gardial, 1996; Massnick, 1997; Zifko-Baliga, 1998).

1.2.2 Identification of Customers

The process of explicitly defining the set of customers in a business organization may be proven quite difficult, given the size of this set and the existence of multiple segments and behavioral groups. In many cases also, the lack of data relative to the set of customers (e.g. a customer database) makes this particular process an even more difficult task. For this reason, when the term "customer" is used, it is necessary to clarify whether it refers to current, past, potential, internal or external customers.

According to the classic approach, a customer is the person who buys a product or a service offered by a business organization, as the purchase process of Figure 1.1 displays (see for example Engel et al., 1978; Engel and Blackwell, 1982). Similarly, potential customers may be considered as the persons that have:

- the need or desire to purchase the product or the service,
- the motive to proceed to this particular purchase,
- the necessary financial resources (cash or credit), and
- the ability to access the locations where the products or the services are made available.

Despite the simplicity of the aforementioned definition, there are several critical issues that need clarification:

- In many cases, the purchaser and the user of a product or a service may be different. Additionally, there might be several individuals involved in the buying purchasing process, having different roles and contributing unevenly in the final purchase decision. Thus, the problem of which of them should be included in a satisfaction measurement program arises.
- Usually, customer should be defined as an entity, rather as a single person, particularly in business-to-business research. However, in this case, it is also difficult to define the term "customer", since no single entities (individuals, organization's departments) decide, buy, and use the product or the service. For example, executive management will often have different requirements and expectations from those of technical users, while corporate officers may have a different view of satisfaction than that of branch plants or operational units (Dutka, 1995).
- In several cases, it is difficult to distinguish current from past customers. For example, is a customer who was making regular monthly purchases for five years and then stopped three months ago a past customer? Is the purchaser of a long-lasting durable good a current customer even if a new purchase has not been made during the last five years? As it is clear, currency depends mainly on the purchase cycle or frequency in the industry examined, and thus, it is neces-

sary for business organizations to establish their own definition of "current customer" probably with the help of an appropriate customer database (Vavra, 2002). Moreover, it is possible to focus on particular segments of current customers, like high value, special interest or vocal/conspicuous customers.

The quality approach offers a different perspective on the definition of customer, since quality is meeting the customer needs in a way that exceeds the customer expectations. In this approach, a customer is the person that assesses the quality of the offered products and services. Consequently, these persons have the ability to express their dissatisfaction, in case that their expectations are not fulfilled (Czarnecki, 1999; Gerson, 1993; Dutka, 1995).

A process-oriented approach may also provide an alternative definition of customer. As Edosomwan (1993) emphasizes, the customer is the person or group that receives the work output. According to this particular definition, the customers may be classified based on the following categories:

1. *Self-unit customers*: All individuals are self-unit customers of themselves. Self-inspection, a disciplined attitude, and a desire for excellence should be a way of life for everyone.
2. *Internal customers*: The personnel of an organization constitutes the set of internal customers, who receive output from one or more internal process owners, or even process outputs performed by suppliers.
3. *External customers*: This category refers to the buyers or users of the final products and services of the business organization.

It should be mentioned that the relation between internal and external customer satisfaction is very strong and important as discussed in section 3.3.

1.3 Evolution of Customers Satisfaction Measurment

The measurement of customer satisfaction has emerged within the field of Total Quality Management (TQM), although it has also been explored by several researchers and theorists from other scientific areas (e.g. marketing). The TQM School formalizes customer satisfaction as a quality component, as appearing in the major quality awards (e.g. Malcolm Baldrige National Quality Award), emphasizing on the exploitation of customer satisfaction data within a business organization (i.e. design and develop products and services that meet customer expectations). On the other hand, the Marketing School explores customer satisfaction from a social-psychological perspective, studying how customer satisfaction is formed and which is the impact on future purchase behavior (Vavra, 1997).

As it is accepted nowadays, the increasing interest in customer satisfaction is closely related to the quality revolution that started in the early 1980s. The TQM researchers realized that the quality improvement of products and services could not only rely on internal metrics and standards of the business organizations, but it had also to be combined with customer information and feedback (Vavra, 1997). Moreover, the quality should be manifested in ways relevant and perceptible to the total set of customers.

Deming (1993) mentions that the customer satisfaction surveys can record the pulse of a company's clientele, given that they analyze and explain customer requirements, while at the same time they can be integrated into the total communication procedure between the business organization and its customers. Deming (1993) and Juran (1988, 1993) consider this communication process with customers as the prime prerequisite for the design, development and improvement of the quality of products and services.

While Deming and Juran focus on describing the necessary information that is collected in customers satisfaction surveys (i.e. customer input and feedback), other researchers from the TQM School emphasize on how a business organization should exploit this information by taking specific improvement actions. The Quality Function Deployment method is a representative example of this particular approach (Hauser and Clausing, 1988).

Generally, the TQM School studies the problem of customer satisfaction measurement from the product or service quality viewpoint (Bounds et al., 1994; Business Week Guide, 1994; Noori and Radford, 1995). In particular, customer satisfaction is considered as a necessary condition for offering high quality products or services. In this context, AT&T in the early 1970s was the first company to introduce a market survey different from these that the other companies used to conduct. This survey was called SAM (Satisfaction Attitude Measurement) and it was a satisfaction mail survey addressed only to customers that had used the technical assistance services of AT&T. Given the success of this effort, it was decided to expand the market survey to the total set of organization's customers, taking the form of a telephone survey (it is now called TELSAM), so as to be integrated into the permanent customer satisfaction measurement program of AT&T.

Regarding the Marketing School, customer satisfaction measurement was initially considered, during 1960-1980, as a problem of consumer behavioral analysis. The most important efforts from this perspective were the following (Vavra, 1997):

1. *Cardozo*: The Cardozo model (1965) is one of the first research efforts in the area of customer satisfaction measurement. This approach is based on some of the major theories of social psychology, aiming at understanding the impact of satisfaction to future customer purchase behavior. In particular, the model combines Helson's "contrast effect" and the Festinger's theory of cognitive dissonance. The adaptation level theory provides a conceptual framework for understanding how consumers form product quality expectations, suggesting that the perceptual judgment of a person to incoming information depends on the individual's current expectation level. The work of Helson (1964) on adaptation level theory, proposes that stimuli, resulting in a displacement of the adaptation level may also change an individual's perception of other information

in the series (i.e. a "contrast effect"). On the other hand, the theory of cognitive dissonance can account for the psychological consequences of disconfirmed expectations, since it proposes that people have a motivational drive to reduce dissonance by changing (or justifying/ rationalizing) their attitudes, beliefs, and behaviors (Festinger, 1957).

2. *Howard and Sheth*: The work of Howard and Sheth (1969) is based on the development of a process model of satisfaction, studied in parallel with their work on consumers' pre-purchase and post-purchase reconciliation of information and feedback. The model is an attempt to pull together a disparate set of variables, which are divided into four main components: (1) inputs, which stimulate the purchasing process (e.g. product-related factors like price, quality, and availability, symbolic factors, i.e. images that stem from the mass media and sales people, and social factors, like family, reference groups, and social class), (2) perceptual constructs, which explain the consumer's cognitive activity in terms of information processing, (3) learning constructs, which represent the results of information itself, and (4) outputs, which include not only the purchase itself but also the implications for perception and learning.

3. *Oliver*: One of the earliest and most cited works regarding customer satisfaction measurement is the model of Oliver (1977, 1980, 1981). Using Helson's adaption theory (Helson, 1964), Oliver suggests that expectations fix a standard of performance, offering a frame of reference for customer judgments. Thus, satisfaction may be viewed as a function of the baseline effect of expectations, modified by perceived disconfirmation (Vavra, 1997). Oliver's approach is commonly referred to as the expectancy disconfirmation theory. Although several variants of the model have been proposed, Oliver's approach establishes a process describing how satisfaction is produced in this expectation disconfirmation framework. If subsequent purchase and consumption (perceived quality) are better that expected (positive disconfirmation), it will result in rating above this reference point, and the delight of this positive disconfirmation will enhance a satisfaction judgment. On the other hand, if ratings are below this reference point, it will result in negative disconfirmation. When the product is as expected, it results simply in confirmation. Further details on Oliver's model are given in section 2.4.2.

Other important efforts from the Marketing School include the research of Day (1977) and Hunt (1977), which are the editors of the Journal of Customer Satisfaction/Dissatisfaction, published on a yearly basis since 1988.

The development and installation of customer satisfaction barometers and business excellence models constitute another important effort in this area. These models are able to give business organizations the opportunity to implement an integrated benchmarking program. The most characteristic examples include the national satisfaction barometers (e.g. American Customer Satisfaction Index, Swedish Customer Satisfaction Barometer) and the quality awards (e.g. Malcolm Baldrige National Quality Award, EFQM excellence model). These approaches are presented analytically in sections 3.1.3 and 7.6.

By the mid-1980's, the focus of both applied and academic research had shifted to the study of discrepancies or gaps regarding organizational perceptions of service quality and the tasks associated with service delivery to customers. The work of Parasuraman et al. (1985, 1988) is the most characteristic example of this Service Quality School. Their multi-item Servqual scale is considered to be one of the first attempts to operationalize the customer satisfaction construct (see section 3.2.2). Major technological progress has also boosted the Service Quality School. For example, customer service centers and complaint departments of business organizations give the opportunity to interact and communicate with a large number of dissatisfied customers. In this framework, several researchers and practitioners had the ability to study this available information and suggest methods to retain customers and improve the level of customer loyalty (see for example Eastman Kodak Company, 1989; Reichheld and Sasser, 1990; Scheslinger and Heskett, 1991)

Other efforts, particularly during 1970-1980, have been focused on studying the relation between the customer satisfaction and the financial performance of a business organization (e.g. profit, sales). Although this relation seems rather logical and self-evident, it is not always strong, since several other internal and/or external factors (e.g. market conditions) may affect the financial results. For this reason, customer satisfaction should be considered as a necessary but not a sufficient condition for the financial success of a company (Vavra, 1995, 1997; Pruden et al., 1996).

Finally, it should be mentioned that numerous researches and studies on employee satisfaction offer a significant contribution in the evolution of satisfaction measurement, as presented in more detail in section 3.3 (Lawler and Hall, 1970; Hackman and Oldham, 1975; Weaver, 1978; Champoux, 1991; Loher et al., 1985; Fried and Ferris, 1987).

1.4 Satisfaction Measurement Programs

1.4.1 Measurement and Sources of Information

Customer satisfaction measurement efforts are usually integrated programs within business organizations, which include not only customer satisfaction metrics, but also other related measures, like customer loyalty and value. Moreover, multiple measures are used for the evaluation of customer satisfaction, since a single indicator is usually not a good predictor of overall performance. The use of multiple satisfaction measures is justified by the following reasons (Czarnecki, 1999):

- Satisfaction is related to the overall consumer behavior. For this reason, the use of a single measure is not able to provide reliable information.

- The use of multiple satisfaction measures is able to verify the integrity and accuracy of collected data.

It is obvious that the existence of multiple customer satisfaction measures implies the usage of multiple information sources from the business organization. Generally, this available information comes from research methods, operational data, marketing/sales channels, and other sources of information, as the representative examples of Table 1.3 indicate.

Table 1.3 Customer satisfaction sources of information (Massnick, 1997)

Category	Examples	
Research methods	Customer surveys	Employee surveys
	Dealer/supplier surveys	Focus groups
	Mystery shoppers	Customer panels
	Customer visits	Industry trade press
Operational data	Complaints	Customer service reports
	Customer comment cards	Engineering/design meetings
	Field service reports	Warranty claims
	Product returns	Employee suggestions
	Telephone activity reports	Quality performance tracking
Marketing/sales channels	Sales contact reports	Customer/competitor advertising
	Trade show intelligence	Sales data analysis
	Lead tracking	Closed accounts
	New product idea suggestions	Customer literature
Other	Benchmarking	Management contacts
	Workshops/seminars	Business literature

The satisfaction measurement systems can generally segregated into the following categories according to the source of the available information (Caddote and Turgeon, 1988; Woodruff and Gardial, 1996):

1. *Direct measurement systems*: These systems are based on data coming directly from the set of customers, like customer satisfaction surveys, customer complaint systems, personal interviews, etc. There are several types of direct customer satisfaction measurement systems, each providing the analysis of the particular problem from a different perspective. For example, while satisfaction surveys may analyze the expectations and the needs of the customers, service and complaint management systems focus mainly on the set of dissatisfied customers, in order to retain customers and increase loyalty levels. The direct methods have a "preventive" character, providing a kind of early warning systems. Thus, they may help managers to indentify improvement actions before potential problems or undesirable situations occur (dissatisfaction, customer complaints, decrease in sales, etc.).

2. *Indirect measurement systems*: Although the indirect measurement systems alone are not able to give a solution to the problem of customer satisfaction measurement, they may offer valuable information to business organizations. These systems are based on data reflecting the outcome/result of customer satisfaction, such as the sales level, the market share, etc. For this reason, the improvement actions that are based on such type of data may be characterized as "remedial", since they try to correct potential problems or undesirable situations that have already occurred.

An alternative classification of the customer satisfaction measurement systems is suggested by Czarnecki (1999) and consists of the following categories:

1. Direct measurement systems, which are usually used when there is a unit or production or an event that is captured in an automated system (e.g. direct recording of customer complaints in a computer for a call center).
2. Indirect measurement systems, which are used when the actual data are not collected at the time the event occurs (e.g. analysis of sales data).
3. Statistical samples, which may be used to develop estimates when whole data are incomplete (i.e. unavailable or difficult to obtain).
4. Interviews and surveys, which constitute the most direct customer satisfaction measurement systems, and they may offer a valuable solution in the case of customer behavioral analysis, or when the measures are perceptual.

Finally, it is worthwhile to mention the importance of developing a customer database or a customer satisfaction information system that will be able to detail interactions with customers. As pinpointed by Czarnecki (1999), a customer satisfaction information system is an automated (or manual) system that:

- collects customer satisfaction perceptions and information in a structured manner,
- stores the results of customer satisfaction measurement activities,
- assists in processing the information,
- segments and stratifies key issues,
- identifies actionable change, and
- links to the organization in order to quickly change processes.

As shown in Figure 1.4, business organizations receive continuously customer information regarding sales (e.g. account number, purchase history, history of sales contacts), basic company information for corporate customers (e.g. revenues, employees, cash flow), or points of customer contact (e.g. complaints, requests, mailings). A customer database may also give the ability to integrate the total available customer information coming from different departments of the organization. Given the technological progress and the available solutions nowadays, this is one the most important challenges that researchers and practitioners in the area of Management Information Systems face, as discussed in section 9.2.

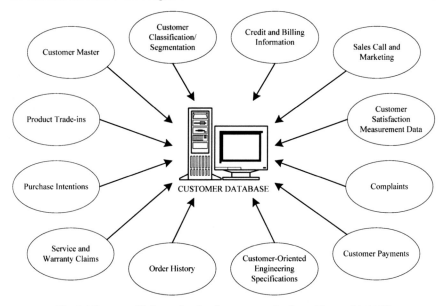

Fig. 1.4 Sources of information for the customer database (Czarnecki, 1999)

1.4.2 Satisfaction Measurement Process

The implementation of a customer satisfaction measurement program should follow the general rules for conducting a market or a customer survey, while at the same time it should adopt the main principles of continuous improvement in a business organization. Furthermore, the measurement process should give the ability to improve these particular programs, given their interactive character.

Although the satisfaction measurement programs do not remain constant due to continuous changes in the set of customers, or even changes in their expectations, needs and preferences, the basic process is rather unvarying.

The main steps of the process for designing and implementing a customer satisfaction measurement program are presented in Figure 1.5, from which the following principles become clear (Naumann and Giel, 1995):

- Customer focus is first of all a top management commitment in the business organization.
- Organization's customer orientation is embedded, at least partially, in the corporate culture.
- Customer satisfaction measurement programs should be considered as sequential and iterative processes.

It is important to note that a customer satisfaction measurement program should be embedded in all the processes of the business organization. To this end, several individual companies have developed their own procedures and standards for measuring customer satisfaction that fit to their structure and operations. Figure 1.6 presents the example of Motorola, where the customer satisfaction measurement program is linked to the six sigma approach developed by this firm.

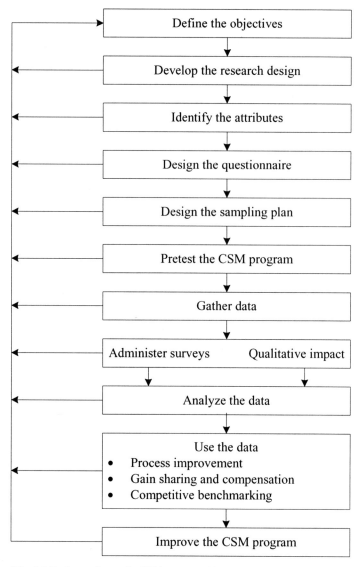

Fig. 1.5 Design and use of a CSM program (Naumann and Giel, 1995)

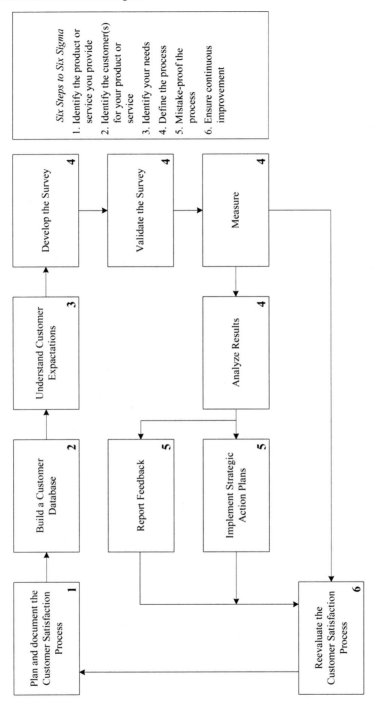

Fig. 1.6 The Motorola customer satisfaction measurement process (Motorola, 1995)

Any customer satisfaction measurement process has the ability to collect qualitative data regarding customer perceptions, something that is not possible using
the mechanisms of a classic market survey (Naumann and Giel, 1995). This way,
the process gives the ability to identify or formulate specific improvement actions.
The goal is not to conduct a survey or to achieve a predetermined score on the results, but rather to satisfy customers, which are the most important element in the
process (Motorola, 1995).

1.4.3 MUSA Approach

The MUSA (MUlticriteria Satisfaction Analysis) method, which is presented in
this book, is a multicriteria model for measuring and analyzing customer satisfaction. The main aim of this section is to illustrate how the MUSA method may be
integrated in a customer satisfaction measurement program.

The method is a preference disaggregation approach following the principles of
ordinal regression analysis (inference procedure). It evaluates the satisfaction level
of a set of individuals (customers, employees, etc.) based on their values and expressed preferences. Using data from satisfaction surveys, the MUSA method aggregates the different preferences in unique satisfaction functions, with the minimum possible errors (see Chapter 3).

The main assumptions related to the development of the MUSA method focus
on the following:

1. *Rational consumer*: This assumption refers to the existence of a set of rational
   customers and is generally met in decision science area.
2. *Satisfaction criteria*: The MUSA method assumes the existence of a set of
   characteristics for the examined product or service, according to which customers evaluate/judge their satisfaction. These characteristics form the set of customer satisfaction criteria and they should follow some fundamental properties
   (see sections 4.1.3 and 7.3.2).
3. *Additive aggregation model*: An additive model aggregating the set of satisfaction criteria is assumed. This has the form of an additive value function, which
   in the context of multicriteria decision analysis should follow the monotonicity
   property (see section 4.2).

Furthermore, it should be emphasized that the MUSA method is based on information directly expressed by customers (i.e. survey data), and thus it should be
integrated into a more general customer satisfaction measurement program.

The main steps for designing and implementing a customer satisfaction survey,
using the MUSA method, are presented in Figure 1.7. The process consists of the
following steps:

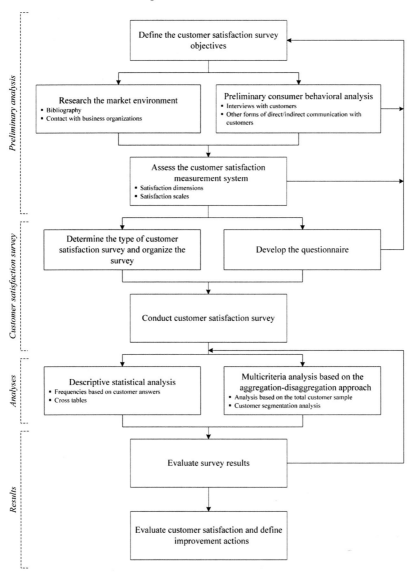

Fig. 1.7 Main steps of the MUSA method

1. *Preliminary analysis*: This step refers to the determination of the problem to be analyzed, and includes the analytical assessment of the objectives of the customer satisfaction survey. It also consists of the preliminary customer behavioral and market environment analysis. Thus, a general viewpoint of the customers, as well as the product/services provided by the business organization may be obtained.

2. *Questionnaire and survey*: Based on the previous results, this step focuses on the development and testing of the questionnaire, the determination of survey parameters, and the survey conduction. Also, several important aspects of the research (sampling, type of survey, survey process, survey network, etc.) should be determined before survey is conducted.

3. *Analyses*: This step refers to data analysis of collected information. The main quantitative approaches that may be applied include statistical methods (descriptive statistics, non-parametric statistics, and correlation analysis) and the multicriteria analysis MUSA method. Furthermore, this step includes a customer segmentation analysis, where discriminating characteristics that determine special customer groups are identified.

4. *Results*: This final step is devoted to the presentation of results and the determination of specific improvement efforts for the business organization. It should also be noted that the validity test of the results may lead to additional analyses of the data set.

Chapter 7 presents in detail the methodology of designing and conducting a customer satisfaction survey, as well as other important issues in this process. Moreover, Chapters 4-6 refer to the mathematical development and the extensions of the MUSA method, while many real-world applications of the MUSA method in customer satisfaction surveys are presented in Chapter 8.

Chapter 2
Basic Methodological Approaches

2.1 Types of Variables and Multivariate Analysis

In the context of quantitative techniques and tools (e.g. data analysis methods and statistical models), the problem of customer satisfaction evaluation presents the following basic characteristics (Wilkie and Pessemier, 1973; Churchill, 1991; Cooper, 1994):

- This particular subject is approached not only as a measurement problem, but also as a problem of understanding and analyzing customer satisfaction. In simple words, it is not enough for a business organization to know if its customers are satisfied or not, but it is necessary for the applied methods and techniques to identify the reasons behind customer satisfaction or dissatisfaction.
- In the majority of practical applications, it is commonly accepted that the data of the problem are based on the customers' judgments and should be directly collected from them. This justifies the necessity of conducting customer satisfaction surveys that results in the collection of a large volume of data.
- This is a multivariate evaluation problem given that customer's global satisfaction depends on a set of variables representing product/service characteristic dimensions. In addition, in several cases, it is necessary to examine and analyze customer behavior in relation to a set of competitive products.

The selection of the appropriate multivariate method depends mainly on the nature and the measurement scale of the variables used in the satisfaction evaluation model. Although extensive research on the measurement theory can be found for alternative levels of measurement, the variables used generally in market surveys may be classified to the following basic categories (Stevens, 1951):

- *Nominal variables*: These variables are only used in order to categorize various objects, and thus the containing information does not have any sense of ranking of preference. The only admissible mathematical operators in this category are

E. Grigoroudis and Y. Siskos, *Customer Satisfaction Evaluation*, International Series
in Operations Research & Management Science 139, DOI 10.1007/978-1-4419-1640-2_2,
© Springer Science + Business Media, LLC 2010

equality "=" and inequality "≠". Thus, if nominal variables are quantified, this is purely for coding reasons (e.g. when developing a database); the numbers assigned to nominal variables carry no magnitude value (Vavra, 1997).

- *Ordinal variables*: These variables indicate the order of objects, according to a particular attribute. Along with the equality and inequality operators, the operators of ">" and "<" are also meaningful in this category. Thus, if numbers are assigned to ordinal variables, these numbers can only indicate order. For example, the central tendency of an ordinal variable may be represented by its median, but the mean cannot be defined. It should be emphasized that the ordinal scale permits the ordering of the objects, but it is unable to specify their distance. For this reason, the arbitrary quantification of an ordinal variable may lead to unexpected and erroneous results in subsequent analyses (Gerson, 1993; Vavra, 1997).
- *Interval variables*: The interval variables use a specific measurement unit and consequently they are able to order objects so that the differences between the values of the scale levels are equal. This means that the aforementioned differences are meaningful and can be compared (Vavra, 1997). A typical example of such scale is the temperature Celsius scale: 40°C is warmer than 20°C (ordering), an increase from 30°C to 40°C is the same with an increase form 40°C to 50°C (equal intervals), and the difference between 20°C and 40°C is twice the difference between 40°C and 50°C (comparing differences). Apart from the allowed operators of the former scales, addition (+) and subtraction (−) can also be used. However, interval variables have no meaningful zero point (usually it is arbitrarily assigned, like in the Celsius scale).
- *Ratio variables*: These variables are similar to interval variables, but with meaningful (non-arbitrary) zero point. Most of the measurement in the physical sciences and engineering is done on ratio scales, like mass, length, time, volume, etc. This scale takes its name form the fact that the measurement is the estimation of the ratio between a magnitude of a continuous quantity and a unit magnitude of the same kind. Since ratios between numbers on a ratio scale are meaningful, operators such as multiplication "*" and division "/" may be carried out directly. In fact, all available mathematical operators can be used for ratio scales.

The variables assessed on a nominal scale are also called categorical or discrete variables, while interval and ratio variables are also denoted as numerical or metric variables.

Examples of different measurement scales used in customer satisfaction surveys are presented in Figure 2.1. As shown, the most frequent use of nominal scales in these types of surveys is in collecting classification information (i.e. variables that may segment the total set of customers). On the other hand, ratio scales seldom apply to the subjective concepts measured in customer satisfaction surveys (Vavra, 1997). In fact the majority of information collected in these surveys uses ordinal variables.

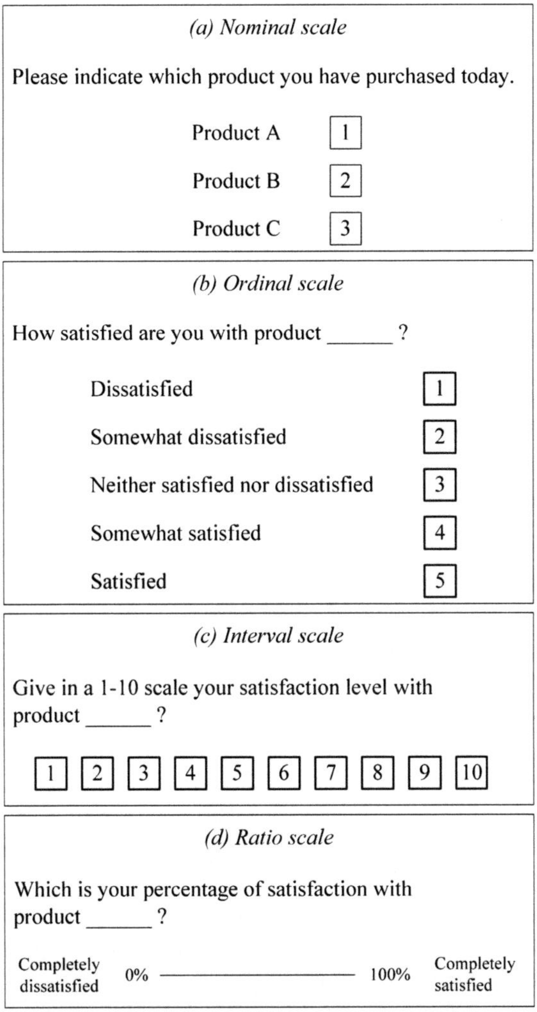

(a) Nominal scale

Please indicate which product you have purchased today.

Product A | 1 |

Product B | 2 |

Product C | 3 |

(b) Ordinal scale

How satisfied are you with product _____ ?

Dissatisfied | 1 |

Somewhat dissatisfied | 2 |

Neither satisfied nor dissatisfied | 3 |

Somewhat satisfied | 4 |

Satisfied | 5 |

(c) Interval scale

Give in a 1-10 scale your satisfaction level with product _____ ?

| 1 | | 2 | | 3 | | 4 | | 5 | | 6 | | 7 | | 8 | | 9 | | 10 |

(d) Ratio scale

Which is your percentage of satisfaction with product _____ ?

Completely dissatisfied   0% ————————— 100%   Completely satisfied

Fig. 2.1 Examples of different measurement scales

More specifically, the main variables considered in a satisfaction survey are directly or indirectly related to the customer satisfaction (e.g. satisfaction level, repurchase intention, loyalty level) or the performance of particular characteristics of the considered product or service. These variables are measured using the following alternatives (see also section 7.3.3):

- Using a quantitative scale (e.g a 1-10 interval) according to which the customer is asked to rate the performance or express his/her satisfaction from a product or from a product's particular characteristic. Attention should be paid to the wording of the question and the direction of the scale, so that the collected data are not biased by these factors (Naumann and Giel, 1995). It should also be noted that the size of the scale may create difficulties to respondents (Oliver, 1997).

• Using a verbal scale of an ordinal form (see for example Figure 2.1). However, as already noted, only simple descriptive statistics should be applied in these ordinal scales. For this reason, in many cases, an a priori arbitrary quantification is used (e.g. 1 for dissatisfied customers, 2 for somewhat dissatisfied customers, etc.). This particular quantification approach has been intensely criticized, because it makes the strong assumption that the "value" given by customer at each satisfaction level is known a priori. Moreover, the assumed linear relation of the satisfaction level "values" is not always compatible with the real market conditions, given that going from one satisfaction level to another neither yields the same "value" to customers nor is proportional to the effort that the organization should make. In addition, this quantification may lead to wrong conclusions, particularly when calculating averages. Finally, this approach does not take into account the demanding level of customers that may vary for different product/service characteristics.

The importance of partial satisfaction dimensions or product characteristics is another parameter included in satisfaction surveys, particularly when simple descriptive statistics are applied. The direct measurement of importance is usually accomplished with the following ways (Hauser, 1991):

• Customers are asked to assign a set of importance points (usually 100) to the defined satisfaction dimensions (this approach is also called constant sum method). Although it is widely used in several cases, its criticism concerns mainly the response difficulty that the customers face when dealing with a large number of satisfaction dimensions, and the fact that customers tend to assess the importance by using groups of 5 or 10 points, thus resulting in data that are not truly continuous.

• Customers are asked to rank the satisfaction dimensions according to their importance preference. This approach may present difficulties in case of a large number of satisfaction dimensions.

• Using an ordinal or an interval scale, similarly to the case of satisfaction judgments. This scale is either defined similarly to the satisfaction scale, or normalized in order to be combined with satisfaction data.

Other alternative techniques for measuring importance are presented by Diener et al. (1985) and Dolinsky (1994), while a large number of researches that mostly refer to employee satisfaction measurement identify the inconsistencies that this particular approach may lead to (Cohen et al., 1972; Bettman et al., 1975; Ryan and Bonfield, 1975; Locke, 1984; Rice et al., 1991; McFarlin and Rice, 1992; Taber and Allinger, 1995; McFarlin et al., 1995). These inconsistencies are caused by the so called "range of affect", or by the fact that the estimated low weight of some attributes does not necessarily imply that these are not considered important by the customers (see section 3.4.1). For this reason, many researchers suggest that the importance should not be based only on information given directly by customers, but it should be estimated using an analytical method (Mobley and Locke, 1970; Blood, 1971; Oliver, 1997).

Taking into account the aforementioned framework, it should be noted that that the selection of the appropriate multivariate method depends also on the objective of the analysis, besides the measurement scale of the considered variables. Vavra (1997) classifies the multivariate statistical techniques that may be used to analyze customer satisfaction by considering two major objectives: explore the relationships in different customer satisfaction data and determine the dependencies in these data (Figure 2.2).

2.2 Simple Quantitative Models

2.2.1 Descriptive Statistics

The simplest technique to analyze satisfaction survey data is to calculate the frequencies of customer responses to particular questions that are assumed critical. More specifically, depending on the applied scale, the percentages of satisfied and dissatisfied customers are calculated and used as a performance measure of the company. In many cases, the selection of satisfaction levels that characterize satisfied or dissatisfied customers depends on the strategy and the general philosophy of the business organization (e.g. some companies use the percentages of "very satisfied" and "satisfied" customers as their performance indicator, while others prefer to use only the percentage of "very satisfied" customers).

This approach does not violate the qualitative nature of the collected information, while in addition, if longitudinal data are available, they may be used in order to evaluate customer satisfaction trends. For example, Dutka (1995) proposes the following statistical approach:

1. Present the frequencies of customer satisfaction data in a time-series format, in order to identify which satisfaction dimensions have been improved and in which satisfaction dimensions additional effort should be put.
2. Apply a statistical hypothesis test in order to investigate potential changes in customer attitude compared to previous time periods.
3. Present the data in statistical quality control charts with predefined control limits.

In case where metric variables are used in the customer satisfaction survey, it is possible to estimate an overall satisfaction index, based on the customer judgments for the performance and importance of the product/service characteristics. The customer satisfaction index *CSI* is calculated using a weighted sum formula (Hill, 1996):

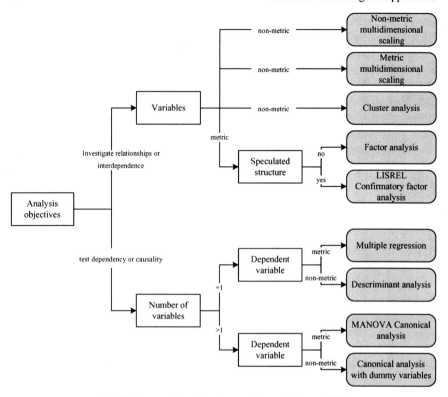

Fig. 2.2 A map of mutlivariate techniques (Vavra, 1997)

$$\begin{cases} CSI = \sum_{i=1}^{n} \overline{b}_i \overline{X}_i \\ \text{with } \overline{b}_i = \frac{1}{M} \sum_{j=1}^{M} b_{ij} \text{ and } \overline{X}_i = \frac{1}{M} \sum_{j=1}^{M} x_{ij} \end{cases} \qquad (2.1)$$

where $\overline{X}_i$ and $\overline{b}_i$ are the average scores of the satisfaction/performance and the importance of the characteristic i, respectively, x_{ij} and b_{ij} are the satisfaction/performance and the importance judgment of customer j for the characteristic i, respectively, n is the number of product/service characteristics, and M is the size of customer sample. In case that different measurement scales are used for the x and b variables, a normalization coefficient should be used in the *CSI* formula.

In several studies, the previous approach is also applied even though only ordinal satisfaction data are available. However, this requires the quantification of the ordinal scale which presents, as already mentioned, a series of problems (see section 2.1). Additional difficulties in analyzing and interpreting these types of results are also mentioned in Oliver (1997) and Vavra (1997).

Other techniques that focus on the reporting and the presentation of results are given by Dutka (1995) and Hill (1996). The most important of them refers to the performance profiles and performance matrices, examples of which are presented in Figure 2.3 (see also section 4.3.5 for a detailed presentation and discussion of performance matrices).

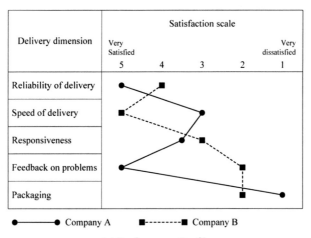

(a) Performance Profile

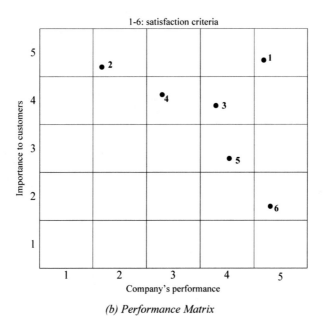

(b) Performance Matrix

Fig. 2.3 Examples of performance profiles and matrices (Hill, 1996)

Descriptive statistics methods are not able to provide an in depth analysis of customer satisfaction. Nevertheless, they can be used either during the preliminary analysis or complementary to other quantitative models.

2.2.2 Basic Statistical Approaches

Multiple regression analysis is one of the most widely used statistical methods for analyzing customer satisfaction data. The method is used to study the relation between the satisfaction/performance of the total set of product's or service's characteristics (independent variables) and the overall customer satisfaction judgment (dependent variable).

The general form of multiple regression equation is as follows:

$$Y = b_0 + b_1 X_1 + b_2 X_2 + \ldots + b_n X_n \tag{2.2}$$

where Y is the overall customer satisfaction judgment, X_i is the customer satisfaction/performance of characteristic i, b_i are the estimated regression coefficients and n is the number of product or service characteristics.

In order to apply multiple regression analysis in customer satisfaction data, the following issues should be emphasized (Grisaffe, 1993; McLauchlan, 1993; Mullet, 1994):

- All the variables in the linear model should be metric, otherwise multiple regression analysis should not be performed. Particularly in the case of ordinal variables, the arbitrary codification of the scales may lead to significant inconsistencies. In addition, if model variables are measured in different scales, a normalization procedure is necessary.
- Beside the overall customer satisfaction with a product/service, the Y variable, may also represent other related aggregated measures, such as customer loyalty level or repurchase intention level.
- The coefficients b_i indicate the contribution of the independent variables to the dependent variable Y. Thus, these coefficients may reveal the importance given by customers to each one of the product's or service's characteristics, and therefore to identify the critical satisfaction dimensions.

The major problems and the criticism of this particular approach focus on the quantification of the satisfaction data and the multicollinearity among the independent variables X_i. In addition, even when a metric scale is used, it is assumed that the model variables are continuous, which is not compatible with the type of the collected information. Moreover, the dependency among the variables X_i may affect the reliability of the results and it is possible to lead to inconsistencies. However, several approaches have been proposed in order to overcome the aforementioned problems (see for example Flury and Riedwyl, 1988).

Detailed presentation of the method is given by Draper and Smith (1967), Daniel and Wood (1980) and Flury and Riedwyl (1988), while applications of multiple regression analysis to market survey data are presented by Kerlinger and Pedhazur (1973), Cohen and Cohen (1983), Dutka (1995) and Vavra (1997).

Another statistical method widely used in analyzing customer satisfaction data is factor analysis. The aim of the method is to study the relation pattern among the product's or service's characteristics.

The main form of the factor analysis equation relates the set of variables with a minimum number of factors as follows (Harman, 1976):

$$X_i = a_{i1}F_1 + a_{i2}F_2 + \ldots + a_{im}F_m \quad \text{with } i = 1, 2, \ldots, n \tag{2.3}$$

where X_i is the customer satisfaction/performance of characteristic i, F_j is factor j, a_{ij} are the estimated coefficients, m is the number of factors, and n is the number of product/service characteristics.

Beside the estimation of a_{ij} coefficients, which are able to investigate the nature and number of underlying dimensions in the survey data, factor analysis also generates data (scores) for every customer on each of the factors uncovered. These derived values for each case are called factor scores and may approximate how customers might have rated the product/service, if they were asked to give their judgments only for the discovered factors (instead of the raw variables that they originally answered). These factor scores may be also used to cluster customers (Vavra, 1997).

In general, factor analysis is used to decompose a data matrix into its bare structural essentials that can efficiently describe the original customer satisfaction data. The reduction of a large number of attributes is the most common application of factor analysis to a customer satisfaction measurement program. Usually, the application process includes the following steps (Dutka, 1995):

1. Create an exhaustive list of product/service characteristics that affect the customer satisfaction, using qualitative survey techniques, like personal interviews or customer focus groups (see section 7.1).
2. Conduct a preliminary customer satisfaction survey using a pilot questionnaire that includes the list of these characteristics.
3. Reduce the number of characteristics into the major evaluative dimensions of customers using factor analysis.
4. Implement the customer satisfaction measurement program using the defined satisfaction dimensions.

The criticism and the problems related to the application of factor analysis to market survey data do not differ from those of multiple regression analysis. In addition, Dutka (1995) notes that during the application of the method, particular attention should be paid to critical issues related to the interpretation of the results (e.g. selecting the appropriate technique to rotate the factor solution).

The mathematical development of the method is presented analytically in many textbooks on multivariate data analysis (see for example Rummel, 1970; Cooley and Lohnes, 1971; Urban and Hauser, 1980; Gorsuch, 1983), while a large number of publications refers to the application of factor analysis in market survey data (Roberts et al., 1971; Hayes, 1992; Naumann and Giel, 1995; Hill, 1996; Vavra, 1997).

2.3 Advanced Quantitative Techniques

2.3.1 Conditional Probability Models

An important category of quantitative tools that may be used in the customer satisfaction measurement problem refers to the conditional probability models. These models follow a regression-type approach, taking into account that the measurement variable has an ordinal form.

The conditional probability models, given customer evaluations for a set of product/service characteristics, estimate a satisfaction probability distribution function, i.e. the probability that a customer belongs to a particular "satisfaction group" (e.g. group of satisfied customers, group of dissatisfied customers, etc.). The main forms of these models include the linear probability model and the logit and probit models.

The linear probability model is a binary regression approach, assuming that customer's overall satisfaction (dependent variable) is a dichotomous variable taking two possible values (i.e. satisfaction or dissatisfaction). The model may be expressed by the following formula:

$$\Pr(Y = 1 | \mathbf{X}) = b_0 + b_1 X_1 + \ldots + b_n X_n \tag{2.4}$$

where Y is the dichotomous variable representing overall customer satisfaction, b_i are the regression coefficients, X_i are the customer satisfaction/performance of characteristic i, and n is the number of product/service characteristics.

It should be noted here that b_i are OLS (ordinary least square) estimates, and thus the linear probability model is used when alternative techniques based on maximum likelihood estimates are computationally difficult. Moreover, in case that Y is a multiple response variable, the model can be extended with the use of dummy variables.

There are several potential statistical problems in the application of linear probability models, although alternative techniques have been proposed in order to overcome these problems. For example, the error terms are heteroskedastic and their distribution is not normal, while without restrictions on b_i, the estimated coefficients can imply probabilities outside the unit interval [0, 1].

The logit analysis is a similar approach where the previous satisfaction probability is given by the logistic function:

$$
\begin{cases}
\Pr(Y=1|\mathbf{X}) = \dfrac{1}{1+e^{-z}} \\[2mm]
\text{with } \quad z = b_0 + b_1 X_1 + \ldots + b_n X_n
\end{cases}
\tag{2.5}
$$

The logit analysis has numerous applications in marketing and other fields (e.g. artificial neural networks, biology, medicine, economics, mathematical psychology). The method, based on a cumulative distribution function, provides the probability of a customer to belong to one of the prescribed satisfaction classes, given his/her satisfaction/performance judgments on a set of product/service characteristics.

For the logit of the previous probability, which is the inverse of the logistic function, it can be shown that:

$$
p = \Pr(Y=1|\mathbf{X}) = \frac{1}{1+e^{-z}} \Rightarrow \frac{p}{1-p} = e^z \Rightarrow
$$

$$
\Rightarrow \mathrm{logit}(p) = \ln\left(\frac{p}{1-p}\right) = z = b_0 + b_1 X_1 + \ldots + b_n X_n
\tag{2.6}
$$

Probit models are similar to logit analysis. The main difference is that the probability $\Pr(Y=1|\mathbf{X})$ is given by the cumulative standard normal distribution function:

$$
\begin{cases}
\Pr(Y=1|\mathbf{X}) = \dfrac{1}{2\sqrt{\pi}} \displaystyle\int_{-\infty}^{z} e^{-\frac{1}{2}u^2}\, du \\[3mm]
\text{with } \quad z = b_0 + b_1 X_1 + \ldots + b_n X_n
\end{cases}
\tag{2.7}
$$

Usually, logit analysis is used as an alternative to probit analysis mainly because of the simplicity of the logistic function and the relatively lower required computational effort (Pindyck and Rubinfeld, 1985). However, these models are very similar since they assume that the probability of a customer j to be satisfied by the offered product or service is described by the relationship:

$$
\Pr(\mathbf{X}_j, \mathbf{b}) = F(b_0 + \mathbf{b}^T \mathbf{X}_j)
\tag{2.8}
$$

where $\mathbf{X}_j$ is the satisfaction vector of customer j for the total set of product/service characteristics and $\mathbf{b}$ is the vector of estimated model parameters. The main difference is that, in order to assess $\Pr(\mathbf{X}_j,\mathbf{b})$, logit analysis uses a cumulative logistic function, while probit analysis a cumulative normal distribution function, as shown in Figure 2.4.

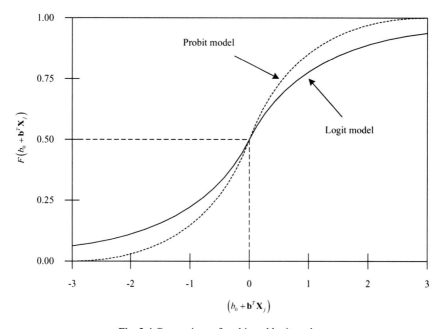

Fig. 2.4 Comparison of probit and logit analyses

Logit and Probit analyses present also similarities with the classification statistical models (e.g. discriminant analysis). However, it should be noted that their purpose is not to classify customers in prescribed satisfaction classes, but to assess the probability that a customer belongs to one of these classes.

Detailed presentation of the binary logit and probit analysis is given by Gnanadesikan (1977), Hanushek and Jackson (1977), Fienberg (1980), Andersen (1990), and Agresti (1996), while the case of multiple response models is presented in Theil (1969), McCullagh (1980), Fienberg (1980) and Agresti (1984, 1990).

The ordered conditional probability models may be considered as an extension of the previous models, taking into account that the dependent variable is ordinal. Moreover, in case of multiple responses, customer satisfaction may be modeled as follows (Agresti, 1984, 1990, 1996):

$$y_j = \begin{cases} 0 & \text{if } y_j^* \leq \mu_0 \\ 1 & \text{if } \mu_0 < y_j^* \leq \mu_1 \\ 2 & \text{if } \mu_1 < y_j^* \leq \mu_2 \\ \vdots \\ a-1 & \text{if } y_j^* > \mu_{a-2} \end{cases} \tag{2.9}$$

where y_j is the overall satisfaction of customer j, a is the number of satisfaction levels (ordinal scale) and μ_m are the estimated model parameters, having a role of thresholds for the dummy variable y_j^*, which is denoted by the following formula:

$$y_j^* = \sum_{i=1}^{n} b_i x_{ij} + \varepsilon_j \tag{2.10}$$

where x_{ij} is the satisfaction/performance judgment of customer j for product/service characteristic i, b_i are the estimated model coefficients, ε_j are the error terms, and n is the number of product/service characteristics.

It should be emphasized that the values $\{0, 1, \ldots, a-1\}$, which the overall satisfaction variable can take, are simply a coding and do not quantify the y_j variable. In addition, the arbitrary quantification of y_j is avoided by using the dummy variable y_j^* and estimating the parameters μ_m. Usually, the thresholds μ_m are normalized by setting $\mu_m = 0$ in order to minimize the model parameters that should be estimated. Moreover, it is assumed that the error terms follow a prescribed probability distribution function (e.g. standard normal distribution, standard logistic distribution). Finally, the aforementioned modeling assumes that all possible values of the overall satisfaction y_j are present in the dataset.

Using equations (2.9) and (2.10), the probability that customer j has expressed for the m-th satisfaction level, given his/her satisfaction/performance judgments $\mathbf{X}_j = (x_{1j}, x_{2j}, \ldots, x_{nj})$ is

$$\Pr(y_j = m) = \Pr(\mu_{m-1} < y_j^* \leq \mu_m) =$$

$$= \Pr\left(\varepsilon \leq \mu_m - \sum_{i=1}^{n} b_i x_{ij}\right) - \Pr\left(\varepsilon \leq \mu_{m-1} - \sum_{i=1}^{n} b_i x_{ij}\right) = \tag{2.11}$$

$$= F\left(\mu_m - \sum_{i=1}^{n} b_i x_{ij}\right) - F\left(\mu_{m-1} - \sum_{i=1}^{n} b_i x_{ij}\right)$$

or alternatively

$$\Pr(y_j \leq m) = F\left(\mu_m - \sum_{i=1}^{n} b_i x_{ij}\right) \tag{2.12}$$

where F is the standard normal distribution function for the ordered probit model and the standard logistic distribution function for the ordered logit model.

The estimation of the parameters b_i and μ_m is based on the maximization of the log-likelihood function L:

$$L = \sum_{k=0}^{a-1} \log F\left(\mu_k - \sum_{i=1}^{n} b_i x_{ij}\right) \tag{2.13}$$

An analytical presentation of the ordered conditional probability models may be found in Gensch and Recker (1979), Fienberg (1980), Wickens (1989), Andersen (1990), and Agresti (1984, 1990, 1996).

The conditional probability models have been mainly applied in the marketing field (market surveys, discrete choice models), although a growing number of real-world applications in customer satisfaction surveys may be found in the literature.

Finally, it should be mentioned that logit and probit analysis may be considered as a special case of loglinear models that constitute an interesting alternative approach to the analysis of multidimensional contingency tables (Knoke and Burke, 1980; Wickens, 1989).

2.3.2 Structural Equation Modeling

Structural equation modeling (SEM) is a statistical technique for measuring relationships among latent variables. It has been around since early in the 20th century originating in the geneticist Sewall Wright's 1916 work (Bollen, 1989). SEM is a technique to specify, estimate, and evaluate models of linear relationships among a set of observed variables in terms of a generally smaller number of unobserved variables (Shah and Goldstein, 2006).

SEM, as a part of the general category of causal modeling, is focused on testing the hypothesis that the relationships among data are consistent with the assumed causal structure. These causal relationships are usually considered linear. Thus, SEM may be considered as an extension of regression models. In fact, SEM is a family of models that also include the following approaches (Raykov and Markoulides, 2000):

- *Path analysis*: Path analysis examines patterns of directional and non-directional relationships only among observed variables. Thus, it allows for the testing of structural relationships among observed variables, when these observed variables are of primary interest or when multiple indicators for latent variables are not available (Shah and Goldstein, 2006).

- *Confirmatory factor analysis*: Confirmatory factor analysis (CFA) models are commonly used to examine patterns of interrelationships among several constructs. CFA assumes that the observed variables are loaded on specific latent variables, which are allowed to correlate. Thus, contrary to explanatory factor analysis, CFA requires that the latent variables and their associated observed variables to be specified before analyzing data (Shah and Goldstein, 2006).

Different examples of causal modeling are presented in Figure 2.5. The simplest causal model may have only two variables: one predictor variable and one outcome variable, as shown in Figure 2.5(a). In this case, the path coefficient is equivalent to the simple correlation coefficient between these two variables. A multiple predictor causal model is depicted in Figure 2.5(b), where three predictor variables are examined, each of which has some level of covariance with the others. In this case, the path coefficients will be equivalent to correlation coefficients, only if the predictor variables are orthogonal. A more complex case is presented in Figure 2.5(c), which refers to a simple path analysis model in which five predictor variables (x_i) affect two outcome variables (y_j). In this diagram, γ_{ij} denote the path coefficients among predictor and outcome variables, while β_{kj} represent the path coefficient among outcome variables. It should be mentioned that this modeling allows predictor variables to affect both of the outcome variables, and thus both direct and indirect effects are possible (e.g. service quality influences loyalty indirectly through customer satisfaction, while loyalty is directly affected by product quality). In addition, error terms ε_j are introduced in the outcome variables and the path analysis model includes the covariance terms (CV) among all possible pairs of predictor variables.

The previous examples illustrate how causal modeling may be generalized in a path analysis context. However, the following remarks should be emphasized for the implementation of path analysis models (Allen and Rao, 2000):

- The variance-covariance matrix is the main input data for this method. In addition, outcome variables are assumed normally distributed and measured in an interval or a ratio scale.
- Path analysis assumes that the relations between variables are linear and additive, while a sufficient number of cases are required to produce stable and robust results.
- Covariance terms among predictor variables should not be omitted, unless there are particular experiential, empirical, or theoretical reasons to do so.
- Using the hypothesized structure or the analytical model equations, it is possible to estimate direct and indirect effects of predictor variables to outcome variables.
- A saturated model (i.e. a model containing paths from each of the predictor variables to all of the dependent variables) will always fit the original data perfectly.

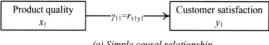

(a) Simple causal relationship

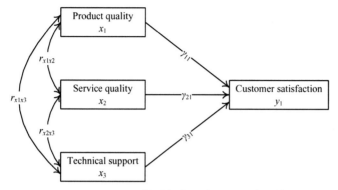

(b) Multiple predictor causal model

(c) Path analysis model with two dependent variables

Fig. 2.5 Examples of causal modeling (Allen and Rao, 2000)

- There are several statistical fitting indicators, but the most well-known is chi-squared, which indicates lack of fit. Moreover, in case of accepting the structural model, the errors should not be correlated.
- Since a linear equation can be written for every outcome variable, path analysis estimates a separate R^2 statistic for each of these equations (R^2 reflects the proportion of dependent variable variance accounted for by the predictor variables).

SEM refers to a general category of path analysis models having measured and latent variables, and thus it may be defined as a hypothesis of a specific pattern of relations among the aforementioned variables. In general, this category of models may be considered as a combination of path analysis and factor analysis.

The use of latent variables is the main difference from path analysis, and thus, SEM models are decomposed into their two main components:

1. The *measurement model*, which explicates the relations between measured and latent variables, and is defined as follows:

$$\begin{cases} y = \Lambda_y \eta + \varepsilon \\ x = \Lambda_x \xi + \delta \end{cases} \tag{2.14}$$

2. The *structural model*, which specifies relationships between latent variables through a structural equation model, and is given by:

$$n = B\eta + \Gamma\xi + \zeta \tag{2.15}$$

Table 2.1 gives the necessary notation for the measurement and the structural model. The measured variables are also called manifest or observed variables, while the terms endogenous and exogenous are model specific (a latent variable is endogenous, if it is determined by variables within the model, while it is exogenous, if its causes lie outside the model).

The main assumptions of the SEM models, using the aforementioned notation, may be summarized in the following (Bollen, 1989):

1. $E(\eta) = E(\xi) = E(\zeta) = E(\varepsilon) = E(\delta) = 0$
2. ε uncorrelated with η, ξ, and δ
3. δ uncorrelated with ξ, η, and ε
4. ζ uncorrelated with ξ
5. $(I-B)$ nonsingular

It can be shown that the covariance matrix for the observed variables derived from raw data is a function of eight parameter matrices: Λ_x, Λ_y, Γ, B, Φ, Ψ, Θ_δ, and Θ_ε. Thus, given a hypothesized model in terms of fixed and free parameters of the eight-parameter matrices, and given a sample covariance matrix for the measured variables, one can solve for estimates of the free parameters of the model. The most common approach for fitting the model to data is to obtain the maximum likelihood estimates of the parameters, and an accompanying likelihood ratio chi-square test of the null hypothesis that the model holds in the population (Shah and Goldstein, 2006).

An example of a SEM model in a case of customer satisfaction measurement is presented in Figure 2.6. The model considers three latent endogenous variables (product quality, service quality, and technical support) and two latent endogenous variables (customer satisfaction and loyalty). As shown, the endogenous variables may affect loyalty directly (e.g. product quality), or indirectly through customer satisfaction (e.g. service quality). Moreover, a number of different measured variables are used in order to define all these latent variables.

Table 2.1 Notation for SEM

Type	Symbol	Dimension	Description
Variables	$\mathbf{x}$	$q \times 1$	Observed indicators of ξ
	$\mathbf{y}$	$p \times 1$	Observed indicators of ζ
	$\boldsymbol{\delta}$	$q \times 1$	Measurement errors for $\mathbf{x}$
	$\boldsymbol{\varepsilon}$	$p \times 1$	Measurement errors for $\mathbf{y}$
	$\boldsymbol{\eta}$	$m \times 1$	Latent endogenous variables
	$\boldsymbol{\xi}$	$n \times 1$	Latent exogenous variables
	$\boldsymbol{\zeta}$	$m \times 1$	Latent errors in equations
Coefficients	$\boldsymbol{\Lambda}_x$	$q \times n$	Coefficient relating $\mathbf{x}$ to ξ
	$\boldsymbol{\Lambda}_y$	$p \times m$	Coefficient relating $\mathbf{y}$ to $\boldsymbol{\eta}$
	$\mathbf{B}$	$m \times m$	Coefficient matrix for latent endogenous variables
	$\boldsymbol{\Gamma}$	$m \times n$	Coefficient matrix for latent exogenous variables
Covariance matrices	$\boldsymbol{\Theta}_\delta$	$q \times q$	$E(\boldsymbol{\delta\delta}')$ covariance matrix of $\boldsymbol{\delta}$
	$\boldsymbol{\Theta}_\varepsilon$	$p \times p$	$E(\boldsymbol{\varepsilon\varepsilon}')$ covariance matrix of $\boldsymbol{\varepsilon}$
	$\boldsymbol{\Phi}$	$n \times n$	$E(\boldsymbol{\xi\xi}')$ covariance matrix of $\boldsymbol{\xi}$
	$\boldsymbol{\Psi}$	$m \times m$	$E(\boldsymbol{\zeta\zeta}')$ covariance matrix of $\boldsymbol{\zeta}$

SEM has been implemented in a large number of software packages, such as LISREL (Jöreskog and Sörbom, 1993, 1996), AMOS (Arbuckle, 1997; Blunch, 2008) and EQS (Bentler, 1995).

It should be emphasized that SEM is a confirmatory rather than an exploratory approach, since its main objective is to determine whether the a priori model is valid, and not to find a suitable model (Shah and Goldstein, 2006). Thus, it is suited to theory testing rather than theory development, although, in several cases, it is used in order to explore alternative structural models.

Generally, the implementation of a SEM analysis should be based on the following main steps (Kline, 1998).

1. Specify the model (the hypotheses in the form of a structural equation model).
2. Determine whether the model is identified.
3. Select measures of the variables represented in the model and collect data.
4. Analyze the model (estimate the model parameters).
5. Evaluate model fit (determine how adequately the model accounts for the data).
6. Re-specify the model and evaluate the fit of the revised model to the same data.

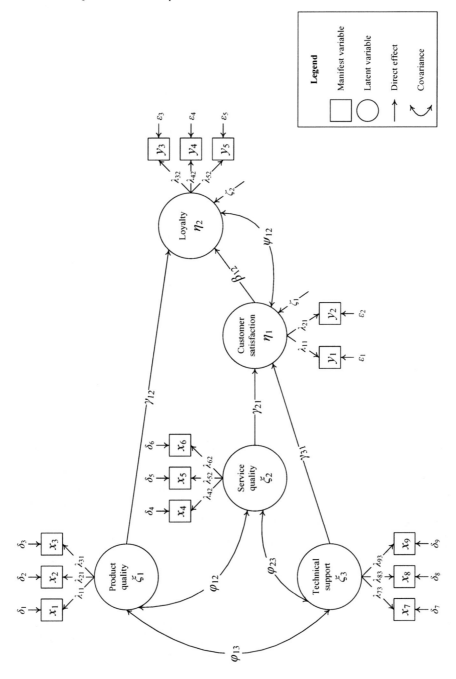

Fig. 2.6 Example of a structural equation model (Allen and Rao, 2000)

The most important strength of SEM is the ability to study latent variables. Since these variables are not directly measured, but estimated in the model from a set of measured variables, SEM models may be used to evaluate complex customer behavioral variables. For example, customer loyalty may not be measured directly, but instead, its measurement may be based on its outcomes (e.g. repurchase intention, complaints, and price elasticity). Another important advantage of SEM models, which justifies their popularity in many scientific fields of study, is that they provide a mechanism for explicitly taking into account measurement error in the observed variables (both dependent and independent) considered in the model (Raykov and Markoulides, 2000). Additionally, SEM models are able to study both direct and indirect effects of various variables included in the model. Direct effects are the effects that go directly from one variable to another, while indirect effects are the effects between two variables that are mediated by one or more intervening variable (Raykov and Markoulides, 2000).

2.3.3 Other Statistical and Data Analysis Models

Satisfaction dimensions related to a customer segment may diversify compared to another segment. Thus, several quantitative methods and techniques aim to identify product or service attributes that best discriminate customer segments, which are assessed according to the expressed satisfaction level (i.e. satisfied vs. dissatisfied customers), or a particular customer characteristic (e.g. frequency of use).

Discriminant analysis is one among the most widely used multivariate methods that, given a customer's satisfaction judgments on set of the product/service characteristics, estimates whether this customer belongs to one of the prescribed satisfaction classes.

Discriminant analysis estimates a z-score for each customer i, based on the following formula:

$$z_j = a_1 x_{1j} + a_2 x_{2j} + \ldots + a_n x_{nj} \tag{2.16}$$

where x_{ij} is the satisfaction judgment of customer j for product/service characteristic i, a_i are the estimated model coefficients, and n is the number of product/service characteristics.

The classification of customers is achieved using these z_j values and the calculation of appropriate cutoff scores. Detailed presentation of the method is given by Cooley and Lohnes (1971) and Klecka (1980).

For applying discriminant analysis in customer satisfaction surveys, the following should be taken into account (Vavra, 1997):

- The assessment of the classification groups constitutes one of the most difficult and important decisions when applying this particular method, given that it refers to the selection of the classification variable (e.g. overall satisfaction, re-purchase intention), as well as the determination of the variable levels that discriminate the particular customer classes.

- The potential problems referring to the application of the method do not differ from these that were mentioned in the case of multiple regression analysis due to the relative similarity of the two methods (e.g. the parameters a_i may be interpreted in the same way with the regression coefficients).
- Usually, the set of customers is divided in two subsets, the first of which is used for the estimation of the model parameters (training set) and the second for testing the reliability the results (test set).
- Stepwise discriminant analysis is a different version of this particular method, which may be used when the set of satisfaction dimensions that classifies customers is not known and defined.

Characteristic examples of discriminant analysis applications to customer satisfaction problems are presented by Dutka (1995) and Vavra (1997).

Another important objective of satisfaction data analyses is the identification of priorities and the development of improvement strategies for the business organization. In this context, conjoint analysis is used to assess the effects of the trade-offs made by customers, when they purchase or express satisfaction evaluations for a particular product or service. According to this method, customers evaluate a series of product or service profiles having different performance levels on a set of defined attributes. This trade-off analysis is able to reveal the relative importance of these component attributes.

Conjoint analysis may be considered as a reasonable extension of customer satisfaction surveys, given that the most important trade-off decisions made by customers include the critical performance dimensions of a product or service that have been identified during the satisfaction survey process. The implementation of conjoint analysis includes the following main steps (Dutka, 1995):

1. Identification of the trade-off choices among the critical performance attributes.
2. Development of an experimental design to measure trade-offs.
3. Conduction of consumer surveys to implement the experimental design.
4. Computation of utility functions that measure the importance of the various trade-offs.
5. Analysis of the impact of changes in the product or service.

A large number of publications refer to the presentation of this particular approach (Green and Rao, 1971; Green and Wind, 1973; Johnson, 1974; Green and Sprinivasan, 1978; Green et al., 1983; Green, 1984), while a detailed review of alternative versions of conjoint analysis is given by Louviere (1988). The applications of the method not only refer to cases of customer satisfaction surveys, but also to general market surveys (Gattin and Wittink, 1982; Joseph et al., 1989; Anderson and Bettencourt, 1993).

Another important data analysis technique refers to correspondence analysis, which is one of the most popular mathematical tools for developing perceptual maps in the marketing field. Customer satisfaction research is an ideal application for perceptual mapping, since the relationship among questionnaire variables (e.g. satisfaction or performance judgments for particular product/service attributes, demographics, competitors' performance) may be investigated (Dutka, 1995).

The most important characteristics of the method, in relation to other statistical models are (Dutka, 1995):

- Correspondence analysis is mainly a descriptive technique providing qualitative information of an explanatory nature, in contrast to discriminant and regression analysis, which are quantitative methods allowing the evaluation of overall customer satisfaction on the basis of a specific mathematical formula.
- The method uses cross-tabulations as input data, thus it can analyze simultaneously row and column variables of this table (e.g. performance attributes in relation to customer demographic characteristics) However, a significant portion of the information from the raw satisfaction survey data is lost.
- Physical interpretations of the axes presented in the perceptual maps are not necessary, in contrast to factor analysis where this particular task is rather difficult. This may be justified by the fact that correspondence analysis relies on point-to-point distances rather than distances from axes.

The detailed development of the method is presented by Hoffman and Franke (1986) and Weller and Romney (1990), while conclusively, it should be noted that conjoint analysis is not able to evaluate and analyze customer satisfaction, but it is usually applied either during the preliminary stage of the data analysis process, or complementary to other methods and techniques.

Other statistical models and quantitative tools, applied for analyzing customer satisfaction, include (Wilk and Gnanadesikan, 1968; Aldenderfer and Blashfield, 1984; Denby et al., 1990; Douglas, 1995; Vavra, 1997; Löthgren and Tambour, 1999, Allen and Rao, 2000):

- Data Envelopment Analysis (DEA)
- Multidimensional scaling
- Confirmatory factor analysis
- Kruskal's relative importance approach
- Cluster analysis
- Canonical correlation analysis
- Dominance analysis
- Probability plotting methods

Finally, recent research efforts in the problem of measuring and analyzing customer satisfaction include approaches from the field of dominance-based rough sets, support vector machines, fuzzy logic, and neural networks.

2.4 Consumer Behavioral Models

2.4.1 Consumer Psychology and Satisfaction

Customer ratings on a set of product/service attributes do not explain why a particular attribute is considered important (or unimportant) and why its perform-ance level is considered excellent (or poor). Thus, this performance approach is not able to reveal the psychological intricacies that customer brings to the firm's product or service. This important shortcoming of customer satisfaction perform-ance analysis is emphasized by several researchers who argue that levels of per-formance exist only as external stimuli to consumers (Oliver, 1977).

The approach of psychology and consumer behavioral analysis is based on the assumption that satisfaction is a mental condition of the customer. The perform-ance evaluation of a provided product or service (or some of their characteristics) is quite subjective and for this reason it should be linked with some comparison standards.

A generic model of consumer behavioral analysis considers the working on a customer's mind as a "black box", implying that consumer's psychology mediated the impact of performance observations on satisfaction judgments (Figure 2.7). Alternative behavioral models try to describe and explain what exactly happens in this "black box" in order to unravel the processing of future performance (Oliver, 1977, 1997).

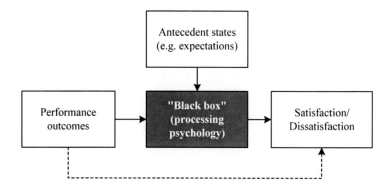

Fig. 2.7 The mediated performance model of satisfaction (Oliver, 1997)

The nature of comparison standards used in this customer satisfaction judgment process received increasing attention during the last years. A typical definition of satisfaction is focused on customer expectations as the main comparison standard (see section 2.1). However, as Woodruff and Gardial (1996) note, there are several comparison standards used by customers, which may vary across stages in a con-sumption process (e.g. pre-purchase, purchase, use, and disposal). These different comparison standards may lead to completely different satisfaction judgments, and they include the following (Woodruff and Gardial, 1996):

- *Expectations*: they represent how the customer believes the product/service will perform.
- *Ideals*: they represent how the customer wishes the product/service would perform.
- *Competitors*: the performance of competitors in the same product/service category may be adopted by customers as a standard for comparison.
- *Other product categories*: products or services in completely different categories may also provide comparison standards for customers.
- *Marketer promises*: they refer to promises that were made by the salesperson, the product/service advertisement, the company spokesperson, or some other form of corporate communication.
- *Industry norms*: they are related to a "model" or average performance level developed by customers with considerable experience in a product category (across companies and brands) or access to industry standards.

2.4.2 Expectancy Disconfirmation

The most important theory for customer satisfaction analysis, in the context of consumer behavior, concerns Oliver's approach (Oliver, 1977, 1980, 1997; Churchill and Suprenant, 1982; Vavra, 1997). According to this particular methodological approach, satisfaction may be defined as a pleasant past-purchasing experience from a product or service given the ante-purchasing expectancy of the customer. The performance judgment process made by customers is presented in Figure 2.8, where the following should be noted:

- Customer perceptions play the most important role in the satisfaction creation process. Perceived performance is not necessarily the same with actual performance, as already emphasized in section 1.1.
- Perceived performance is compared with a standard that may refer to customer expectations (Oliver, 1997), or other comparison standards, as already mentioned (Woodruff and Gardial, 1996).
- The previous comparison results in disconfirmation, i.e. the difference between what was expected and what was received.
- Satisfaction is the evaluation or feeling that results from the disconfirmation process. As Woodruff and Gardial (1996) urge, it is not the comparison itself (i.e. the disconfirmation process), but it is the customer's response to the comparison, given the emotional component of satisfaction.
- Finally, satisfaction feeling leads to various attitude and behavioral outcomes, such as repeat purchase intentions, word of mouth, brand loyalty, etc.

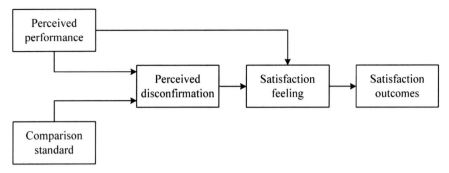

Fig. 2.8 Expectancy disconfirmation model (Woodruff and Gardial, 1996)

The aforementioned comparison process of the customer given his/her expectations is the key concept of this particular methodology. For this reason, Oliver's approach is also called as expectancy disconfirmation model.

The existence of an indifference zone is an important aspect of the expectance disconfirmation process, since it suggests that disconfirmation and performance level are not proportionally related. This zone, which is also called attitude of acceptance in the assimilation-contrast theory, indicates that, from the consumer's perspective, there may be some latitude within which product performance may vary but it still fulfills the consumer's needs (Figure 2.9).

An analytical review of the expectancy disconfirmation model, which is one of the dominant theories of customer satisfaction influencing several research efforts, may be found in Churchill and Suprenant (1982), Yi (1991), and Erevelles and Leavitt (1992).

2.4.3 Fornell's model

Fornell's satisfaction model (Johnson and Fornell, 1991; Anderson and Fornell, 1991; Anderson and Sullivan, 1991; Anderson, 1994; Fornell, 1995) constitutes the basic measurement and analysis tool that is used in both the American Customer Satisfaction Index (ACSI) and the Swedish Customer Satisfaction Barometer (SCSB), as analytically presented in section 7.6.

This particular approach is based on an economic structural model that links different customer satisfaction measures (e.g. expectations, loyalty, complaints, etc.) with specific and pre-defined formulas. Given these defined relations between included variables, the model produces a system of cause and effect relationships.

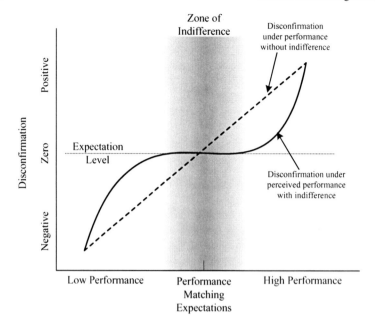

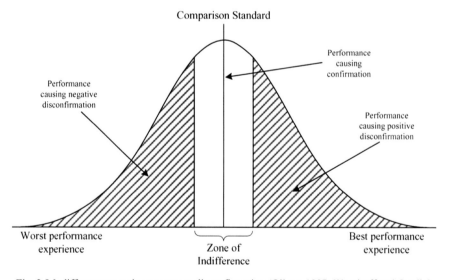

Fig. 2.9 Indifference zone in expectancy disconfirmation (Oliver, 1997; Woodruff and Gardial, 1996)

Generally, as presented in Figure 2.10, the model variables are analyzed in the following main categories:

1. *Satisfaction causes*: One of the most important assumptions of the model is that customer satisfaction has three antecedents: perceived quality, perceived value,

and customer expectations. The positive relation between customer satisfaction and perceived quality is consistent with several studies from marketing and consumer behavioral analysis (Churchill and Suprenant, 1982; Westbrook and Reilly, 1983; Tse and Wilton, 1988; Yi, 1991; Fornell, 1992). According to Deming (1981) and Juran and Gryna (1988), the evaluation of perceived quality should take into account the customization of the product or service to customer needs, as well as the product/service reliability. On the other hand, the quality/price ratio may be considered as the main estimate of perceived value, since it is used by customers for comparing similar products and services (Johnson, 1984). Another determinant of satisfaction refers to customer expectations (Oliver, 1980; Van Raaij, 1989). While perceived quality and value are based on recent customer experiences, customer expectations refer to all previous product/service purchase and usage experiences.

2. *Satisfaction*: Customer satisfaction is evaluated using a set of additional parameters, like disconfirmation of expectations and distance from the ideal product/service. These parameters are weighted in order to provide final estimates, while it should be noted that the model assumes that the previous three antecedents may be positively related (Howard, 1977; Johnson et al., 1995).

3. *Satisfaction results*: Following Hirschman's (1970) exit-voice, the consequences of customer satisfaction are focused on customer complaints and loyalty (Fornell and Wernefelt, 1987, 1988). Loyalty is the main dependent variable in the model because of its value as a proxy for profitability.

In this approach, customer satisfaction is based on multiple indicators and it is measured as a latent variable using Partial Least Squares (PLS). PLS is able to estimate this causal model and it is preferred because it is an iterative procedure that does not impose distributional assumptions on the data. PLS estimates weights for the variable measures that maximize their ability to explain customer loyalty as the ultimate endogenous or dependent variable (Fornell et al., 1996).

Furthermore, confirmatory factor analysis and linear equation modeling have been conducted to validate the relationships depicted in the model and the overall framework (Vavra, 1997).

2.4.4 Other Behavioral Models

There are several approaches from social psychology and consumer behavioral analysis that have been used in the customer satisfaction analysis problem. These approaches attempt to give a clearer understanding on how and why satisfaction is created, rather than to provide a quantitative measurement framework.

One of the most important categories of these approaches refers to motivation theories. As already noted, satisfaction is related to the fulfillment of customer needs. Thus, motivation theories may be used in order to indentify needs and study human motivation.

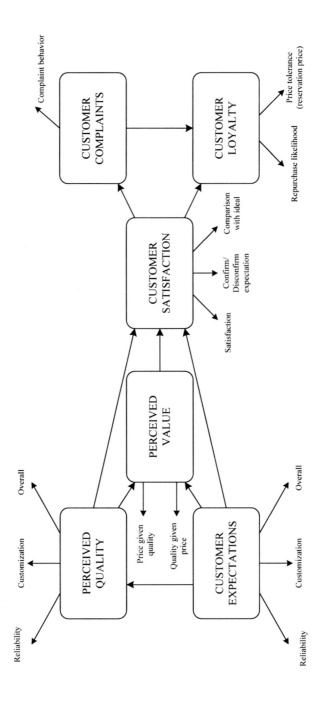

Fig. 2.10 Fornell's satisfaction model (Vavra, 1997)

In this context, early research efforts were focused not only on the determination, but also on the hierarchy of human needs (Murray, 1938; McClelland, 1961; Kassarjian, 1974; Horton, 1974). Maslow's need hierarchy is one the most popular approaches on human motivation. This hierarchy is often presented as a pyramid, and consists of the following stages (Maslow, 1943):

1. *Physiological needs*: biological needs necessary for human survival, like food, water, sleep, etc.
2. *Safety needs*: needs for safety and security, which include personal and financial security, health and well-being, etc.
3. *Love needs*: needs for love, affection and belongingness; they are also referred as needs for affiliation.
4. *Esteem needs*: needs for both the self-esteem and the esteem a person gets from others.
5. *Need for self-actualization*: need for self-fulfillment; self-actualization is described as a person's need to be and do that for which the person was "born to do".

The previous stages are presented in order of importance: the higher needs in this hierarchy only come into focus when the lower needs are met. It should be noted that later Maslow (1970) added a sixth stage: need for self-transcendence (i.e. the need to integrate with the human community rather than to remain as an individualist pursuing self-goals).

Alternative categorizations and hierarchies of human needs have also been proposed in the works of Herzberg et al. (1959), McClelland (1961), Alderfer (1972), and Alderfer et al. (1974).

The contribution of motivation theories to the customer satisfaction analysis problem is focused on the determination of "critical" satisfaction dimensions (Swan and Combs, 1976; Maddox, 1981). Product or service attributes may be classified to satisfiers and dissatisfiers, i.e. attributes that may cause satisfaction and dissatisfaction, respectively, according to their performance. Moreover, it should be mentioned that motivation theories have been focused on job satisfaction studies (see for example Herzberg et al., 1959; Herzberg, 1966, 1968). Oliver (1997) notes that these approaches are not widely adopted in consumer behavior, because they are not capable of generating an exhaustive set of satisfaction drivers, or even of choice criteria.

Another alternative behavioral approach refers to the equity theory, where equity is also referred as fairness, rightness, or deservingness to other entities, whether real or imaginary, individual or collective, person or non-person (Oliver, 1997). The "rule of justice", as proposed by Homans (1961) is the main concept of the equity theory: *"...A person's reward in exchange with other should be proportional to his/her investment..."*

Homan's approach suggests an outcome/input ratio, while reward and investment are used in a rather generic way. For example, in the customer satisfaction problem, customer reward may refer to the satisfaction caused by the usage of a product/service, or by the performance of its attributes. Similarly, investment may refer to the effort, time, or money paid by the customer in order to purchase or use a particular product/service.

According to the equity theory, satisfaction may be seen as the outcome of comparing rewards to investments, taking into account:

- the expectations (or predictions) of the customer,
- the rewards and investments of the company or the seller, and
- the rewards and investments of other customers.

A large number of studies referring to the application of the equity theory in the customer behavioral analysis problem may be found in the literature (Huppertz et al., 1978; Huppertz, 1979; Fisk and Coney, 1982; Mowen and Grove, 1983; Brockner and Adsit, 1986; Goodwin and Ross, 1990; Martins and Monroe, 1994; Lapidus and Pinkerton, 1995), while in several cases the approach is combined with the expectancy disconfirmation theory (Fisk and Young, 1985; Oliver and DeSarbo, 1988).

Finally, a relatively new approach in the context of social psychology that may be used in this particular problem is the regret theory. Since in many cases satisfaction is considered as a comparison outcome, the regret theory suggests that this outcome includes those that might have happened or those that did happen to another consumer who made a different choice of product/service (Bell, 1980; Loomes and Sugden, 1982). For example, a consumer may regret about his/her purchasing decision, thinking that he/she might have purchase an alternative product/service, or even take no purchasing decision at all.

The formulation of these comparison standards, i.e. the way a consumer thinks what might have happened, is mainly based on the following (Oliver, 1997):

- proactive observation (personal intentional direct observations),
- vicarious experience (observing the outcome of others who have made alternative choices), and
- simulation (imagine what might have happened in a hypothetical situation).

The effects of these comparison results on customer satisfaction are analytically presented in Figure 2.11.

The regret theory is one of the most recent research directions of consumer behavioral analysis that studies the customer satisfaction problem, while in several cases its applications are combined with marketing choice models (Harrison and March, 1984; Roese and Olson, 1993; Boninger et al., 1994; Roese, 1994).

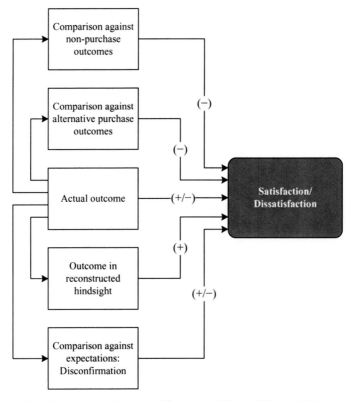

Fig. 2.11 Regret and hindsight effects on satisfaction (Oliver, 1997)

Chapter 3
Other Methodological Approaches

3.1 Quality Approach

3.1.1 Customer Satisfaction and TQM

Over the years, several definitions of quality have been proposed and the concept of quality has been radically evolved (Reeves and Bednar, 1994). Most of the early studies were developed in the context of manufacturing firms and quality was essentially defined as conformance to specifications (Muffatto and Panizzolo, 1995). The early efforts for measuring and analyzing quality in a business environment were focused on the inspection of tangible attributes and characteristics of the product, using statistical/process quality control techniques. The study of employee attitude, the development of motivation theories and techniques, and the research of human behavior (employees or customers) were developed in parallel, but independently from the product control process. In addition, marketing research, new product development methodologies, and customer service approaches were developed without any direct relation with the quality processes within business organizations.

However the increased importance of the service sector has led to a major shift in the way researchers and practitioners have defined and approached quality. The modern approach provides an externally focused definition of quality by embodying the customer dimension: quality is delighting the customers by fully meeting their needs and expectations.

The change of orientations has been reinforced by the development of Total Quality Management (TQM), which is a management approach for an organization, centered on quality, based on the participation of all its members and aiming at long-term success through customer satisfaction, and benefits to all members of the organization and to society (ISO 8402:1994).

E. Grigoroudis and Y. Siskos, *Customer Satisfaction Evaluation*, International Series in Operations Research & Management Science 139, DOI 10.1007/978-1-4419-1640-2_3, © Springer Science + Business Media, LLC 2010

Although different management philosophies have been developed in the context of TQM, customer satisfaction is the core concept in all of them. For example, Deming (1986) emphasizes that the consumer is by necessity the most important part of the production system, since without a consumer, there is no reason to produce (the consumer is the end-user of whatever product and service is being supplied). As Deming points out, the only meaningful definition of quality is that which the consumer specifies, and for this reason, several researchers suggest that Deming's definition of quality is based on the user's perspective. Juran (1988) also sees quality as a concept that can only be usefully defined by the consumer. He introduced a widely adopted definition of quality, "fitness for use", which describes the extent to which a product successfully serves the purpose of the user. Furthermore, his "spiral progress in quality" demonstrates his quality improvement process in a TQM environment, where customer input and feedback is necessary to direct product design and improvement (Figure 3.1).

Other definitions of quality in the TQM area are presented in Table 3.1, where it should be emphasized that although quality leaders may have their own ideas on how quality should be defined, it is clear that all point in the same direction: quality should be judged by customers.

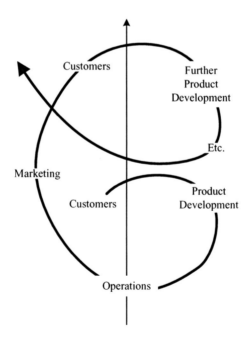

Fig. 3.1 Juran's spiral of progress in quality (Juran, 1988)

Table 3.1 Some definitions of quality (Campbell et al., 2002; Chandrupatla, 2009)

Author	Definition
W. Edwards Deming	Aimed at meeting the needs of the consumer, present and future.
Joseph Juran	Fitness for use (fitness for use refers to product features that meet customer needs or freedom from deficiencies).
Philip Crosby	Conformance to requirements (quality is not "elegance" or "goodness").
Armand Feigenbaum	Based upon a customer's actual experience with a product/service measured against his/her requirements.
Drucker	What the customer gets out of product/service and is willing to pay for.
Robert Peach	The totality of characteristics of an entity that bear on its ability to satisfy stated and implied needs.
ISO 9000	The degree to which a set of inherent characteristics fulfills requirements (requirements are needs or expectations).
American Society for Quality (ASQ)	Excellence in goods and services, especially to the degree they conform to requirements and satisfy customers.

Beside customer focus, TQM recognizes the significant interaction among the traditional quality processes of products or services, the behavior and motivation of the employees, the relationships with the suppliers, the development of new products, and the production process (Dutka, 1995).

Total customer service is one of the most important outcomes of a TQM project. In a total customer service environment, the organization (Stephen and Weimerskirch, 1994):

- systematically monitors the performance and reliability of its services;
- compares its performance against competition, and, if necessary, modifies and improves its service processes.

Consequently, customer satisfaction has the most important role in the development process of a TQM environment, given that it is based on the needs, the expectations and, generally, the voice of the customers. This way, emphasis is given on the customer's perspective for the added value of product and services. In general, products and services may be considered as solutions to specific customers problems.

Within the frame of TQM, the concept of customer gets a new wider dimension so as to cover not only the external, but also the internal customers (employees). Also, the terms "quality" and "satisfaction" are not defined based on internal rules and standards of the organization, but they are determined by customers themselves through a process of comparing alternative products and competitive companies.

3.1.2 Quality Management Systems

A quality management system helps business organizations to develop clear requirements, communicate policies and procedures, monitor work performance, and improve teamwork. It is defined as a management system to direct and control an organization with regard to quality (ISO 9000:2000). The purpose of a quality management system is to establish a framework of reference points, ensuring that whenever a process is performed, the same information, methods, skills and controls are used and applied in a consistent manner (Dale, 1999).

The ISO 9000 standards are the most widely used quality management systems. They were developed by the International Standards Organization (ISO), which was formed by the United Nations in 1947. The main principles of ISO 9000:2000, which is the current family of quality standard, include the following:

1. Customer focus
2. Leadership
3. Involvement of people
4. Process approach
5. System approach to management
6. Continual improvement
7. Factual approach to decision making
8. Mutually beneficial supplier relationships

The new family of ISO quality management standards comprises three individual standards:

- ISO 9000 (Quality management systems: Fundamentals and vocabulary)
- ISO 9001 (Quality management systems: Requirements)
- ISO 9004 (Quality management systems: Guidelines for performance improvements)

It should be noted that business organizations are certified according to the ISO 9001, while the other standards are complementary and each adds a dimension to the development of an effective quality management system.

The ISO 9000 family of standards promotes the adoption of a process approach when developing, implementing and improving a quality management system. This process approach is shown in Figure 3.2, where the adoption of a Plan-Do-Check-Act cycle for managing these processes is clearly presented. The role of customer in the integrated quality management system is crucial, since it drives all the processes of the organization. As emphasized by Hill (1996), customers, not management, are the starting point of the quality management system; the role of management is to ensure that customer requirements are determined and are met with the aim of enhancing customer satisfaction.

A detailed and practical process approach for developing and conducting customer satisfaction surveys within the ISO 9001:2000 standard is proposed by Vavra (2002). His approach consists of five main stages:

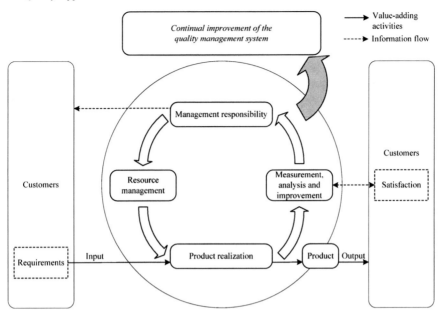

Fig. 3.2 Process view of the ISO 9000 standards

1. Discovery (understand customer satisfaction and its role in standard).
2. Design and deployment (define the process of customer satisfaction measurement).
3. Deduction (define how customer satisfaction data will be analyzed).
4. Discourse (decide about the reporting of the results).
5. Development (identify ways to stimulate continual improvement).

Consequently, it is clear that the central purpose of a quality management system is to ensure that the organization provides goods or services that satisfy customers. However, although a quality standard contains specific requirements in order to enhance customer satisfaction, the business organizations have the ability to develop their own approaches to the customer satisfaction measurement problem. Thus, by adopting the quality philosophy and meeting the requirements of the standard, they may develop programs for measuring customer satisfaction that best fit their structures and processes.

3.1.3 Business excellence models

Business excellence has been evolved within the quality movement and may be described as an effective quality management using appropriate tools and knowledge for the success of the organization. Business excellence is based on the management of resources, which leads to organizational learning and solution to prob-

lems, by creating a team environment and an orientation to achieve specific results. Different business excellence models are implemented in many countries
worldwide trying to assist organizations to improve their performance (Bohoris,
1995; Vokurka et al., 2000; Cauchick, 2001). These models provide the guidelines
for effective quality management and may be used as self assessment models. Although, a large number of national business excellence models and quality awards
have been proposed, the most important of them include the Deming Prize, the
Malcolm Baldrige National Quality Award, and the European Foundation for
Quality Management Excellence Model.

The Deming Prize was the first business excellence model established in 1951.
It was developed by the Union of Japanese Scientists and Engineers to commemo-
rate Dr Deming's contribution to the Japanese industry and to further promote the
continuing development of quality control in Japan (Porter and Tanner, 1998). The
Deming Prize has a total of five categories: Deming Prize for Individuals, Deming
Application Prize, Deming Application Prize for Small Companies, Deming Application Prize for Divisions, and Quality Control Award for Factories. Non-
Japanese companies have been allowed to apply for and receive the Deming Prize
since 1984. The aim of this quality award is to evaluate company's quality assurance policies and activities, company-wide quality control practices, as well as the
results achieved by the application of statistical techniques and quality circles. The
Prize is given to companies that have achieved distinctive performance through
the application of company-wide quality control. The evaluation criteria of the
Deming Prize are divided into the following ten categories of equal importance:

1. Policies
2. Organization and its management
3. Education and dissemination
4. Collection, dissemination and use of information of quality
5. Analysis
6. Standardization
7. Control
8. Quality assurance
9. Effects
10. Planning for the future

The Malcolm Baldrige National Quality Award (MBNQA) was established in
1987 by the United Stated (US) government as a statement of national intention to
provide quality leadership and improve the competitiveness of US companies. It is
currently administered by the National Institute of Standards and Technology
(NIST), with the American Society of Quality (ASQ) assisting in the application
review process, preparation of award documents and other administrative duties
(Vokurka et al., 2000). The award is assigned annually to companies and organizations that excel in quality management practice and performance. Three awards
may be given annually in each of six categories (the education and healthcare
categories were added in 1999, while a government and nonprofit category was
added in 2007):

1. Manufacturing
2. Service company
3. Small business
4. Education
5. Healthcare
6. Nonprofit

Organizations that apply for the MBNQA are judged by an independent board of examiners. Recipients are selected based on achievement and improvement in seven performance criteria, as presented in Figure 3.3: Leadership, Strategic Planning, Customer and Market Focus, Measurement, Analysis, and Knowledge Management, Human Resources Focus, Process Management, and Business Results. Each one these main performance dimensions is divided in more specific items (Table 3.2).

The MBQNA has sustained a number of major modifications since its introduction and continues to change every year. These modifications concern the number and weights of the criteria, the categories of the evaluation dimensions and the evaluation process. Maybe the most important modifications of the award concern the substantial focus given on the business results since 1995 (450 out of 1000 point values) and the introduction of society results in 2003.

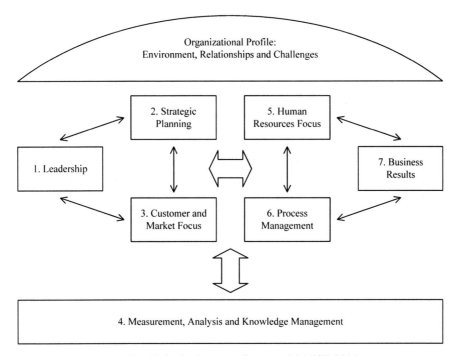

Fig. 3.3 MBNQA business excellence model (NIST, 2006)

Table 3.2 MBNQA examination criteria (NIST, 2006)

Criteria	Items
1. Leadership	1.1 Organizational leadership
	1.2 Social responsibility
2. Strategic Planning	2.1 Strategy development
	2.2 Strategy deployment
3. Customer and Market Focus	3.1 Customer and market knowledge
	3.2 Customer relationships and satisfaction
4. Measurement, Analysis and Knowledge Management	4.1 Measurement and analysis of organizational performance
	4.2 Information and knowledge management
5. Human Resources Focus	5.1 Work systems
	5.2 Employee learning and motivation
	5.3 Employee wellbeing and satisfaction
6. Process Management	6.1 Value criterion processes
	6.2 Support processes
7. Business Results	7.1 Customer-focused results
	7.2 Product and service results
	7.3 Financial and market results
	7.4 Human resource results
	7.5 Organizational effectiveness results
	7.6 Governance and social responsibility results

The European Foundation for Quality Management (EFQM) was founded by 14 of the leading Western European businesses in 1988, when several major companies in Europe realized that their only way of surviving in business was to give much greater attention to quality (Bohoris, 1995). In recognition of achievement as a feature of the policy of the EFQM, the European Quality Award (EQA) was established in 1991 with the support of the European Organization for Quality (EOQ) and the European Commission (EC). In 2006, the award was renamed as the European Excellence Award (EEA) to reflect the changing environment of the EFQM and its members. It is reviewed and updated on a 3-year cycle, with input from members and academia.

The EFQM excellence model is based on nine criteria (Figure 3.4), which are divided into "Enablers" and "Results". The "Enablers" criteria cover what an organization does, while the "Results" criteria refer to what an organization achieves and the revealing assumption is that "Results" are caused by "Enablers". The nine main evaluation criteria are divided into a number of subcriteria as shown in Table 3.3. The model has a scoring system similar to that used in the MBNQA model, with 500 points allocated to the "Enablers" and 500 points allocated to the "Results".

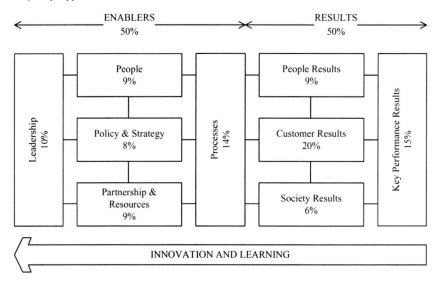

Fig. 3.4 EFQM business excellence model (EFQM, 2006)

The EFQM model is based on the premise that excellent results with respect to performance, customers, people and society are achieved through leadership driving policy and strategy, people, partnerships and resources, and processes (EFQM, 2006). It is underpinned by the fundamental concept of continuous improvement and by the Plan-Do-Check-Act cycle of Deming. The scores of the model are derived using the RADAR process, which is a scoring matrix and evaluation tool assisting discipline and consistency in self-assessment. RADAR refers to Results (what an organization achieves), Approach (what an organization plans to do and the reasons for it), Deployment (extent to which an organization uses the approach and what it does to deploy it), and Assessment and Review (what an organization does to assess and review both the approach and the deployment of the approach).

An alternative business excellence model has been proposed by Kanji (1998), who applied a structural modeling approach in order to establish a Business Excellence Index (BEI). This index is a means of measuring customers', employees' and shareholders' satisfaction simultaneously within an organization, so as to obtain a comprehensive evaluation of the organizational performance (Kanji, 2001). The structural model links together the prime (leadership), the four principles (delight the customer, management by fact, people based management and continuous improvement), and the four core concepts (customer focus, process performance, people performance and improvement culture) to provide forces of excellence in an organization (Figure 3.5).

All the previous business excellence models and quality awards provide a non-prescriptive framework that recognizes that there are many approaches to achieving sustainable excellence.

Table 3.3 EFQM criteria and subcriteria (EFQM, 2006)

Criteria	Subcriteria
1. Leadership	1a. Leaders develop the mission, vision and values and are role models of a culture of Excellence.
	1b. Leaders are personally involved in ensuring the organization's management system is developed, implemented and continuously improved.
	1c. Leaders are involved with customers, partners and representatives of society.
	1d. Leaders motivate, support and recognize the organization's people.
2. Policy and Strategy	2a. Policy and Strategy are based on the present and future needs and expectations of stakeholders.
	2b. Policy and based on information from performance measurement, research, learning and creativity related activities.
	2c. Policy and Strategy are developed, reviewed and updated.
	2d. Policy and Strategy are deployed through a framework of key processes.
	2e. Policy and Strategy are communicated and implemented.
3. People	3a. People resources are planned, managed and improved.
	3b. People's knowledge and competencies are identified, developed and sustained.
	3c. People are involved and empowered.
	3d. People and the organization have a dialogue.
	3e. People are rewarded, recognized and cared for.
4. Partnership and Resources	4a. External partnerships are managed.
	4b. Finances are managed.
	4c. Buildings, equipment and materials are managed.
	4d. Technology is managed.
	4e. Information and knowledge are managed.
5. Processes	5a. Processes are systematically designed and managed.
	5b. Processes are improved, as needed, using innovation in order to fully satisfy and generate increasing value for customers and other stakeholders.
	5c. Products and Services are designed and developed based on customer needs and expectations.
	5d. Products and Services are produced, delivered and serviced.
	5e. Customer relationships are managed and enhanced.
6. Customer Results	6a. Perception Measures.
	6b. Performance Indicators.
7. People Results	7a. Perception Measures.
	7b. Performance Indicators.
8. Society Results	8a. Perception Measures.
	8b. Performance Indicators.
9. Key Performance Results	9a. Key performance Outcomes.
	9b. Key performance Indicators.

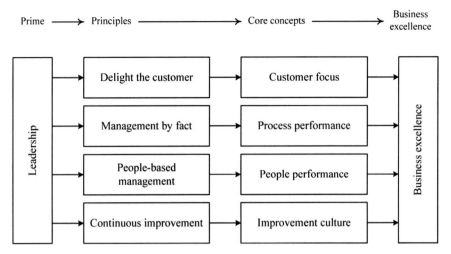

Fig. 3.5 Kanji's business excellence model (Kanji, 1998)

However, customer-focus is a fundamental concept in these self-assessment approaches, since it should be present in the organization's philosophy, structure, processes, and results. The term "customer" refers mainly to external customers, although employee satisfaction and results are also considered. Within the frame of business excellence models, the external customer is defined as anyone outside the organization who receives products, services, or some other benefits from it, such as service users, clients, beneficiaries, members, funders, the general public, other services, stakeholders, and targeted groups.

There are several studies that have found a positive correlation between the adoption of a business excellence model and the improved organizational results, though the main contribution of these approaches is that they are based on TQM-oriented criteria that allow self-assessment on an ongoing basis and thus, they may be used as a measuring stick for performance comparison with other business organizations.

3.2 Service Quality

3.2.1 Ideal Point Approach

The "ideal point" is one of the earliest approaches in marketing that offer a consumer comparative standard. It is based on a process whereby the features of a product or service are compared with the performance of an "ideal" product, as defined by customers.

The overall quality judgment of a customer for a given brand, in comparison to the ideal brand, is given by the following equation (Ginter, 1974):

$$Q_j = 100 - \sum_{i=1}^{n} \mathrm{Pr}_{ij} \left| P_{ij} - I_i \right| \tag{3.1}$$

where Q_j is the quality judgment of brand j, Pr_{ij} is the probability that brand j possesses attribute i, P_{ij} is the performance level of brand j on attribute i, I_i is the ideal level of attribute i, and n is the number of attributes.

In order to apply this particular approach, using equation (3.1), the following should be taken into account (Oliver, 1997):

- The model assumes that customers are able to assess the probabilities Pr_{ij} and that all attributes are equally important.
- The absolute value in equation (3.1) ensures the validity of the results in case of quality attributes that constitute non-monotonic criteria. However, this assumes that negative and positive deviations from ideal levels are equally undesirable to customers.
- The overall quality judgment Q_j is defined in the interval [0, 100], while $Q_j = Q_{ideal} = 100$ holds only in the case that the brand j has ideal performance levels for all of its attributes.
- Customer judgments are measured using quantified qualitative scales (see Figure 3.6).

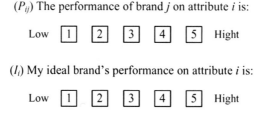

(P_{ij}) The performance of brand j on attribute i is:

Low   [1]   [2]   [3]   [4]   [5]   Hight

(I_i) My ideal brand's performance on attribute i is:

Low   [1]   [2]   [3]   [4]   [5]   Hight

Fig. 3.6 Measurement scales for the ideal point approach (Oliver, 1997)

During the evaluation process, at which this particular model focuses on the post-purchase customer behavior, it is possible to assume that the customer has already observed performance levels, and now holds them with some degree of certainty, so that $\mathrm{Pr}_{ij} = 1$. In this case, equation (3.1) becomes (Jan-Benedict and Steenkamp, 1990):

$$Q_j = 100 - \sum_{i=1}^{n} \left| P_{ij} - I_i \right| \tag{3.2}$$

As Cadotte et al. (1987) note, the ideal product/service may be either a fictitious product/service that reflects the customer needs and expectations, or the dominant, in terms of quality, product/service in the market. The former case refers to the product/service, which is truly the best brand, while the latter refers to the best product/service that can be offered (a proxy for the ideal standard).

3.2.2 Servqual

The Servqual model is the most widely adopted approach in the area of service quality measurement and management, having numerous real-world applications and academic researches. The model may be considered as an extension of the ideal point approach, adopting the "service gaps" theory (see section 1.2.1) and the expectancy disconfirmation paradigm (Parasuraman et al., 1985, 1988, 1991, 1994; Zeithaml et al., 1990).

The principles of the Servqual model are based on the assumption that satisfaction is related to the size and direction of disconfirmation of a person's experience vis-à-vis his/her initial expectations (Churchill and Surprenant, 1982; Smith and Houston, 1982; Parasuraman et al., 1985). In fact, the model identifies five potential gaps occurring in the service delivery process (Figure 3.7):

1. *Gap 1*: between customers' expectations and management's perceptions about these expectations.
2. *Gap 2*: between management's perceptions of customers' expectations and service quality specifications.
3. *Gap 3*: between service quality specifications and service delivery.
4. *Gap 4*: between service delivery and external communications to customers about service delivery.
5. *Gap 5*: between customers' expectations and their perceptions on service quality.

As noted by Zeithaml et al. (1990), the conceptual model of Figure 3.7 may provide a good understanding of service quality and its determinants, while at the same time, it implies a logical process which companies can employ to measure and improve quality of services.

The first four gaps are identified as functions of the way in which service is delivered, while Gap 5 pertains to the customer. As such, it is considered to be the true measure of service quality. However, the key to closing Gap 5 is to close Gaps 1-4. As shown in Table 3.4, different reasons may cause these service quality gaps, and thus, different strategies and tactics may be applied in order to close them (see for example Zeithaml et al., 1990).

Further studies have extended the concept of Gap 5 to what is called a "zone of tolerance" (Figure 3.8). The zone of tolerance depends on the desired service level (the quality level that customer believe that can and should receive) and the adequate service level (the minimum quality level that customers are willing to accept). The final customer perception of service quality is compared to this zone of tolerance. The previous three service levels (i.e. desired, adequate, and perceived) may define the following measures:

$$\begin{cases} MSA = Perceived\ Service - Adequate\ Service \\ MSS = Perceived\ Service - Desired\ Service \end{cases} \tag{3.3}$$

where *MSA* is the measure of service adequacy and *MSS* is the measure of service superiority.

The Servqual model was originally measured on ten aspects of service quality: reliability, responsiveness, competence, access, courtesy, communication, credibility, security, understanding or knowing the customer, and tangibles. However, in early 1990s, the model has been refined, taking into account the results of various statistical analyses, revealing a significant correlation among the initial ten dimensions. The final service quality dimensions, that are able to capture facets of all the ten originally conceptualized dimensions, are the following:

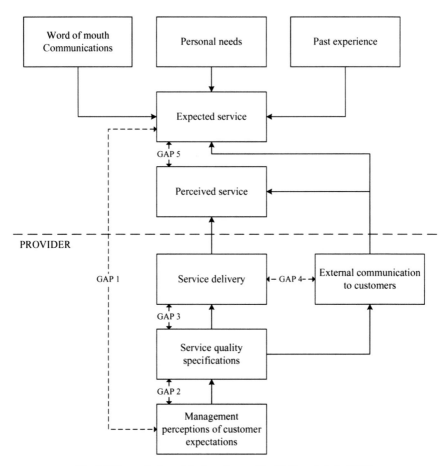

Fig. 3.7 Conceptual model of service quality (Zeithaml et al., 1990)

Table 3.4 Factors contributing to service quality gaps (Zeithaml et al., 1990)

Service quality gap	Key reasons
Gap 1	Lack of marketing research orientation
	Inadequate upward communication from contact personnel to management
	Too many levels of management
Gap 2	Inadequate commitment to service quality
	Lack of perception of feasibility
	Inadequate task standardization
	Absence of goal setting
Gap 3	Role ambiguity
	Role conflict
	Poor employee-job fit
	Poor technology-job fit
	Inappropriate supervisory control systems
	Lack of perceived control
	Lack of teamwork
Gap 4	Inadequate horizontal communication (particularly among operations, marketing, and human resources, as well as across branches)
	Propensity to overpromise in communications

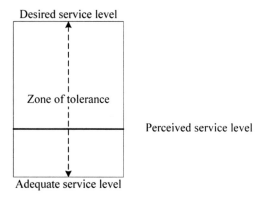

Fig. 3.8 Zone of tolerance

1. Tangibles (appearance of physical facilities, personnel, and communication materials).
2. Reliability (ability to perform the promised service dependably and accurately).
3. Responsiveness (willingness to help customers and provide prompt service).
4. Assurance (knowledge and courtesy of employees and their ability to convey trust and confidence).
5. Empathy (caring, individualized attention the firm provides its customers).

These major service quality dimensions are further divided into a set of 22 variables/items, which are able to assess the aforementioned dimensions and develop the Servqual instrument.

The calculation of the Servqual score in a particular service quality dimension is based on the following formula:

$$G_i = \frac{1}{n_i} \sum_{j=1}^{n_i} (P_{ij} - I_{ij}) \tag{3.4}$$

where G_i is the quality gap (perceived service quality) of dimension i, P_{ij} and I_{ij} are the performance perception and the excellence expectation for item j in dimension i, respectively, and n_i is the number of items in dimension i.

For collecting the necessary data, a predefined questionnaire is used that includes two major parts: the first one refers to the measurement of customer expectations based on his/her exceptional level of a service quality item, while the second contains questions for evaluating customer perception for these items. Usually a 7-point Likert scale is used in order to measure perceptions and expectations, as presented in Figure 3.9.

There are two basic variations of the Servqual model: the unweighted and the weighted model. The unweighted model is based on the following formula:

$$G = \frac{1}{5M} \sum_{k=1}^{M} \sum_{t=1}^{5} G_{kt} \tag{3.5}$$

where G is the overall Servqual score (i.e. company's overall service quality gap), G_{kt} is the Servqual score of customer k for dimension t, and M is the number of customers.

On the other hand the weighted model takes into account the importance of service quality dimension as expressed by customers. Dimension weights are usually estimated by asking customers to allocate a total of 100 importance points to the defined service quality dimensions, although alternative approaches may be found in the literature. The overall Servqual score is then given by the formula:

(P_{ij}) The performance of item j of service quality dimension i is excellent:

Strongly Disagree $\boxed{1}$ $\boxed{2}$ $\boxed{3}$ $\boxed{4}$ $\boxed{5}$ $\boxed{6}$ $\boxed{7}$ Strongly Agree

(I_{ij}) An excellent company should have a high performance on item j of service quality dimension i :

Strongly Disagree $\boxed{1}$ $\boxed{2}$ $\boxed{3}$ $\boxed{4}$ $\boxed{5}$ $\boxed{6}$ $\boxed{7}$ Strongly Agree

Fig. 3.9 Measurement scales for the ideal point approach (Oliver, 1997)

$$G = \frac{1}{M} \sum_{k=1}^{M} \sum_{t=1}^{5} w_{kt} G_{kt} \qquad (3.6)$$

where w_{kt} is the weight of customer k for dimension t.

Regardless of the variation of the Servqual model, Zeithaml et al. (1990) propose a number of additional analyses that may be performed, including mainly the following:

- Comparative analysis for each service quality dimension or detailed item.
- Estimation of Servqual scores for each customer and analysis of different customer segments having distinguished perceptions for service quality.
- Comparison analysis of customer perceptions and expectations over time.
- Comparison of company's Servqual scores against competitor scores.

In the context of the Servqual model, service quality is defined as the degree and direction of discrepancy between consumer perceptions and expectations. In their discussion, Parasuraman et al. (1988) assert that the Servqual scale deals with perceived quality and looks specifically at service quality, not customer satisfaction. They state that *"...perceived service quality is a global judgment or attitude concerning the superiority of service whereas satisfaction is related to a specific transaction..."*

The relationship between customer satisfaction and service quality has been a matter of considerable debate during the last decades. In fact, two major approaches may be found (Galloway, 1999): customer satisfaction may be considered as an antecedent of service quality, as in the Servqual model, or service quality may be assumed to be an antecedent of customer satisfaction, as in the expectancy disconfirmation approach. Other researchers suggest that neither satisfaction nor service quality may be antecedent to the other (McAlexander et al., 1994; Dabholkar et al., 2000), or propose a non-recursive relationship between the two constructs (Cronin and Taylor, 1992).

The assumption made for the relationship between customer satisfaction and service quality may also affect the concept of customer expectations. Parasuraman et al. (1985, 1988) emphasize that the term "expectation" is used differently in the service quality literature than in the marketing literature. They note that service expectations do not represent predictions about what service providers would offer, but rather what they should offer. This definition is somehow vague in terms of the meaning of "should"; it is the reason why Parasuraman et al. (1985, 1988) have noted that the service expectations concept is *"...intended to measure customers' normative expectation..."*, and these expectations represent an "ideal standard" of performance.

Despite its similarities with the ideal point approach, it should be noted that the Servqual model focuses on the estimation of the quality gap that can get either positive or negative values (Oliver, 1997).

3.2.3 Other Service Quality Models

The service sector has become the dominant element of the economy, encompassing a diverse and complex range of organizations and enterprises. On the other hand, quality plays an important role for the survival and development of business organizations in the modern environment. The previous remarks justify the importance of service quality, since several empirical studies have found that service quality is related to the organization's financial results (e.g. market share, profitability, asset turnover).

The main characteristic of service quality management is that quality is not easily identifiable and measurable due to inherent characteristics of services, which make them different from goods. Service quality is more difficult to define and measure than product quality, because services appear to have the following characteristics (Ghobadian et al., 1994):

- *Inseparability of production and consumption*: Production and consumption of many services are inseparable, and thus the high visibility of the conversion process means that it is not possible to hide mistakes or quality shortfalls. In labor intensive services, quality occurs during service delivery, usually in an interaction between the client and the contact person from the service firm. The consumer's input becomes critical to the quality of service performance.
- *Intangibility of service*: Most services cannot be counted, measured, inventoried, tested, and verified in advance of sale to assure quality. Because of intangibility, the firm may find it difficult to understand how consumers perceive their services and evaluate service quality. Moreover, in service organizations frontline staff and physical facilities fulfill the dual functions of production and marketing, since they are viewed by the potential customer as signs of quality.
- *Perishability of services*: Services are perishable and cannot be stored in one time period for consumption at a later date. As a result, the organization should provide the service right, first time, every time. This is because, unlike manufactured goods, the quality of services cannot be inspected before consumption.
- *Heterogeneity of services*: Service performance varies from producer to producer, from customer to customer, and from day to day. Consistency of behavior from service personnel is difficult to assure because what the firm intends to deliver may be entirely different from what the consumer receives.

As a result, services require a distinct framework for quality explication and measurement.

The Servqual model developed in this context constitutes the most widespread service quality measurement approach. However, despite its popularity, Servqual has received a large number of criticisms referring to different aspects of the model:

- The model is only applicable to service provision cases and it is not suitable for any business providing tangible products of any kind, whether as a manufacturer or distributor (Hill, 1996).

- It is adequate to measure only perceptions in service quality research and unnecessary to measure expectations (Cronin and Taylor, 1992).
- Servqual is more appropriate for measuring post-transaction satisfaction than for measuring customers' underlying satisfaction with a service or an organization (Cronin and Taylor, 1994).
- "Transaction specific quality" is a distinct concept from "relationship quality" (Teas, 1993; Bitner and Hubbert, 1994).
- The 22 items grouped into five dimensions is a far too rigid approach. Even amongst service providers, the criteria used to measure customer satisfaction cannot be standardized to the same 22 factors (Hill, 1996).
- Consumers use standards other than expectations to evaluate service quality, and thus the term expectation is polysemic (Teas, 1993; Iacobucci et al., 1994).

Buttle (1996) gives an analytical review of the Servqual construct, as well as a thoroughly presentation of the theoretical and operational criticisms to the model.

The previous debate forced researchers to propose alternative service quality models. For example, Cronin and Taylor (1992, 1994) questioned the conceptual basis of the Servqual scale and found it confusing with service satisfaction. They suggested that the expectation component of the Servqual model should be discarded, and service quality should depend only on performance. So, they proposed the Servperf model, an unweighted performance-based scale, as a better method for measuring service quality. In order to calculate the service quality scores, the following formula is used:

$$SQ_k = \sum_{i=1}^{n} P_{ki} \tag{3.7}$$

where SQ_k is the perceived service quality for customer k, P_{ki} is the perception of customer k with respect to the performance of a service firm on attribute i, and n is the number of attributes.

Other service quality models have also been proposed focusing on different aspects of customer perceptions, customer satisfaction, service quality, and the relationship among them. The most characteristic approaches include the following:

- The technical and functional quality model (Grönroos, 1984).
- Organizational service quality improvement model (Moore, 1987).
- Service quality trade-off continuum (Haywood-Farmer, 1988).
- Synthesized model of service quality (Brogowicz et al., 1990).
- Modified service journey model (Nash, 1988).
- Attribute and overall affect model (Dabholkar, 1996).
- Perceived quality and satisfaction model (Spreng and Mckoy, 1996).
- PCP (Pivotal, Core, and Peripheral) attribute model (Philip and Hazlett, 1997).
- Retailed service quality and perceived value model (Sweeney et al., 1997).
- Internal service quality model (Frost and Kumar, 2000).
- Behavioral service quality model (Beddowes et al., 1987).

The previous list is not exhaustive, although it is representative of the research that has been done in the service quality field during the last decades.

Regardless the ongoing debate on the relationship among service quality, customer satisfaction, and customer expectations, the alternative service quality approaches, and, particularly the Servqual model, have been widely applied and have proved that they are able to provide insight into the customer satisfaction analysis problem.

3.3 Employee Satisfaction Modeling

3.3.1 Background

The increasing importance of human resources for business organizations is evident in modern management systems. Though these systems adopt different approaches, employees are considered as internal customers of the organization and employee satisfaction as an important driver for business success. The role and importance of employee satisfaction is crucial, as well, for the effectiveness of a TQM program.

Employee satisfaction is probably the most frequently studied concept in organizational sciences, with over 5,000 articles and dissertations having been written on the topic since 1992 (Cranny et al., 1992). Robbins and Coulter (1996) stated that employee satisfaction is an employee's general attitude towards his/her job. Katzell (1964) argues that if there is a consensus about employee satisfaction, it is the verbal expression of an incumbent's evaluation of his/her job. On this basis, it is an affective or hedonic tone, for which the stimuli are events or conditions experienced in connection with jobs or occupations. Employee satisfaction has been defined as *"a pleasurable or positive emotional state resulting from the appraisal of ones job or job experiences"* (Locke, 1976). According to Cranny et al. (1992) employee satisfaction is an affective -that is, emotional- reaction to one's job, resulting from the incumbent's comparison of actual outcomes with those that are desired (expected, deserved, etc.).

Evidently, there is no single definition about employee satisfaction. It is a rather complex concept and is often referred to as job satisfaction, though there are different opinions about it. Furthermore, it is not clear if there are specific measurement dimensions or if employee satisfaction just reflects an emotional state. The problems concerning the clear definition of employee satisfaction refer mostly to the complexity of the topic, the subjectivity and the quality nature of the concept of satisfaction, the difficulties occurred when comparing with other standards, as well as the differently oriented scientists involved in the research.

During the last twenty years, a large number of studies have investigated the relationship between employee satisfaction and specific job characteristics, with often contradictory results. Most of them have originated from the field of social psychology and are based on human behavioral theories, while others emphasize the importance of employee satisfaction in a TQM context.

The linkage between employee satisfaction and business performance has also historically been challenged by many researchers (Vroom, 1964; Bernhardt et al., 2000). Moreover, job satisfaction has been shown to relate positively with specific facets of performance like organizational citizenship behavior (Smith et al., 1983; Organ, 1988), which is employee behavior that is not formally required in a job description but is nevertheless critical for organizational success (e.g. helping co-workers, volunteering for extra assignments).

Similarly to job satisfaction, affective commitment is an important determinant of organizational performance. Whereas satisfaction denotes positive emotions toward a particular job, organizational commitment is the degree to which an employee feels loyal to a particular organization (Mueller et al., 1992; Price, 1997). A large body of research has investigated the linkage between overall job satisfaction and organizational commitment (Elliot and Hall, 1994; Fletcher and Williams, 1996). At the individual level of analysis, research has shown high affective commitment to be related to high levels of job performance (Mowday et al., 1974; Steers, 1977), high job involvement (Blau, 1985; Brooke et al., 1988), high job satisfaction (Kanungo, 1982; Mathieu and Farr, 1991), and low absenteeism (Koch and Steers, 1978; Mathieu and Kohler, 1990).

An even more widely accepted relationship refers to employee satisfaction and employee turnover. Turnover is one of the most widely studied outcomes of both satisfaction and commitment, and it is based on the axiomatic connection that researchers make between employee attitudes and behaviors (Bluedorn, 1982; Mowday et al., 1982). Research in employee turnover is primarily concerned with voluntary turnover defined as *"individual movements across the membership boundary of a social system which is initiated by the individual"* (Price, 1997). Models of employee turnover almost universally propose a negative relationship between satisfaction and turnover (Hom and Griffeth, 1991, 1995).

Some more recent researches have shown that employee satisfaction can be linked to customer satisfaction (Tornow and Wiley, 1991; Tompkins, 1992). Schlesinger and Zomitsky (1991) found that employees' perception of service quality positively relates to both job satisfaction and employee self-perceived service capability. This point of view is represented in Figure 3.10, through the cycle of good service. This diagram suggests that customer satisfaction yields to profits, which can improve payments and therefore employee satisfaction. This, in turn, is able to improve employees' performance, which will increase the level of customer satisfaction, and so on (Schlesinger and Heskett, 1991).

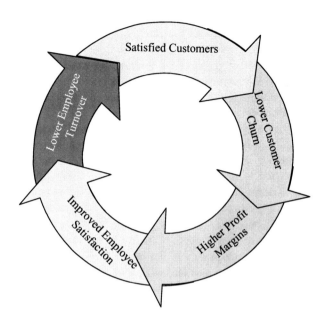

Fig. 3.10 The cycle of good service (Schlesinger and Heskett, 1991)

Another related interesting concept concerns job security, which is critical for influencing work-related outcomes. For example, job security is an important determinant of employee health (Kuhnert et al., 1989), physical and psychological wellbeing of employees (Jacobson, 1991; Kuhnert and Palmer, 1991), employee turnover (Arnold and Feldman, 1982), employee retention (Ashford et al., 1989; Iverson, 1996), job satisfaction (Ashford et al., 1989), and organizational commitment (Ashford et al., 1989; Iverson, 1996).

Finally, several studies have investigated the linkage between employee satisfaction and other additional important factors. Some of them involve job stress (Elangovan, 2001), wages and communication level (Pincus, 1986; Goris et al., 2000), organizational size (Kovach, 1978; Kalleberg and van Buren, 1996), compensation system (Heneman and Schwab, 1985; Heneman and Judge, 2000), and various employees' demographic characteristics such as education level (Vollmer and Kinney, 1955), age (Vollmer and Kinney, 1955; Rhodes, 1983), and marital status (Federico et al., 1976).

3.3.2 Employee Satisfaction and TQM

The first attempts of quality measurement and analysis were focused on the inspection of specific tangible features and characteristics of the product by using statistical quality control and process control techniques. The analysis of employee attitude, the development of motivation methods and techniques, and the investigation of human behavior (employees or customers) were evolved simultaneously, but independently of the products' process control. TQM integrates all the activities of a business organization that are capable to influence the quality of outcomes. This approach acknowledges the substantial interaction of the classic quality operations of products or services, the behavior and motivation of employees, the relationship with the suppliers, as well as the development of new products (Dutka, 1995).

Advocates of TQM hold that the goal of customer satisfaction is achieved through top management commitment to creating an organizational climate that empowers employees and focuses all efforts on this goal. One of the basic concepts in the TQM approaches is that a successful organization needs to have its employees satisfied. Additionally, TQM practices consider as necessary requirements the continuous training of employees, their empowerment and their participation in management decisions. The customer satisfaction focus requires the interaction between front-line employees and customers to be pleasant experiences (especially for the customer). The latter is facilitated by empowered and highly motivated employees who are satisfied with their jobs as a result of their involvement and perception of the emphasis that the organizational culture places on quality. Furthermore, Fulford and Enz (1995) found employee perception of empowerment to have an impact on employee loyalty, concern for others (including customers), and satisfaction. The implication of this finding is that enhancing employee service capability through empowerment contributes to employee job satisfaction, job commitment, pride of workmanship, and what Anderson et al. (1994) called *"employee fulfillment or the degree to which employees feel that the organization continually satisfies their needs"*. Thus, a positive relationship between leadership and commitment, and employee empowerment (leading to job satisfaction) with customer satisfaction is assumed. In almost all of the TQM literature, employee involvement, empowerment, and top management leadership and commitment are identified as crucial elements of a successful TQM program (Deming, 1982; Brower, 1994).

3.3.3 Employee Satisfaction Approaches

A number of different methods have also been proposed as an attempt to study the concept of employee satisfaction. These alternative studies concern mostly various quantitative methods or other approaches based on psychology behavioral analysis.

In general, behavioral models are based on the assumption that job satisfaction is an intellectual condition of the employee. Thus, assessing job satisfaction is quite subjective and it should be compared with other "standards". The most known approaches about employees' behavior concern Maslow's Hierarchy of Needs Theory, Herzberg's Dual Factor Theory, and Hackman-Oldham's Job Characteristics Theory.

The Job Characteristics Theory (Hackman and Oldham, 1980) is the most influential approach of how job characteristics affect people. The basis of the theory is that people can be motivated by the intrinsic satisfaction they find in doing job tasks: when they find their work to be enjoyable and meaningful, people like their jobs and will be motivated to perform their jobs well.

Figure 3.11 illustrates this approach and shows how core characteristics of jobs induce psychological states that in turn lead to job performance, job satisfaction, motivation, and turnover. The five core characteristics are thought to lead to three psychological states:

1. Skill variety, task identity, and task significance combined induce experienced meaningfulness of work.
2. Autonomy leads to feelings of responsibility.
3. Feedback results in knowledge of results about the products of work.

The three psychological states in turn contribute to important outcomes of job satisfaction and motivation of employees.

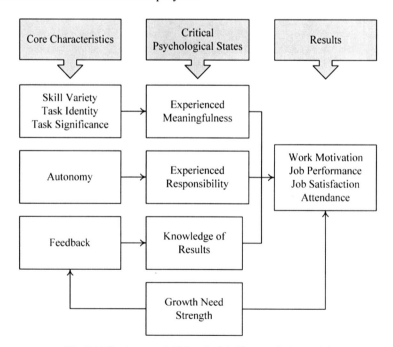

Fig. 3.11 Hackman and Oldham's Job Characteristics model

Another major approach of job satisfaction characteristics concerns Herzberg's Dual Factor Theory (Herzberg et al., 1959), which proposes that an employee's motivation to work is best understood when the respective attitude of that employee is understood. That is, the internal concept of attitude which originates from a state of mind, when probed, should reveal the most pragmatic information for managers with regard to the motivation of workers. In his approach to studying the feelings of people toward their work, or their attitudes, Herzberg et al. (1959) set out to answer three questions:

1. How can one specify the attitude of any individual toward his or her job?
2. What causes these attitudes?
3. What are the consequences of these attitudes?

As a result of their inquiry about the attitudes of employees, Herzberg et al. (1959) developed two distinct lists of factors. One set of factors caused happy feelings or a good attitude within the worker, and these factors, on the whole, were task-related. The other grouping was primarily present when feelings of unhappiness or bad attitude were evident, and these factors, Herzberg claimed, were not directly related to the job itself, but to the conditions that surrounded doing that job. The first group is called motivators (job factors), while the second group is named hygiene factors (extra-job factors), as shown in Table 3.5.

Motivators refer to factors intrinsic within the work itself, like the recognition of a task completed. Conversely, hygienes tend to include extrinsic entities, such as relations with co-workers, which do not pertain to the worker's actual job. According to Herzberg, motivators cause positive job attitudes because they satisfy the worker's need for self-actualization. The presence of these motivators has the potential to create great job satisfaction; however, in the absence of motivators, Herzberg says, dissatisfaction does not occur. On the contrary, hygiene factors, which simply "move" (cause temporary action), have the potential to cause great dissatisfaction, if they are absent, while their presence does not provoke a high level of satisfaction.

Table 3.5 Factors affecting employee satisfaction according to Herzberg theory

Motivators	Hygiene factors
Recognition	Salary
Achievement	Interpersonal relations - supervisor
Possibility of growth	Interpersonal relations - subordinates
Advancement	Interpersonal relations - peers
Responsibility	Supervision - technical
Work itself	Company policy and administration
	Working conditions
	Factors in personal life
	Status
	Job security

3.3.4 Employee Satisfaction Dimensions

The assessment of employee satisfaction dimensions is extremely important for researchers because it gives primarily the ability to define, in some way, the concept of employee satisfaction. The various related studies examine the relation between employee satisfaction and specific aspects or facets of the job. Most of them were applied in order to find out which parts of the job produce satisfaction or dissatisfaction. Several scales have been developed in order to assess employee satisfaction from their job, the most popular of which concern the Job Satisfaction Survey, the Job Descriptive Index, the Minnesota Satisfaction Questionnaire, the Job Diagnostic Survey, the Job in General Scale, and the Michigan Organizational Assessment Questionnaire.

The Job Satisfaction Survey (JSS) (Spector, 1985) assesses nine facets of job satisfaction, as well as overall satisfaction. These facets are:

1. Pay (satisfaction with pay and pay raises)
2. Promotion (satisfaction with promotion opportunities)
3. Supervision (satisfaction with the person's immediate supervisor)
4. Fringe benefits (satisfaction with fringe benefits)
5. Contingent rewards (satisfaction with rewards, not necessarily monetary, given for good performance)
6. Operating conditions (satisfaction with rules and procedures)
7. Co-workers (satisfaction with co-workers)
8. Nature of work (satisfaction with the type of work done)
9. Communication (satisfaction with communication within the organization)

The scale contains 36 items and uses a summated rating scale format, which is very popular in this field. Each of the nine facet subscales contains four items, and a total satisfaction score can be computed by combining all of the items.

The Job Descriptive Index (JDI) (Smith et al., 1969) has probably been the most popular facet scale among organizational researchers. It may also have been the most carefully developed and validated scale. The JDI assesses five facets: work, pay, promotion, supervision and co-workers. The entire scale contains 72 items with either 9 or 18 items per subscale. Each item is an evaluative adjective or short phrase that is descriptive of the job. The JDI uses a 3-point response scale: "Yes", "Uncertain", or "No".

The Minnesota Satisfaction Questionnaire (MSQ) (Weiss et al., 1967) is another satisfaction scale that has been very popular among researchers. The MSQ comes in two forms: a 100-item long version and a 20-item short form. It uses two groups of subscales: the extrinsic and intrinsic satisfaction subscales. Extrinsic satisfaction concerns aspects of work that have little to do with the job tasks or work itself (e.g. pay), while intrinsic satisfaction refers to the nature of job tasks themselves, and how people feel about the work they do. The 20 facets of the MSQ are in many cases more specific than the JDI or JSS and include: activity, independence, variety, social status, supervision (human relations), supervision (technical),

moral values, security, social service, authority, ability utilization, company policies and practices, compensation, advancement, responsibility, creativity, working
conditions, co-workers, recognition, and achievement.

The Job Diagnostic Survey (JDS) (Hackman and Oldham, 1975) is an instrument that has been developed to study the effects of job characteristics on people.
It contains subscales to measure the nature of the job and job tasks, motivation,
personality, psychological states (cognitions and feelings about job tasks), and reactions to the job. One of the reactions is job satisfaction. The JDS is considered
to be a facet measure because it covers several areas of job satisfaction, specifically growth, pays, security, social, and supervision, as well as global satisfaction.
The individual subscales contain 2-5 items each, and the format of the facet items
is a 7-point scale ranging from "Extremely dissatisfied" to "Extremely satisfied"
(for the global satisfaction the 7-point scale ranges from "Disagree strongly" to
"Agree strongly").

The Job in General Scale (JIG) (Ironson et al., 1989) was designed to assess
overall job satisfaction rather than facets. Its format is the same as the JDI, and it
contains 18 items. Each item is an adjective or short phrase about the job in general rather than a facet, while the total score is a combination of all items. The JIG
is a good choice for the assessment of overall job satisfaction when this is of interest rather than facets. Often, facet scales are used to assess general satisfaction by
combining all of the individual facet scores. This can be justified by the fact that
facets often correlate well with overall job satisfaction.

The Michigan Organizational Assessment Questionnaire (MOAQ) contains a
three-item overall satisfaction subscale (Camman et al., 1979). The MOAQ is
rather simple and short, which makes it ideal for use in questionnaires that contain
many scales. For each item, a 7-point Likert type response scale is used, ranging
form "Strongly disagree" to "Strongly agree". Responses are numbered from 1 to
7, respectively, and the items are summed to yield an overall job satisfaction
score.

The problem of assessing a universally accepted set of employee satisfaction
dimensions has been studied extensively in other research efforts. A representative
set of these satisfaction dimensions may include:

1. Company effectiveness (development of specific strategy and goals, quality
   continuous improvement, customer focus)
2. Communication (means and tools, quality of communication, access to information)
3. Relationships (with managers and colleagues)
4. Empowerment (responsibilities, awareness of company's goals and strategy,
   participation in decision making)
5. Job characteristics (job tasks, work insurance, work environment)
6. Career (fair system of performance measurement, career development, opportunities for personal growth)
7. Reward (payment and other benefits, recognition of personal efforts)

Table 3.6 presents additional examples of characteristic factors that affect employee satisfaction, revealing the different perspectives that may be examined to analyze this concept.

Table 3.6 Characteristic dimensions of employee satisfaction

Van Saane et al. (2003)	Shikdara and Das (2003)
Job's content	Vagueness of the job's objectives
Autonomy	Importance of the job's objective
Personal growth	Autonomy
Payment-rewards	Work conditions
Career development	Payment - rewards
Supervision	Supervision
Communication	Career development
Colleagues	Colleagues
Importance of job	Multiple skills
Work load	Communication
Requirements of work	
Sibbald et al. (2000)	**Seo et al. (2004)**
Payment – rewards	Environment (work opportunities)
Work load	Psychological variables (positive and negative
Recognition of personal efforts	sentimentality)
Opportunity to use specific skills	Organization (autonomy, vagueness of respon-
Autonomy	sibilities, conflict of responsibilities, work load,
Job variety	lack of resources, relationships with colleagues
Work conditions	and supervisors, personal growth, routine, jus-
Responsibilities	tice, career opportunities, payment - rewards)
Colleagues	
Pressure	

Finally, it should be noted that while most of the researchers focus on measuring employee satisfaction, other believe that measuring and trying to decrease employee dissatisfaction may have better results for an organization. According to Crow and Hartman (1995), employers should not solely focus on improving job satisfaction in an effort to improve organizational effectiveness, because an employee's level of job satisfaction is a result of a multiplicity of factors, most of which cannot be influenced by the employer. Organizations can influence basic things like pay, working conditions and supervision; however personal job satisfaction may be so complicated that it is beyond the influence of the employer. In short, employers should be responsible for removing sources of job dissatisfaction rather than trying to improve employee satisfaction. From a practical, business standpoint, one of the management's primary roles is to remove road-blocks to effective performance and thus to eliminate obvious sources of job dissatisfaction in terms, for example, of pay inequities, abusive supervision, favoritism, poor working conditions, poor communications and poor performance.

3.4 Other Approaches

3.4.1 Kano's model

The theory of attractive quality according to Kano et al. (1984) originated because of the lack of explanatory power of a one-dimensional recognition of quality. In particular, the one-dimensional view of quality can explain the role of certain quality attributes where both satisfaction and dissatisfaction vary in accordance with performance. However, this approach cannot explain the role of other quality attributes where customer satisfaction (or dissatisfaction) is not proportional to their performance. In this case, fulfilling the individual product/service requirements does not necessarily imply a high level of customer satisfaction (or the opposite, i.e. dissatisfaction does not occur, although the performance of a product/service attribute is relatively low). A characteristic example of this situation is presented by Witell and Löfgren (2007): people are satisfied if a package of milk extends the expiration and dissatisfied if the package shortens the expiration; however, for a quality attribute such as leakage, people are not satisfied if the package does not leak, but they are very dissatisfied if it does.

Kano's model classifies the quality attributes into different quality dimensions (Kano et al., 1984), as presented also in Figure 3.12:

1. *Must-be quality*: These quality attributes are taken for granted when fulfilled but result in dissatisfaction when not fulfilled. The customer expects these attributes, and thus views them as basics. Customers are unlikely to tell the company about them when asked about quality attributes; rather they assume that companies understand these fundamentals of product design (Watson, 2003).
2. *One-dimensional quality*: These attributes result in satisfaction when fulfilled and result in dissatisfaction when not fulfilled. They are also referred as "the-more-the-better" quality attributes (Lee and Newcomb, 1997). The one-dimensional attributes are usually spoken and they are those with which companies compete.
3. *Attractive quality*: These quality attributes provide satisfaction when fully achieved but do not cause dissatisfaction when not fulfilled. They are not normally expected by customer, and thus they may be described as surprise and delight attributes. For this reason, these quality attributes are often left unspoken by customers.
4. *Indifferent quality*: These attributes refer to aspects of a product that are neither good nor bad, and thus, they cannot create satisfaction or dissatisfaction.
5. *Reverse quality*: This category is similar to the one-dimensional quality, but it refers to a high degree of achievement resulting in dissatisfaction, and vice versa (i.e. a low degree of achievement resulting in satisfaction). Thus they may be characterized as "the-less-the-better" quality attributes.

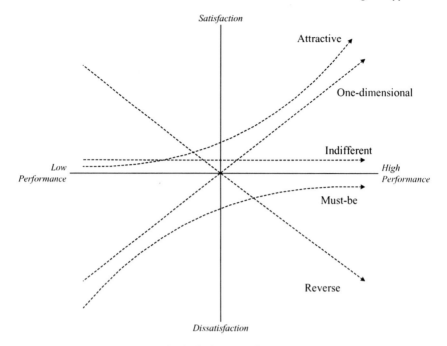

Fig. 3.12 The Kano diagram

The theory of attractive quality is inspired by Herzberg's work on job satisfaction. In particular, Herzberg's Dual Factor Theory (see section 3.3.3) posits that the factors that cause job satisfaction are different form the factors that cause dissatisfaction (Herzberg et al., 1959). Using this context, Kano's model suggests distinguishing customer satisfaction and dissatisfaction, taking into account the degree of achievement.

Kano's approach may give insight into the relationship between the importance of quality attributes and the customer requirements for these attributes. As Kano et al. (1984) note, customers may be communicating different levels of importance in their explicit judgments of importance. In simple words, the theory of attractive quality suggests that the importance of a quality attribute is not constant, but it is affected by the category in which this attribute is assigned, as well as its performance level.

According to Kano (2001), quality attributes are dynamic and can change over time. In particular, a successful attribute follows a life cycle from being indifferent, to attractive, to one-dimensional, to must-be.

Using the Kano's model, customer requirements are better understood, since the product/service criteria that have the highest impact on customer satisfaction or dissatisfaction can be identified. Classifying product/service requirements into must-be, one-dimensional and attractive categories may be useful to identify priorities for product development.

Moreover, the approach may provide valuable help in trade-off situations during the product development stage. If two product/service requirements cannot be met simultaneously due to technical or financial reasons, the attribute with the highest impact on customer satisfaction may be chosen. Discovering and fulfilling attractive requirements may be also very important since it offers significant opportunities for differentiation. A product or service that merely satisfies the must-be and one-dimensional requirements is perceived as average and therefore, interchangeable. The attractive attributes are the key to beating the competition in the marketplace (Hinterhuber et al., 1994).

Must-be, one-dimensional and attractive requirements differ, as a rule, in the utility expectations of different customer segments. Using this as a starting point, customer-tailored solutions for special problems can be elaborated and this may guarantee an optimal level of satisfaction in the different customer segments.

In order to classify quality attributes into the five aforementioned dimensions, Kano et al. (1984) use a specific questionnaire that contains pairs of customer requirement questions, that is, for each customer requirement two questions are asked:

1. How do you feel if a given feature is present in the product (functional form of the question)?
2. How do you feel if that given feature is not present in the product (dysfunctional form of the question)?

Using a predefined preference scale and the evaluation table of Figure 3.13, each customer requirement may be classified into the five dimensions of the Kano's model (Löfgren and Witell, 2008). The dimension designated as questionable contains skeptical answers and is used for responses in which it is unclear whether the responder has understood the question. Finally, in order to decide on the classification of a quality attribute, the proportion of respondents (statistical mode) who classifies a given attribute in a certain category is used (i.e. the attribute is assigned into the category with the highest frequency according to customer answers). Several variations of this classification procedure have been proposed, referring mostly to alternative quality dimensions and evaluation scales. Löfgren and Witell (2008) present a thoroughly review of these alternative approaches.

However, the previous procedure does not take into account that quality attributes are in fact random variables and customer responses form a probability distribution function on the main categories of the Kano's model. Thus, the statistical mode is not always a good indicator of central tendency. Furthermore, different market segments usually have different needs and expectations, so sometimes it is not clear whether a certain attribute can be assigned to a specific category. For this reason, several indices have been proposed to aid the classification process of quality attributes (Löfgren and Witell, 2008). A simple approach is to calculate the average impact on satisfaction and dissatisfaction for each quality attribute. Berger et al. (1993) introduced the *Better* and *Worse* averages, which indicate how strongly an attribute may influence satisfaction or, in case of its non-fulfillment customer dissatisfaction:

$$\begin{cases} Better = \dfrac{A+O}{A+O+M+I} \\[2ex] Worse = -\dfrac{O+M}{A+O+M+I} \end{cases} \qquad\qquad (3.8)$$

where A, O, M, and I are the attractive, one-dimensional, must-be, and indifferent responses, respectively (i.e. percentage of customers assigning a given attribute to a certain category).

Customer Requirements ⇨ ⇩		Dysfunctional				
		Like	Expect	Neutral	Accept	Dislike
Functional	Like	Q	(A) Q	A	A	O
	Expect	(R) Q	(I) Q	I	I	M
	Neutral	R	I	I	I	M
	Accept	R	I	I	I	M
	Dislike	R	R	R	R	Q

A: Attractive quality	I: Indifferent quality
O: One-dimensional quality	R: Reverse quality
M: Must-be quality	Q: Questionable result

Fig. 3.13 Kano evaluation table (Lee and Newcomb, 1997)

The pairs of *Better* and *Worse* averages can be plotted in a two-dimensional diagram representing the impact of quality attributes on satisfaction or dissatisfaction (Figure 3.14), and thus a clearer view for the classification of quality attributes may be obtained.

An alternative classification approach is presented in section 5.4.2, using a dual importance diagram, which combines the derived and stated importance of quality attributes (i.e. the weights of attributes as estimated by a regression-type model and straightforwardly expressed by customers, respectively).

Consequently, the theory of attractive quality may give a valuable explanation about the relationship between the degree of sufficiency of a quality attribute and the customer satisfaction with that attribute. Based on this approach, it can be recognized that customer satisfaction is more than a one-level issue as traditionally examined. Moreover, it may not be enough to merely satisfy customers by meeting their basic and spoken requirements, particularly in a highly competitive environment.

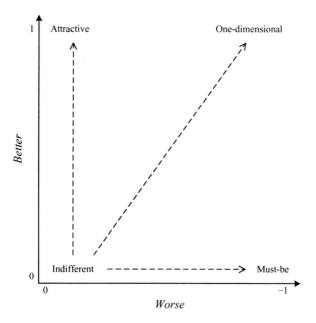

Fig. 3.14 Two-dimensional representation of Kano quality categories (Berger et al., 1993)

Finally, Kano's model has often been combined with various methods of assessing product and service development, such as quality function deployment (Griffin and Hauser, 1993; Matzler et al., 1996; Huiskonen and Pirttilä, 1998; Shen et al., 2000), Servqual (Tan and Pawitra, 2001), and others (see for example the review of Löfgren and Witell, 2008).

3.4.2 Customer Loyalty

Several researchers urge that customer satisfaction is not able to provide a reliable measure for the performance or the quality level of a business organization, particularly in a highly competitive environment. Instead, they suggest that measuring customer loyalty may give a better understanding of consumer behavior in terms of repeat purchases, and thus improve corporate financial results (Stewart, 1995).

Although, customer loyalty and satisfaction are strongly related, they are not identical. Previous research efforts have found that (Griffin, 1995; Vandermerwe, 1996; Oliver, 1997; Hill and Alexander, 2006):

- Customer satisfaction and loyalty are strongly related; however their relation is rather nonlinear (Figure 3.15).
- Loyalty is considered as the main consequence of customer satisfaction.
- Satisfaction is a necessary but not a sufficient condition for customer loyalty.

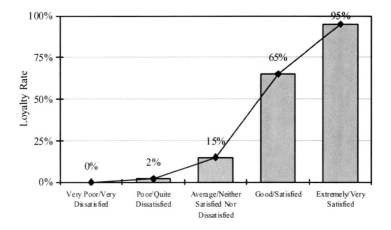

Fig. 3.15 A characteristic link between satisfaction and loyalty (Hill and Alexander, 2006)

Until mid 1970s, customer loyalty measurement was mainly based on analyzing repurchase and brand choice data, using classical statistical methods and data
analysis techniques (Newman and Werbel, 1973; Bass, 1974). Modern approaches
are based on the works of Jacoby (1971, 1975), Jacoby and Kyner (1973), Jacoby
and Chestnut (1978), Tarpey (1974, 1975), and Elrond (1988), in which the definition of loyalty depends on a positive commitment level by customers, instead of
purchase (or repurchase) actions for a product or service. In particular, Oliver
(1997) provides the following definition:

> *"...Customer loyalty is a deeply held commitment to rebuy or repatronize a preferred
> product or service consistently in the future, despite situational influences and marketing
> efforts having the potential to cause switching behavior..."*

The critical factors that affect customer loyalty are the commitment to a brand
and the repeat purchase rate. According to Dick and Basu (1994), customer loyalty
may be examined by relating attitude and repeat purchasing (relative attitude is the
degree to which the consumer's evaluation of one alternative brand is dominated
by that of another). In this context, true loyalty exists only when repeat patronage
coexists with high relative attitude. This approach is also adopted by Griffin
(1995), who distinguishes four types of loyalty (Figure 3.16):

1. *No loyalty*: For several reasons some customers do not develop loyalty to certain products or services, since both repeat patronage and relative attachment
   are low. Some marketeers suggest that businesses should avoid targeting these
   buyers because they will never be loyal customers, while others believe that if a
   reasonably frequent need for a product/service exists, potential efforts may increase the relative attachment, and thus customers may switch to another loyalty segment.
2. *Inertia loyalty*: A low level of attachment coupled with high repeat purchase
   produces inertia loyalty, which means that customers usually buy out of habit.

The primary reasons for buying are based on non-attitudinal/situational factors (e.g. convenience). These customers feel some degree of satisfaction, or at least no real dissatisfaction. Thus, it is possible to turn inertia loyalty into a higher form of loyalty by courting the customer and increasing the product/service differentiation.

3. *Latent loyalty*: A high relative attitude combined with low repeat purchase signifies latent loyalty. In this case situational effects rather than attitudinal influences determine repeat purchase (e.g. inconvenient store locations, out-of-stock situations, influence of other people). Dick and Basu (1994) outline that managerial efforts are best focused on removing the obstacles to patronage, for example by extending the branch network.

4. *Premium loyalty*: Premium loyalty is produced when high level of attachment and repeat patronage coexists. It is the preferred type of loyalty for all customers and any business. Premium loyalty is achieved when the company has developed and communicated a proposition that clearly has long-term benefits for the customer, and when the customer modifies his/her behavior to remain loyal over time.

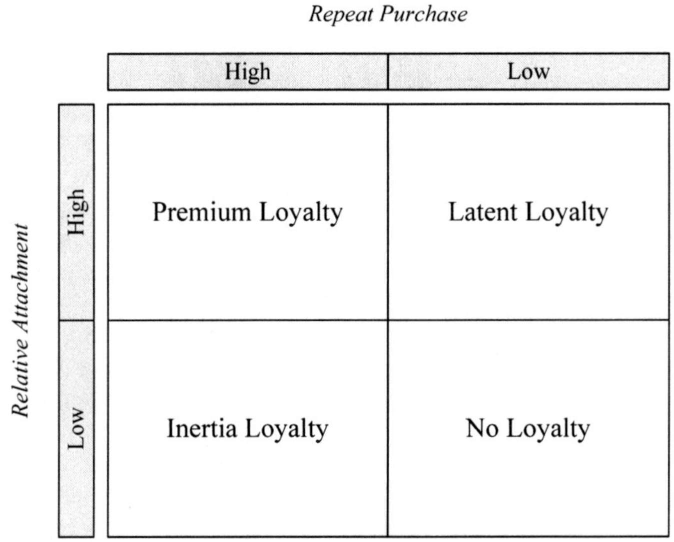

Repeat Purchase

	High	Low
High *Relative Attachment*	Premium Loyalty	Latent Loyalty
Low	Inertia Loyalty	No Loyalty

Fig. 3.16 Types of loyalty (Griffin, 1995)

Although several alternative types of loyalty have been proposed, all of them follow the aforementioned framework and combine the different types of repurchase patterns with customer's attitude toward the company or brand, as presented in Table 3.7. However, all these categorizations of different types of loyalty are able to give a better understanding and provide alternative assessments for this concept.

Table 3.7 Examples of different types of loyalty (Hill and Alexander, 2006)

Types of loyalty	Example	Degree of allegiance
Monopoly loyalty	Rail commuters	Low
Cost of change loyalty	Financial software	Medium
Incentivized loyalty	Frequent business flyers	Low to medium
Habitual loyalty	Petrol station	Low
Committed loyalty	Football club	High

Customer loyalty is not a constant and one-dimensional concept, but it is a rather dynamic process having different stages and evolving over time. The main customer loyalty stages are presented in Figure 3.17 and include (Griffin, 1995; Hill and Alexander, 2006):

1. *Suspects*: Suspects include everyone who may buy the examined product/service. Suspects are either unaware of the offering or they have no inclination to buy it.
2. *Prospects*: A prospect is someone who has the need for the examined product/service, as well as the ability to buy it. Prospects are potential customers who have some attraction toward the company, but they have not taken the step of purchase yet.
3. *First-time customers*: These are the customers who have purchased the products or services offered (usually once, although the category may include some repeat buyers). First-time customers have no real feeling of affinity toward the company.
4. *Repeat customers*: Repeat customers are people who have purchased the examined product/service two or more times. They have positive feelings of attachment toward the organization, but their support is passive, rather than active, apart from making purchases.
5. *Clients*: Clients buy regularly all the product or services offered by a business organization, if they have the need for them. Usually, there is a strong relation between the organization and a client, positively affecting his/her switching behavior.
6. *Advocates*: Advocates are clients who additionally support the organization by talking about it and/or recommending it to others.
7. *Partners*: This is the strongest form of customer-supplier relationship, which is sustained because both parties see partnership as mutually beneficial.

Other alternative approaches for assessing the different levels of customer loyalty are proposed in the context of consumer behavioral analysis and social psychology (Crosby and Taylor, 1983; Kuhl, 1985, 1986; Stum and Thiry, 1991; Bagozzi et al., 1992; Reichheld, 1993).

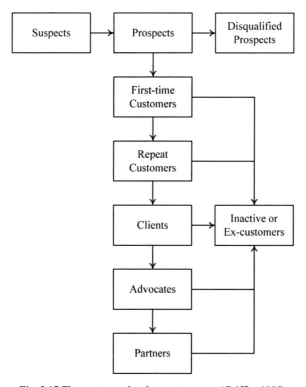

Fig. 3.17 The customer development process (Griffin, 1995)

A large number of research efforts focus on the measurement and analysis of customer loyalty, by applying different techniques and tools (Jarvis and Wilcox, 1976; Raju, 1980; Belch, 1981; Sproles and Kendall, 1986; Tranberg and Hansen, 1986; Czepiel and Gilmore; 1987, Morris and Holman, 1988; Mittal and Lee, 1989; Snyder, 1991; McDonald, 1993; Bawden, 1998). The most important approaches are based on the following:

- Repeat purchase data or patterns (e.g. purchase frequency and quantity).
- Ratio of brand in the region of acceptance to those in the region of rejection (i.e. the ratio of the number of brands that a customer would definitely use to the number of brands that he/she would never use).
- Attitudinal scales (e.g. repurchase intention, recommendation to others).

An alternative interesting approach is presented by Oliva et al. (1992, 1995) who modeled the relation between customer loyalty and satisfaction using a catastrophe model (these models are used in order to describe nonlinear "jumps" once a threshold level of a critical variable is attained).

Taking into account the definition of customer loyalty, as well as the aforementioned measurement approaches, it is clear that since loyalty is a commitment from customers, it is not possible to directly measure it. Instead, it seems more appropriate to measure its consequences, in terms of customer repurchase behavior, and its drivers according to customer's attachment to the examined brand.

Satisfaction surveys may also be used in order to analyze customer loyalty by applying the following process (Hill, 1996):

1. Evaluate the level of customer satisfaction not only for the examined product/service, but also for those of the main competitors.
2. Segment the total set of customers using a cross table that contains the results of the previous measurement.
3. Determine different strategies for each one of the previous segments (e.g. communicate with customers, develop an appropriate database, establish a loyalty club), taking into account the different levels of customer loyalty.

Other research efforts are focused on the determination of business strategies for improving customer retention, increasing purchase budget, evaluating customer trust, or studying further the relation between customer satisfaction and purchase intention (Howard, 1977; Mazursky et al., 1987; Tellis, 1988; Beatty et al., 1988; McQuarrie, 1988; Kasper, 1988; Mazursky and Geva, 1989; Bagozzi and Warshaw, 1990; Wernefelt, 1991; Bagozzi, 1993; Cheong, 1993; Ping, 1994; Morgan and Dev, 1994; Keaveney, 1995).

Chapter 4
MUSA: Multicriteria Satisfaction Analysis

4.1 Introduction to Multicriteria Decision Analysis

4.1.1 Decision Problem Modeling

Multicriteria analysis includes methods, models and approaches that aim to aid the decision-makers to handle semi-structured decision problems with multiple criteria (Siskos and Spyridakos, 1999). Multiple criteria decision problems belong in the category of "ill-structured problems", given that their rational solution does not preexist, but constitutes an objective of research usually through an interactive process.

The main theoretical multicriteria analysis approaches are the following (Figure 4.1):

1. The *value system approach* or *multiattribute utility theory* aims to develop a value system that aggregates the decision-maker's preferences on the total set of criteria, based on strict assumptions, like complete and transitive relation (Fishburn, 1970, 1972, 1982; Keeney and Raiffa, 1976; Keeney, 1992; Von Winterfeldt and Edwards, 1993; French, 1993; Kirkwood, 1997). The estimated value system provides a quantitative way to aid the final decision.

2. The *outranking relations approach*, using a non compensatory process, aims to the development of outranking relations that allow the incomparability among the decision actions (Roy, 1976, 1985, 1989, 1990; Vanderpooten, 1989; Brans and Mareschal, 1990; Vincke, 1992; Roy and Bouyssou, 1993). This particular approach is not bounded into a mathematical model but it results in partial preference structures of the decision actions. Thus, it aids the decision-maker in taking a "good" decision.

E. Grigoroudis and Y. Siskos, *Customer Satisfaction Evaluation*, International Series
in Operations Research & Management Science 139, DOI 10.1007/978-1-4419-1640-2_4,
© Springer Science + Business Media, LLC 2010

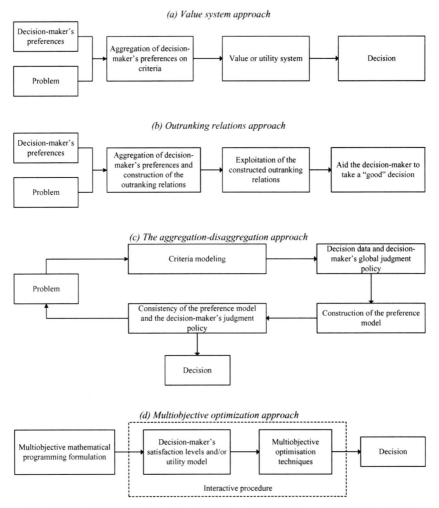

Fig. 4.1 Theoretical approaches of multicriteria analysis (Siskos and Spyridakos, 1999)

3. The *aggregation-disaggregation approach* aims to analyze the behavior and the cognitive style of the decision-maker (Siskos, 1980; Jacquet-Lagrèze and Siskos, 1982; Jacquet-Lagrèze, 1984, 1990; Siskos and Yannacopoulos, 1985; Siskos et al., 1993). Special iterative interactive procedures are used, where the components of the problem and the decision maker's global judgments are analyzed and then they are aggregated into a value system. The main aim of the approach is to aid the decision-maker to improve his/her knowledge on the problem's state and his/her way of preferring that entails a consistent decision to be achieved.

4. The *multiobjective optimization approach* constitutes an extension of mathematical programming, aiming to solve problems with no discrete alternative ac-

tions and more than one objective functions (Evans and Steuer, 1973; Zeleny, 1974, 1982; Zionts and Wallenius, 1976, 1983; Jacquet-Lagrèze et al., 1987; Siskos and Despotis, 1989; Korhonen and Wallenius, 1990; Wierzbicki, 1992; Jaszkiewicz and Slowinski, 1995). The solution is estimated through iterative procedures which lead to achieving the decision-maker's satisfactory levels on the criteria, constructing a utility model in order to select the solutions assessed by a utility maximization procedure, or a combination of the two aforementioned methods.

The general methodological framework for modeling decision-making problems within the field of multicriteria decision analysis includes four successive and interactive stages as Figure 4.2 displays (Roy, 1985; Roy and Bouyssou, 1993).

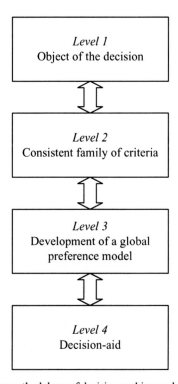

Fig. 4.2 Modeling methodology of decision-making problems (Roy, 1985)

Level 1: Object of the decision

The decision is analyzed in a finite or continuous set of actions A on which a problematic is determined. Roy (1985) distinguishes four referential problematics, each of which does not necessarily preclude the others. They can be employed separately or in a complementary way in all phases of the decision-making process. The four problematics are the following:

- *Problematic α*: Choosing one action from *A* (choice).
- *Problematic β*: Sorting the actions in well defined categories, which are given in a preference order (sorting).
- *Problematic γ*: Ranking the actions from the best one to the worst one (ranking).
- *Problematic δ*: Describing the actions in terms of their performances on the criteria (description).

Level 2: Consistent family of criteria

The result of the implementation of an action can be modeled using a number of consequences or actions (Roy, 1985). These consequences are, generally, numerous and concern many aspects (time, cost, security, quality, etc.). A criterion may be considered as a tool allowing to aggregate a set of evaluations on consequences related to a particular "point of view" (Bouyssou, 1989). These points of view represent the different axes along which the decision-maker justifies and transforms his/her preferences. The comparisons deduced from each of these criteria should therefore be interpreted as partial preferences.

Level 3: Development of the global preference model

This stage refers to the development of a global preference model which aggregates the marginal preferences on the criteria. The actions of set *A* are globally compared based on this model and the problematic that has been defined during stage 1.

Level 4: Decision-aid

Decision-aid tries to provide answers to questions raised by actors involved in a decision process, using a clearly specified model (Bouyssou, 1989). Its aim is to enable the decision-maker to enhance the degree of conformity and coherence between the evolution of a decision-making process and the value systems and objectives involved in this process (Roy, 1989). This stage is actually supplementary to the previous one given that a solution provided by a model is not directly understandable and exploitable in the field of decision making and/or negotiation.

The process of modeling a consistent family of criteria $\{g_1, g_2, ..., g_n\}$ is probably the most important stage of the multicriteria decision-making methodology. Generally, a criterion is any monotonic variable that reflects the decision-maker's preferences. A criterion can be either quantitative, in which case it is expressed using a continuous scale (time, cost, etc.), or qualitative, in which case a conventional monotonic scale of discrete values is used.

Each criterion is a non-decreasing real valued function defined on set *A*, as follows:

$$g_i : A \rightarrow [g_{i*}, g_i^*] \subset \mathbb{R} / a \rightarrow \mathbf{g}(a) \in \mathbb{R} \qquad (4.1)$$

where $[g_{i*}, g_i^*]$ is the criterion evaluation scale, g_{i*} and g_i^* are the worst and the best level of criterion i, respectively, $g_i(a)$ is the evaluation or performance of action a on criterion i, and $\mathbf{g}(a)$ is the vector of performances of action a on the n criteria.

From the above definitions the following preferential situations should be determined:

$$\begin{cases} g_i(a) > g_i(b) \Leftrightarrow a \succ b \ (a \text{ is preferred to } b) \\ g_i(a) = g_i(b) \Leftrightarrow a \succ b \ (a \text{ is indifferent to } b) \end{cases} \quad \forall a, b \in A \qquad (4.2)$$

As noted, the criteria are models allowing to compare alternative actions of the problem that have the following fundamental properties:

1. *Monotonicity*: The partial preferences modeled by each criterion have to be consistent with the global preferences expressed on the alternatives. Thus, if for a couple of actions a and b it holds that $g_i(a) = g_i(b) \ \forall \ i \neq j$ and $g_j(a) > g_j(b)$, then action a is preferred to action b.
2. *Exhaustiveness*: The family of criteria should contain every important point of view. In particular, this condition implies that if for a couple of actions a and b it holds that $g_i(a) = g_i(b) \ \forall \ i$, then actions a and b are indifferent.
3. *Non redundancy*: This property implies the exclusion of unnecessary criteria from the family. This means that the suppression of a criterion g from the family will lead to a set of criteria satisfying the first two properties.

Such a set of functions/variables is called *consistent family of criteria* and represents the set A in $\mathbb{R}^n$, as Figure 4.3 displays. Other important qualities for a family of criteria are the legibility and the operationality properties. Roy and Bouyssou (1993) note that other desirable conditions can also be imposed on a family of criteria (e.g. ceteris paribus comparisons on a sub-family of criteria). Usually, the construction process of a consistent family of criteria leads to reconsider the definition of some criteria, to introduce new ones, to aggregate some of them, etc.

In multicriteria analysis four types of criteria are used with the following properties:

- *Measurable criterion*: This criterion enables the preferential comparison of intervals of the evaluation scale. It may be distinguished in the following subtypes (Vincke, 1992): true-criterion (without any threshold), semi-criterion (with indifference threshold), and pseudo-criterion (with indifference and preference thresholds).
- *Ordinal criterion*: This criterion defines only an order on set A; thus the evaluation scale is discrete (qualitative criterion).
- *Probabilistic criterion*: It covers the case of uncertainty in the actions' performances modeled by probability distributions.
- *Fuzzy criterion*: The performances of the actions are intervals of the criterion's evaluation scale.

An analytical discussion of the properties and the development of a consistent family of criteria, particularly in the case of a customer satisfaction measurement problem, are given in Chapter 7.

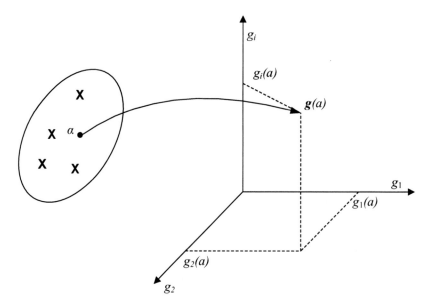

Fig. 4.3 Representation of set A in multicriteria modeling

4.1.2 The Aggregation-Disaggregation Approach

In decision-making involving multiple criteria, the basic problem stated by analysts and decision-makers concerns the way that the final decision should be made. In many cases, however, this problem is posed in the opposite way: assuming that the decision is given, how is it possible to find the rational basis through which the decision was made? Or equivalently, how is it possible to assess the decision-maker's preference model leading to exactly the same decision as the actual one, or at least the most "similar" decision?

The philosophy of preference disaggregation in multicriteria analysis is to assess/infer preference models from given preferential structures and to address decision-aiding activities through operational models within the aforementioned framework. The aggregation-disaggregation approach accepts that both the decision and the criteria are susceptible of progressive processing mutually structured in time.

In the traditional aggregation paradigm, the criteria aggregation model is known a priori, while the global preference is unknown. On the contrary, the philosophy of disaggregation involves the inference of preference models from given global preferences (Figure 4.4).

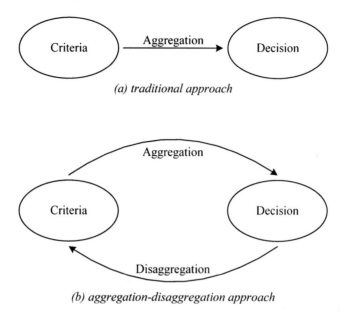

(a) traditional approach

(b) aggregation-disaggregation approach

Fig. 4.4 Different approaches for decision problems

In order to use global preference as datum, Jacquet-Lagrèze and Siskos (2001) note that the clarification of the decision-maker's global preference necessitates the use of a reference set of actions A_R. In most of the cases, this set should be:

1. a set of past decision alternatives (A_R: past actions), or
2. a subset of decision actions, especially when A is large ($A_R \subset A$), or
3. a set of fictitious actions, consisting of performances on the criteria, which can be easily judged by the decision-maker to perform global comparisons (A_R: fictitious actions).

In each of the above cases the decision-maker is asked to externalize and/or confirm his/her global preferences on the set A_R taking into account the performances of the reference actions on all criteria.

The models of this particular category are based on the principle that the result of a decision can either be observed (in case of decisions with a repetitive character), or collected by the decision-maker (through dialogic procedures). The main aim is the extrapolation of the resulted preference system in the set of decision actions A.

Figure 4.5 presents the interactive process of the aggregation-disaggregation approach. It should be noted that in case of inconsistency between the decision maker and the developed preference model, either the family of criteria or the decision data are reconsidered.

The aggregation-disaggregation approach was initially founded by Hammont et al. (1977), while UTA methods (Siskos, 1980; Jacquet-Lagrèze and Siskos, 1982; Siskos and Yannacopoulos, 1985) may be considered as the main initiatives and the most representative examples in this particular field. A detailed presentation of the UTA methods family, the UTA-based decision support systems, and the overall progress made in this field can be found in Jacquet-Lagrèze and Siskos (2001) and Siskos et al. (2005). Finally, a large number of publications refers to applications of the aggregation-disaggregation approach (Siskos, 1986; Siskos and Zopounidis, 1987; Zopounidis, 1987; Siskos and Assimakopoulos, 1989; Hatzinakos et al., 1991; Oral et al., 1992; Siskos and Matsatsinis, 1993; Siskos et al., 1994, 1995a 1995b, 2001b; Jacquet-Lagrèze, 1995; Baourakis et al., 1996; Zopounidis et al., 1996, 1999; Zopounidis and Doumpos, 1998, 1999; Diakoulaki et al., 1999; Matsatsinis and Siskos, 1999, 2003; Beuthe et al., 2000; Spyridakos et al., 2000).

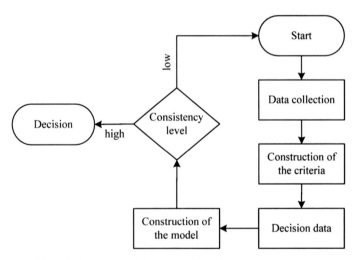

Fig. 4.5 The process of the aggregation-disaggregation approach

4.1.3 Multiattribute Utility Theory

Multiattribute Utility Theory (MAUT) is based on the assumption that, in any decision problem, a real valued function U defined on set A exists, which the decision-maker, consciously or not, wishes to maximize (Roy and Vincke, 1981). MAUT lies on the utility theory of von Neumann and Morgenstern (1947) and it was originally evolved in the 60's from the work of Adams and Fagot (1959), Yntema and Torgerson (1961), Miller and Starr (1969), and others. Although enormous publications deal with the theoretical development and the applications of MAUT, the methodological background of the theory can be found in Gorman

(1959, 1968), Fishburn (1966, 1967, 1970, 1972, 1982), Huber (1974), Keeney and Raiffa (1976), Vincke (1992), Keeney (1992), Dyer et al. (1992), French (1993), and Von Winterfeldt and Edwards (1993).

A real valued function, which aggregates the criteria $\{g_1, g_2, ..., g_n\}$ is assessed so that:

$$\begin{cases} U(a) > U(b) \Leftrightarrow a \succ b \quad (a \text{ is preferred to } b) \\ U(a) = U(b) \Leftrightarrow a \sim b \quad (a \text{ is indifferent to } b) \end{cases} \quad \forall a, b \in A \qquad (4.3)$$

The existence of such a function $U(.)$ under certainty is founded based on the following fundamental assumptions:

- complete comparability of the alternative actions, and
- transitivity of the preferences of the alternative actions.

Moreover, the existence of an additive value function under certainty and the properties of the decision-maker's preferences are based on the concept of preferential independence (Keeney and Raiffa, 1976; Roy and Vincke, 1981; Keeney, 1992):

Definition 1 (preferential independence)
Let $F = \{g_1, g_2, ..., g_n\}$ and $K \subset F$: K is preferentially independent in F, if the preferences between actions, which are only different for criteria in K, do not depend from their values on the criteria in $F \setminus K$.

Theorem 1
If K_1 and K_2 are preferentially independent in F, and $K_1 \cap K_2 = \varnothing$, then $K_1 \cup K_2$ and $K_1 \cap K_2$ are preferentially independent in F.

Definition 2 (mutual preferential independence)
The criteria $g_1, g_2, ..., g_n$ are mutually preferentially independent, if $\forall K \subset F$, K is preferentially independent in F.

Theorem 2
Given a set of criteria $\{g_1, g_2, ..., g_n\}$ $(n \geq 3)$, an additive value function

$$u(g_1, g_2, ..., g_n) = \sum_{i=1}^{n} u_i(g_i) \qquad (4.4)$$

exists iff the criteria are mutually preferentially independent, where u_i is a value function over g_i.

Formal proofs of this theorem are found in Debreu (1960), Pruzan and Jackson (1963), Fishburn (1970), and Krantz et al. (1971).

Though several forms of the additive value function U have been proposed, the most familiar formulas are:

Generic additive form

$$\begin{cases} U(a) = \sum_{i=1}^{n} u_i\left(g_i(a)\right) \\ u_i(g_{i*}) = 0, \quad u_i(g_i^*) = 1 \end{cases} \qquad i = 1, 2, \dots, n \qquad (4.5)$$

where $a \in A$, u_i is a non-decreasing function of g_i for every alternative action a, and g_{i*} and g_i^* are the worst and the best value of the criterion g_i, respectively.

Weighted additive form

$$\begin{cases} U(a) = \sum_{i=1}^{n} w_i g_i(a) \\ \sum_{i=1}^{n} w_i = 1 \quad \text{with} \quad w_i \geq 0 \quad i = 1, 2, \dots, n \end{cases} \qquad (4.6)$$

where $a \in A$, u_i is a non-decreasing function of g_i for every alternative action a, and w_i is the weight of u_i; it is obvious that this formula is a special case of the generic additive form.

The weights (importance coefficients, scaling factors) w_i emphasize the concept of tradeoff, which is another fundamental base of MAUT. Roy and Vincke (1981) note that since a function U, which aggregates the criteria $\{g_1, g_2, \dots, g_n\}$, exists, there must also exist functions w_{ij} measuring the amount that the decision-maker is willing to concede on criterion j to obtain a unit on criterion i. Hence, the weight w_{ij} is called the tradeoff between the i-th and the j-th criteria.

Remark 1
In the case of a weighted additive form, if the functions U and g_i are sufficiently regular, then

$$w_{ij} = \frac{\partial U / \partial g_j}{\partial U / \partial g_i} \qquad (4.7)$$

In general, the tradeoffs support an interactive process between the analyst and the decision-maker aiming to the evaluation of U. Among others, Keeney (1981, 1992) and Kirkwood (1997) describe such an analytical interactive process in order to evaluate the set of weights.

Tradeoffs can also be used in tests of preferential independence, as shown by the following theorem (Ting, 1971):

Theorem 3
K is preferentially independent in F, iff

$$\frac{\partial w_{ij}}{\partial g_k} = 0 \quad \forall i, j \in K, \quad \forall k \in F \setminus K \tag{4.8}$$

Finally, it should be noted that several analytical methods and techniques are addressed to the construction of an additive value function, such as the midvalue splitting technique, and the lock-step procedure presented by Keeney and Raiffa (1976), as well as the MIIDAS system (Siskos et al., 1999).

4.2 The MUSA Method

4.2.1 Main Principles and Notations

The MUSA (MUlticriteria Satisfaction Analysis) method is a multicriteria pref-erence disaggregation approach that provides quantitative measures of customer satisfaction, considering the qualitative form of customers' judgments (Siskos et al., 1998; Grigoroudis and Siskos, 2002). The main objective of the MUSA method is the aggregation of individual judgments into a collective value function, assuming that customer's global satisfaction depends on a set of n criteria or vari-ables representing service/product characteristic dimensions (Figure 4.6). This set of criteria is denoted as $\mathbf{X} = (X_1, X_2, \ldots, X_n)$ where a particular criterion i is repre-sented as a monotonic variable X_i. This way, the evaluation of customer's satisfac-tion can be considered as a multicriteria analysis problem.

These criteria are regarded as satisfaction dimensions and justify the aggrega-tion-disaggregation character of the MUSA method. Several methods for develop-ing satisfaction dimensions, as well as real-world examples are presented analyti-cally in Chapters 7-8.

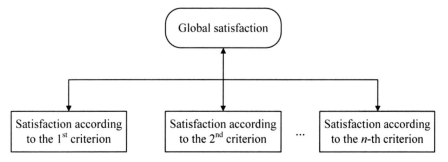

Fig. 4.6 Aggregation of customer's preferences

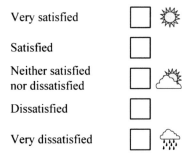

Fig. 4.7 A sample of an ordinal satisfaction scale

The required information is collected via a simple questionnaire in which the customers evaluate the provided product/service, i.e. they are asked to express their judgments, namely their global satisfaction and their satisfaction with regard to the set of discrete criteria. A predefined ordinal satisfaction scale is used for these customers' judgments, as the one presented in Figure 4.7.

The MUSA method assesses global and partial satisfaction functions Y^* and X_i^*, respectively, given customers' judgments Y and X_i. It should be noted that the method follows the principles of ordinal regression analysis under constraints using linear programming techniques (Jacquet-Lagrèze and Siskos, 1982; Siskos and Yannacopoulos, 1985; Siskos, 1985). The ordinal regression analysis equation has the following form (Table 4.1 presents model variables):

$$Y^* = \sum_{i=1}^{n} b_i X_i^* \quad \text{with} \quad \sum_{i=1}^{n} b_i = 1 \tag{4.9}$$

where the value functions Y^* and X_i^* are normalized in the interval [0, 100], and b_i is the weight of criterion i.

Table 4.1 Variables of the MUSA method

Variable	Description
Y	Customer's global satisfaction
α	Number of global satisfaction levels
y^m	The m-th global satisfaction level ($m = 1, 2, ..., \alpha$)
n	Number of criteria
X_i	Customer's satisfaction according to the i-th criterion ($i = 1, 2, ..., n$)
α_i	Number of satisfaction levels for the i-th criterion
x_i^k	The k-th satisfaction level of the i-th criterion ($k = 1, 2, ..., \alpha_i$)
Y^*	Value function of Y
y^{*m}	Value of the y^m satisfaction level
X_i^*	Value function of X_i
x_i^{*k}	Value of the x_i^k satisfaction level

The normalization constraints for the value functions Y^* and X_i^* can be written as follows:

$$\begin{cases} y^{*1} = 0, \ y^{*\alpha} = 100 \\ x_i^{*1} = 0, \ x_i^{*\alpha_i} = 100 \ \text{ for } \ i = 1, 2, \ldots, n \end{cases} \tag{4.10}$$

Furthermore, because of the ordinal nature of Y and X_i the following preference conditions are assumed:

$$\begin{cases} y^{*m} \leq y^{*m+1} \Leftrightarrow y^m \preceq y^{m+1} \ \text{ for } \ m = 1, 2, \ldots, \alpha - 1 \\ x_i^{*k} \leq x_i^{*k+1} \Leftrightarrow x_i^k \preceq x_i^{k+1} \quad \text{ for } \ k = 1, 2, \ldots, \alpha_i - 1 \end{cases} \tag{4.11}$$

where $\preceq$ means "less preferred or indifferent to".

It should be noted that the value/satisfaction functions Y^* and X_i^* are non-decreasing functions in the ordinal scales Y and X_i, respectively. A detailed presentation of the concept and the properties of these functions are given in the next sections.

The principles and the initiative methodological frame of the MUSA method have been developed by Siskos et al. (1998) and Grigoroudis et al. (2000), while a discussion and a more detailed presentation of the method may also be found in Grigoroudis and Siskos (2002).

4.2.2 Model Development

The MUSA method infers an additive collective value function Y^*, and a set of partial satisfaction functions X_i^* from customers' judgments. The main objective of the method is to achieve the maximum consistency between the value function Y^* and the customers' judgments Y.

Based on the modeling presented in the previous section, and introducing a double-error variable, the ordinal regression equation becomes as follows:

$$\tilde{Y}^* = \sum_{i=1}^{n} b_i X_i^* - \sigma^+ + \sigma^- \tag{4.12}$$

where $\tilde{Y}^*$ is the estimation of the global value function Y^*, and σ^+ and σ^- are the overestimation and the underestimation error, respectively.

Formula (4.12) holds for a customer who has expressed a set of satisfaction judgments. For this reason, a pair of error variables should be assessed for each customer separately (Figure 4.8).

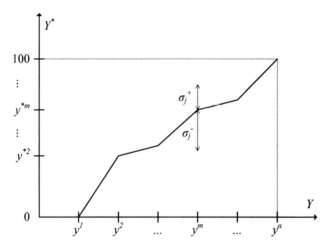

Fig. 4.8 Error variables for the j-th customer

Through formula (4.12) it is easy to note the similarity of the MUSA method with the principles of goal programming modeling, ordinal regression analysis, and particularly with the additive utility models of the UTA family (Jacquet-Lagrèze and Siskos, 1982, 2001; Siskos and Yannacopoulos, 1985; Despotis et al., 1990; Siskos et al., 2005).

According to the aforementioned definitions and assumptions, the customers' satisfaction evaluation problem may be formulated as a linear program (LP) in which the goal is the minimization of the sum of errors under the constraints:

- ordinal regression equation (4.12) for each customer,
- normalization constraints for Y^* and X_i^* in the interval [0, 100], and
- monotonicity constraints for Y^* and X_i^*.

Removing the monotonicity constraints, the size of the previous LP can be reduced in order to decrease the computational effort required for the search of the optimal solution. This is effectuated via the introduction of a set of transformation variables, which represent the successive steps of the value functions Y^* and X_i^* (Siskos and Yannacopoulos, 1985; Siskos, 1985). The transformation equation can be written as follows (see also Figure 4.9):

$$\begin{cases} z_m = y^{*m+1} - y^{*m} & \text{for } m = 1,2,...,\alpha - 1 \\ w_{ik} = b_i x_i^{*k+1} - b_i x_i^{*k} & \text{for } k = 1,2,...,\alpha_i - 1 \text{ and } i = 1,2,...,n \end{cases} \tag{4.13}$$

It is very important to mention that using these variables, the linearity of the model is achieved since equation (4.12) presents a non-linear model (the variables Y^* and X_i^* as well as the coefficients b_i should be estimated).

Using equation (4.13), the initial variables of the MUSA method can be written as:

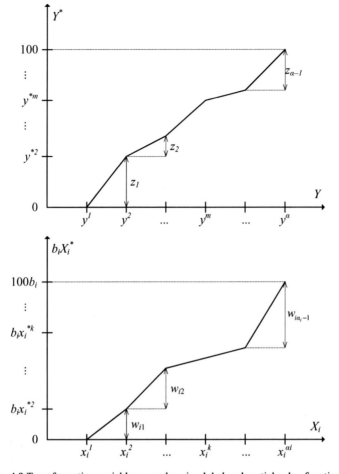

Fig. 4.9 Transformation variables z_m and w_{ik} in global and partial value functions

$$\begin{cases} y^{*m} = \sum_{t=1}^{m-1} z_t & \text{for } m = 2,3,\ldots,\alpha \\ b_i x_i^{*k} = \sum_{t=1}^{k-1} w_{it} & \text{for } k = 2,3,\ldots,\alpha_i \text{ and } i = 1,2,\ldots,n \end{cases} \quad (4.14)$$

In particular, assume that customer j has expressed his/her satisfaction judgments y^{t_j} and $x^{t_{ij}}$ using the ordinal scales Y and X_i, respectively, i.e.:

$$\begin{cases} y^{t_j} \in Y = \left\{ y^1, y^2, \ldots, y^{t_j}, \ldots, y^{\alpha} \right\} \\ x_i^{t_{ij}} \in X_i = \left\{ x_i^1, x_i^2, \ldots, x_i^{t_{ij}}, \ldots, x_i^{\alpha_i} \right\} \quad \text{for } i = 1, 2, \ldots n \end{cases} \tag{4.15}$$

Hence, introducing the z_m and w_{ik} variables, and using formula (4.13), the ordinal regression equation (4.12) becomes as follows:

$$\sum_{m=1}^{t_j-1} z_m = \sum_{i=1}^{n} \sum_{k=1}^{t_{ji}-1} w_{ik} - \sigma^+ + \sigma^- \quad \forall j \tag{4.16}$$

Therefore, the final LP formulation of the method may be written:

$$\begin{cases} [\min] F = \sum_{j=1}^{M} \sigma_j^+ + \sigma_j^- \\ \text{subject to} \\ \sum_{i=1}^{n} \sum_{k=1}^{t_{ij}-1} w_{ik} - \sum_{m=1}^{t_j-1} z_m - \sigma_j^+ + \sigma_j^- = 0 \quad \forall j \\ \sum_{m=1}^{\alpha-1} z_m = 100 \\ \sum_{i=1}^{n} \sum_{k=1}^{\alpha_i-1} w_{ik} = 100 \\ z_m \geq 0, \ w_{ik} \geq 0, \ \sigma_j^+ \geq 0, \sigma_j^- \geq 0 \quad \forall i, j, k, m \end{cases} \tag{4.17}$$

where M is the number of customers; the structure of the previous LP suggests that it is more useful to solve the dual LP.

The calculation of the initial model variables is based on the optimal solution of the previous LP, since:

$$\begin{cases} b_i = \frac{1}{100} \sum_{t=1}^{\alpha_i-1} w_{it} & \text{for } i = 1, 2, \ldots, n \\ y^{*m} = \sum_{t=1}^{m-1} z_t & \text{for } m = 2, 3, \ldots, \alpha, \\ x_i^{*k} = 100 \dfrac{\sum_{t=1}^{k-1} w_{it}}{\sum_{t=1}^{\alpha_i-1} w_{it}} & \text{for } i = 1, 2, \ldots, n \text{ and } k = 2, 3, \ldots, \alpha_i \end{cases} \tag{4.18}$$

4.2.3 Stability Analysis

The stability analysis is considered as a post-optimality analysis problem, considering that the MUSA method is based on a linear programming modeling. In this context, it should be noted that in several cases, particularly in large-scale LPs, the problem of multiple or near optimal solutions appears.

The MUSA method applies a heuristic method for searching near optimal solutions (Siskos, 1984). These solutions have some desired properties, while the heuristic technique is based on the following:

- In several cases, the optimal solutions are not the most interesting, given the uncertainty of the model parameters and the preferences of the decision-maker (Van de Panne, 1975).
- The number of the optimal or near optimal solutions is often huge. Therefore, an exhaustive search method (reverse simplex, Manas-Nedoma algorithms) requires a lot of computational effort.

As shown in Figure 4.10, the post-optimal solutions space is defined by the polyhedron:

$$\begin{cases} F \leq F^* + \varepsilon \\ \text{all the constraints of LP (4.17)} \end{cases} \qquad (4.19)$$

where F^* is the optimal value of the objective function of LP (4.17), and ε is a small percentage of F^*.

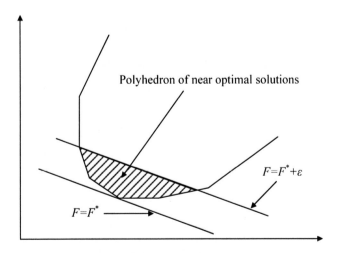

Fig. 4.10 Post-optimality analysis (Jacquet-Lagrèze and Siskos, 1982)

According to the aforementioned remarks, during the post-optimality analysis stage of the MUSA method, n LPs (equal to the number of criteria) are formulated and solved. Each LP maximizes the weight of a criterion and has the following form:

$$\begin{cases} [\max] F' = \sum_{k=1}^{a_i-1} w_{ik} \ \ \text{for} \ \ i = 1, 2, \ldots, n \\ \text{subject to} \\ F \leq F^* + \varepsilon \\ \text{all the constraints of LP (4.17)} \end{cases} \qquad (4.20)$$

The average of the optimal solutions given by the n LPs (4.20) may be considered as the final solution of the problem. In case of instability, a large variation of the provided solutions appears in the post-optimality analysis, and the final average solution is less representative.

4.3 Results of the MUSA method

4.3.1 Value Functions and Criteria Weights

The estimated value/satisfaction functions are the most important results of the MUSA method, considering that they show the real value, in a normalized interval [0, 100], that customers give for each level of the global or marginal ordinal satisfaction scale. The form of these functions indicates the customers' degree of demanding; Figure 4.11 presents an example of three (global or marginal) value functions referring to customer groups with different demanding levels:

- *Neutral customers*: the value function has a linear form; the more satisfied these customers express they are, the higher the percentage of their fulfilled expectations.
- *Demanding customers*: this refers to the case of a convex value function; customers are not really satisfied, unless they receive the best quality level.
- *Non-demanding customers*: this refers to the case of a concave value function; customers express that they are satisfied, although only a small portion of their expectations is fulfilled.

The customers' satisfaction global and partial value functions Y^* and X_i^*, respectively, are mentioned as additive and marginal value or utility functions, respectively, and their properties are determined in the context of multicriteria analysis. Particularly, the collective value function Y^* represents the customers' preference value system and indicates the consequences of the satisfaction criteria.

Moreover, the MUSA method assumes that Y^* and X_i^* are monotonic, non-decreasing, discrete (piecewise linear) functions.

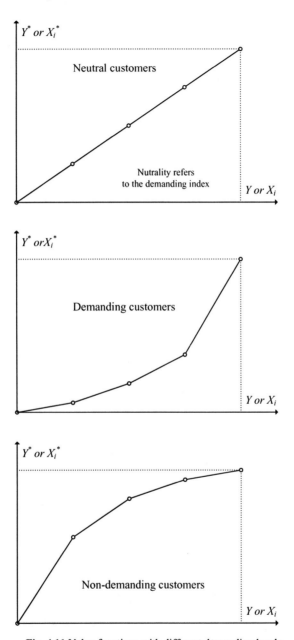

Fig. 4.11 Value functions with different demanding levels

The satisfaction criteria weights represent the relative importance of the assessed satisfaction dimensions, given that $b_1+b_2+...+b_n = 1$. Thus, the decision of whether a satisfaction dimension is considered as "important" by the customers, is also based on the number of assessed criteria. The properties of the weights are also determined in the context of multicriteria analysis, and it should be noted that the weights are basically value tradeoffs among the criteria, as presented in the previous sections.

4.3.2 Average Satisfaction Indices

The assessment of a performance norm, globally and per satisfaction criteria as well, may be very useful in customer satisfaction analysis and benchmarking. The average global and partial satisfaction indices, S and S_i, respectively, are used for this purpose, and may be assessed according to the following equations (see also Figure 4.12):

$$\begin{cases} S = \dfrac{1}{100} \sum_{m=1}^{a} p^m y^{*m} \\ S_i = \dfrac{1}{100} \sum_{k=1}^{a_i} p_i^k x_i^{*k} \quad \text{for } i = 1,2,\ldots,n \end{cases} \tag{4.21}$$

where p^m and p_i^k are the frequencies of customers belonging to the y^m and x_i^k satisfaction levels, respectively.

As noted in Figure 4.12, the average satisfaction indices are basically the mean value of the global or marginal value functions, normalized in the interval [0, 100%].

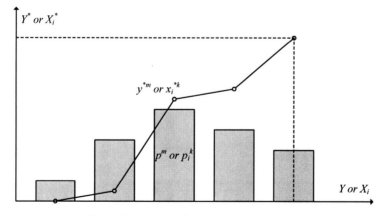

Fig. 4.12 Average satisfaction index assessment

4.3.3 Average Demanding Indices

The need of assessing a set of average demanding indices has been raised in previous sections, given the following advantages:

- a quantitative measure is assessed for the concept of customers' demanding, and
- the information provided by the added values is fully exploited.

The average global and partial demanding indices, D and D_i, respectively, are assessed as follows (see also Figure 4.13):

$$
\begin{cases}
D = \dfrac{\displaystyle\sum_{m=1}^{a-1}\left(\dfrac{100(m-1)}{\alpha-1}-y^{*m}\right)}{100\displaystyle\sum_{m=1}^{a-1}\dfrac{m-1}{\alpha-1}} & \text{for } \alpha > 2 \\[6mm]
D_i = \dfrac{\displaystyle\sum_{k=1}^{a_i-1}\left(\dfrac{100(k-1)}{\alpha_i-1}-x_i^{*k}\right)}{100\displaystyle\sum_{k=1}^{a_i-1}\dfrac{k-1}{\alpha_i-1}} & \text{for } \alpha_i > 2 \text{ and } i=1,2,\ldots,n
\end{cases}
\tag{4.22}
$$

Using a simple progression formula, equation (4.22) may also be written as follows:

$$
\begin{cases}
D = \dfrac{1-\left(\bar{y}^{*}/50\right)}{1-(2/\alpha)} & \text{for } \alpha > 2 \\[4mm]
D_i = \dfrac{1-\left(\bar{x}_i^{*}/50\right)}{1-(2/\alpha_i)} & \text{for } \alpha_i > 2 \text{ and } i=1,2,\ldots,n
\end{cases}
\tag{4.23}
$$

where $\bar{y}^{*}$ and $\bar{x}_i^{*}$ are the mean values of functions Y^{*} and X_i^{*}, respectively.

The average demanding indices are normalized in the interval $[-1, 1]$ and the following possible cases hold:

- $D = 1$ or $D_i = 1$: customers have the maximum demanding level.
- $D = 0$ or $D_i = 0$: this case refers to the neutral customers.
- $D = -1$ or $D_i = -1$: customers have the minimum demanding level.

These indices represent the average deviation of the estimated value curves from a "normal" (linear) function (Figure 4.13). This means that the demanding indices can take different values for different levels of the ordinal satisfaction scale. For example, a sigmoid value function can give a zero average demanding index. In this case, if additional detailed analysis is required, a set of discrete demanding functions may be assessed as follows:

$$\begin{cases} D(y^m) = y^{*m+1} - y^{*m} & \text{for } m = 1, 2, \ldots \alpha - 1 \\ D(x_i^k) = x_i^{*k+1} - x_i^{*k} & \text{for } k = 1, 2, \ldots, \alpha_i - 1 \text{ and } i = 1, 2, \ldots, n \end{cases} \tag{4.24}$$

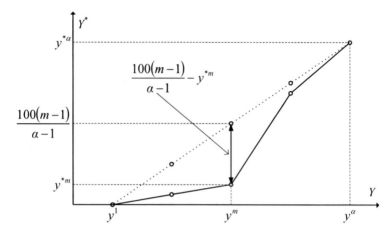

Fig. 4.13 Average demanding index assessment

Demanding indices are used in customer behavior analysis. They may also indicate the extent of company's improvement efforts: the higher the value of the demanding index, the more the satisfaction level should be improved in order to fulfill customers' expectations.

4.3.4 Average Improvement Indices

The output of improvement efforts depends on the importance of the satisfaction dimensions and their contribution to dissatisfaction as well. The average improvement indices show the improvement margins on a specific criterion, and they are assessed according to the following equation:

$$I_i = b_i(1 - S_i) \quad \text{for } i = 1, 2, \ldots, n \tag{4.25}$$

These indices are normalized in the interval [0, 1] and it can be proved that:

$$\begin{cases} I_i = 1 \Leftrightarrow b_i = 1 \wedge S_i = 0 \\ I_i = 0 \Leftrightarrow b_i = 0 \vee S_i = 1 \end{cases} \quad \text{for } i = 1, 2, \ldots, n \tag{4.26}$$

The average improvement indices are used for the development of a series of improvement diagrams, as presented in the next sections.

4.3.5 Action Diagrams

Combining weights and average satisfaction indices, a series of action diagrams can be developed (Figure 4.14). These diagrams indicate the strong and the weak points of customer satisfaction, and define the required improvement efforts.

The action diagrams are also mentioned as decision, strategic, perceptual, and performance-importance maps (Dutka, 1995; Motorola, 1995; Naumann and Giel, 1995), or gap analysis (Hill, 1996; Woodruff and Gardial, 1996; Vavra, 1997), and they are similar to SWOT (Strengths-Weaknesses-Opportunities-Threats) analysis.

Each of these maps is divided into quadrants, according to performance (high/low) and importance (high/low) that may be used to classify actions:

- *Status quo* (low performance and low importance): Generally, no action is required, given that these satisfaction dimensions are not considered as important by the customers.
- *Leverage opportunity* (high performance/high importance): This area can be used as advantage against competition. In several cases, these satisfaction dimensions are the most important reasons why customers have purchased the product/service under study.
- *Transfer resources* (high performance/low importance): Regarding the particular satisfaction dimension, company's resources may be better used elsewhere (i.e. improvement of satisfaction dimensions located in the action opportunity quadrant).
- *Action opportunity* (low performance/high importance): These are the criteria that need attention; improvement efforts should be focused on these, in order to increase the global customer satisfaction level.

This grid can be also used in order to identify priorities for improvement. The bottom right quadrant is obviously the first priority, for the attributes are important to customers but company's performance is rated moderately low. The second priority may be given to the satisfaction criteria in the top right quadrant, especially if there is a significant improvement margin. The third priority issues are indicated in the bottom left quadrant; although these issues are not terribly pertinent at the time of the analysis, they may be more important in the future, and company's performance is certainly not good. Finally, last priority for improvement should be given to the criteria in the top left quadrant, because this category is the least important and company's performance is relatively good. Apparently, priorities for improvement may vary among different companies, depending on the potential capabilities of improving the particular category.

As shown in Table 4.2, there are two types of action diagrams:

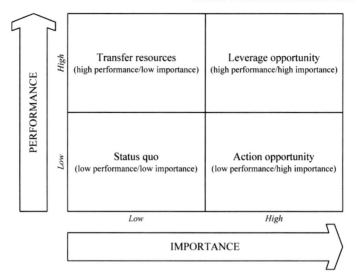

Fig. 4.14 Action diagram (Motorola, 1995)

Table 4.2 Types of action diagrams

Type	Axis	Variables	Interval	Cut-off level
Raw	Importance	b_i	[0, 1]	$1/n$
	Performance	S_i	[0, 1]	0.5
Relative	Importance	$b_i' = \dfrac{b_i - \bar{b}}{\sqrt{\sum_i (b_i - \bar{b})^2}}$	[−1, 1]	0.0
	Performance	$S_i' = \dfrac{S_i - \bar{S}}{\sqrt{\sum_i (S_i - \bar{S})^2}}$	[−1, 1]	0.0

$\bar{b}$ and $\bar{S}$ are the mean values of the criteria weights and the average satisfaction indices, respectively.

1. *Raw action diagrams*: They use the weights and the average satisfaction indices as they are calculated by the MUSA method. The importance axis refers to the criteria weights b_i, which take values in the range [0, 1]. It is assumed that a criterion is important if $b_i > 1/n$, considering that the weights are based on the number of criteria. On the other hand, the performance axis refers to the average satisfaction indices S_i, which are also normalized in the interval [0, 1]. The cut-off level defines if a particular criterion has high or low performance, and it has been chosen to be equal to 0.5 (50%). This is a rather arbitrary assumption, which can be reconsidered depending upon the case.

2. *Relative action diagrams*: These diagrams use the relative variables b_i' and S_i' in order to overcome the assessment problem of the cut-off level for the importance and the performance axis. This way, the cut-off level for the axes is recalculated as the centroid of all points in the diagram. This type of diagram is very useful, if points are concentrated in a small area because of the low-variation appearing for the average satisfaction indices (e.g. in case of a highly competitive market).

4.3.6 Improvement Diagrams

The action diagrams can indicate which satisfaction dimensions should be improved, but they cannot determine the output or the extent of improvement efforts. For this reason, combining the average improvement and demanding indices, a series of improvement diagrams can be developed.

As shown in Figure 4.15, each of these maps is divided into quadrants according to demanding (high/low), and effectiveness (high/low), that may be used to rank improvement priorities:

- *1st priority*: this area indicates direct improvement actions, since these dimensions are highly effective and customers are not demanding.
- *2nd priority*: it includes satisfaction dimensions that have either a low demanding index or a high improvement index.
- *3rd priority*: it refers to satisfaction dimensions that have small improvement margin and need substantial effort.

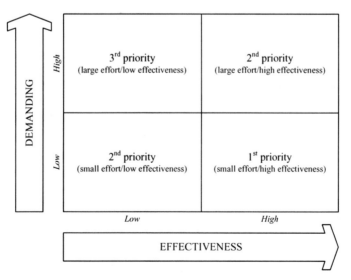

Fig. 4.15 Improvement diagram

Similar to the previous section, there are two types of improvement diagrams (Table 4.3):

1. *Raw improvement diagrams*: They use the average improvement and demanding indices as they are calculated by the MUSA method.
2. *Relative improvement diagrams*: The cut-off level for the axes is recalculated as the centroid of all points in the diagram; these relative diagrams use the normalized variable I_i'.

Table 4.3 Types of improvement diagrams

Type	Axis	Variables	Interval	Cut-off level
Raw	Effectiveness	I_i	[0, 1]	0.5
	Demanding	D_i	[−1, 1]	0.0
Relative	Effectiveness	$I_i' = \dfrac{I_i - \overline{I}}{\sqrt{\sum_i (I_i - \overline{I})^2}}$	[−1, 1]	0.0
	Demanding	D_i	[−1, 1]	0.0

$\overline{I}$ is the mean value of the average improvement indices.

4.4 A Numerical Example

Assume the case of a customer satisfaction survey conducted for a service providing business organization, with the following data:

- Customers' global satisfaction depends on three main criteria: product, purchase process, and additional service (Figure 4.16). Although this is not a consistent family of criteria, it can be used to illustrate the implementation of the MUSA method.
- The ordinal satisfaction scale is presented in Figure 4.16, and it is the same for both the global and the partial satisfaction judgments.
- Table 4.4 presents the data of the satisfaction survey that include satisfaction judgments for a set of 20 customers.

During the 1st implementation step of the MUSA method, the initial LP (4.17) is formulated and solved using the data of Table 4.4. As shown in Table 4.5, for the optimal solution found, the sum of errors equals 0. It is important to mention the existence of multiple optimal solutions in this initial LP.

The 2nd implementation step of the method concerns the post-optimality analysis, where three LPs (equal to the number of problem criteria) are solved, each of them maximizing the weight of the corresponding satisfaction criterion. The final solution of the model variables is calculated as the average of the post-optimal solutions obtained from the aforementioned LPs (Table 4.6). Despite the small sample size, it is worth to mention the relatively high stability of the results.

In the last implementation step, the main results of the MUSA method (criteria weights, average satisfaction, demanding, and improvement indices) are calculated, as shown in Table 4.7.

Moreover, given the formula (4.18) and the information provided by Tables 4.6 and 4.7, the value function curves (Figure 4.17) and the action and improvement diagrams (Figures 4.18 and 4.19) are created.

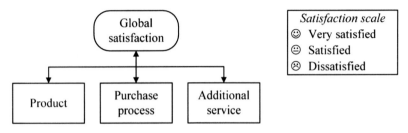

Fig. 4.16 Criteria and satisfaction scales for the numerical example

Table 4.4 Data set for the numerical example

Customer	Global satisfaction	Product	Purchase process	Additional service
1	Satisfied	Very satisfied	Satisfied	Dissatisfied
2	Dissatisfied	Dissatisfied	Dissatisfied	Dissatisfied
3	Very satisfied	Very satisfied	Very satisfied	Very satisfied
4	Satisfied	Very satisfied	Dissatisfied	Satisfied
5	Dissatisfied	Dissatisfied	Dissatisfied	Dissatisfied
6	Very satisfied	Very satisfied	Very satisfied	Very satisfied
7	Satisfied	Very satisfied	Dissatisfied	Very satisfied
8	Satisfied	Very satisfied	Dissatisfied	Very satisfied
9	Satisfied	Satisfied	Satisfied	Satisfied
10	Dissatisfied	Dissatisfied	Dissatisfied	Dissatisfied
11	Satisfied	Satisfied	Very satisfied	Dissatisfied
12	Dissatisfied	Dissatisfied	Dissatisfied	Dissatisfied
13	Very satisfied	Very satisfied	Very satisfied	Very satisfied
14	Satisfied	Satisfied	Very satisfied	Dissatisfied
15	Dissatisfied	Dissatisfied	Dissatisfied	Dissatisfied
16	Very satisfied	Very satisfied	Very satisfied	Satisfied
17	Very satisfied	Very satisfied	Very satisfied	Very satisfied
18	Very satisfied	Very satisfied	Very satisfied	Satisfied
19	Satisfied	Satisfied	Satisfied	Satisfied
20	Dissatisfied	Satisfied	Dissatisfied	Dissatisfied

Table 4.5 Optimal solution of the initial LP

Variable	Value
w_{11}	0.0
w_{12}	25.0
w_{21}	25.0
w_{22}	25.0
w_{31}	25.0
w_{32}	0.0
z_1	50.0
z_2	50.0
F^*	0.0

Table 4.6 Post-optimality results for the numerical example

	w_{11}	w_{12}	w_{21}	w_{22}	w_{31}	w_{32}	z_1	z_2
max b_1	10.00	22.50	22.50	22.50	22.50	0.00	55.00	45.00
max b_2	0.00	23.75	23.75	28.75	23.75	0.00	47.50	52.50
max b_3	0.00	20.00	20.00	30.00	30.00	0.00	50.00	50.00
Average	3.33	22.08	22.08	27.08	25.42	0.00	50.83	49.17

Table 4.7 Main results for the numerical example

Criterion	Weight	Average Satisfaction index	Average demanding index	Average improvement index
Product	25.42%	53.28%	0.74	0.12
Purchase process	49.17%	46.74%	0.10	0.26
Additional service	25.42%	55.00%	−1.00	0.11
Global satisfaction	-	50.33%	−0.02	-

Given the results of the numerical example, the following points raise:

- A very low satisfaction level appears for the customers' set (average global satisfaction index 50.33%). This result is also justified by the statistical frequencies of the sample (30% of the customers are globally dissatisfied).
- Regarding the satisfaction dimensions, the criterion of the "purchase process" seems to be the most important (weight 47.17%), while at the same time, it presents the lowest satisfaction index (46.74%).
- This result is also demonstrated in the related action diagram that suggests this particular criterion as a critical satisfaction dimension.

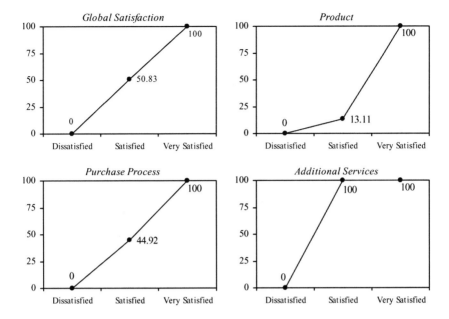

Fig. 4.17 Value functions for the numerical example

Therefore, the improvement efforts should focus on the "purchase process" criterion as the related improvement diagram also suggests. Additionally, other improvement efforts may concern the criterion of "additional service" mostly due to the observed low demanding level.

As shown in the numerical example, the main advantage of the MUSA method is that it fully considers the qualitative form of customers' judgments and preferences. Moreover, the development of a set of quantitative indices and perceptual maps makes possible the provision of an effective support for the satisfaction evaluation problem.

A detailed discussion on several extensions of the MUSA method and the reliability evaluation of the provided results are given in Chapter 6, while Chapter 8 presents the implementation of the MUSA method in real-world satisfaction evaluation problems. These applications refer mostly to customers or employees of business organizations.

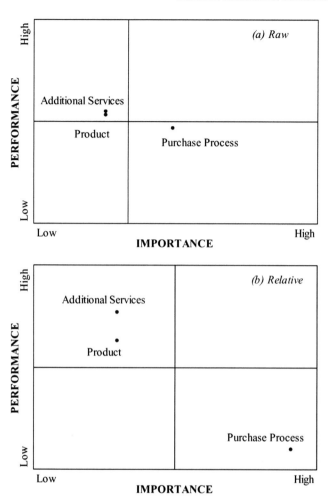

Fig. 4.18 Action diagrams for the numerical example

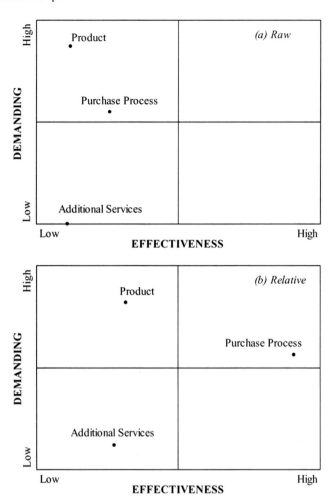

Fig. 4.19 Improvement diagrams for the numerical example

Chapter 5

Extensions of the MUSA Method

5.1 Strictly Increasing Value Functions

Some of the most common potential implementation problems of the MUSA method, which may affect the reliability of the provided results, include the following:

- In several cases with unstable results, it appears that $y^{*m} = y^{*m+1}$ or $x_i^{*k} = x_i^{*k+1}$ (Jacquet-Lagrèze and Siskos, 1982).
- Cases where $b_i = 0$ for some criteria X_i should be avoided.

Assessing a set of preference thresholds may overcome these problems. Thus, in this extension, it is assumed that Y^* and X_i^* are monotonic and strictly increasing functions in order to consider the strict preferential order of the scales of some or all the satisfaction criteria. Taking into account the hypothesis of strict preferences, the conditions of equation (4.11) become as follows:

$$\begin{cases} y^{*m} < y^{*m+1} \Leftrightarrow y^m \prec y^{m+1} & \text{for } m = 1, 2, \ldots, \alpha - 1 \\ x_i^{*k} < x_i^{*k+1} \Leftrightarrow x_i^k \prec x_i^{k+1} & \text{for } k = 1, 2, \ldots, \alpha_i - 1 \text{ and } i = 1, 2, \ldots, n \end{cases} \tag{5.1}$$

where $\prec$ means "strictly less preferred".

Based on (5.1), the following conditions occur:

$$\begin{cases} y^{*m+1} - y^{*m} \geq \gamma & \text{for } m = 1, 2, \ldots, \alpha - 1 \\ b_i x_i^{*k+1} - b_i x_i^{*k} \geq \gamma_i & \text{for } k = 1, 2, \ldots, \alpha_i - 1 \text{ and } i = 1, 2, \ldots, n \end{cases} \tag{5.2}$$

where γ and γ_i are the preference thresholds for the value functions Y^* and X_i^*, respectively (with $\gamma, \gamma_i > 0$).

E. Grigoroudis and Y. Siskos, *Customer Satisfaction Evaluation*, International Series
in Operations Research & Management Science 139, DOI 10.1007/978-1-4419-1640-2_5,
© Springer Science + Business Media, LLC 2010

Introducing the preference thresholds in the basic variables (4.13) of the MUSA method, the following relations are obtained:

$$\begin{cases} z_m \geq \gamma \\ w_{ik} \geq \gamma_i \end{cases} \Leftrightarrow \begin{cases} z_m - \gamma \geq 0 \\ w_{ik} - \gamma_i \geq 0 \end{cases} \Leftrightarrow \begin{cases} z'_m \geq 0 & \text{for } m = 1, 2, \dots, \alpha \\ w'_{ik} \geq 0 & \text{for } k = 1, 2, \dots, \alpha_i - 1 \\ & \text{and } i = 1, 2, \dots, n \end{cases} \tag{5.3}$$

where it is set:

$$\begin{cases} z_m = z'_m + \gamma & \text{for } m = 1, 2, \dots, \alpha \\ w_{ik} = w'_{ik} + \gamma_i & \text{for } k = 1, 2, \dots, \alpha_i - 1 \text{ and } i = 1, 2, \dots, n \end{cases} \tag{5.4}$$

The thresholds γ and γ_i represent the minimum step of increase for functions Y^* and X_i^*, respectively (Figure 5.1), and it can be proved that in this case, the minimum weight of a criterion X_i becomes $\gamma_i(\alpha_i - 1)$.

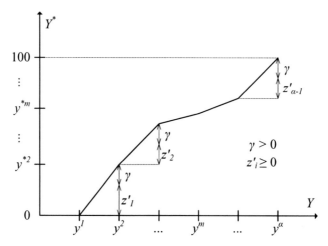

Fig. 5.1 Preference threshold for the value function Y^*

Using the previous formulas, the generalized MUSA method reads:

$$\begin{cases}
[\min]F = \sum\limits_{j=1}^{M} \sigma_j^+ + \sigma_j^- \\[2mm]
\text{subject to} \\[2mm]
\sum\limits_{i=1}^{n}\sum\limits_{k=1}^{t_{ij}-1} w'_{ik} - \sum\limits_{m=1}^{t_j-1} z'_m - \sigma_j^+ + \sigma_j^- = \gamma(t_j - 1) - \sum\limits_{i=1}^{n}\gamma_i(t_{ij}-1) \quad \forall j \\[2mm]
\sum\limits_{m=1}^{a-1} z'_m = 100 - \gamma(\alpha - 1) \\[2mm]
\sum\limits_{i=1}^{n}\sum\limits_{k=1}^{a_i-1} w'_{ik} = 100 - \sum\limits_{i=1}^{n}\gamma_i(a_i - 1) \\[2mm]
z'_m \geq 0,\ w'_{ik} \geq 0,\ \sigma_j^+ \geq 0, \sigma_j^- \geq 0 \quad \forall\, i,j,k,m
\end{cases} \qquad (5.5)$$

where t_j and t_{ij} are the judgments of customer j for global and partial satisfaction, respectively, as defined in expression (4.15).

The proposed extension consists the generalized form of the MUSA method, since the basic form (4.17) is a special case where $\gamma = \gamma_i = 0$, $\forall\, i$.

The post-optimality analysis results of this extended version for the numerical example of section 4.4 are presented in Table 5.1, while Table 5.2 shows a comparison analysis between the basic and the generalized MUSA method. In this table, the significant improvement of the achieved stability should be noted: the mean standard deviation of the results obtained during the post-optimality analysis stage decreases from 3.9 to 0.8.

Table 5.1 Post-optimality results for the numerical example (Generalized MUSA method)

	w_{11}	w_{12}	w_{21}	w_{22}	w_{31}	w_{32}	z_1	z_2
max b_1	4.00	23.00	25.00	23.00	23.00	2.00	52.00	48.00
max b_2	2.00	23.25	25.25	24.25	23.25	2.00	50.50	49.50
max b_3	2.00	22.50	24.50	24.50	24.50	2.00	51.00	49.00
Average	2.67	22.92	24.92	23.92	23.58	2.00	51.17	48.83

Table 5.2 Comparison analysis of the post-optimality analysis results

	Basic MUSA method $(\gamma = \gamma_i = 0)$			Generalized MUSA method $(\gamma = \gamma_i = 2)$		
	b_1	b_2	b_3	b_1	b_2	b_3
max b_1	**32.50**	45.00	22.50	**27.00**	48.00	25.00
max b_2	23.75	**52.50**	23.75	25.25	**49.50**	25.25
max b_3	20.00	50.00	**30.00**	24.50	49.00	**26.50**
Standard deviation	5.24	3.12	3.28	1.05	0.62	0.66

It should be emphasized that the following conditions occur, in order to avoid negative values in the right-hand constraints of LP (5.5):

$$
\begin{cases}
\gamma(\alpha - 1) \leq 100 \\
\sum_{i=1}^{n} \gamma_i (\alpha_i - 1) \leq 100
\end{cases}
\tag{5.6}
$$

For example, in case where $\gamma = \gamma_i \ \forall \ i$, the previous conditions take the following form:

$$
\gamma \leq \min \left\{ \frac{100}{(\alpha - 1)}, \frac{100}{\sum_{i=1}^{n}(\alpha_i - 1)} \right\}
\tag{5.7}
$$

5.2 Multiple Criteria Levels

In several cases, during the assessment process of a consistent family of criteria, it seems rather useful to assume a value or treelike structure, as presented in Figure 5.2. This structure is also mentioned as "value tree" or "value hierarchy" (Keeney and Raiffa, 1976; Keeney, 1992; Kirkwood, 1997).

The first criteria level includes the main satisfaction dimensions in a general form (e.g. personnel), while the second level considers more detailed characteristics (personnel's friendliness, skills, etc.). It should be noted that the number of levels might not be uniform across a value hierarchy. The total set of main criteria, as well as each of the subcriteria sets should satisfy the properties of a consistent family of criteria.

In this particular case, the formulation of the MUSA method is based on the additional assessed variables of Table 5.3, and therefore the ordinal regression analysis equation reads:

$$
\begin{cases}
Y^* = \sum_{i=1}^{n} b_i X_i^* \\
\sum_{i=1}^{n} b_i = 1
\end{cases}
\text{and}
\begin{cases}
X_i^* = \sum_{j=1}^{n_i} b_{ij} X_{ij}^* \\
\sum_{j=1}^{n_i} b_{ij} = 1
\end{cases}
\text{for } i = 1, 2, \ldots, n
\tag{5.8}
$$

where the value functions Y^*, X_i^*, and X_{ij}^* are normalized in the interval [0, 100].

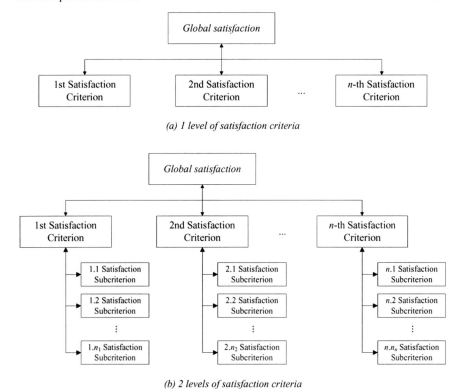

(a) 1 level of satisfaction criteria

(b) 2 levels of satisfaction criteria

Fig. 5.2 Multiple criteria levels extension

Table 5.3 Additional variables of the MUSA method (2 criteria levels)

Variable	Description
n_i	Number of subcriteria for the i-th criterion
X_{ij}	Customer's satisfaction according to the j-th subcriterion of the i-th criterion ($j = 1, 2, ..., n_i$, $i = 1, 2, ..., n$)
α_{ij}	Number of satisfaction levels for the j-th subcriterion of the i-th criterion
x_{ij}^k	The k-th satisfaction level for the j-th subcriterion of the i-th criterion ($k = 1, 2, ..., \alpha_{ij}$)
X_{ij}^*	Value function of X_{ij}
x_{ij}^{*k}	Value of the x_{ij}^k satisfaction level
b_i	Weight for the i-th criterion
b_{ij}	Weight for the j-th subcriterion of the i-th criterion

Similarly to (4.13), the new additional variables representing the successive steps of the value functions X_{ij}^* are assessed as follows:

$$w_{ijk} = b_i b_{ij} x_{ij}^{*k+1} - b_i b_{ij} x_{ij}^{*k} \quad \text{for } k = 1, 2, \ldots, \alpha_{ij} - 1,$$
$$j = 1, 2, \ldots n_i \quad \text{and} \quad i = 1, 2, \ldots, n \tag{5.9}$$

Thus, the LP (4.17) takes the following form:

$$
\begin{cases}
[\min] F_1 = \displaystyle\sum_{q=1}^{M} (\sigma_q^+ + \sigma_q^-) + \frac{1}{n} \sum_{q=1}^{M} \sum_{i=1}^{n} (\sigma_{qi}^+ + \sigma_{qi}^-) \\[2ex]
\text{subject to} \\[1ex]
\displaystyle\sum_{i=1}^{n} \sum_{k=1}^{t_{qi}-1} w_{ik} - \sum_{m=1}^{t_q-1} z_m - \sigma_q^+ + \sigma_q^- = 0 \quad \forall q \\[2ex]
\displaystyle\sum_{j=1}^{n_i} \sum_{k=1}^{t_{qij}-1} w_{ijk} - \sum_{k=1}^{t_{qi}-1} w_{ik} - \sigma_{qi}^+ + \sigma_{qi}^- = 0 \quad \forall i,q \\[2ex]
\displaystyle\sum_{m=1}^{a-1} z_m = 100 \\[2ex]
\displaystyle\sum_{i=1}^{n} \sum_{k=1}^{a_i-1} w_{ik} = 100 \\[2ex]
\displaystyle\sum_{i=1}^{n} \sum_{j=1}^{n_i} \sum_{k=1}^{a_{ij}-1} w_{ijk} = 100 \\[2ex]
z_m, w_{ik}, w_{ijk}, \sigma_q^+, \sigma_q^-, \sigma_{qi}^+, \sigma_{qi}^- \geq 0 \quad \forall i,j,k,m,q
\end{cases}
\tag{5.10}
$$

The new model variables are calculated according to the following formulas:

$$
\begin{cases}
b_{ij} = \dfrac{\displaystyle\sum_{t=1}^{\alpha_{ij}-1} w_{ijt}}{\displaystyle\sum_{t=1}^{\alpha_i-1} w_{it}} \quad \forall i,j \\[4ex]
x_{ij}^{*k} = 100 \dfrac{\displaystyle\sum_{t=1}^{k-1} w_{ijt}}{\displaystyle\sum_{t=1}^{\alpha_{ij}-1} w_{ijt}} \quad \forall i,j \text{ and } k = 2,3,\ldots,\alpha_{ij}
\end{cases}
\tag{5.11}
$$

while the global satisfaction function and the weights and partial value functions for the main criteria can be written as follows:

$$\left\{\begin{array}{ll} b_i = \dfrac{\displaystyle\sum_{t=1}^{a_i-1} w_{it}}{100} & \forall i \\[10pt] y^{*m} = \displaystyle\sum_{t=1}^{m-1} z_t & \text{for } m = 2,3,\ldots,\alpha \\[10pt] x_i^{*k} = 100\dfrac{\displaystyle\sum_{t=1}^{k-1} w_{it}}{\displaystyle\sum_{t=1}^{a_i-1} w_{it}} & \forall i \text{ and } k = 2,3,\ldots,\alpha_i \end{array}\right. \tag{5.12}$$

The stability analysis of LP (5.10) can also be considered as a post-optimality problem, where $\sum n_i$ LPs are formulated and solved, each of them maximizing the weight b_{ij} of every subcriterion. The LPs have the following form:

$$\left\{\begin{array}{l} [\max]F_1' = \displaystyle\sum_{k=1}^{a_{ij}-1} w_{ijk} \quad \forall i,j \\[10pt] \text{subject to} \\[6pt] F_1 \le F_1^* + \varepsilon \\[6pt] \text{all the constraints of LP (5.10)} \end{array}\right. \tag{5.13}$$

where F_1^* is the optimal value for the objective function of LP (5.10), and ε is a small percentage of F_1^*; the final solution may be calculated as the average of the optimal solutions of these LPs.

5.3 Alternative Objective Functions

This section discusses the issue of selecting alternative objective functions during the post-optimality analysis process. The basic form of the MUSA method (see section 4.2.3) proposes the solution of n LPs that maximize the weight b_i of each criterion.

Alternatively, the simultaneous solution of n LPs that minimize the weight b_i of each criterion may be considered. In this case, $2n$ LPs should be formulated and solved:

$$\begin{cases} [\max]F' = \sum_{k=1}^{a_i-1} w_{ik} \ \text{ and } \ [\min]F' = \sum_{k=1}^{a_i-1} w_{ik} \ \text{ for } i=1,2,\dots,n \\ \text{subject to} \\ F \le F^* + \varepsilon \\ \text{all the constraints of LP (4.17)} \end{cases}$$ (5.14)

Another alternative approach considers the search of near optimal solutions that maximize the preference thresholds. This approach overcomes the problem of selecting appropriate values for these parameters that are known to affect the stability of the model (Srinivasan and Shocker, 1973), while the estimated optimal values γ and γ_i maximize the discrimination of the preference conditions (Beuthe and Scanella, 2001). In this particular case, the post-optimality analysis includes the solution of $n+1$ LPs of the following form:

$$\begin{cases} [\max]F' = \gamma \ \text{ and } \ [\max]F' = \gamma_i \ \text{ for } i=1,2,\dots,n \\ \text{subject to} \\ F \le F^* + \varepsilon \\ \text{all the constraints of LP (5.5)} \end{cases}$$ (5.15)

Similarly to the previous case, the maximization of the successive steps of the value functions Y^* and X_i^* (w_{ik} and z_m variables) may be considered during the post-optimality process (Beuthe and Scannella, 1996):

$$\begin{cases} [\max]F' = z_m \ \text{ and } \ [\max]F' = w_{ik} \ \forall i,m,k \\ \text{subject to} \\ F \le F^* + \varepsilon \\ \text{all the constraints of LP (4.17)} \end{cases}$$ (5.16)

In this particular approach, the stability analysis includes the solution of $(\alpha-1) + \sum_{i=1}^{n}(\alpha_i-1)$ LPs.

A final alternative approach, in the context of ordinal regression analysis, considers the minimization of the difference between the maximum and the minimum value of the error variables σ_j^+ and σ_j^- in the case where $F^* > 0$ (Despotis et al., 1990). This particular approach corresponds to the minimization of the L_∞ norm of errors. This way, the LP of the post-optimality analysis takes the following form:

$$\begin{cases} [\min] F' = m_e \\ \text{subject to} \\ F \leq F^* + \varepsilon \\ m_e - \sigma_j^+ \geq 0 \quad \forall j \\ m_e - \sigma_j^- \geq 0 \quad \forall j \\ \text{all the constraints of LP (4.17)} \end{cases} \tag{5.17}$$

where m_e is the maximum value of the error variables σ_j^+ and σ_j^-.

Table 5.4 summarizes all the aforementioned proposed alternative approaches for the post-optimality analysis of the MUSA method. It should be noted that the average of the optimal solution of these alternative LPs have been considered as a representative final solution. Based on the information provided in this table and considering the nature of the proposed extensions, the following points raise:

1. The satisfaction criteria are usually competitive and therefore, it is not necessary to consider simultaneously the maximization and minimization of the criteria weights. For this reason, the MUSA I method is very similar to the generalized MUSA method (for $\gamma = \gamma_i = 0$).
2. The MUSA III version is actually an extension of the MUSA II method, since the following conditions hold:

$$\begin{cases} \gamma \leq \min_m \{z_m\} \\ \gamma_i \leq \min_k \{w_{ik}\} \quad \forall i \end{cases} \tag{5.18}$$

3. Usually, the minimization of the L_∞ norm of errors (MUSA IV) is of limited support to this particular case, although it is an important tool of the post-optimality problem in the context of ordinal regression analysis. This extension distributes equally the error values to the total set of customers, and in this way, the collective method is not able to "correct" potential discriminated judgments. Additionally, it should be noted that this version applies only if $F^* > 0$, and therefore it cannot overcome the stability analysis problem (multiple or near optimal solutions).

The implementation of all different approaches to the numerical example of section 4.4 reveals the high stability of the results for this particular data set (Table 5.5).

Finally, it should be noted that the idea of preference thresholds, which is introduced in the generalized MUSA method, may also be combined with the alternative post-optimality analyses presented in this section.

Table 5.4 Alternative objective functions in the post-optimality analysis

Extension	Objective function	Remarks
Gen. MUSA	$[\max]F' = b_i$	Basic model with preference thresholds
MUSA I	$[\max]F' = b_i$, $[\min]F' = b_i$	Maximization-minimization of weights
MUSA II	$[\max]F' = \gamma$, $[\max]F' = \gamma_i$	Maximization of preference thresholds
MUSA III	$[\max]F' = z_m$, $[\max]F' = w_{ik}$	Maximization of value functions' successive steps
MUSA IV	$[\max]F' = m_e$	Minimization of the L_∞ norm of errors

Table 5.5 Summarized results of alternative post-optimality analysis approaches

	Basic MUSA method ($\gamma = \gamma_i = 0$)	Generalized MUSA method ($\gamma = \gamma_i = 2$)	MUSA I	MUSA II	MUSA III	MUSA IV
b_1	25.42	25.58	26.46	26.21	26.51	25.00
b_2	49.17	48.83	48.75	49.25	49.06	50.00
b_3	25.42	25.58	24.79	24.54	24.43	25.00

5.4 Modeling Preferences on Criteria Importance

5.4.1 Model Development

A customer satisfaction survey may include, besides the usual performance questions, preferences about the importance of the criteria. Using such questions, customers are asked either to judge the importance of a satisfaction criterion using a predefined ordinal scale, or rank the set of satisfaction criteria according to their importance (Figure 5.3).

Based on such importance questions, each one of the satisfaction criteria can be placed in one of the following categories $C_1, C_2, \ldots, C_q$, where C_1 is the most important criterion class and C_q is the less important criterion class. Considering that C_l, with l the class index, are ordered in a 0-100% scale, there are T_{q-1} thresholds, which define the rank and, therefore, label each one of the classes (see Figure 5.4). Thus, the evaluation of preference importance classes C_l is similar to the estimation of thresholds T_l.

An ordinal regression approach may also be used in order to develop the weights estimation model. Using the notations of the MUSA method, assume that $\hat{b}_{ij}$ is the preference of customer j about the importance of criterion i. Then, the following cases exist (Grigoroudis and Spiridaki, 2003):

1. If $\hat{b}_{ij} \in C_1$, that is customer j considers criterion i as the most important, then:

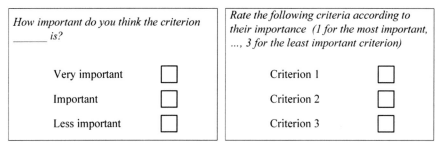

Fig. 5.3 Example questions for preferences on criteria importance

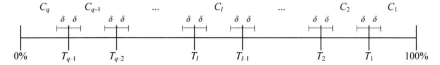

Fig. 5.4 Preference importance classes

$$\sum_{k=1}^{a_i-1} w_{ik} - 100T_1 - \delta + S_{ij}^- \geq 0 \qquad (5.19)$$

2. If $\hat{b}_{ij} \in C_l$, that is customer j considers criterion i in the importance class l, then $(l = 2, 3, \ldots, q-1)$:

$$\begin{cases} \sum_{k=1}^{a_i-1} w_{ik} - 100T_{l-1} + \delta - S_{ij}^+ \leq 0 \\ \sum_{k=1}^{a_i-1} w_{ik} - 100T_l - \delta + S_{ij}^- \geq 0 \end{cases} \qquad (5.20)$$

3. If $\hat{b}_{ij} \in C_q$, that is customer j considers criterion i as the least important, then:

$$\sum_{k=1}^{a_i-1} w_{ik} - 100T_{q-1} + \delta - S_{ij}^+ \leq 0 \qquad (5.21)$$

In the previous formulas, it should be noted that S_{ij}^+ and S_{ij}^- are the overestimation and underestimation error, respectively, for the j-th customer and the i-th criterion. Also, δ is a small positive number, which is used in order to avoid cases where $b_{ij} = T_l \; \forall \; l$, while criteria weights are considered through the following expression:

$$\sum_{t=1}^{a_i-1} w_{it} = 100 b_i \tag{5.22}$$

Furthermore, a minimum value may be assumed for thresholds T_l in order to increase the discrimination of the importance classes. Thus, the following conditions occur:

$$\begin{cases} T_{q-1} \geq \lambda \\ T_{q-2} - T_{q-1} \geq \lambda \\ \vdots \\ T_1 - T_2 \geq \lambda \end{cases} \tag{5.23}$$

where λ is a positive number with $\lambda \leq (100/n)$, since the maximum value that λ may take cannot exceed the criteria weights (if they are all of equal importance).

According to the previous notations and assumptions, the following linear constraints may be formulated:

$$\left. \begin{array}{l} \sum_{k=1}^{a_i-1} w_{ik} - 100T_1 - \delta + S_{ij}^- \geq 0 \qquad \hat{b}_{ij} \in C_1 \\[2ex] \left. \begin{array}{l} \sum_{k=1}^{a_i-1} w_{ik} - 100T_{l-1} + \delta - S_{ij}^+ \leq 0 \\[2ex] \sum_{k=1}^{a_i-1} w_{ik} - 100T_l - \delta + S_{ij}^- \geq 0 \end{array} \right\} \;\; \hat{b}_{ij} \in C_l \;\; l=2,\ldots,q-1 \\[3ex] \sum_{k=1}^{a_i-1} w_{ik} - 100T_{q-1} + \delta - S_{ij}^+ \leq 0 \quad \hat{b}_{ij} \in C_q \end{array} \right\} \; \forall i,j \tag{5.24}$$

$$\sum_{i=1}^{n} \sum_{k=1}^{a_i-1} w_{ik} = 100$$

The final model for the estimation of weights may be formulated through the following LP (Grigoroudis and Spiridaki, 2003):

$$
\begin{cases}
[\min]\Phi = \sum_{i=1}^{n}\sum_{j=1}^{M} S_{ij}^{+} + S_{ij}^{-} \\
\text{subject to} \\
\text{constraints (5.24)-(5.23)} \\
w_{ik} \geq 0,\ S_{ij}^{+} \geq 0, S_{ij}^{-} \geq 0 \quad \forall\, i, j, k
\end{cases}
\tag{5.25}
$$

An alternative objective function that could be minimized in the previous LP is the following (Zopounidis and Doumpos, 2001):

$$
\Phi = \sum_{k=1}^{q}\ \sum_{\forall b_{ij}\in C_k} \frac{S_{ij}^{+} + S_{ij}^{-}}{m_k}
\tag{5.26}
$$

where m_k is the number of customers' judgments in the class C_k.

Similarly to the MUSA methods, a post-optimality analysis should be considered, where the following LPs are formulated and solved:

$$
\begin{cases}
[\max]\Phi' = \sum_{k=1}^{a_i-1} w_{ik} \quad \text{for } i = 1, 2, \ldots, n \\
\text{subject to} \\
\Phi \leq \Phi^{*} + \varepsilon \\
\text{all the constraints of LP (5.25)}
\end{cases}
\tag{5.27}
$$

where Φ^{*} is the optimal value of the objective function of LP (5.25), and ε is a small percentage of Φ^{*}; the average of the optimal solutions of the previous LPs is taken as a representative final solution for the model variables w_{ik}.

Other alternative approaches for the post-optimality criteria may also be considered (Zopounidis and Doumpos, 2001; Beuthe and Scanella, 1996, 2001). In the first approach, $q-1$ LPs (equal to the number of thresholds), are formulated and solved. These LPs maximize the thresholds T_l and have the following form:

$$
\begin{cases}
[\max]T_l \quad \text{for } l = 1, 2, \ldots, q - 1 \\
\text{subject to} \\
\Phi \leq \Phi^{*} + \varepsilon \\
\text{all the constraints of LP (5.25)}
\end{cases}
\tag{5.28}
$$

Other approaches maximize δ or the sum $T_l+\delta$ using the following LP:

$$
\begin{cases}
[\max]\ \delta \quad \text{or} \quad [\max]\ T_l + \delta \quad \text{for} \quad l = 1, 2, \ldots q - 1 \\
\text{subject to} \\
\Phi \leq \Phi^* + \varepsilon \\
\text{all the constraints of LP (4-25)} \\
\lambda \geq \delta
\end{cases}
\tag{5.29}
$$

The previous modeling is a sorting ordinal regression model, following the principles of preference disaggregation, and particularly the UTADIS methods (Zopounidis and Doumpos, 2001; Doumpos and Zopounidis, 2002).

5.4.2 Derived vs. Stated Importance

The straightforward customer preference for the weight of a satisfaction criterion which is evaluated through importance questions is defined as stated importance. Derived importance is estimated by a regression-type quantitative technique using customer judgments for the performance of this set of criteria (e.g. MUSA method). A common problem faced while analyzing data from customer satisfaction surveys is the comparison of stated and derived importance for a set of satisfaction dimensions.

Interestingly, derived importance by a preference disaggregation model and stated importance that is given to each criterion by the customers are seldom the same. It is not unreasonable to say that customers tend to rate every criterion as important, when asked freely (Naumann and Giel, 1995). Because of the tendency of customers to rate almost everything as important, the researchers are often wary of self-explicated importance data and derived importance data are considered generally more reliable.

Nevertheless, the comparison between derived and stated importance can give valuable information. It enables a company to identify what attributes the customers rate as important and see how these agree with truly important and truly unimportant attributes. Moreover, it helps the company identify unspoken motivators or even expected or cost of entry attributes. This approach also agrees with the principles of Kano's approach for defining different quality levels and may give the ability to classify customer requirements.

The presented methodology consists of the following main steps (Grigoroudis and Spiridaki, 2003):

1. In the first step, performance and importance data are collected using a simple questionnaire. In particular, customers are asked about their level of satisfaction/dissatisfaction from each criterion (see Figure 4.7), while at the same time, they are asked to express their level of importance for each criterion (see Figure 5.3).

2. Based on the performance satisfaction judgments, derived importance is estimated using the MUSA method. Moreover, the straightforward customer preferences for satisfaction criteria weights are used in the model presented in this section in order to estimate stated importance.
3. In the last step, stated and derived importance results are comparatively examined through a dual importance diagram that defines different quality levels in agreement with Kano's approach and gives the ability to classify customer requirements.

This diagram contains the normalized results of stated and derived importance (similarly to the relative action and improvement diagrams presented in sections 4.3.5 and 4.3.6). These results may help a business organization to identify what attributes are rated as important by customers and, at the same time, see how these attributes differ in importance when modeled by a regression-type quantitative technique.

The dual importance diagram is divided in four quadrants (Figure 5.5). Quadrants (i) and (ii) include the dimensions that are truly important to the customers. These are the main characteristics that management and production should focus on. Quadrants (i) and (iv) include the important dimensions according to the customers' free statement. These are the dimensions that marketing should focus on. When a characteristic appears in quadrant (i) or (iii) there is an agreement between derived and stated importance. On the other hand, in quadrants (ii) or (iv) there is a disagreement between the stated and derived importance. This disagreement is an indication that these dimensions require further analysis.

According to Lowenstein (1995), the dual importance diagram may be linked with the Kano's model and its three basic categories of product/service requirements:

- Quadrants (i) and (iii) correspond to the characteristics that are truly important or truly unimportant for the customers (one-dimensional characteristics). Both the model and the customers agree on them giving the company a more valid view and a better-grounded direction.
- Quadrant (ii) includes the characteristics that the MUSA method evaluates as being very important, while the customers judge as less important when they are asked straightforward. These characteristics are called "unspoken motivators" and represent dimensions to which the company should pay attention. They may affect (positively or negatively) future clientele, although the customers consider them of low importance.
- Finally, quadrant (iv) includes the characteristics that the model estimates as less important, while the customers rate them as very important. These usually include expected or cost-of-entry services (e.g. service/product guarantees). A company should keep such characteristics at a level at least as high as the ones of their competitors in order to keep its clientele, or offer extra, unexpected services to gain competitive advantage.

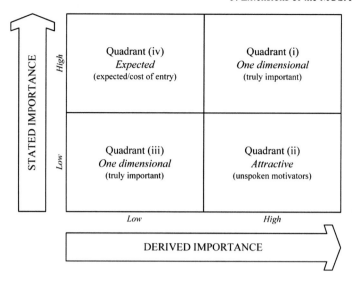

Fig. 5.5 Dual importance diagram (Lowenstein, 1995)

5.4.3 Combining Performance and Importance Judgments

A different approach for criteria importance preferences is presented in this section. The main purpose of this analysis is to examine whether additional information about criteria weights can improve the results of the MUSA method.

Using together customers' performance and importance judgments, an extension of the MUSA method may be modeled as a Multiobjective Linear Programming (MOLP) problem:

$$
\begin{cases}
[\min]F = \sum_{j=1}^{M} \sigma_j^+ + \sigma_j^- \\
[\min]\varPhi = \sum_{i=1}^{n}\sum_{j=1}^{M} S_{ij}^+ + S_{ij}^- \\
\text{subject to} \\
\text{all the constraints of LPs (4.17) and (5.25)}
\end{cases}
\qquad (5.30)
$$

Since competitiveness of the objective functions is the main characteristic of MOLP problems, searching for a solution that optimizes both F and $\varPhi$ is rather pointless. The above problem may be solved using any MOLP technique (e.g. compromise programming, global criterion approach, etc.). Here, an alternative heuristic method, consisting three steps, is presented (Grigoroudis et al., 2004):

Step 1:
Solve the following LP:

$$\begin{cases} [\min] F = \sum_{j=1}^{M} \sigma_j^+ + \sigma_j^- \\ \text{subject to} \\ \text{all the constraints of LPs (4.17) and (5.25)} \end{cases} \tag{5.31}$$

Step 2:
Minimize the errors S_{ij}^+ and S_{ij}^- using the following LP:

$$\begin{cases} [\min] \Phi = \sum_{i=1}^{n} \sum_{j=1}^{M} S_{ij}^+ + S_{ij}^- \\ \text{subject to} \\ F \leq F^* + \varepsilon_1 \\ \text{all the constraints of LPs (4.17) and (5.25)} \end{cases} \tag{5.32}$$

where F^* is the optimal value of the objective function of LP (5.31), and ε_1 is a small percentage of F^*.

Step 3:
Perform stability analysis (formulate and solve n LPs where each one maximizes the weight of a criterion):

$$\begin{cases} [\min] F' = \sum_{k=1}^{a_i - 1} w_{ik} \quad \text{for } i = 1, 2, \ldots, n \\ \text{subject to} \\ F \leq F^* + \varepsilon_1 \\ \Phi \leq \Phi^* + \varepsilon_2 \\ \text{all the constraints of LPs (4.17) and (5.25)} \end{cases} \tag{5.33}$$

where F^*, Φ^* are the optimal values of the objective functions of LPs (5.31)-(5.32), and ε_1, ε_2 are small percentages of F^* and Φ^*, respectively; similarly to the basic MUSA method, the final solution is calculated as the average of the optimal solutions of the previous LPs.

A detailed discussion about modeling preferences on criteria importance in the framework of the MUSA method, as well as real-world applications of the aforementioned approaches are given by Grigoroudis and Spiridaki (2003) and Grigoroudis et al. (2004).

5.5 Other Extensions

5.5.1 A Customer Satisfaction Barometer Model

The main principles of the MUSA method may also be used in order to develop a customer satisfaction barometer model. In this extension, called MUSA+ model, a sample of customers evaluates all the satisfaction criteria (global and partial) for a set of competitive companies. Thus, the MUSA+ model may be characterized as a satisfaction benchmarking analysis.

The MUSA+ estimation model can be written as follows:

$$
\left\{
\begin{aligned}
& [\min] F = \sum_{j=1}^{M} \sum_{t=1}^{T} \sigma_{tj}^{+} + \sigma_{tj}^{-} \\
& \text{subject to} \\
& \sum_{i=1}^{n} \sum_{k=1}^{q_{tij}-1} w_{ik} - \sum_{m=1}^{q_{tj}-1} z_{m} - \sigma_{tj}^{+} + \sigma_{tj}^{-} = 0 \quad \forall j, t \\
& \sum_{m=1}^{a-1} z_{m} = 100 \\
& \sum_{i=1}^{n} \sum_{k=1}^{a_{i}-1} w_{ik} = 100 \\
& z_{m} \geq 0,\; w_{ik} \geq 0,\; \sigma_{tj}^{+} \geq 0,\; \sigma_{tj}^{-} \geq 0 \quad \forall\, i, j, k, m, t
\end{aligned}
\right.
\tag{5.34}
$$

where M is the number of customers, T is the number of competitive companies, q_{tj} and q_{tij} are the global and partial satisfaction judgments of customer j ($j = 1, 2, .., M$) for company t ($t = 1, 2, .., T$) with:

$$
\left\{
\begin{aligned}
& y^{q_{tj}} \in Y = \left\{ y^{1}, y^{2}, ..., y^{q_{tj}}, ..., y^{a} \right\} \\
& x_{i}^{q_{tij}} \in X_{i} = \left\{ x_{i}^{1}, x_{i}^{2}, ..., x_{i}^{q_{tij}}, ..., x_{i}^{a_{i}} \right\} \quad \text{for } i = 1, 2, ... n
\end{aligned}
\right.
\tag{5.35}
$$

Alternative objective functions of LP (5.34) may also be considered, taken into account additional information on the sample of customers or the set of competitive companies. For example, if a different number of customers have evaluated the set of companies, the error variables may be weighted according to the market share of each company:

$$F = \sum_{t=1}^{T} \frac{C_t}{M_t} \sum_{j=1}^{M} (\sigma_{tj}^+ + \sigma_{tj}^-) \tag{5.36}$$

where C_t are the sales of company t and M_t is the number of customer evaluating company t.

Similarly to the original MUSA method, the MUSA+ model includes also a post-optimality analysis stage in order to overcome the problem of model stability. Thus, the final solution of the problem is calculated by exploring multiple or near optimal solutions of the LP (5.34).

Based on this solution and using formulas (4.18) and (4.22), the value functions, the criteria weights, and the average demanding indices can be directly calculated. However, in the MUSA+ method, the average satisfaction indices are re-assessed for every competitive company, using the following formulas:

$$\begin{cases} S_t = \dfrac{1}{100} \sum_{m=1}^{\alpha} p_t^m y^{*m} & \text{for } t = 1, 2, \ldots T \\[4mm] S_{ti} = \dfrac{1}{100} \sum_{k=1}^{\alpha_i} p_{ti}^k x_i^{*k} & \text{for } i = 1, 2, \ldots, n \text{ and } t = 1, 2, \ldots T \end{cases} \tag{5.37}$$

where S_t, S_{ti} are the average global and partial satisfaction indices and p_t^m, p_{ti}^k are the frequencies of customers belonging to the y^m and x_i^k satisfaction levels, for company t.

Using a weighted sum formula, an industry satisfaction barometer may also be estimated as follows:

$$\begin{cases} SI = \dfrac{1}{\displaystyle\sum_{t=1}^{T} C_t} \sum_{t=1}^{T} C_t S_t \\[6mm] SI_i = \dfrac{1}{\displaystyle\sum_{t=1}^{T} C_t} \sum_{t=1}^{T} C_t S_{ti} & \text{for } i = 1, 2, \ldots n \end{cases} \tag{5.38}$$

where SI and SI_i are the industry's average global and partial satisfaction indices, respectively, and C_t are the sales of company t.

In the MUSA+ method, the satisfaction benchmarking analysis is mainly based on the comparative performance diagrams. These diagrams present the average satisfaction indices of a particular company in relation to the performance of the other competitive companies. They are divided into four quadrants and can be used as a benchmarking tool in order to assess the performance of the different characteristics of the company against the competitors (Figure 5.6):

1. *Competitive advantages* (high performance/better than competition): this area indicates the competitive advantages of the company.
2. *Struggle quadrant* (high performance/worst than competition): it refers to criteria for which even though the company has high performance, it is still lower than the performance of the competitors as there is a high competition; these criteria are worth to improve, only if they are important to customers.
3. *Competitive disadvantages* (low performance/worst than competition): this area indicates the competitive disadvantages of the company.
4. *Waiting quadrant* (low performance/better than competition): it concerns the criteria for which the company has low performance but they are still better than the competitors; these criteria need special monitoring as potential changes in the future may convert them to critical points or competitive advantages.

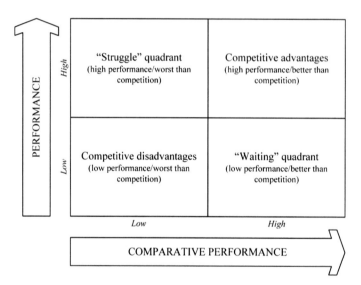

Fig. 5.6 Comparative performance diagrams

There are alternative comparative performance measures that can be used in these diagrams. The performance of a satisfaction criterion for a particular company can be compared with:

- the average of the sector (mean value of the satisfaction indices for the total set of competitive companies),
- the best company in the market (i.e. the company with the highest average global satisfaction index), or

- the best-in-class company (i.e. the company with the highest satisfaction index in this particular criterion).

It should be noted that usually a relative form of the aforementioned diagrams is used, in order to overcome the problem of assessing the cut-off levels for horizontal and vertical axes (see action and improvement diagrams in sections 4.3.5 and 4.3.6).

An analytical discussion of the MUSA+ method is given by Grigoroudis et al. (2007a), while Grigoroudis and Siskos (2004) present the development of a satisfaction barometer for the transportation-telecommunications sector, based on a draft version of the method.

5.5.2 Combining Cardinal and Ordinal Input Data

In several cases, customer satisfaction judgments are expressed in a cardinal form. These data may refer to the performance of a particular characteristic of the product/service (ratio scale), or satisfaction judgments in predefined numerical intervals (interval scale).

For example, assume that customers express their overall satisfaction using a 0-10 numerical scale (where 0 means absolutely dissatisfied and 10 means absolutely satisfied) and their partial satisfaction using the ordinal scales X_i, so that:

$$\begin{cases} y^j \in Y = \left\{0,1,\ldots,y^j,\ldots,10\right\} \\ x_i^{t_{ij}} \in X_i = \left\{x_i^1,x_i^2,\ldots,x_i^{t_{ij}},\ldots,x_i^{a_i}\right\} & \text{for } i = 1,2,\ldots n \end{cases} \qquad (5.39)$$

Hence, assuming that $y^{*m} = 10y^m = 10m$ for $m = 0, 1, \ldots, 10$, the ordinal regression equation (4.12) of the basic MUSA method becomes as follows:

$$10y^j = \sum_{i=1}^{n}\sum_{k=1}^{t_{ij}-1} w_{ik} - \sigma^+ + \sigma^- \quad \forall j \qquad (5.40)$$

Using these cardinal data, the z_m variables may be removed and the new LP formulation may be written:

$$
\left\{
\begin{aligned}
& [\min]\, F = \sum_{j=1}^{M} \sigma_j^+ + \sigma_j^- \\[2mm]
& \text{subject to} \\[2mm]
& \sum_{i=1}^{n} \sum_{k=1}^{t_{ij}-1} w_{ik} - \sigma_j^+ + \sigma_j^- = 10 y^j \quad \forall j \\[2mm]
& \sum_{i=1}^{n} \sum_{k=1}^{a_i-1} w_{ik} = 100 \\[2mm]
& w_{ik} \geq 0,\ \sigma_j^+ \geq 0, \sigma_j^- \geq 0 \quad \forall\, i,j,k,m
\end{aligned}
\right.
\tag{5.41}
$$

A post-optimality analysis stage should be also considered in this case, similarly to the basic MUSA method. Moreover, the assumed linear form of the value function Y^* yields $D = 0$, while the global average satisfaction index is given by the following formula:

$$
S = \frac{1}{100} \sum_{m=0}^{10} p^m 10m = \frac{1}{10} \sum_{m=0}^{10} mp^m
\tag{5.42}
$$

where p^m is the frequency of customers belonging to the m-th overall satisfaction level.

All the other variables, like b_i, x_i^k, S_i, and D_i are calculated similarly to the basic MUSA method (see Chapter 4). A detailed discussion of the aforementioned model and applications to e-learning evaluation problems are given by Matsatsinis et al. (2003).

5.5.3 Additional Constraints and Optimality Criteria

The LP formulation of the MUSA method gives the ability to consider additional constraints regarding special properties of the assessed model variables. One of the most interesting extensions concerns additional properties for the assessed average indices.

For example, a linkage between global and partial average satisfaction indices may be assumed, since these indices are considered as the main performance indicators of the business organization. In particular, the global average satisfaction index S is assessed as a weighted sum of the partial satisfaction indices S_i:

$$
S = \sum_{i=1}^{n} b_i S_i \Leftrightarrow \sum_{m=1}^{\alpha} p^m y^{*m} = \sum_{i=1}^{n} b_i \sum_{k=1}^{a_i} p_i^k x_i^{*k}
\tag{5.43}
$$

Using formulas (4.18) and (4.21), the above equation becomes as follows:

$$\sum_{m=2}^{a} p^m \sum_{t=1}^{m-1} z_t = \sum_{i=1}^{n} \sum_{k=2}^{a_i} p_i^k \sum_{t=1}^{k-1} w_{it} \tag{5.44}$$

In the case of the generalized MUSA method, the preference thresholds γ and γ_i should be introduced, and equation (5.44) is written:

$$\sum_{i=1}^{n} \sum_{k=2}^{a_i} p_i^k \sum_{t=1}^{k-1} w_{it} - \sum_{m=2}^{a} p^m \sum_{t=1}^{m-1} z_t = \sum_{m=2}^{a} p^m \gamma(m-1) - \sum_{i=1}^{n} \sum_{k=2}^{a_i} p_i^k \gamma_i (k-1) \tag{5.45}$$

Similarly, a weighted sum formula may be assumed for the average demanding indices:

$$D = \sum_{i=1}^{n} b_i D_i \tag{5.46}$$

Using formulas (4.18) and (4.22), the previous equation can be written in terms of the MUSA variables:

$$\frac{\sum_{m=1}^{a-1} 100(m-1) - (a-1)\sum_{t=1}^{m-1} z_t}{a(a-1)} = \sum_{i=1}^{n} \frac{\sum_{k=1}^{a_i-1}(k-1)\sum_{t=1}^{a_i-1} w_{it} - (a_i-1)\sum_{t=1}^{k-1} w_{it}}{a_i(a_i-1)} \tag{5.47}$$

Alternatively, formulas (4.23) may also be used, while in the case of the generalized MUSA method, equation (5.47) should be modified by introducing the variables z'_m and w'_{ik} (see formula (5.4)).

The equations (5.44) and (5.47) may be introduced as additional constraints in the LP (4.17). However, these additional properties of average indices should be used carefully, since their form does not guarantee a feasible solution of the LP, especially in case of inconsistencies between global and partial satisfaction judgments. For this reason, the aforementioned equations may be written using a goal programming formulation and used alternatively as post-optimality criteria.

Another extension of the MUSA method refers to the objective function of the initially formulated LP. The objective function assessed in section 4.2.2 concerns the sum of errors variables σ^+ and σ^- and does not take into account the distribution of customer judgments to the assessed overall satisfaction levels. Therefore, using this optimality criterion, it is expected to have large values of the error variables, when particular levels of overall satisfaction have been chosen by a small percentage of customers.

In order to overcome this problem, an alternative approach is to weight the errors according to the overall satisfaction frequencies. This weighted sum of errors has the following form:

$$F_w = \sum_{m=1}^{a} \frac{1}{p^m} \sum_{j \in Y^m} (\sigma_j^+ + \sigma_j^-) \qquad\qquad (5.48)$$

where p^m is the frequency and Y^m is the set of customers belonging to the y^m over-all satisfaction level.

The minimization of the previous objective function may be introduced as an alternative optimality criterion in the basic MUSA method, as well as in the extensions presented in this Chapter. Moreover, it should be noted that the formula (5.48) assumes that $p^m \neq 0$. In cases where $p^m = 0$, it is not possible to estimate the additive value function in this particular point y^{*m}, since there are no customers that have selected level y^m of the overall satisfaction ordinal scale. Thus, in these cases, the overall satisfaction scale should be reconsidered, probably by combining some adjacent satisfaction levels.

5.6 Discussion and Future Research

The MUSA method is based on the principles of multicriteria analysis, and particularly on aggregation-dissaggregation approach and linear programming modelling. The implementation of the method in customer satisfaction surveys is able to evaluate quantitative global and partial satisfaction levels and to determine the strong and the weak points of a business organisation,

The main advantage of the MUSA method is that it fully considers the qualitative form of customers' judgements and preferences, as expressed in a customer satisfaction survey. This way the proposed methodology does not arbitrarily quantify the collected information. Other advantages of the method include the following:

- The post-optimality analysis stage gives the ability to achieve a sufficient stability level concerning the provided results, while the LP formulation offers a flexible model development, as illustrated by the large number of extensions and variations presented in this Chapter.
- The provided results are focused not only on the descriptive analysis of customer satisfaction data, but they are also able to assess an integrated benchmarking system. This way, they offer a complete information set including: value functions, criteria weights, average satisfaction, demanding and improvement indices, action and improvement diagrams, etc.
- All these results are sufficient enough to analyze in detail the satisfaction evaluation problem, and to assess the reliability of the method's implementation.
- A significant effort has been devoted in order for all the provided results to be easily and directly understood. For this reason, the indices' sets are assessed in a normalized [0, 100%] interval.

As already noted, the MUSA method is based on a very flexible modeling, which gives the ability to consider the analyst's preferences and modify model development in accordance with the special characteristics of the examined customer satisfaction measurement problem. For example, any combination of the extensions of the MUSA method presented in this Chapter may be considered.

The potential implementation problems of the MUSA method concern the model assumptions and the quality of the collected data, which is however something common in all regression analysis models.

The logical inconsistency of customer satisfaction data affects directly the reliability and the stability of the results. Examples of such inconsistencies may refer to cases where customers appear very satisfied to the whole set of criteria, while they are overall dissatisfied with the product/service provided (and vice-versa). The main cause of this problem is that the satisfaction criteria set is not a consistent family of criteria, or even the customers are not rational decision-makers. During the implementation process of the MUSA method, a preliminary stage for searching such inconsistencies should be applied. If the problem appears in a small portion of customers, the particular data should be removed, while in the opposite case the defined satisfaction criteria set should be reconsidered.

Another problem that may appear concerns the existence of distinguished customer groups with different preference value systems (value functions, criteria weights, etc.). This problem can be identified by the high variance of the variables during the post-optimality analysis and is due to the collective nature of the MUSA method. The segmentation of the total set of customers into smaller groups according to particular characteristics (e.g. age, sex) is the most reliable solution to the aforementioned problem.

Future research regarding the MUSA method is mainly focused on comparison analysis with other alternative satisfaction measurement approaches like statistical models, data analysis techniques, fuzzy sets, and other advanced prediction methods (e.g. neural networks). Moreover, the problem of selecting appropriate values for the parameters of the method (preference thresholds, ε value) and its impact to the reliability and stability of the provided results should be studied.

The implementation of the MUSA method requires complete and correctly answered questionnaires as input data, which cannot always be achieved. Missing data analysis and data mining techniques may be used to overcome this problem by filling in the empty cells in the data table (Matsatsinis et al., 1999).

Other extensions of the method may include:

- The development of an extended MUSA method in a customer satisfaction survey for a set of competitive companies, given that the currently presented version is focused on the satisfaction evaluation problem for a single business organization.
- The assessment of a "critical" satisfaction level that can relate customer satisfaction level and repurchase probability. Hill (1996) notes several research efforts for the determination of a customer tolerance band. Furthermore, combining MUSA method with several brand choice models, the segmentation of the

total set of customers into smaller groups with different loyalty levels can be achieved. A pilot survey in the context of multicriteria analysis is proposed by Grigoroudis et al. (1999a).

Finally, it is interesting to analyze the relation between the results of the MUSA method and the financial indices (market share, profit, etc.) of a business organization. Although customer satisfaction is a necessary but not a sufficient condition for the financial viability, several researches have shown that there is a significant correlation among satisfaction level, customer loyalty, and company's profit (Dutka, 1995; Naumann and Giel, 1995).

Chapter 6
Advanced Topics on the MUSA method

6.1 Computational Issues

The computational difficulty of the MUSA method is based on the number of variables and the number of constraints in the formulated LP. The method consists of two distinct stages: in the first stage an initial LP is solved in order to obtain an optimum value for the selected error function, while in the second stage a heuristic algorithm is used (solving a number of LPs) in order to explore the multiple or near optimal solutions space.

As a rule, the computational effort (CE) of a single LP may be estimated using the following expression:

$$CE \propto N_v \cdot N_c^2 \tag{6.1}$$

where N_v and N_c are the number of variables and constraints of the LP, respectively.

For example, the initial LP in the basic, and the generalized, MUSA method has $M + 2$ constraints and $2M + (\alpha-1) + \sum(\alpha_i - 1)$ variables, while in the post-optimality analysis stage n LPs are solved having $M + 3$ constraints (the number of variables remains the same). Without loss of generality, we may assume that $\alpha = \alpha_i \ \forall i$, and therefore, the computational effort for the basic MUSA method is:

$$CE \propto \left[2M + (n+1)(\alpha - 1)\right]\left[(M + 2)^2 + n(M + 3)^2\right] \tag{6.2}$$

where M is the number of customers, n is the number of criteria, and α is the number of overall (or marginal) satisfaction levels.

As shown in expression (6.2), the computational difficulty of the MUSA method is heavily affected by the number of customers (see also Figure 6.1),

E. Grigoroudis and Y. Siskos, *Customer Satisfaction Evaluation*, International Series
in Operations Research & Management Science 139, DOI 10.1007/978-1-4419-1640-2_6,
© Springer Science + Business Media, LLC 2010

which is quite reasonable, since M determines the number of cases in a regression-type model.

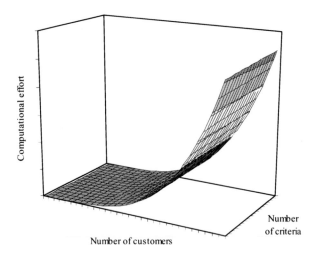

Fig. 6.1 Computational difficulty for the basic MUSA method

For this reason, the Dual Linear Program (DLP) of the MUSA formulation may be considered, in order to reduce the computational effort. In the case of the basic MUSA method, LP (4.17) may be written in the following form:

[min] $\mathbf{1}'_{2M} \boldsymbol{\sigma}$

subject to

$$
\begin{bmatrix} \boldsymbol{\Theta} \\ \mathbf{1}'_{\sum_i (a_i-1)} \\ \mathbf{0}'_{\sum_i (a_i-1)} \end{bmatrix} \mathbf{w} + \begin{bmatrix} \boldsymbol{\Psi} \\ \mathbf{0}'_{(a-1)} \\ \mathbf{1}'_{(a-1)} \end{bmatrix} \mathbf{z} + \begin{bmatrix} \boldsymbol{\Lambda} \\ \mathbf{0}'_{2M} \\ \mathbf{0}'_{2M} \end{bmatrix} \boldsymbol{\sigma} = \begin{bmatrix} \mathbf{0}_M \\ 100 \\ 100 \end{bmatrix} \tag{6.3}
$$

with $\mathbf{w}, \mathbf{z}, \boldsymbol{\sigma} \geq 0$

where $\mathbf{w}$, $\mathbf{z}$, and $\boldsymbol{\sigma}$ are the vectors of the model variables, $\mathbf{1}_x$ and $\mathbf{0}_x$ are vectors of size x with ones and zeros, respectively, $\boldsymbol{\Theta}$ and $\boldsymbol{\Psi}$ are matrices of size $M \times \sum(a_i-1)$ and $M \times (a-1)$, respectively, where θ_{ij} and ψ_{ij} are given according to formula (4.16), and $\boldsymbol{\Lambda}$ is a matrix of size $M \times 2M$ having the following form:

$$\Lambda = \begin{bmatrix} -1 & 1 & 0 & 0 & \ldots & 0 & 0 \\ 0 & 0 & -1 & 1 & \ldots & 0 & 0 \\ \vdots & & & & \ddots & \vdots & \vdots \\ 0 & 0 & 0 & 0 & \ldots & -1 & 1 \end{bmatrix}$$

The dual of LP (6.3) can be written as follows:

[max] $100u_{M+1} + 100u_{M+2}$

subject to

$$\begin{bmatrix} \mathbf{\Theta}' & \mathbf{1}_{\sum_i (a_i-1)} & \mathbf{0}_{\sum_i (a_i-1)} \\ \mathbf{\Psi}' & \mathbf{0}_{(a-1)} & \mathbf{1}_{(a-1)} \end{bmatrix} \mathbf{u} \le 0 \tag{6.4}$$

$-1 \le u_i \le 1$ for $i = 1, 2, \ldots, M$

u_i free of sign $\forall i$

where $\mathbf{u}$ is the vector of dual variables with size $M + 2$.

The complexity of DLP (6.4) is based only on $(a-1) + \sum(a_i-1)$ constraints, since $-1 \le u_i \le 1$ are just boundary constraints. Thus the computational difficulty of DLP (6.4) is significantly smaller compared to the original LP (4.17).

It should be noted that the previous discussion refers only to the basic or the generalized MUSA method. The computational difficulty changes if we consider alternative objective functions for the post-optimality analysis stage. As shown in Table 6.1, the alternative MUSA methods presented in section 5.3 have different number of constraints and variables, while a different number of LPs has to be solved during the post-optimality analysis stage. Figure 6.2 shows the computational effort for these extensions of the MUSA method for a given number of criteria n and satisfaction levels a and a_i (the computational effort has been estimated using formula (6.1)). As expected, the complexity appears smaller for the generalized MUSA and the MUSA II methods, while MUSA III variation requires the highest computational effort.

6.2 Reliability Evaluation and Error Indicators

6.2.1 Average Fitting Indices

The reliability evaluation of the results is mainly related to the level of fitting to the customer satisfaction data, and the stability of the post-optimality analysis results.

Table 6.1 Problem size of alternative post-optimality approaches

Extension	Number of LPs	Number of constraints	Number of variables
Generalized MUSA	n	$M+3$	$2M+(\alpha-1)+\sum_{i=1}^{n}(\alpha_i-1)$
MUSA I	$2n$	$M+3$	$2M+(\alpha-1)+\sum_{i=1}^{n}(\alpha_i-1)$
MUSA II	$n+1$	$M+3$	$2M+\alpha+\sum_{i=1}^{n}\alpha_i$
MUSA III	$(\alpha-1)+\sum_{i=1}^{n}(\alpha_i-1)$	$M+3$	$2M+(\alpha-1)+\sum_{i=1}^{n}(\alpha_i-1)$
MUSA IV	1	$3M+3$	$2M+\alpha+\sum_{i=1}^{n}(\alpha_i-1)$

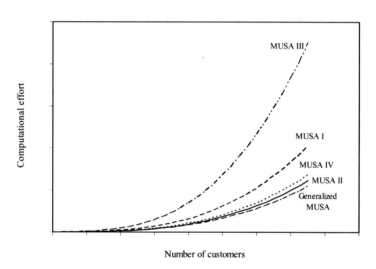

Fig. 6.2 Computational difficulty for the alternative MUSA methods

The fitting level of the MUSA method refers to the assessment of a preference collective value system (value functions, weights, etc.) for the set of customers with the minimum possible errors. For this reason, the optimal values of the error variables indicate the reliability of the value system that is evaluated.

Although several fitting measures may be assessed, all these indicators depend on the optimum error level and the number of customers. Grigoroudis and Siskos (2002) propose the following simple average fitting index AFI_1:

$$AFI_1 = 1 - \frac{F^*}{100M} \tag{6.5}$$

where F^* is the minimum sum of errors of the initial LP, and M is the number of customers.

AFI_1 is normalized in the interval $[0, 1]$, and it is equal to 1 if $F^* = 0$, i.e. when the method is able to evaluate a preference value system with zero errors. Similarly, AFI_1 takes the value 0 only when the pairs of the error variables σ_j^+ and σ_j^- take the maximum possible values. It is easy to prove that $\sigma_j^+ \cdot \sigma_j^- = 0 \;\; \forall j$, i.e. the optimal solution has at least one zero error variable for each customer, given that the MUSA method is similar to goal programming modeling (Charnes and Cooper, 1961).

An alternative fitting indicator is based on the percentage of customers with zero error variables, i.e. the percentage of customers for whom the estimated preference value systems fits perfectly with their expressed satisfaction judgments. This average fitting index AFI_2 is assessed as follows:

$$AFI_2 = \frac{M_0}{M} \tag{6.6}$$

where M_0 is the number of customers for whom $\sigma^+ = \sigma^- = 0$

Although the previous fitting indicators are rather simple and can be easily calculated, they present several disadvantages. For example, AFI_1 may rarely take large values, since usually $F^* \ll 100M$. This is justified by the fact that it is unreasonable all the error variables in a regression-type model to have their maximum possible values, i.e. $\sigma_j^+ + \sigma_j^- = 100 \;\; \forall j$. For this reason, AFI_1 usually overestimates the fitting ability of the MUSA method. On the other hand, AFI_2 examines only the existence of non-zero errors, without taking into account the values of these error variables. For this reason, in several cases AFI_2 underestimates MUSA's fitting level. Additionally, the values of AFI_2 may not give a reliable indication for the overall fitting ability of the MUSA method, since a small (or high) value of AFI_2 does not imply a respective small (or high) sum of errors.

To overcome these disadvantages, a new fitting indicator may be assessed, which will be able to examine separately every level of overall satisfaction and to calculate the maximum possible error value for each one of these levels. As shown in Figure 6.3, for the estimation of y^{*m}, $0 \leq y^{*m} \leq 100$ holds and thereby, the maximum overestimation (σ^+) and underestimation (σ^-) errors are $100 - y^{*m}$ and y^{*m}, respectively. Thus, the overall maximum error for every overall satisfaction level is the maximum of the previous expressions.

Using this approach, an alternative formulation of AFI_1 may be developed. The new average fitting index AFI_3 takes into account the maximum values of the error variables for every global satisfaction level, as well as the number of customers that belongs to this level:

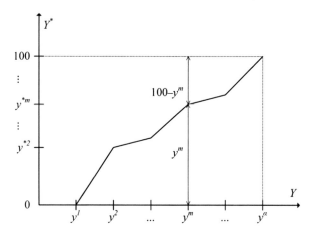

Fig. 6.3 Maximum error values for the m-th overall satisfaction level

$$AFI_3 = 1 - \frac{F^*}{M\sum_{m=1}^{\alpha} p^m \max\left\{y^{*m}, 100 - y^{*m}\right\}}$$ (6.7)

where p^m is the frequency of customers belonging to the y^m satisfaction level.

Consequently, AFI_3 may be considered as a variation of AFI_1, for which $AFI_3 \leq AFI_1$ can be proved to hold. Although AFI_3 appears more reliable, all of the aforementioned average fitting indicators are highly affected by potential inconsistencies in customer satisfaction judgments. Therefore, the examination of all these indices may give a more complete view for the fitting ability of the MUSA method.

6.2.2 Other Fitting Indicators

One of the most useful tools, which may serve as an alternative fitting indicator of the MUSA method, is the variance diagram of the added value curve. This variance diagram (Figure 6.4) shows the value range that the customers' set gives for each level of the ordinal satisfaction scale. Therefore, it can be considered as a confidence interval for the estimated added value function.

This diagram depends upon the estimated satisfaction values and the optimal values of the error variables as well. The development process of this diagram consists of the following steps (Grigoroudis and Siskos, 2002):

Step 1:
For each customer j, the evaluated satisfaction value $\tilde{y}_j^{*m}$ is calculated according to the formula:

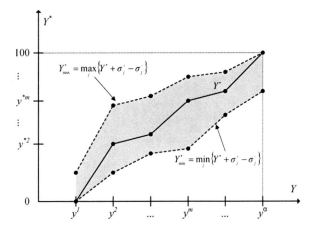

Fig. 6.4 Variance diagram of the added value curve

$$\tilde{y}_j^{*m} = y^{*m} + \sigma_j^+ - \sigma_j^-$$ (6.8)

where y^{*m} is the satisfaction value of level m, and σ_j^+, σ_j^- are the corresponding error variables for customer j.

Step 2:
The maximum and minimum satisfaction curves y_{max}^{*m} and y_{min}^{*m} accordingly, are calculated for each level m of the ordinal satisfaction scale, using the following formula:

$$\begin{cases} y_{max}^{*m} = \max_j \left\{ \tilde{y}_j^{*m} \right\} \\ y_{min}^{*m} = \min_j \left\{ \tilde{y}_j^{*m} \right\} \end{cases} \quad \text{for } m = 1, 2, \ldots, \alpha$$ (6.9)

Another fitting indicator is the prediction table of global satisfaction, which is developed in a similar way according to the following steps (Grigoroudis and Siskos, 2002):

Step 1:
For each customer j, the evaluated satisfaction value $\tilde{y}_j^{*m}$ is calculated according to (6.8).

Step 2:
Based on the previous value, the evaluated satisfaction level $\tilde{y}_j^m$ is calculated for each customer j, according to the formula:

$$\tilde{y}_j^m = \begin{cases} y_j^1 & \text{if } \tilde{y}_j^{*m} \le \dfrac{y^{*2}}{2} \\[2mm] y_j^2 & \text{if } \dfrac{y^{*2}}{2} < \tilde{y}_j^{*m} \le \dfrac{y^{*3} + y^{*2}}{2} \\[2mm] \vdots \\[2mm] y_j^\alpha & \text{if } \tilde{y}_j^{*m} > \dfrac{100 + y^{*\alpha-1}}{2} \end{cases} \tag{6.10}$$

Step 3:

Using the actual (as expressed by the customers) and the estimated level of global satisfaction, y_j^m and $\tilde{y}_j^m$ accordingly, the number of customers belonging to each of these levels is calculated.

The general form of a prediction table is presented in Figure 6.5, and includes the following results for each actual and evaluated satisfaction level:

- N_{ij}: the number of customers that have declared to belong to global satisfaction level i, while the model classifies them to level j.
- R_{ij}: the percentage of customers of actual global satisfaction level i that the model classifies to level j.
- C_{ij}: the percentage of customers of estimated global satisfaction level j that have declared to belong to level j.

R_{ij} and C_{ij} are calculated according to the formulas:

$$R_{ij} = \frac{N_{ij}}{\displaystyle\sum_{i=1}^{\alpha} N_{ij}}, \quad C_{ij} = \frac{N_{ij}}{\displaystyle\sum_{j=1}^{\alpha} N_{ij}} \quad \forall i,j \tag{6.11}$$

while the overall prediction level (*OPL*) is based on the sum of the main diagonal cells of the prediction table, and it represents the percentage of correctly classified customers:

$$OPL = \frac{\displaystyle\sum_{i=1}^{\alpha} N_{ii}}{\displaystyle\sum_{i=1}^{\alpha}\sum_{j=1}^{\alpha} N_{ij}} \tag{6.12}$$

In general, it should be mentioned that the fitness of the MUSA method is not satisfactory when a high percentage of customers appears away from the main diagonal of the prediction table, i.e. a significant number of customers having declared to be very satisfied is predicted to have a low satisfaction level and vice versa.

		Predicted Global Satisfaction Level			
		$\tilde{y}^1$	$\tilde{y}^2$	$\tilde{y}^j$	$\tilde{y}^a$
	y^1	N_{11} R_{11} C_{11}	N_{12} R_{12} C_{12} ...	N_{1j} R_{1j} C_{1j} ...	N_{1a} R_{1a} C_{1a}
	y^2	N_{21} R_{21} C_{21}	N_{22} R_{22} C_{22} ...	N_{2j} R_{2j} C_{2j} ...	N_{2a} R_{2a} C_{2a}
		$\vdots$			$\vdots$
	y^i	N_{i1} R_{i1} C_{i1}	N_{i2} R_{i2} C_{i2} ...	N_{ij} R_{ij} C_{ij} ...	N_{ia} R_{ia} C_{ia}
		$\vdots$			$\vdots$
	y^a	N_{a1} R_{a1} C_{a1}	N_{a2} R_{a2} C_{a2} ...	N_{aj} R_{aj} C_{aj} ...	N_{aa} R_{aa} C_{aa}

(Left vertical label: Actual Global Satisfaction Level)

Fig. 6.5 Prediction table of global satisfaction

6.2.3 Average Stability Index

The stability of the results provided by the post-optimality analysis is not related to the degree of fitness of the MUSA method. More specifically, during the post-optimality stage, n LPs are formulated and solved, which maximize repeatedly the weight of each criterion. The mean value of the weights of these LPs is taken as the final solution, and the observed variance in the post-optimality matrix indicates the degree of instability of the results. Thus, an average stability index ASI may be assessed as the mean value of the normalized standard deviation of the estimated weights:

$$ASI = 1 - \frac{1}{n}\sum_{i=1}^{n}\frac{\sqrt{n\sum_{j=1}^{n}\left(b_i^j\right)^2 - \left(\sum_{j=1}^{n}b_i^j\right)^2}}{100\sqrt{n-1}} \tag{6.13}$$

where b_i^j is the estimated weight of the i-th criterion in the j-th post-optimality analysis LP.

ASI is normalized in the interval $[0, 1]$, and it should be noted that when this index takes its maximum value, then:

$$ASI = 1 \Leftrightarrow b_i^j = b_i \quad \forall i, j \qquad\qquad (6.14)$$

where b_i is the final estimated weight for criterion i.

On the other hand, if ASI takes its minimum value, then:

$$ASI = 0 \Leftrightarrow b_i^j = \begin{cases} 1 & \text{if } i = j \\ 0 & \text{if } i \neq j \end{cases} \quad \forall i, j \qquad\qquad (6.15)$$

It should be emphasized that the aforementioned stability index refers to the basic or the generalized MUSA method. In case of alternative objective functions during the post-optimality analysis stage, formula (6.13) should be modified taking into account the number of LPs solved during this stage (see Table 6.1).

Generally, apart ASI, the variance of the weights during post-optimality analysis (see section 9.5.4) is also able to provide valuable information for the stability analysis of the results provided by the MUSA method. This diagram can give a confidence interval for the estimated weights, and can identify possible competitiveness in the criteria set, i.e. the existence of certain customer groups with different importance levels for the satisfaction criteria.

6.3 Selection of Parameters and Thresholds

6.3.1 Preference Thresholds

The problem of selecting appropriate model parameters is focused on the preference values γ, γ_i, and the tradeoff threshold ε during the post-optimality analysis.

In this section, it is examined how different values of these parameters may affect the fitting and stability level of the MUSA results. For this reason, a large number of indicative customer satisfaction data sets have been used. These data sets present different characteristic properties (e.g. number of criteria, number of satisfaction levels, consistency of judgments and stability level, etc.). One of the most important results of this analysis is that the selection of preference thresholds γ and γ_i depends mainly on the stability of the results.

In particular, in case of stable results, the average fitting index AFI_1, as well the average stability index ASI, have high values (~100%) for $\gamma = \gamma_i = 0$. The increase of γ and γ_i will cause a relatively small reduction of the fitting and stability level of the results, as shown in Figure 6.6(a). This finding may be justified by the fact that the preference thresholds provide a lower bound for the model variables z_m and w_{ik} (see formula (5.3)). For example, by increasing γ_i, the MUSA method is forced to assign a minimum weight of $\gamma_i(a_i-1)$ to each criterion. Thereby, the initially achieved fitting and stability level of the results is decreased. Consequently, in case of stable results, it is preferred to set $\gamma = \gamma_i = 0$ (or at least very small values for the preference thresholds).

In case of unstable results, *ASI* may take rather small values (e.g. <50%) for $\gamma = \gamma_i = 0$, while AFI_1 may retain a relatively high level (e.g. >80%). Figure 6.6(b) reveals a competitive relation between *ASI* and AFI_1 in this case: the increase of preference thresholds γ and γ_i may improve the stability of the results, but it will decrease the fitting level of the model. As previously noted, this is justified by the fact that the preference thresholds determine the minimum value of the criteria weights. Thus, in case of instability, the increase of γ and γ_i will decreas the variability observed in the post-optimality table, and therefore, it will increase the average stability index.

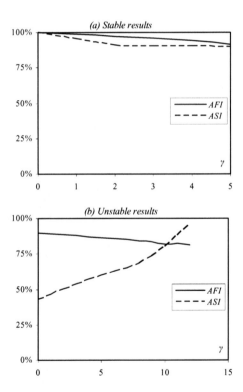

Fig. 6.6 Modification of AFI_1 and *ASI* for different values of γ

Generally, the process proposed in Figure 6.7 should be considered when selecting appropriate values for the preference thresholds γ and γ_i. This process is based on the work of Jacquet-Lagrèze and Siskos (1982) in the area of ordinal regression modeling. Moreover, it should be emphasized that special attention should be given when modifying the preference thresholds, because of the following main reasons:

- An arbitrarily large increase of the preference thresholds may falsify the customer satisfaction data set; large values of γ and γ_i require stronger assumptions for the preference conditions (5.1).
- Based on the assessed values of γ_i the minimum weight of criterion i is γ_i (a_i–1). This assumption should be verified by the decision-maker.

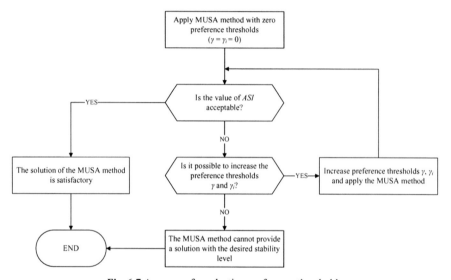

Fig. 6.7 A process for selecting preference thresholds

6.3.2 Post-optimality Thresholds

The post-optimality threshold ε does not affect the fitting ability of the model, since all the alternative fitting indices do not depend on the post-optimality results. Moreover, it should be noted that usually, in real world applications, $F^* > 0$, and thus ε may be assessed as a small percentage of the optimal value of the objective function F.

Similarly to the previous analyses, a large number of customer satisfaction data sets have been used, in order to examine the effect of post-optimality threshold on the stability level of the MUSA results. These experiments show that the increase of ε causes a decrease of the average stability index *ASI*, regardless of the stability level of results. This is rather expected, since an increase of ε implies an increase of the near optimal solutions space (see Figure 4.10).

As shown in Figure 6.8, the decrease of *ASI* is larger in case of unstable results because F^* is larger and, thus, the overall tradeoff value $(1+\varepsilon)F^*$ is larger in the post-optimality analysis. For this reason, the results presented in Figure 6.8(a)-(b) are not straightforward comparable (i.e. for the same value of ε, the tradeoff value $1+\varepsilon)F^*$ is larger for unstable results than for stable results).

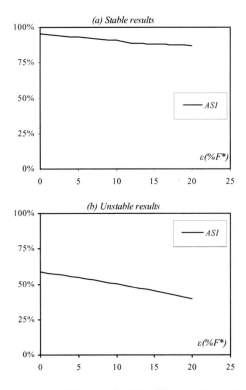

Fig. 6.8 Modification of *ASI* for different values of ε

Consequently, ε is a near optimal solutions threshold that should be always selected as a small percentage of F^*. The modification of ε should take into account the following:

- A very large value of ε will falsify the information provided by the post-optimality analysis, and decrease the stability ability of the model.
- A very low value of ε will not give the ability to explore the near optimal solutions space during post-optimality analysis.

6.4 Experimental Comparison Analysis

6.4.1 Design of the simulation process

The experimental research is the most important approach for comparing alternative methodologies. The main aim of this section is to present an experimental comparison analysis for different customer satisfaction evaluation models. The comparison concerns the MUSA method and the ordered conditional probability models (ordered Logit-Probit analysis), since all these models require the same type of input data, while they respect the qualitative form of the examined variables.

The first stage of the experimental comparison analysis refers to the design of the simulation process and aims at generating customer satisfaction data sets with different predefined characteristics. In particular, the data generation procedure is based on the principal that customer behavior (satisfaction judgments) may be explained through an explicitly defined set of value functions for a set of satisfaction criteria.

As Figure 6.9 shows, the data generation algorithm for the presented experiment consists of the following main steps:

Step 1:
In this initial step, the main parameters of the data sets are defined. These parameters include:

1. The number of satisfaction criteria n.
2. The number of the overall satisfaction levels α, as well as the number of the satisfaction levels of each satisfaction criterion α_i ($i = 1, 2, \ldots, n$).
3. The deviation level D_e (with $D_e \in [0, 1]$).
4. The desirable size of the data set M.

In addition, a set of value functions for the overall satisfaction Y^* and the marginal satisfaction $b_i X_i^*$ ($i = 1, 2, \ldots, n$) is selected in this step. For these value functions, the following monotonicity and normalization constraints must hold:

$$\begin{cases} y^{*1} = 0 \ \text{ and } \ y^{*a} = 100 \\ y^{*m} \le y^{*m+1} \quad m = 1, 2, \ldots a - 1 \end{cases}$$

$$\begin{cases} b_i x_i^{*1} = 0 \ \text{ and } \ \sum_{i=1}^{n} b_i x_i^{*a_i} = 100 \quad i = 1, 2, \ldots, n \\ b_i x_i^{*k} \le b_i x_i^{*k+1} \quad k = 1, 2, \ldots a_i - 1 \ \text{ and } \ i = 1, 2, \ldots, n \end{cases} \tag{6.16}$$

where it should be noted that the marginal value functions are written in a non-normalized form, in order to reduce the number of parameters; this way, it is not necessary to estimate the criteria weights.

Step 2:
The main properties of the data set are defined through this step. These properties are largely determined by the value functions assessed in the previous step. However, generating random data based on these value functions does not guarantee a consistent data set. For this reason, in the current step, a matrix of excluding values for every possible data combination is developed. This matrix is assessed according to the following formula:

$$E(i_1, i_2, \ldots i_n) = \begin{cases} 0 \text{ if } \exists k : \left| \sum_{j=1}^{n} b_j x_j^{i_j} - y^{*k} \right| \leq D_e \\ 1 \text{ otherwise} \end{cases} \quad i_j = 1, 2, \ldots, \alpha_i \qquad (6.17)$$

The matrix $E(.)$ is able to determine if any data combination $(i_1, i_2, \ldots, i_n)$ is consistent, thus $E(i_1, i_2, \ldots, i_n) = 0$, or inconsistent thus $E(i_1, i_2, \ldots, i_n) = 1$.

Step 3:
The last step refers to the data generation process according to the aforementioned properties and assumptions. This process may be considered as a type of Monte Carlo simulation analysis. Analytically, the procedure consists of the following steps:

1. Generation of a set of random numbers $(v_1, v_2, \ldots, v_n)$, which corresponds to the satisfaction of a fictitious customer for each one of the defined satisfaction criteria. These numbers are generated randomly, i.e. $v_j \sim U(1, \alpha_j)$, respecting the selected satisfaction levels.
2. If the previous data combination is inconsistent, that is $E(i_1, i_2, \ldots, i_j) = 1$, these numbers are rejected and a new random data set is generated. In the opposite case, the optimal level of the overall value function y^{*m} is calculated. In order to achieve the maximum consistency between y^{*m} and the data combination $(v_1, v_2, \ldots, v_n)$ the following is applied:

$$\left| \sum_{j=1}^{n} b_j x_j^{*v_j} - y^{*m} \right| = \min_k \left| \sum_{j=1}^{n} b_j x_j^{*v_j} - y^{*k} \right| \qquad (6.18)$$

3. The values $(y^{*m}, v_1, v_2, \ldots, v_n)$ are added in the data set and the previous steps are repeated starting with the generation of a new set of random numbers $(v_1, v_2, \ldots, v_n)$. The algorithm ends when the desired data set size is reached.

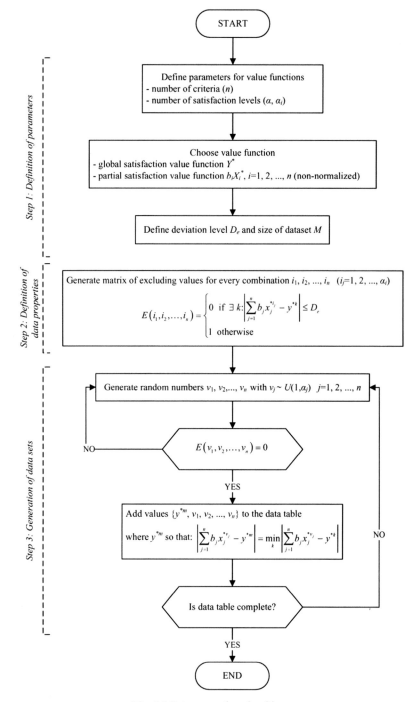

Fig. 6.9 Data generation algorithm

Using the presented algorithm, 16 different customer satisfaction data sets have been generated. These data sets are characterized by four different properties, as shown in Table 6.2. For each one of these properties (deviation level, number of customers, number of criteria, and number of satisfaction scales), 2 different values have been chosen, based on a series of pre-tests that are able to discriminate the results estimated by the MUSA method and the Logit-Probit analysis. This is the main reason for the large difference of the chosen deviation levels (5% and 40%). Moreover, the selected size of the data sets (500 and 1000 customers) is similar to the number of customers participating in real-world satisfaction surveys.

Table 6.2 Properties of the generated data sets

Deviation level (D_e)	Number of customers (M)	Number of criteria (n)	Number of satisfaction levels $(\alpha=\alpha_i)$
0.05-0.40	500-100	3-5	3-5

Finally, it should be noted that different families of value functions have been defined for each one of these generated data sets. Similarly, these sets of value functions present different characteristics, concerning the weights of the criteria and the shape of the assumed curve:

- The coefficient of variation may be used in order to measure differences in the distribution of criteria weights. For the defined value functions, the coefficient of variation for the selected weights ranges in [0.43, 0.73] with an average of 0.53.
- As noted in section 4.3.3, the average demanding indices are able to indicate the shape of a value function. For the defined value functions, these indices have the maximum possible range (i.e. [−1, 1]), with an average of −0.01.

Finally, for reasons of simplicity and without loss of generality, an equal number of satisfaction levels have been assumed for the selected overall and marginal value functions, i.e. $\alpha = \alpha_i \ \forall \ i$.

6.4.2 Simulation Results

The generated customer satisfaction data sets are used in order to compare the evaluation results provided by the MUSA method, as well as other alternative models. The presented results do not focus on the analysis of customer satisfaction, but rather on how these models behave for each one of the experimental data sets.

Table 6.3 presents a summary of the simulation results for the MUSA method. The fitting level of the MUSA method is rather high, since AFI_1 ranges between 87.9% and 99.1%, with an average of 94.5% for the generated data sets. This justifies the ability of the MUSA method to effectively evaluate a value system for the set of customers. However, *ASI* appears to have smaller values. Although this index has an average of 75.1%, there are particular data sets where the MUSA method is not able to achieve a high level of stability. Since *ASI* is calculated from the results of the post-optimality analysis, these data sets refer to the cases where customers' judgments do not appear homogenous. This probably indicates a comparative relation among the criteria weights, given the variability observed in the post-optimality analysis table, and it is caused by the chosen high deviation level D_e. Finally, in order to examine if the MUSA method is able to accurately estimate the defined experimental parameters, the hit rate ability of the model is calculated. In this case, the hit rate is defined as the average absolute deviation between the initially assumed and the finally estimated criteria weights. As shown in Table 6.3, the estimation accuracy of the MUSA is relatively high, since the hit rate ranges between 82% and 99.2%, with an average of 93.9%. However, it should be noted that the increase of the number of parameters for the value functions, increases the degrees of freedom of the MUSA method, and thus the hit rate is decreased.

Table 6.3 Simulation results for the MUSA method

Index	Statistics	Value
AFI_1	Range	0.879-0.991
	Average	0.945
ASI	Range	0.120-0.986
	Average	0.751
Hit rate	Range	0.820-0.992
	Average	0.939

Another important objective of the experimental analysis is to examine the influence of the parameters of the MUSA method to the fitting and the stability level of the estimated results. For this reason, a series of one-way ANOVA analyses have been performed in order to analyze the influence of each parameter of the experiment to the calculated *AFI* and *ASI* indices. Tables 6.4 and 6.5 present the summary results for this analysis of variance, from where the following points raise:

- The chosen deviation level of the experiment does not affect *ASI*, but influences *AFI*. This is more or less expected, since D_e determines the consistency of the satisfaction judgments and therefore it is strongly related with the fitting ability of the MUSA method.
- The size of the data set (number of customers) does not seem to affect the fitting and stability level of the MUSA method.
- Similarly, both *AFI* and *ASI* are not influenced by the chosen number of criteria and the number of satisfaction levels. However, these parameters may have a greater impact on the stability level (*p*-value less than 10%).

- The distribution of criteria weights, as measured by the average coefficient of variation, seems to affect *ASI* because large differences in the selected criteria weights generate data sets with heterogeneous customer preferences, which lead to an increased variability in the post-optimality analysis.

Table 6.4 Summary results for one-way ANOVA (*AFI*)

Factors	SS	df	MS	F	p-value
Deviation level	0.013	1	0.013	32.477	0.000
Number of customers	0.000	1	0.000	0.000	0.985
Number of criteria	0.000	1	0.000	0.011	0.917
Number of satisfaction levels	0.000	1	0.000	0.011	0.917
Distribution of weights	0.001	3	0.000	0.206	0.890

Table 6.5 Summary results for one-way ANOVA (*ASI*)

Factors	SS	df	MS	F	p-value
Deviation level	0.036	1	0.036	0.501	0.491
Number of customers	0.000	1	0.000	0.000	0.993
Number of criteria	0.202	1	0.202	3.385	0.087
Number of satisfaction levels	0.202	1	0.202	3.385	0.087
Distribution of weights	0.618	3	0.206	5.920	0.010

Similarly to the previous analysis, the generated customer satisfaction data sets have been used in the conditional probability models. As presented in section 2.3.1, the estimated parameters of these models include the threshold values of the dummy dependent variable y^* (overall satisfaction) and the coefficients of the independent variables x_i (marginal satisfaction) in the regression formula (this formula relates y^* and x_i in a weighted sum expression). Since the conditional probability models have a different philosophy (assumptions, interpretation of parameters, etc.) compared to the MUSA method, a straightforward comparison of the results provided by this approaches is not possible. However, the thresholds of the dummy dependent variables may indicate the shape of the overall value function, while the regression coefficients represent a measure of the relative importance for the satisfaction criteria.

The simulation results for the ordered Probit and Logit analysis are presented in Tables 6.6 and 6.7, where a summary of t-test statistics is given for each one of the aforementioned parameters (the p-value represents the probability of error under the hypothesis of accepting the values of the estimated parameters). Overall, it appears that the fitting ability of these models is satisfactory, since in most of the generated data sets the p-value is small ($p < 0.0001$). However, in many cases (almost 40% of the generated data sets) the Probit and Logit models are not able to achieve a high fitting level. These cases do not only concern data sets where the

MUSA method is not able to provide reliable results, but they also refer to data sets where *AFI* and *ASI* indicators of the MUSA method have relatively high values. Finally, it should be noted that the estimated results of the Probit analysis do not differ significantly from those provided by the Logit analysis.

Table 6.6 Simulation results for the Probit model

Parameters	Index	Statistics	Value
Thresholds	*t*-test	Range	0.000-26.040
		Average	14.581
	p-value	Range	0.000-1.000
		Average	0.125
Regression coefficients	*t*-test	Range	−5.878-19.410
		Average	5.793
	p-value	Range	0.000-1.000
		Average	0.292

Table 6.7 Simulation results for the Logit model

Parameters	Index	Statistics	Value
Thresholds	*t*-test	Range	0.000-22.709
		Average	13.351
	p-value	Range	0.000-1.000
		Average	0.125
Regression coefficients	*t*-test	Range	−5.417-18.246
		Average	5.584
	p-value	Range	0.000-1.000
		Average	0.272

Apart from the fitting and stability analyses, the prediction table of global satisfaction (see Figure 6.5) may also be used in order to compare the estimated results of the MUSA method and the conditional probability models. To this end, formula (6.12) is used to calculate the *OPL* for each one of the generated data sets. A summary of the analysis, regarding the prediction ability of these alternative models, is given in Table 6.8, where it should be noted that for all the examined data sets, the *OPL* of the MUSA method is higher compared to the other models.

Table 6.8 Overall prediction level for alternative models

Model	Range	Average
MUSA	0.701-1.000	0.885
Probit analysis	0.622-1.000	0.784
Logit analysis	0.622-1.000	0.764

Furthermore, in case of highly consistent and homogenous data sets, a high prediction index appears for all alternative approaches. In general, the most important differences between the prediction levels achieved by the MUSA method and the Logit-Probit analysis concerns data sets with greater number of estimated parameters (e.g. number of criteria, number of satisfaction levels, etc.). Moreover, it seems that the size of the data sets does not affect the *OPL*, while the prediction index between the Probit and the Logit analysis is similar for all the data sets of the experiment.

The main result of the presented experimental comparison analysis is the high prediction ability of all alternative models, although *OPL* is slightly higher for the MUSA method. However, the fitting and stability level of the MUSA method is significantly higher compared to the conditional probability models for all data sets of the experiment. Moreover, in case of inconsistent and non-homogenous data, poor stability results may appear for all alternative approaches.

The presented experiment may be considered as a pilot analysis, since a larger number of data sets is required, in order to increase the reliability of the findings. Moreover, additional parameters and desired properties of the generated data sets may be examined (e.g. parameters of the MUSA method). The presented results examine the effect of several parameters to the fitting and the stability level of the MUSA method using one-way ANOVA analysis. For this reason, future research may focus on other alternative customer satisfaction evaluation models or examine how several combinations of these parameters may affect the reliability of the results. Finally, it should be noted that the development of an unbiased data generation process for satisfaction judgments is rather difficult, since it requires a strong assumption about the preference model of the customers. In the presented experiment, this assumption appears through the assumed value functions during the first step of the simulation process.

Chapter 7
Customer Satisfaction Surveys and Barometers

7.1 Research Methodologies

Customer satisfaction research methodologies may be divided, according to their content and objectives, into qualitative and quantitative research (Dutka, 1995).

The main aim of qualitative research is to obtain detailed information and additional explanations on customers' attitude and opinions. This justifies the exploratory nature of qualitative research. The main characteristics of qualitative research include the following (Taylor and Bogdan, 1975):

- Open-ended (probing) questions are used, and thus customer responses are not given in a predefined format.
- The number of respondents is small, but the research gives the ability to analyze in detail customer behavior.
- The results are based on responses given by customers, as well as on observation.
- Usually generalization of results is not possible.

The most typical examples of customer satisfaction qualitative research are discussed in Dutka (1995), Naumann and Giel (1995), Woodruff and Gardial (1996), and Kessler (1996) and concern mainly in-depth interviews, focus groups, observations, and advisory groups.

In-depth interviews are personal interviews with customers, which generally do not have a formal structure. Thus, questions are rather general and nondirective and customer responses are not given according to a predefined set of choices, but instead allow the respondent to state whatever thoughts occur (Dutka, 1995). However, although a structured questionnaire is not used, the interviewer should prepare a detailed discussion outline and control the interview by providing the necessary order and structure. Usually, the interview is rather lengthy (1-2 hours)

E. Grigoroudis and Y. Siskos, *Customer Satisfaction Evaluation*, International Series
in Operations Research & Management Science 139, DOI 10.1007/978-1-4419-1640-2_7,
© Springer Science + Business Media, LLC 2010

and it is recorder in order to avoid bias created by interviewer. Since the interview will attempt to draw out attitudes and beliefs which respondents find difficult to articulate, well practiced interview skills and a good understanding of appropriate interview techniques are necessary (Hill, 1996).

On the other hand, focus groups refer to discussions involving a group of customers (5-10 persons) who share common characteristics. The participants have a free discussion for about two hours expressing opinions, viewpoints, and perceptions about a predefined topic. Similarly to in-depth interviews, a discussion outline is necessary. The role of the moderator (facilitator) is important since he/she uses this outline to ensure that the relevant topics are covered in sufficient depth, to offer well-prepared questions for discussion, and to keep the session on track in terms of both content and time (Dutka, 1995). The purpose of focus groups is the same as in-depth interviews, i.e. to improve the understanding of all aspects of the customer-supplier relationship (Hill, 1996). The main difference refers to potential interactions among the participants, which often stimulate thinking in a manner not possible with other interviewing techniques.

The information collected by focus groups heavily depends on the synthesis of the group. For this reason, it is usually preferable to recruit a number of participants having different characteristics (Gerson, 1993). An analytical presentation of planning and conducting focus groups may be found in Taylor and Bogdan (1975), Krueger (1980), Greenbaum (1988), and Morgan (1988), whereas special cases of semi-structured interviews are presented in Reynolds and Gutman (1988).

In several cases, customers have difficulties in articulating their relationship to products or services, since they are not always consciously aware of their needs and expectations. In addition, interviewers may be inhibiting, time consuming and biased by the perspective of the interviewer, while responses may also be insincere (social desirability bias). Thus, in order to overcome these problems, direct observation is preferred (Woodruff and Gardial, 1996). In this context, the collected qualitative information is based on the observation of customers during the purchase or use of a product or service (sometimes it may cover customers' post-usage evaluations). There are several and quite different observation techniques. Some of them have the form of official observations by employees trained for this particular task, or they may be done by employees that have a direct contact with costumers (e.g. salesmen, technicians, etc.). In other cases, observations use video recording to reveal areas of customer dissatisfaction. A large number of publications refer either to more general issues about observation techniques (Taylor and Bogdan, 1975; Webb et al., 1981; Denzin, 1989; Griffin and Houser, 1993) or to their usage in customer satisfaction applications (Woodruff et al., 1993; Naumann and Giel, 1995; Kessler, 1996; Woodruff and Gardial, 1996; Massnick, 1997).

Finally, advisory groups are another type of qualitative research that is very similar with focus groups. Advisory groups are volunteer groups of customers that meet at regular intervals to provide in-depth suggestions and direction to a company (Kessler, 1996). Sometimes, other experts are also included (e.g. community or industry leaders, retired CEOs). The main difference compared to focus groups is that advisory groups are more homogenous and they are set up to provide input over time, since they are considered to last for a long period (usually 1-2 years).

Table 7.1 presents the main advantages and disadvantages of the most important types of qualitative research (in-depth interviews and focus groups), while a more detailed comparative analysis is given by Griffin and Houser (1993) and Woodruff and Gardial (1996).

Contrary to the previous options, the aim of quantitative research is to develop statistically reliable information from sample data that can be generalized to a larger population (Dutka, 1995). Quantitative research uses a relatively short structured questionnaire, while the survey sample should be large enough in order to provide a statistically reliable set of responses. The collected information is also analyzed using specific statistical techniques and quantitative tools. In the case of customer satisfaction measurement, this type of research is focused on the quantification of satisfaction information and its tracking and comparison over time. The most frequently used types of quantitative research are mail surveys, personal interviews, and telephone surveys (Gerson, 1993; Massnick, 1997).

Table 7.1 Comparing main qualitative research options (adopted from Dutka, 1995)

Type of research	Advantages	Disadvantages
In-depth interviews	Complex questions can be explored.	Cost is greater than with other methodologies.
	More in-depth responses are obtained.	
	Responses that might be viewed negatively by a group are easier to obtain.	Time for completion is longer.
		Number of completed interviews is smaller.
	Use of visual aids is very effective.	
	Medium skill level is required for interviewers.	Aggregating information from individual interviews is rather difficult.
	Customer's reactions may be observed.	Difficult to determine changes in customer attitudes over time.
	Customers are more likely to participate (than with focus groups).	
Focus groups	Complex questions can be explored.	Responses may be affected by other customers.
	Group interactions generate information that is not otherwise obtainable.	
	More in-depth responses are obtained.	It is difficult to analyze in details the group attitudes and expectations.
	It is an excellent method for generating ideas.	Results cannot be generalized to a larger population.
	Use of visual aids is very effective.	Information is almost qualitative than quantitative.
	Heterogeneity may cause creative argument.	A skilled facilitator is required.
	Participation can be attractive to customers.	The interpretation and analysis of responses are rather difficult.
	Customer's reactions may be observed.	Group synthesis may discourage participation.

Mail surveys constitute a typical type of quantitative research that is widely used by business organizations, given the relatively lower cost. Mail surveys can easily cover different geographical areas and large customer samples. Moreover, technology may provide effective solutions regarding the management of collected information (e.g. data entry, customer database development). Mail surveys appear as a good solution in cases where directly contacting customer (e.g. by telephone or personal meeting) is difficult or impossible.

On the other hand, personal interviews have a form of direct communication with customers, and thus they help in establishing a customer relationship philosophy. This is the main reason why they are preferred in many cases by business organizations, although they present several disadvantages (high cost, experienced interviewers, etc.). Personal interviews also allow for observing and analyzing customers' reactions, while at the same time interviewers may give explanations and use visual prompts.

Finally, telephone surveys seem to combine the most important characteristics of the previous quantitative research options. In particular, a telephone survey is a form of personal contact with customers, while at the same time, it can easily cover distanced geographical areas and large customer samples. The most important advantages of telephone surveys are their ability to reduce non-response bias and, using modern technologies, to provide immediate availability of data.

The most important advantages and disadvantages of the aforementioned types of quantitative satisfaction research are presented in Table 7.2, while several publications present analytically the various alternatives of organizing and conducting these surveys (Dillman, 1978; Frey, 1983; Erdos, 1983; Gerson, 1993).

It should be emphasized that choosing qualitative or quantitative research is not an either-or situation, and as noted by Dutka (1995), these methodologies should be combined in order to maximize their individual strengths (see section 7.2).

An alternative classification of survey researches, based on the different types of interviewing processes, is given by Varva (1997, 2002):

1. Self-administrated, such as mail or fax questionnaire.
2. Interviewer administrated, like personal interview, telephone interview, and chat room interview.
3. Machine administrated, such as Internet questionnaire, email interview diskette-in-the-mail questionnaire, kiosk administrated, and interactive TV interview.

Finally, other types of research methods may be used to collect customer satisfaction information, including the following (Kessler, 1996):

- *Lost customer surveys*: They are mainly interviews with customers who have stopped buying the examined product or service (or significantly reduced their usage).
- *"Mystery" shopper*: They pose as customers of the examined organization and test the offered service quality.

- *New customer feedback*: It refers to a specially designed survey initiated after the customer has sampled the product or service.

Table 7.2 Comparing main quantitative research options (adopted from Dutka, 1995)

Type of research	Advantages	Disadvantages
Mail surveys	Cost is sometimes lower per completed interview (depending on response rate).	Response rate is generally much slower and lower than with other methodologies.
	Respondents are under no pressure to provide quick answers.	Bias due to non-response is greater (than with telephone surveys).
	Different geographical areas may be easily covered.	Quality control is difficult or impossible (questions can be skipped, open-ended responses are not probed, etc.).
	There is no interviewer bias.	
	Questionnaire completion is unintrusive and anonymous.	Information from open-ended questions can be negligible and incomplete, since probing by interviewer is not possible.
	Customers may decide how and when they will respond.	The questionnaire has to be short and questions should be simple.
Personal interviews	Interviewing can be monitored and supervised, thus quality control is easier.	The cost is relatively high, especially in business markets.
	The questionnaire may be less simple.	Time for completion is longer.
	Customer's reactions may be observed and analyzed.	Interviews need good planning and control if an accurate sample is to be achieved.
	It is a two-way communication that allows explanations and prompts.	It is difficult to cover different geographical areas.
	Visual prompts are possible.	Interviewer bias may be greater.
	It is an opportunity to directly and personally communicate with customers.	Questionnaire completion may be intrusive.
		Interview should not be interrupted.
		Interviewers should be well trained.
Telephone surveys	Interviewing can be monitored and supervised, thus quality control is easier.	Cost may be higher than with mail surveys (depending on response rate).
	Response rate is much greater than with mail surveys, thus reducing bias associated with non-response.	Some respondents may be difficult to reach by telephone.
	Time to complete the project is shorter.	Telephone interviewers often generate quick responses, allowing inadequate time for in-depth thinking.
	Different geographical areas may be easily covered.	
	Cost is lower than with personal interviews and may not be greater than with mail surveys.	Interviewer bias may be greater.
		Questionnaire completion may be intrusive.
	The questionnaire may be less simple.	Interview should not be interrupted.
	It is a two-way communication that allows explanations and prompts.	Visual aids are impractical though not possible.
	Results may be available shortly.	Interviewers should maintain respondents' interest and concentration.

- *Perceptual research*: It measures how a total customer pool perceives the examined organization compared to the competition.
- *Real time fixes*: It is not a separate tool, but happens when an interviewer/employee is talking to a customer (e.g. customer calls to complaint or the employee observes that a customer is dissatisfied and offers to help).
- *Transaction reports*: They are feedback pieces of transactions that may also help to fix potential problems.
- *Usability tests*: They reveal how people use the products, and may help segmenting customer base.
- *Win/Loss reports*: They usually investigate the reasons why a company won or lost a competitive bid.

Although customer satisfaction surveys appear similar to other types of marketing research and public opinion measurement, it should be emphasized that they are very special survey situations. As Vavra (1997) underlines, customer satisfaction measurement should be a census (all customers should be given the opportunity to participate) and it should be implemented in a continuous basis, while a marketing research is based on a statistically representative sample which is conducted when collecting particular information is required. In addition, customer satisfaction measurement is not only focused on collecting customer-related information, but it also aims at communicating with customers.

7.2 Survey Planning and Preliminary Analysis

The first and one of the most important stages of a customer satisfaction measurement program concerns the survey planning. It is mainly a preliminary stage that aims at avoiding potential errors and ensuring appropriate results by designing an effective research process.

The general process of a customer satisfaction survey planning is presented analytically in Figure 7.1 and consists of the following main steps:

1. *Determine survey objectives*: It is the most important step in this general process, since it may affect all the other steps when designing and conducting a customer satisfaction survey.
2. *Determine satisfaction dimensions*: In this step, the set of customer satisfaction dimensions, as well the related hierarchy should be determined (see section 7.3.2).
3. *Determine measurement process*: Based on the survey objectives and the applied customer satisfaction measurement program, the detailed measurement process should be determined in this step. In addition it should be integrated with other corporate processes and information from the organization (e.g. customer call centers, complaint management systems, total quality programs).
4. *Determine sample size and survey procedure*: This particular step concerns the determination of the sampling process (type of sampling process, sample size,

etc.). Moreover, the type of survey and the communication procedure with customers should also be determined.

5. *Develop questionnaire*: Based on the decisions made during the previous steps,
   the questionnaire is developed. The importance of this step is justified by the
   fact that the questionnaire is the main survey instrument (see section 7.3.1).
6. *Test questionnaire and refine*: This final step refers mainly to the pilot survey,
   which aims at testing the effectiveness of the research methodology (see section 7.4.1).

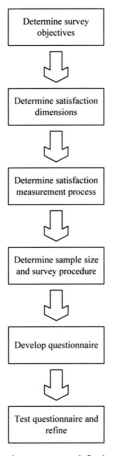

Fig. 7.1 Main steps in customer satisfaction survey planning

During the implementation of a customer satisfaction measurement program,
the complementary use of qualitative and quantitative research should be emphasized. As shown in Figure 7.2 the entire process is inherently interactive and illustrates that in fact, there is no problem of choosing between these two types of research. The process usually starts with a qualitative research (depth interviews,

focus groups, etc.) in order to develop an exhaustive list of satisfaction attributes. Then, this list is reduced and the main satisfaction dimensions are determined (see section 7.3.2). Based on this information, the quantitative research is conducted and the results obtained from the customer satisfaction survey are validated. Finally, the new customer satisfaction program should be redesigned, taken into account potential revisions and improvements (e.g. revised satisfaction dimensions).

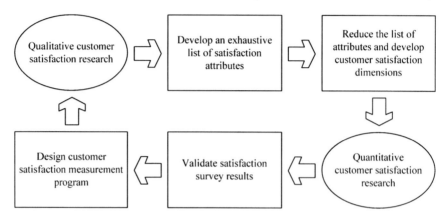

Fig. 7.2 Combining qualitative and quantitative research

In general, a qualitative satisfaction survey is combined with additional secondary data, which are available by the business organization or by other external sources. This research is the main part of the preliminary analysis, which is an exploratory stage in any research project. The main aim of the preliminary analysis is to ensure that the researcher understands enough about the composition and attitudes of the target population to draw an accurate sample and to design an appropriate questionnaire (Hill, 1996).

Finally, determining when customer satisfaction surveys should be conducted is another important issue that often is not given enough attention. In most of the cases, satisfaction surveys are conducted at regular time intervals, usually on an annual basis. Although this selection of certain times of the year looks arbitrary, Vavra (1997) notes that there are two general explanations: convention and events. In the first case, customer satisfaction is surveyed on a yearly basis when the organization's resources are available and it is usually combined with the preparation of the organization's planning (e.g. financial, strategic). In the second case, some major events (e.g. yearly industry conference, end of tourist season) may trigger administration of a satisfaction survey. However, there is no enough justification why a period of 365 days, or any other time interval, gives the optimum frequency for conducting customer satisfaction surveys. In fact, this decision should take into account the market trends and the implicit customers' attitude change (Hill, 1996). Thus, in case of a new company or product/service, intense competition or short market cycle, the satisfaction survey should be conducted more frequently, while in the opposite situation (stable market conditions, long market cycle, etc.) the frequency may be smaller.

However, many researchers urge that customer satisfaction should be measured continuously, in order to reinforce organization's commitment to quality. A continuously ongoing customer satisfaction program may help to establish a permanent customer satisfaction, and thus support business organizations to adopt a continuous improvement philosophy. Besides, in many cases when there is a direct contact with costumers, the satisfaction information is constantly available.

7.3 Questionnaire Design

7.3.1 Main principles

Questionnaire's content and structure are critical factors for the success of any marketing survey. In fact, it has been said that a survey is only as good as the questions it asks (Dutka, 1995).

Although many believe that the questionnaire development is a relatively simple, straightforward task, this is not true, since preparing an effective questionnaire requires both experience and patience. There are several decisions that have to be taken in the questionnaire design process, like the contents of the questionnaire (what it will be asked), the type of questions, including wording and measurement scales (how it will be asked), as well as the structure of the questionnaire (order of questions).

In any case, it should be emphasized that a questionnaire is a communication tool between an organization and its customers (Naumann and Giel, 1995). However, it is not a one-way communication device, whereby information is collected from customers, but rather an interactive communication tool. Figure 7.3 presents the different steps in this two-way communication process, where, as in any communication form, there is the risk of erroneous coding or decoding of the transmitted information.

Although there is no analytical methodological framework for questionnaire design in survey research, the major principles that should be considered are (Fowler, 1993):

- The questionnaire should be kept simple and comprehensive.
- The questions should be specific and single-minded.
- The structure of the questionnaire should help respondents to give their answers.

In this context, Vavra (1997) notes that the rule of thumb for successful question writing is to *"keep it short, keep it simple, and single-minded"*, namely KIS[3]. Following these critical rules, a questionnaire helps in maximizing the participation of respondents and ensuring the reliability and validity of the collected information.

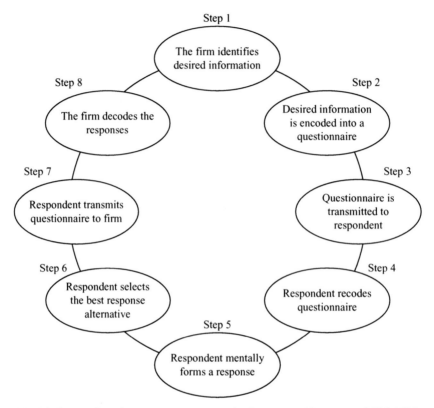

Fig. 7.3 The questionnaire as a two-way communication process (Naumann and Giel, 1995)

Usually, a questionnaire designed for customer satisfaction surveys consists of the following main sections (Dutka, 1995; Naumann and Giel, 1995; Vavra, 1997):

1. *Introduction*: This section welcomes customers explaining several issues of the satisfaction survey, such as the reasons why the survey is conducted, how the particular customer has been selected, and also the reasons for which the customer should participate in the survey.
2. *Demographics*: The questions contained in this section are related to the basic demographic characteristics of the customers, like gender, age, marital status, etc. Furthermore, other customer characteristics that may segment the customer sample may be also included in this section (e.g. purchase preferences, frequency of use, etc.). This information gives the ability to examine if the sample is representative, and to perform additional segmentation analyses based on variables that are believed to discriminate customer population.

3. *Satisfaction questions*: This is the core part of the questionnaire, since it refers to questions about the overall and partial satisfaction based on the assessed dimensions and measurement scales (see sections 7.3.2 and 7.3.3). Usually, these questions have the form of performance judgments taking into account the different attributes of the examined product or service.

4. *Behavioral questions*: This section concerns the general customer behavior or attitude. The questions included usually refer to the satisfaction consequences or outcomes, like repurchase intentions, probability of recommending the product/service to other consumers, etc.

An important issue of the questionnaire is the order of questions. As a general rule, simple questions that are easily answered should appear first (Converse and Presser, 1986). Furthermore, the overall satisfaction question may be placed before or after the partial satisfaction questions (i.e. satisfaction/performance judgments for particular attributes of the examined product/service). The researchers that favor the first option note that systematic errors are avoided by applying this approach. This is because customers, by answering the overall satisfaction question firstly, have the ability to interpret the meaning of this question and "naturally" give their judgment. Several researchers pinpoint that negative customer responses will be increased if the overall satisfaction question is firstly asked (Wittink and Bayer, 1994). On the other hand, if the overall satisfaction question is asked after the evaluation of partial satisfaction dimensions, the consistency of collected information will be increased. This is because customers have the ability to give their overall judgment taking into account their previous answers. This particular approach is preferred when an additive assessment model is used (e.g. MUSA method). Moreover, with this approach it is possible to identify potential consistency problems that may arise due to incomplete sets of satisfaction dimensions.

In any case, it should be noted that the overall satisfaction question is considered necessary, and thus it should always be included in a satisfaction questionnaire (Oliver, 1997), given its aforementioned ability to examine the consistency of customer judgments. Moreover, an overall customer satisfaction question offers an additional variable for any kind of data analysis.

As a matter of fact, in several cases it is preferable to measure overall satisfaction with more than one question/variable (Hausknecht, 1990). Detailed examples of alternative forms and presentation formats of overall customer satisfaction question are presented by Hauser (1991), Wittink and Bayer (1994), Gale (1994), and Ryan et al. (1995).

Another important issue in questionnaire design concerns the wording of questions, which always requires experience, skill, and attention to detail (Dutka, 1995). Payne's (1951) book *"The art of asking questions"* is considered classic in questionnaire wording, while several other publications study how collected information is affected by alternative wording of questions (Converse and Presser, 1986; Fowler, 1993, 1995; Schuman and Presser, 1996).

Finally, it is important in several cases to provide customer with additional information and guidelines in order to help the questionnaire completion process. According to Alreck and Settle (1995) these guidelines may include the explanation of the satisfaction dimensions that will be evaluated, the criterion on which this evaluation will be based on, the way in which the provided measurement scale will be used, and the way in which the response should be given.

Several other particular issues for the questionnaire design in customer satisfaction surveys (e.g. satisfaction dimensions, measurement scales, common errors) are discussed in sections 7.3.2, 7.3.3, and 7.4.2.

7.3.2 Satisfaction Dimensions

Determining the detailed factors that affect customer satisfaction is an important stage in any satisfaction survey. These factors may appear having different forms, depending on the perspective from which someone studies the satisfaction measurement problem. Thus, the term "satisfaction dimensions" is frequently related with other concepts, like product/service attributes, measures of effectiveness, measures of performance, criteria, customer requirements, etc. Although related, these terms present significant differences: e.g. dimensions may refer to aggregated factors, attributes mainly concern product/service characteristics, and customer requirements are associated with desired end-states. However, as already mentioned, all these terms may be considered as an attempt to identify factors that may specify customer satisfaction from different viewpoints.

The applied measurement technique may also affect the way these factors should be studied. For example, in the context of the MUSA method, these satisfaction dimensions should comprise a consistent family of criteria having the properties of monotonicity, exhaustiveness, and non-redundancy (see also section 4.1.1). In addition, the MUSA method requires that the assessment of satisfaction dimensions should follow the principles of criteria modeling in the context of multicriteria decision analysis and preference aggregation/disaggregation, as shown in Figure 7.4 (see also Roy, 1985; Roy and Bouyssou, 1993).

Similarly, in the context of Multiattribute Utility Theory, a hierarchical structure is used in order to model objectives, attributes (achievement of objectives), and values (Keeney, 1992). Thus, in addition to the previous properties, Keeney and Raiffa (1976) and Kirkwood (1997) suggest that the set of criteria, as well as their hierarchical structure, should be operational, decomposable, and minimal. In particular, fundamental objectives may help in creating and evaluating alternatives, identifying decision opportunities, and guiding the entire decision-making process, while their hierarchy should have the following properties (Keeney, 1992):

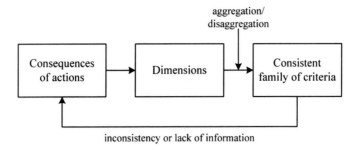

Fig. 7.4 Modeling process of decision criteria

1. *Essential*, to indicate consequences in terms of the fundamental reasons for interest in the decision situation.
2. *Controllable*, to address consequences that are influenced only by the choice of alternatives in the decision context.
3. *Complete*, to include all fundamental aspects of the consequences of the decision alternatives.
4. *Measurable*, to define objectives precisely and to specify the degrees to which objectives may be achieved.
5. *Operational*, to render the collection of information required for an analysis reasonable considering the time and effort available.
6. *Decomposable*, to allow the separate treatment of different objectives in the analysis.
7. *Non-redundant*, to avoid double-counting of possible consequences.
8. *Concise*, to reduce the number of objectives needed for the analysis of a decision.

The previous framework of multiple criteria decision modeling may be used in the assessment process of customer satisfaction criteria. Although, this is not a decision situation with multiple actions (or alternatives), customers may be considered as decision-makers who evaluate a product or service according to their preference or value system.

Organization's internal knowledge and data (e.g. salespersons reports, company records for customer complaints or critical incidents) are the initial source of information that may be used in determining customer satisfaction criteria. Additionally, this information may encourage employees' involvement in the customer satisfaction measurement program. However, the process should be extended beyond the company and into the arena of customer, particularly when requirements and expectations are to be defined (Dutka, 1995). As emphasized by several researchers, satisfaction measurement should be always studied from the customer's perceptive, thus a direct communication with customers is always necessary (having any of the forms discusses in section 7.1).

In several cases it is useful to assess the satisfaction criteria using a value or treelike structure, as mentioned in section 5.2. There are two main approaches to developing this value hierarchy (Kirkwood, 1997), which are based on whether or not sources of customer satisfaction or dissatisfaction are available:

1. *Bottom-up approach*: It is appropriate when sources of customer satisfaction or dissatisfaction are known. The previous detailed attributes are aggregated into more general satisfaction dimensions in order to develop the value hierarchy. According to this approach, customers with different levels of satisfaction/dissatisfaction are examined to determine the ways in which they differ.
2. *Top-down approach*: It is preferred in situations where the aforementioned information is not available. The approach decomposes customer overall satisfaction into a set of detailed characteristics (related to the product/service or the organization) that affect it. The process is repeated by subdividing these characteristics into more detailed components, until the consequences of this decision problem are fully described and the aforementioned properties are satisfied (Kirkwood, 1997).

Detailed examples of developing value hierarchies in the criteria assessment process may be found in Keeney and Raiffa (1976), Keeney (1981, 1988, 1992), Buede (1986), Bouyssou (1989), Corner and Kirkwood (1991), Gustafson et al. (1992), Dutka (1995), and Kirkwood (1997).

Other approaches used to identify satisfaction dimensions, mainly originated from the marketing field, are based on the means-end theory, which also assumes a hierarchical representation of how customers view products or services. In particular, it suggests that the product-customer relationship may be represented by three levels, as shown in Figure 7.5: attributes (what the product/service is, its features, its component parts or activities), consequences (what the product does for the user, the outcomes, desired or undesired), and the desired end-states (the user's core values, purposes and goals). Woodruff and Gardial (1996) emphasize that several characteristics of this hierarchy should be considered in practical applications. For example, the levels of this hierarchy are interconnected in the sense that lower levels are the means by which the higher level ends are achieved. Moreover, the level of abstraction and the stability over time increase at higher levels in the hierarchy.

In this context, Woodruff and Gardial (1996) propose a methodology for identifying strategically important customer value dimensions as shown in Figure 7.6. Initially, a large and exhaustive list of value dimensions is developed (usually by conducting a series of personal interviews with customers), which is then reduced taking into account three main criteria: similarity, actionability, and importance to customers (see also Vinson et al., 1977; Gutman, 1982; Gutman and Alden, 1985; Perkins and Reynolds, 1988).

Laddering theory also offers a methodological framework for identifying the relations among customers' motives, requirements, and attributes. Reynolds and Gutman (1988) have developed a process for developing such a hierarchy, consisting of the following main steps (Vavra, 1997):

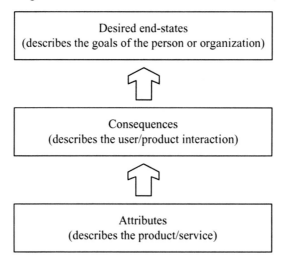

Fig. 7.5 A value hierarchy (Woodruff and Gardial, 1996)

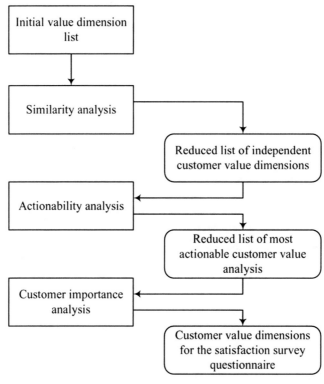

Fig. 7.6 Determining the importance of customer value dimensions (Woodruff and Gardial, 1996)

1. Utilize a technique that may discover the product attributes which will be used in the hierarchy, like preference ordering, occasion differences, or the repertory grid (Kelly, 1955; Reynolds and Gutman, 1988).
2. Select the most important attributes, and use them in a series of directed, importance probing questions (i.e. for each attribute, first ask customer why it is important to him/her, then ask why the reason from the first question is important, and finally ask in what way the answer to the second question is important to him/her).
3. Code the attributes, requirements, and motives generated from the previous steps, and tabulate their relationship.
4. Create finally a hierarchical value grip displaying the overall linkage of performance attributes, requirements, and motives.

Generally, using customer requirements in order to identify satisfaction attributes is a common approach, since customer needs play an important role in the definition of product/service quality (see section 3.1). In fact, Juran (1988) suggests that needs may be represented in a three-level hierarchical structure that takes into account the customer requirements, the consequences, and the end-benefits of these requirements.

Several researches have attempted to determine a universally accepted set of satisfaction criteria, or performance attributes that may serve as satisfaction items. For example, Garvin (1988) proposes eight distinct dimensions of product quality:

1. Performance (basic operating characteristics).
2. Features (secondary characteristics added to basic features).
3. Reliability (probability that product will operate over time).
4. Conformance (degree to which a product's design and operating characteristics meet established standards).
5. Durability (measure of product life).
6. Serviceability (speed, courtesy, competence, and ease of repair).
7. Aesthetics (subjective personal judgments regarding how a product looks, feels, sounds, tastes, or smells).
8. Perceived quality (general image of the company, reputation, and other subjective perceptions based on advertising, brand name, etc.).

Dutka (1995) offers a similar list of dimensions that may be used in the assessment of satisfaction criteria. This list contains performance attributes related to the product, the service, or the purchase process (Table 7.3). The Servqual model may also provide a similar list for the case of service quality (see section 3.2.2). All these efforts focus on developing a common framework for customer satisfaction measurement, as analytically discussed in section 7.5.1.

According to Oliver (1997), none of the previous research attempts for developing a set of customer satisfaction criteria can be successfully generalized. Usually, these lists have to be modified in practical applications by adding, deleting or changing particular attributes in order to best fit the examined business organization. For example, additional service quality dimensions have been proposed in practical implementations of the Servqual method, although it is a generally accepted methodology having numerous applications (see for example Doll and Torkzadeh, 1988; Holmlund and Kock, 1995). Thus, these lists may only provide general guidelines in the assessment process of satisfaction criteria. On the contrary, in the case of employee satisfaction measurement, it is much easier to develop a generally accepted list of satisfaction criteria, based on the applied framework (Hackman and Oldham, 1975; Loher et al., 1985; Fried and Ferris, 1987; Champoux, 1991).

Based on the previous discussion, it is evident that the customer satisfaction criteria may be business-related or they may refer to the product/service performance. However, customer satisfaction dimensions should not be confused with the decision criteria that a consumer uses in the product/service purchasing process (Oliver, 1997). Although these different sets of attributes may appear quite similar, the customer has additional knowledge regarding the product/service usage in the case of customer satisfaction measurement.

Finally, other categories of customer satisfaction criteria may be found in the literature. For example, Dutka (1995) suggests two main categories for the attributes used in customer satisfaction surveys:

- Transaction attributes (how a single contact is perceived).
- Image attributes (overall perceptions with the customer-company experience).

This categorization should be taken into account, given that image-related attributes may affect customer judgments regarding transaction-based attributes. Furthermore, overall satisfaction is most likely based on satisfaction from a series of individual transactions.

Table 7.3 Universal performance attributes (Dutka, 1995)

Category	Attributes
Attributes related to the product	Value price relationship Product quality Product benefits Product features Product design Product reliability and consistency Range of product or services
Attributes related to service	Guarantee or warranty Delivery Complaint handling Resolution of problems
Attributes related to purchase	Courtesy Communication Ease of convenience of acquisition Company reputation Company competence

In a similar context, Vavra (1997) mentions that customer satisfaction surveys usually tap three relatively distinct areas of customer-company interaction, which include: transaction performance (measure of performance associated with a particular customer-company interaction or its intermediates), functional performance (measure of performance in satisfying customer needs), and reliability performance (measure of performance over time).

7.3.3 Satisfaction Scales

As already mentioned in section 2.1, there are four major types of measurement scale: nominal, ordinal, interval, and ratio. The quantitative technique that will be used to analyze data depends mainly on the selected type of measurement scale.

There are several different scales that have been proposed in the context of customer satisfaction surveys, depending on the measurement item or the presentation form.

According to Woodruff and Gardial (1996) the measurement scales used in customer satisfaction surveys include the following main categories (Figure 7.7):

1. *Performance perceptions*: This category refers to the performance measurement of a product's/service's attributes (Figure 7.7a). Usually, customers are asked to rate these attributes on a poor-to-excellent scale. This is the typical approach when the aim is to evaluate satisfaction drivers (i.e. particular attributes that determine overall satisfaction feelings).

2. *Disconfirmation perceptions*: In these scales the main aim is to evaluate whether a customer perceives that the performance of a product or service on particular satisfaction dimensions exceeds (positive disconfirmation), equals (confirmation), or falls below (negative disconfirmation) a complexity standard (see also section 2.4.2). Since this is a comparison scale, it ranges from "much worse" to "much better" according to the selected comparison standard (Figure 7.7b). The problem of choosing between performance and disconfirmation scales is studied by Gardial et al. (1994).

3. *Satisfaction feelings*: This category refers to the measurement of customer's overall satisfaction and dissatisfaction feelings. There are two major approaches when using this scale: the cognitive (evaluative) and the emotional approach. The former uses the words "satisfaction" and "dissatisfaction" as anchor phrases at each end of the defined scale (Figure 7.7c), while the latter focuses on the emotional perspective of customer's evaluation, which may range from mild to strong (Figure 7.7d). The importance of measuring emotional feelings and emotional commitment has been stressed by several researchers (Edwards et al., 1994). Morevoer, alternative measurement scales may be used in order to evaluate customers' satisfaction feelings or emotions (Hausknecht, 1988, 1990).

4. *Satisfaction outcome*: There are several satisfaction outcomes which are frequently measured in customer surveys. These outcomes include repurchase in-

tentions, word of mouth, customer commitment or loyalty, and repeat buying. Usually, customers are asked to answer what are the chances that he/she will buy the product/service again, recommend it to family/friends, etc. using a scale ranging from "no chance" to "certain I will" (Figure 7.7e).

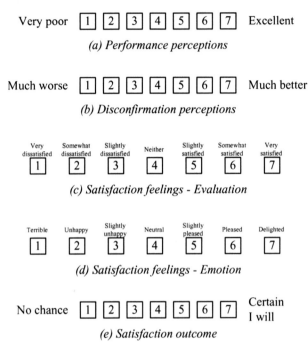

(a) Performance perceptions

(b) Disconfirmation perceptions

(c) Satisfaction feelings - Evaluation

(d) Satisfaction feelings - Emotion

(e) Satisfaction outcome

Fig. 7.7 Satisfaction scale types according to Woodruff and Gardial (1996)

Another classification of measurement scales for customer satisfaction surveys is given by Vavra (1997) and includes the following categories:

1. *Verbal scales*: This category mainly concerns ordinal scales and it is preferred in many cases since several researchers believe that this is the most colloquial way of assessing the respondent's state of mind. Such scales provide a continuum of verbal responses in a graduated order (Figure 7.8a). As already emphasized, the major disadvantage of this approach is the quantification of the scale, i.e. the estimation of the difference between the various scale levels. The choice of an appropriate vocabulary is also a difficult task in many situations. Special cases in this particular category are the scales having a checklist format where customers are asked to give a binary response (i.e. Yes/No) for the adequacy of a given service or the incidence of a given problem.
2. *Numeric scales*: This category usually refers to interval scales and attempts to overcome the problem of arbitrary quantification mentioned in the previous category. These scales are also more likely to escape the problem of multidi-

mensionality, although several researchers prefer to combine verbal and numerical scales in order to further assure that the employed scale is unidimensional. Usually, the number of satisfaction levels is assessed in such a way so as to be easily understood by customers (e.g. 0-10, 1-10, or 1-100), as shown in Figure 7.8b. One of most common problems in these scales refers to possible mixed meaning of the end-points.

3. *School grading scales*: These scales are used for performance measurement adopting a "school grading system", where grade A represents "excellent" and grade F represents "failing" (Figure 7.8c). The main advantage of this approach is that respondents are familiar and may easily understand the meaning of not only the end-points, but also the points in between. However, a school grading scale has an ordinal form, and thus it has similar disadvantages.

4. *Pictorial scales*: These particular scales are able to introduce an air of informality and humanness to a questionnaire. They appear as a useful approach when conducting face-to-face or self-completion surveys. These scales use pictures or graphs, instead of words, in order to depict the degree of gradation on the satisfaction scale. Usually, these pictures take the form of "smiley" faces or thermometers (Figure 7.8d).

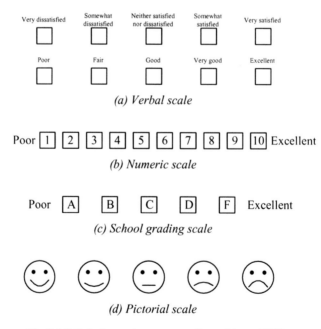

(a) Verbal scale

Poor $\boxed{1}$ $\boxed{2}$ $\boxed{3}$ $\boxed{4}$ $\boxed{5}$ $\boxed{6}$ $\boxed{7}$ $\boxed{8}$ $\boxed{9}$ $\boxed{10}$ Excellent

(b) Numeric scale

Poor $\boxed{A}$ $\boxed{B}$ $\boxed{C}$ $\boxed{D}$ $\boxed{F}$ Excellent

(c) School grading scale

(d) Pictorial scale

Fig. 7.8 Satisfaction scale types according to Vavra (1997)

Another commonly applied measurement scale in customer satisfaction surveys refers to the semantic differential response scale. In this scale, a number of intervals separate two "bipolar" adjectives, i.e. adjectives of opposite meaning (Vavra,

1997). The end-points of the scale usually describe a satisfaction feeling or a performance attribute of the examined product or service (Figure 7.9a). Semantic differential response scales may be considered as a variation of pictorial scales, particularly when geometric figures of diminishing size are used in order to indicate different shadings of opinion.

Finally, Likert scales are the most widely used scales in any survey research (Likert, 1932; Lissitz and Green, 1975; Hayes, 1992; Dutka, 1995; Hill, 1996). These scales are designed to measure degrees of agreement with a specific statement. Figure 7.9b presents a typical Likert scale, but it should be noted that alternative forms of this scale, regarding its size or wording, have been proposed. Usually in customer satisfaction surveys, these statements refer to the adequate performance of a particular product's or service's attribute. Similar to the previous case, Likert scaling is a bipolar scaling method.

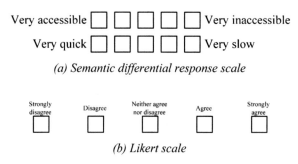

(a) Semantic differential response scale

(b) Likert scale

Fig. 7.9 Other satisfaction scale types (Hill, 1996)

It should be noted that the aforementioned types of measurement scales may be combined, when this is possible (e.g. verbal scales with smileys). Moreover, as noted in section 2.1, the type of measurement scale restricts the set of alternative quantitative techniques that will be used to analyze satisfaction data. In any case, the arbitrary quantification of a measurement scale should be avoided, since it may affect the validity of the collected information.

Other special cases of measurement scales used in customer satisfaction surveys are (Edwards and Keeney, 1946; Lodge, 1981; Hayes, 1992; Hill, 1996; Vavra, 1997):

- Magnitude estimation
- Thurstone's method of equal appearing intervals
- Guttman's scalogram
- SIMALTO (Simultaneous Multi Attribute Level Trade Off) scale

Vavra (1997) presents a comprehensive review of measurement scales in customer satisfaction research, while a large number of publications refers to the study of alternative methods for developing satisfaction scales (Fishbein, 1967; Dawes, 1972; Reckase, 1990), or the evaluation of product/service quality in relation to customer's satisfaction and expectations (Maslow, 1970; Graham and Balloun, 1973; Cohen, 1983; Sirgy, 1986).

Several researchers argue on the selection of the appropriate number of measurement levels in a customer satisfaction scale (Gerson, 1993; Dutka, 1995; Naumann and Giel, 1995; Vavra, 1997; Oliver, 1997). An odd number of levels implies the existence of a neutral level in the measurement scale and assumes that neutrality is an acceptable answer. Advocates of this approach emphasize that a neutral level simply gives, in many cases, an easy option to customers or it is used by them to express their indifference, instead of their neutrality. Regarding the size of the satisfaction scale, it should be noted that there is no universally accepted rule. However, the size of the scale should not be very small in order to ensure the reliability of the collected information, while at the same time it should not be too large so that customers may distinguish the meaning of the different levels of the scale. Oliver (1997) suggests that the number of satisfaction levels should not be smaller than three and larger than ten, while Hayes (1992) notes that satisfaction scales with more than five measurement levels do not offer any additional accuracy. Usually, customers tend to decrease the size of the scale when too many measurement levels are used.

In general, satisfaction scales should be tested during the pilot survey phase, giving emphasis on the wording and the direction of the measurement levels (Vavra, 1997). Moreover, satisfaction scales should be verified taking into account the consistency of survey results with additional corporate available information (Woodruff and Gardial, 1996).

Another important issue is raised when considering the "Do not know" option. Several researchers argue that this particular option should not be given to customers since it offers an easy way out, alleviating them from mentally working a question to reach a real point of view. Vavra (1997) notes that, in many cases, customers must have some impression, no matter how vague, of an organization's performance on all elements of its operation and products. Thus, he believes that in most satisfaction surveys it is fair to force customers to give their judgments. On the other hand, other researchers emphasize that this particular choice is an important piece of information that should not be distorted. Besides, in several situations, it is not practically possible for customers to provide an answer, due to lack of necessary knowledge. In any case, if some customers have not given their judgments in some particular questions, then this customer segment should be analyzed separately and these results should be compared to the other part of the customer sample.

Other issues that should be considered in developing customer satisfaction scales are the following:

- It is preferable to use uniform measurement scales in satisfaction questionnaires, in order to minimize the effort required by the customer to give his/her judgments (Gerson, 1993; Vavra, 1997).
- In several cases, the responses to a particular question are heavily skewed to the upper end-point ("excellent" or "extremely satisfied" level). Since it is im-

portant to have questions that produce a reasonable variation, this scale should be revised by skewed to the most frequently used end-point (Naumann and Giel, 1995; Oliver, 1997; Vavra, 1997). This problem occurs either because customers usually find it difficult to express negative judgments or because there is a highly competitive market environment (Hill, 1996).

- The set of satisfaction dimensions, even in the case of quantitative attributes (e.g. cost, waiting time) should rather be evaluated based on qualitative scales, in order to accurately record customers' perception (Oliver, 1997).

7.4 Critical Issues in Satisfaction Surveys

7.4.1 Pilot Survey

The pilot survey is the final step in the planning process of a customer satisfaction survey, aiming at testing the effectiveness of the research methodology. Usually this pretesting is focused on the questionnaire (or the interview process), which is the main survey instrument. In general, there are two different types of pilot testing (Naumann and Giel, 1995; Vavra, 1997):

- *Declared pretest*: In this case the participating customer is told that the survey is a pretest (either in the introduction or at the completion of the questionnaire). Usually this pretest has a form of personal interviews, where participants are asked to comment on particular aspects of the questionnaire (e.g. what is the meaning of a specific question, if any parts of questions are difficult to understand or confusing, and how they can be better asked).
- *Undeclared pretest*: In this case the respondent is not informed that he/she participates in a pilot survey. Thus, the whole interview process can be tested in "real-world" conditions. For example, the time required for customers to complete the questionnaire may be recorded in order to reveal potential improvements. Undeclared pretests give also the ability to directly observe customer reactions in different parts of the questionnaire.

Conclusively, the main objectives of pilot surveys are to test whether survey questions are fully understood by respondents and to examine the effectiveness of the questionnaire in terms of structure, presentation, etc. In case of a customer satisfaction pilot survey, additional scaling and measurement issues may be tested (i.e. appropriateness of satisfaction scale).

The sample size of a pilot survey is mainly a subjective decision of the survey administrator, since there are no rules or formulas that can tell how large the pretest should be (Naumann and Giel, 1995). Usually, this sample size depends on the complexity of the issues being studied and the size of the full survey. However, it should be noted that participants in the pilot study should be excluded from the final sample, while the sample of the pilot survey should contain all different customer groups that are to participate in the full satisfaction survey.

Several researchers suggest that the questionnaire may be initially tested by organization's internal customers (Naumann and Giel, 1995). This way, the employees have the ability to give specific comments and remarks and actively participate in the customer satisfaction program. Then, the pilot survey is conducted in a set of external customers, and this process is repeated as many times as necessary, in order to ensure the reliability and the validity of the collected information.

7.4.2 Potential Problems and Errors

In general, the potential problems and errors that appear in the conduction of satisfaction surveys do not significantly differ from those of any ordinary consumer-oriented market survey.

A critical requirement for customer satisfaction survey conduct is the fulfillment of the main survey objectives. For example, if the aim of the survey is the performance evaluation of particular attributes of the product or service and the estimation of certain quantitative indices, then a quantitative survey in a large sample of customers is considered necessary. On the other hand, if the aim of the survey is mainly to explore and study customer behavior, a qualitative survey should be preferred (e.g. personal interviews, focus groups).

The general issues that should be taken into account when conducting customer satisfaction surveys may be summarized in the following (Naumann and Giel, 1995):

1. *Volatility*: It is concerned with the stability of attitudes over time. There is some evidence that the more important a particular issue is to a customer, the less volatile the attitudes will be. Also, attitudes tend to be more volatile when a customer experiences conflict among different attributes.
2. *Bias*: It occurs when a customer's response is influenced by factors other than true attributes. These factors may cover a large number of different issues, like sampling, wording of questions, scaling, sequencing, etc.
3. *Validity*: There is a number of different validity concepts, such as content, construct, predictive, and convergent validity. In simple words, validity indicates whether a question (or a survey) measures what it is supposed to measure (construct validity).
4. *Meaningfulness*: The information collected from customers should be meaningful, which means that respondents' answers should not only be sincere, but the respondents should have the necessary knowledge to form accurate answers. Answers may lack meaningfulness for a variety of reason. For example, a common mistake is that because a specific topic is important to the researcher, it is assumed that it is also equally important to respondents, which is not always true.

5. *Awareness and salience*: They are two related issues that may also determine meaningfulness. Awareness refers to the respondent's knowledge and experience, while salience concerns the importance of a particular issue to the respondent. Generally, the more important the issue, the higher the level of awareness. Moreover, the higher the level of respondent awareness, the more meaningful the responses will be.

6. *Reliability*: It is the ability to get consistent answers, time after time, with repeated samples. The reliability of a questionnaire (or a survey) is largely a function or a result of the aforementioned issues.

In particular, reliability and validity are the most frequently discussed issues in any survey. The value of a measured variable contains a systematic and a random error component, beside the true value of the variable. So, validity is related to systematic errors, while reliability concerns random errors. Although several types of validity may be assessed, the most important of them are the following (Vavra, 1997):

1. *Content validity*: It occurs when the experiment provides adequate coverage of the subject being studied. This includes measuring the right things as well as having an adequate sample.

2. *Construct validity*: It is determined by the extent to which a question represents an underlying construct (e.g. customer loyalty) and the extent to which the question relates to other associated constructs (e.g. repurchase intention, satisfaction) in an expected way.

3. *Predictive validity*: It refers to the degree to which a question can predict (or correlate with) other measures of the same construct that will be measured at some time in the future.

4. *Convergent validity*: It occurs when measures of constructs that are expected to correlate do so. This is similar to concurrent validity (which looks for correlation with other tests).

On the other hand, reliability is the extent to which a measure or an entire survey yields the same result on repeated trials, or simply how well the observed satisfaction scores are related to the true satisfaction score (Hayes, 1992). Since in customer satisfaction surveys the true level of satisfaction is unknown, it is not possible to calculate the correlation between the observed and the true scores. However, there are several ways to estimate the reliability of a questionnaire. The most common of them refers to internal consistency estimates (how well the items in the scale are interrelated) and include the following (Hayes, 1992):

- *Split-half reliability*: The method estimates internal consistency by dividing the scale into halves (e.g. odd vs. even items, first half of scale vs. last half of scale), then correlating the scores on these halves.
- *Cronbach's alpha*: This estimate of reliability is calculated using the variance of individual items and covariances between the items.

As implied from the analysis of the previous critical factors, marketing surveys, and in particular customer satisfaction surveys, are subject to a wide variety of potential errors. Although these errors may be caused by several factors, the main sources of errors include the following (Dutka, 1995):

1. *Sampling errors*: This category includes statistical errors that appear as a result of determining customer sample, usually because not every member of the population is included in the sample.
2. *Coverage errors*: These errors occur because the population was not defined correctly, and they justify the importance of defining who the customer is, before interviewing. For example, in some cases, satisfaction surveys are oriented to frequent customers, mainly because their contact or other information is available to organizations.
3. *Non-response errors*: This particular category refers to the bias caused by members of the sample who were not finally included in the survey. These errors depend mainly on the implemented type of survey (see section 7.1).
4. *Interviewer errors*: These errors are caused by interviewers who affect, by any means, the reliability of customer answers (e.g. by not following instructions, or by commenting questions and reinforcing particular response patterns).
5. *Respondent errors*: This category concerns errors that occur when customers do not give accurate information due to misunderstandings, lack of knowledge, or loss of interest, particularly in cases of lengthy surveys.
6. *Questionnaire errors*: This category refers to all type of errors related to the content and the structure of the questionnaire (e.g. wording, scales, and order of questions).
7. *Administrative errors*: These errors include data entry and analysis mistakes and refer to the business organization or the consultant who administrates the survey.

Regarding questionnaire errors, it should be emphasized that situations where customers are unable to respond to certain questions are rather common. This may occur because responders do not fully understand a particular question, or because they do not have the necessary knowledge to provide an accurate response (Naumann and Giel, 1995; Hill, 1996). A typical example in customer satisfaction surveys refers to the case where "technical" or "special" terms are used in the wording of the questionnaire. Usually, only the personnel of the business organization are familiar with these terms. Another example concerns particular questions that may have a different meaning or interpretation by the set of customers. For example, it is not clear if the question "How much satisfied are you by the quality of the products?" refers to the number of defects, the quality/price ratio, or the product's durability (product's life).

Consequently, choosing appropriate wording is one the most important factors that should be taken into account during the questionnaire development phase. Besides the necessary aforementioned clarity of questions, other important issues should be also considered. For example, double-barreled questions should be avoided (e.g. the answer to a question "how satisfied are you from the quality and variety of the products?" is not clear in which attributes refers to). Thus, questions should be specific having a single issue or topic. Also, questions should be kept as simple and short as possible, since lengthy and complex tasks increase the probability of misinterpretation and confusion (e.g. questions that ask customers to recall past events or answer to hypothetical questions).

As already noted, the survey should be developed so as to ensure sincere responses. However, several components of the survey (e.g. interviewer, questionnaire) may force particular response patterns, particularly when its objectives are not clearly defined and accepted. For example, some companies combine the customer satisfaction survey conduct with several promotional activities, although these projects should be implemented separately.

In addition, customers should be given the ability to freely express possible negative judgments regarding their satisfaction from products/services or particular attributes of them. However, in several cases dissatisfied customers are asked to exert additional effort in order to give their judgments. Thus, several managers prompt that satisfaction surveys should be accompanied with an integrated complaint management system, in order to assure customers that negative judgments are worthy of being expressed. So, if there are no particular important reasons (e.g. lotteries), the anonymity of the participants is preferable, particularly when measuring customer satisfaction from a set of competitive products or services (Naumann and Giel, 1995).

Other important issues that should be considered when developing a customer satisfaction questionnaire are:

- Greater attention should be paid when asking sensitive questions (e.g. income questions). These questions are related to the concepts of privacy and confidentiality, which may vary over time, between cultures and other subgroups, and between individuals. Usually, it is better to avoid such questions, but if this is not possible, then effects in the questionnaire design phase should be countered (e.g. use open-ended questions).
- The quantitative tools that will be used to analyze data should be defined before conducting the survey. So, questions that have no apparent usefulness and any rational meaning should be excluded from the survey. On the other hand, the questionnaire should contain all the required information for the intended analyses.
- One should always stress the critical importance of the pilot survey, since this is the only way to test the questionnaire in "real-world" conditions (see also section 7.4.1).
- In several cases, the time in which a survey is conducted affects directly or indirectly the content of the collected information. This is evident is cases where some periodical factors may influence the products or services offered (e.g. tourism services).
- The results of a customer satisfaction survey should bee cross-validated by other corporate sources of information, if this is necessary.

Finally, declining customer response rates are becoming a major problem today. This is not specific to satisfaction surveys but rather to every survey research activity. Low response rates may be caused by a variety of reasons, like the fact that some people are tired of surveys and must be enticed to respond to them. Several customers are also suspicious that customer satisfaction surveys provide a cover for company's promotional activities, while others doubt that survey results may be effectively used in order to improve the quality of the offered products or services. Finally, low response rates may occur when customers do not really have enough time to participate in the survey. It should be reminded that participating in a customer satisfaction survey is time and labor intensive from the customer's perspective (Vavra, 1997).

There are several techniques that are able to increase the response rate in customer satisfaction surveys. These techniques include, amongst others, the following (DeMaio 1980; Dutka, 1995):

- Personalization of the communication process (e.g. personal salutation in an attached letter in case of a mail survey).
- Reminding actions regarding the participation in the survey (e.g. follow-up mails or telephone calls).
- Incenting customers to respond (e.g. gifts, lotteries, coupons).
- Minimizing respondent's effort (e.g. stamped envelope ready for mailing).

Several research efforts have concentrated in evaluating the increase of response rates in marketing surveys, when adopting one of the previous approaches (Hensley, 1974; Goodstadt et al., 1977; Frey, 1983; Lavrakas, 1987). However, it should be noted that the response rates depend on the entire set of the factors engaged in a satisfaction survey (survey planning, questionnaire content, time and place of the survey, etc.).

In general, business organizations should communicate survey results, as well as any decided improvement actions to customers. This may help to establish a "customer relationship" mentality and a continuously interactive communication between the organization and its customers.

7.5 Customer Satisfaction Barometers

7.5.1 Developing Satisfaction Barometers

The development and installation of a permanent customer satisfaction barometer provides the ability to evaluate current and future company's performance. Thus, a business organization has the opportunity to implement an integrated benchmarking program. The national satisfaction barometers presented in this section constitute the most important efforts of generic satisfaction barometers that refer to a group of business sectors or national economies.

The national satisfaction barometers provide useful information regarding consumer behavior given a uniform way of customer satisfaction measurement. These efforts count almost 20 years of life and focus mainly on the development of a customer satisfaction index that supplements the existing national measurement indices of each economy (e.g. consumer price index). This way, although the satisfaction level is evaluated in both micro- and macro-economical level, these applications do not concern satisfaction surveys of individual companies.

However, these customer satisfaction barometers may be considered as uniform, independent, national measures of consumer's experiences with the purchase and consumption of goods and services. The main objective of these barometers is to provide an economic indicator able to track trends in customer satisfaction and quality of goods and services produced in a national economy. As a result, provided results constitute broad-based benchmarks of any business organization, given the uniform way of measurement.

The indicators provided by these barometers may be considered as additional macroeconomic variables for understanding national economic health and development. In most of the cases, national customer satisfaction barometers apply a cause-and-effect econometric model that links customers' evaluations of their experiences with products and services to their overall satisfaction. The estimated satisfaction indices are linked, in turn, to critical behavioral consequences of satisfaction, like customer retention and price tolerance. Thereby, the satisfaction barometers may help to examine future consumer behavior, and allow managers and investors to relate satisfaction to future streams of income.

According to Fornell (2003a), the strong relation between customer satisfaction and national economic growth is justified by the economic imperative to create a satisfied customer: *"Firms that do well by their customers are rewarded with more business from buyers and more capital from investors. In the aggregate, this is how jobs and economic growth are created."* Considering that customer satisfaction barometers aim at capturing actual customer experiences, they are able to balance quantity and quality of economic output. This is extremely important because it is widely accepted that sustainable economic growth cannot be achieved by improving production and deteriorating quality level.

The most important widely developed national or international customer satisfaction index models include the Swedish Customer Satisfaction Barometer (SCSB), the American Customer Satisfaction Index (ACSI), the German Customer Satisfaction Barometer (GCSB), and the European Customer Satisfaction Index (ECSI). In this context, additional models in other countries have been also developed (e.g. Norway, Malaysia, Switzerland, Korea, South Africa, etc.). Usually, these satisfaction barometers adopt a causal modeling, so that satisfaction may be linked with satisfaction drivers and satisfaction results. This is consistent with the argument that user experienced quality can be considered both as a lagging and a leading indicator, in a sense that it is able to show what the company had done to its customers, and what the customers would do to the company, respectively (Fornell, 2003a).

7.5.2 Satisfaction Barometers and Economic Growth

Several research efforts have tried to link national customer satisfaction values with economic data (Fornell, 2001b; Andreassen and Olsen, 2004). These empirical studies are mainly focused on either national or corporate economic growth, although there is a debate over whether changes of satisfaction scores have implications for the broader economy or whether they only matter to individual companies (Barta and Chaker, 2001).

The Gross Domestic Product (GDP) is the most common measure of national economic growth, despite the strong criticism often made by economists. GDP is a measure of quantity of economic output, given that it records the sum of the value of all buyer-seller transactions. On the other hand, customer satisfaction barometers provide a measure of the quality of growth, considering that it is based on true consumption experiences. As a result, positive experiences contribute to increased customer demand and stimulate household spending. The latter is extremely important to economic growth, since consumer spending is usually the largest part of GDP.

The relationship of GDP per capita growth and changes of customer satisfaction scores in Sweden (SCSB), USA (ACSI), and Germany (GCSB) is presented in Figure 7.10. As shown, GDP and national customer satisfaction results do not move together always closely, even if lag of variables is considered. Fornell (2003b) notes that other factors, like spending orientation (durable/non durable goods), interest rates, and price rebates, may also affect this linkage.

Thus, it is clear that consumer spending is the key variable for explaining the link between customer satisfaction and national economic growth (Fornell and Stephan, 2002; Fornell, 2002, 2003a). Satisfied customers are able to increase spending because they are more likely to repurchase, buy more frequently and are less sensitive to price increases. As Fornell (2001a) emphasizes, the linkage between customer satisfaction and spending is confirmed by the fact that most buys are repeat purchases, or ongoing commitments in the case of services. However, this linkage is not always clear or direct, as shown in Figure 7.11. Several researchers note that consumer spending may increase, even though satisfaction declines due to several other factors (e.g. prices, household savings, etc.). On the other hand, negative consumer confidence about the economy and its future may result to lower spending levels, without a relative decrease in satisfaction scores. Several other researchers, studying the linkage between satisfaction and spending, emphasize also the "law of diminishing satisfaction" (i.e. the more we consume, the less the satisfaction with the same product/service is).

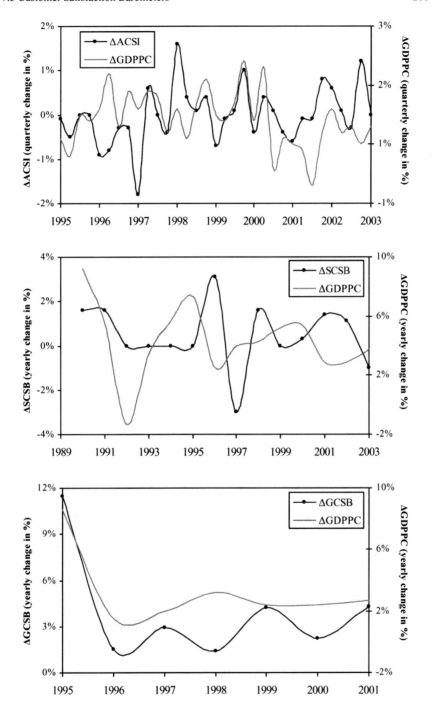

Fig. 7.10 Change in satisfaction scores and GDP per capita growth

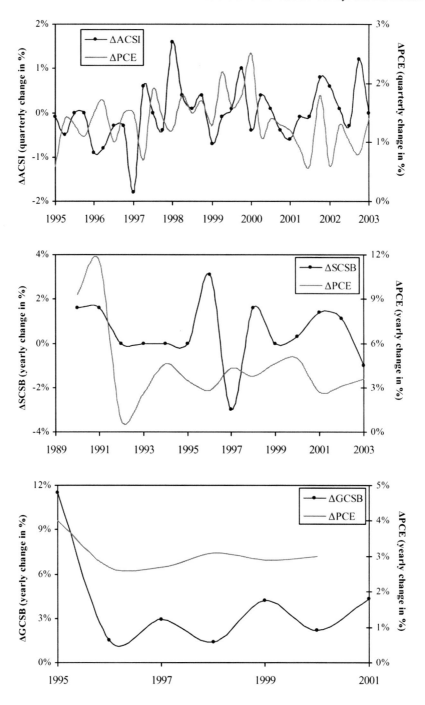

Fig. 7.11 Changes in customer scores and consumer spending growth

It should be noted that consumer spending is assumed to be driven by the aggregated household wealth (income, savings, earning from stock market, etc.). Thus, if customers are spending beyond their means, consumer expenditures are unlikely to continue increasing, even if satisfaction levels are relatively high. However, recent empirical studies have shown that housing income and wealth have a weak impact, although significant, on consumption: only 8% of the variation in consumer spending is explained by combined changes in income and housing wealth (Fornell and Stephan, 2002; Case et al., 2001).

Furthermore, usually consumer spending is related to the uncertainty of the general economic environment, as perceived by customers, including interest rates, inflation, energy prices, wages, unemployment, etc. In this context, several survey-based indicators have been proposed, like Consumer Sentiment Index (CSI) and Consumer Confidence Index (CCI). All the previous factors are assumed to influence the overall consumer's "willingness to pay", although recent studies shown that consumer sentiment/confidence has a weak only impact on customer satisfaction (Fornell and Stephan, 2002). Particularly, as noted by Fornell (2005), increase in interest rates is similar to price increase, in the sense that credit becomes more expensive. Moreover, a change in interest rates may affect the value of a satisfied customer because discounting of future income does not remain stable. This may affect corporate plans for improving customer satisfaction.

Several researches have also studied the relationship between customer satisfaction and economic growth in a corporate level. Using national customer satisfaction data, several studies show that improvement in customer satisfaction has a significant and positive impact on firms' profitability. Ittner and Larcker (1998) and Anderson et al. (2004) show that 1% change in ACSI can lead to a \$240-275 million improvement in firm value. Using similar data, Gruca and Rego (2005) found that a 1% increase in ACSI results to an increase of \$55 million in a firm's net operational cash flow next year and a decrease of 4% in cash flow variability. Other researchers used the SCSB and found that a 1% increase in satisfaction leads to a 2.37% increase in ROI (Return on Investment), while a 1-point increase in SCSB for 5 years is worth about \$94 million or 11.4% of current ROI (Anderson et al., 1994, 1997; Anderson and Mittal, 2000). The relationship between customer satisfaction and stock prices has also been studied, showing that ACSI scores are significantly related to market value of equity (Fornell et al., 2006).

All the aforementioned studies are based on the principle that a satisfied customer is more profitable than a dissatisfied one. In addition, customer satisfaction is an important indicator of the general health of the company, since it is usually related to motivated and loyal employees, good products, and effective management.

However, a decrease in revenues during one period may lead to an increase in customer satisfaction the next period, since financial difficulties often pressure companies to try harder and improve customer service (e.g. airlines sector after 9/11 and telecommunication industry during 2003 in the US). Furthermore, corporate earnings may be affected by the competitiveness of the sector, because alternative products/services and switching costs affect the overall consumer behavior.

Increasing sales may also often lead to lower customer satisfaction, if the acquisition of new customers is not handled well. Thus, customer satisfaction is often considered as a necessary but not sufficient condition for company's growth: high levels of customer satisfaction lead to company's growth, but company's growth does not always lead to satisfied customers.

7.6 Examples of Satisfaction Barometers

7.6.1 Swedish Customer Satisfaction Barometer

The Swedish Customer Satisfaction Barometer (SCSB) was the first truly national satisfaction index, established in 1989. The SCSB counts approximately 20 years of life and the results are given every year. It is conducted under the supervision of the University of Michigan-National Quality Research Centre and the Swedish Post Office.

The required data are collected through a telephone survey from a sample of approximately 23,000 customers, while currently more than 130 companies participate in this survey. The survey is designed to obtain a nationally representative sample of customers of major companies in 32 of Sweden's largest industries. The companies surveyed in each industry sector are the largest share firms such that cumulative market share is more than 70% (Fornell, 1992).

The questionnaire employs 10-point scales to access each respondent's expectations, perceived quality, satisfaction and retention behavior. An example of the questionnaire for the auto industry is presented in Figure 7.12.

The analysis is based on the Fornell's approach (see Figure 2.10), while the model is self-weighting and estimates the indices and the strength of relationships between the variables in order to maximize the explanation of customer satisfaction, as expressed by the sample of customers. Figure 7.13 presents the SCSB model, while the Swedish national results for the overall customer satisfaction index are shown in Figure 7.14.

The main characteristic of the approach is the multiple equations that correlate customers' values and perception for quality with their satisfaction and their loyalty, as it is expressed through price elasticity and repurchase intentions (Fornell, 1992; Johnson et al., 2001).

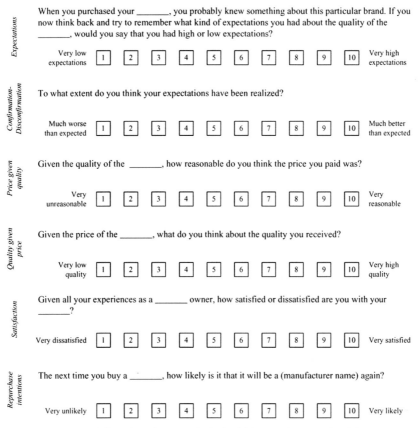

Fig. 7.12 Questionnaire example in the SCSB (Anderson et al., 1994)

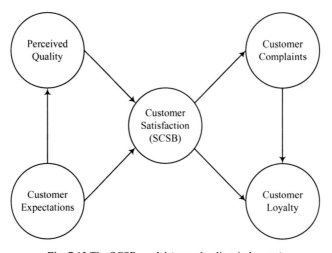

Fig. 7.13 The SCSB model (www.kvalitetsindex.org)

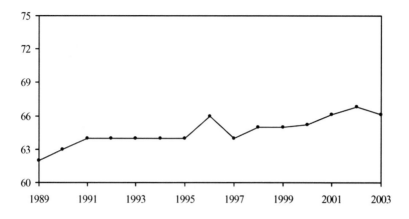

Fig. 7.14 SCSB results for 1989-2003

7.6.2 American Customer Satisfaction Index

The American Customer Satisfaction Index (ACSI) was established in 1994 following several years of development and pre-testing. It is produced through a partnership of the University of Michigan Business School, the American Society for Quality, and Arthur Andersen. The National Quality Research Centre (NQRC) at the University of Michigan Business School is responsible for researching and producing the ACSI (Fornell et al., 1996; National Quality Research Center, 1998, 2000).

The ACSI follows the general modeling and survey methodology of the SCSB adapted in the distinct characteristics of the U.S. economy and it can be considered as an effort to develop an index similar to the national consumer price index. The model links antecedents or causes of customer satisfaction (customer expectations, perceived quality and value) with satisfaction values and consequences or outcomes of customer satisfaction (customer complaints, loyalty), as shown in Figure 7.15 (Anderson and Fornell, 2000).

The ACSI model reports scores on a 0-100 scale at the national level, measuring 7 economic sectors, 39 industries (including e-commerce and e-business), and more than 200 companies and federal/local government agencies. As shown in Figure 7.16, the economic sectors measured, produce almost 73% of the Gross Domestic Product (GDP). The number of interviews increases constantly: current sample size contains more than 65,000 customers, while more than 500,000 respondents have been interviewed since the baseline study in 1994 (Bryant, 2003).

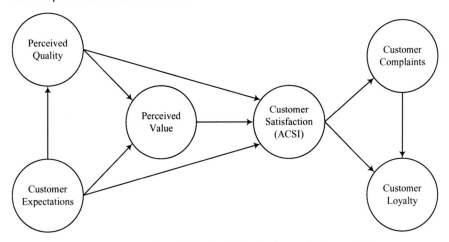

Fig. 7.15 The ACSI model (National Quality Research Center, 1998)

Using the causal analysis, the weights of the indicator variables as well as the relationship between the latent variables are estimated with a partial least squares method (Anderson and Fornell, 2000). Each company in the ASCI is weighted within its industry by its most recent years' revenue. Also, relative sales by each industry are used to determine each industry's contribution to the respective sector index (National Quality Research Center, 1998). Thus, the calculation of ACSI in each level is based on a simple weighted average model. In addition to the satisfaction scores, the ACSI provides scores for the causes and consequences of customer satisfaction and their relationships.

All companies, industries and economic sectors in the ACSI were measured at the same time only for the baseline year (1994). Since that baseline year, ACSI is updated quarterly, on a rolling basis, with new data for one or two sectors replacing data from the prior year. Thus, ACSI provides analytical results at different levels, i.e. for each economical sector, industry or a set of selective companies included in the survey. The ACSI results for the overall customer satisfaction index are presented in Figure 7.17, while an example of detailed results for the examined industries is shown in Figure 7.18.

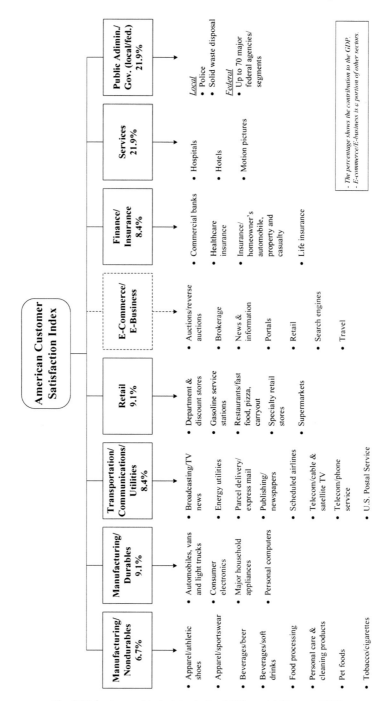

Fig. 7.16 Sectors and industries in the ACSI model (Bryant, 2003)

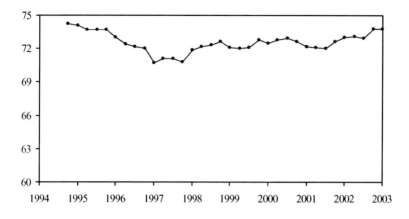

Fig. 7.17 ACSI results for 1989-2003

7.6.3 German Customer Satisfaction Barometer

The German Customer Satisfaction Barometer (GCSB) has been established by the German Marketing Association e.V. and the Deutsche Post AG and operates on a yearly basis since 1992. Its general philosophy focuses on the following points (Meyer and Dornach, 1996):

- Supplying single industries and suppliers with data to determine their position and deficiencies in market according to customers' perspective.
- Information on the customers' expectations as well as on the way through which they are modified.
- Continuous information and controlling of customer satisfaction measures.
- Developing and strengthening the customer orientation philosophy of the German industries, companies, organizations and institutions.

The required data are collected through a computer-aided telephone survey (CATI: Computer Assisted Telephone Interviewing) based on a random sample of approximately 45,000 customers, covering more than 50 industry sectors.

The results of the GCSB are shown in Figure 7.19, while it should be noted that this barometer provides analytical results for different customer segments and industry sectors, including customer satisfaction on detailed quality attributes (Figure 7.20).

The GCSB does not assume a causal model for customer satisfaction, like SCSB and ACSI, and is mainly a survey-based approach. The GCSB approach analyzes a simple questionnaire that consists of (Meyer, 1994, 1996):

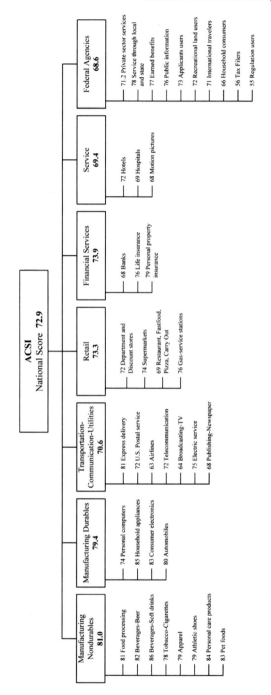

Fig. 7.18 ACSI results for different industries for year 2000 (National Quality Research Center, 2000)

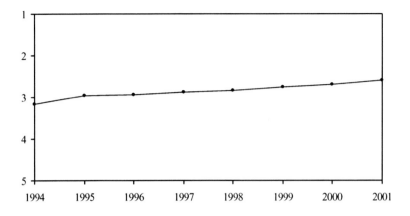

Fig. 7.19 GCSB results for 1989-2003

- Overall customer satisfaction rating.
- Customer retention questions (recommendation, repurchase intention).
- Satisfaction rating for the quality attributes of the product/service surveyed.

The GCSB supplies important data to German companies in order to implement internal, industry or international benchmarks. However, as Meyer and Dornach (1996) state, traditional quantitative performance indicators such as market share or profitability should be combined with customer satisfaction and loyalty indicators provided by GCSB. Finally, it should be noted that GCSB includes also an employee satisfaction survey.

7.6.4 European Customer Satisfaction Index

The development of the European Customer Satisfaction Index (ECSI) has been prompted by the successful application of ACSI and SCSB. ECSI was founded by the European Organization for Quality (EOQ), the European Foundation for Quality Management (EFQM) and the European Academic Network for Customer-oriented Quality Analysis, and supported by the European Commission (DG III). Although a pilot survey was conducted during 1999, where only 11 countries participated and limited number of sectors (retail, banking, telecommunications, and supermarkets) was included, the ECSI has not been able so far to provide broad-based results (Grønholdt et al., 2000; Kristensen et al., 2000; Grigoroudis and Siskos, 2004).

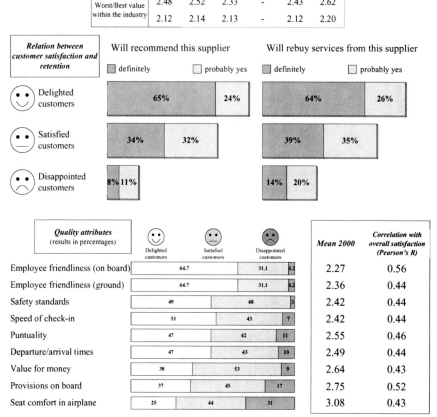

Fig. 7.20 GCSB detailed results for the airline industry

The ECSI model constitutes a modified adaptation of the ACSI model (Figure 7.21), which links customer satisfaction to its determinants and, in turn, to its consequence (Grønholdt et al., 2000). The determinants of customer satisfaction are perceived company image, customer expectations, perceived quality and perceived value. An important difference of the model compared to ACSI is that perceived quality is conceptually divided into "hardware" quality (quality of the product/service attributes) and "humanware" quality (associated customer interactive elements in service, like personal behavior and atmosphere of the service environment).

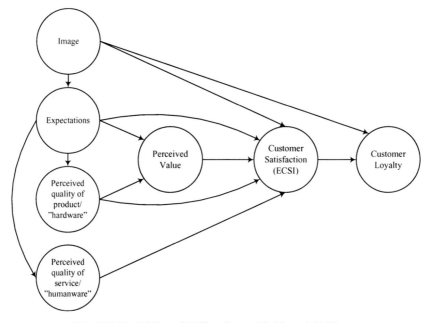

Fig. 7.21 The ECSI model (Ciavolino and Dahlgaard, 2007)

The ECSI model provides the ability to produce 4 levels of satisfaction indices, similarly to ACSI results:

- National customer satisfaction indices.
- Economical sector indices.
- Specific industry indices.
- Scores for companies and organizations within the survey.

7.6.5 Other Satisfaction Barometers

Other important customer satisfaction index models, developed during the last decade, that are able to provide systematic results, include the Norwegian Customer Satisfaction Barometer (NCSB), the Korean Customer Satisfaction Index (KCSI), the Malaysian Customer Satisfaction Index (MCSI), and the Swiss Index of Customer Satisfaction (SWICS) (Kadir et al., 2000; Johnson et al., 2001; Winnie and Kanji, 2001). Furthermore, several countries are conducting a preliminary analysis and design the installation of national satisfaction barometers, like Canada, Australia, Brazil, Argentina, and Mexico.

Additional attempts for developing a customer satisfaction barometer may refer to syndicated or multiclient surveys, which provide the ability of comparison analysis with the most important competitors.

For example, one of the first industries that have conducted syndicated satisfaction surveys was U.S. automotive industry. The American auto industry has been using surveys since 1978 to help dealers measure their performance against other competitors in order to identify operations that needed improvement. In some cases, the surveys have become unwieldy 100-questions documents (Massnick, 1997). The National Automobile Dealers Association (NADA) intervened in 1994 with a much shorter recommended approach to determining a customer satisfaction index. This approach provides a uniform methodology for measurement based on defined satisfaction dimensions (Table 7.4).

Table 7.4 NADA's survey satisfaction dimensions (Massnick, 1997)

	Purchase	Service
Partial dimensions	1. Cleanliness and condition of the car	1. Easiness of getting a service appointment
	2. Courteousness and professionalism of the salesperson	2. Explanation of repairs
	3. Sales transaction handling of the business/financial department	3. Service time
	4. Explanation of warranty and maintenance schedule	4. Proper repairs
	5. Explanation of owner's manual and operating controls	5. Service fees
Overall dimensions	1. Overall satisfaction from the purchase of the new car	1. Overall satisfaction from the service experience
	2. Overall satisfaction from the purchase and delivery process	2. Recommend (for service)
	3. Recommend (for purchase)	

7.6.6 Comparison and Discussion

Most of the aforementioned satisfaction index models have a common methodological background, which is based on a set of cause and effect relationships. Nevertheless, the comparison of these causal models reveals the following differences:

- Compared to the ACSI model, in the original SCSB perceived quality and perceived value appear as one merged variable (perceived value).
- In the ECSI model, the "hard" and "soft" aspects of perceived quality are considered separately, introducing two distinct variables. Additionally, the model includes corporate image as a latent variable having direct effects on customer expectations, satisfaction, and loyalty.
- In NCSB model, Servqual instrument is introduced to evaluate quality, while customer expectations are replaced by corporate image, based on evidence

from empirical studies, showing that expectations exert little influence to satisfaction (see Johnson et al., 2001).

- The consumer complaint variable is considered differently in these satisfaction index models, given that in many cases, customers rarely complain even if they are dissatisfied with products or services. For example, in the NCSB, it is replaced by complaint handling, while the ECSI model does not include such a variable as satisfaction consequence.

The GCSB adopts a completely different approach, aggregating customer judgments in a single satisfaction-to-dissatisfaction scale, while no system of cause and effect relationship exists. Although the GCSB survey includes measures other than satisfaction, there is no satisfaction model per se.

The aforementioned differences in the methodological approaches constitute the most important disadvantage for comparing customer satisfaction across different industries and countries, although several studies have tried to overcome the problem of variation in methodological practices (Johnson and Fornell, 1991; Martensen et al., 2000; Johnson et al., 2001; Johnson et al., 2002; Grigoroudis and Siskos, 2004). Johnson et al. (2002) suggest that observed differences in satisfaction results by SCSB, ACSI, and GCSB are relatively predictable and meaningful. Their results are mainly focused on the following:

- Satisfaction is systematically higher for products, more intermediate for services and retailers, and lower for public agencies.
- Satisfaction is also predictably higher in the United States than in Germany or Sweden.

These arguments may be justified by differences in the considered countries, which are able to affect the degree to which customers are provided with market offerings that satisfy their needs.

Almost all of the aforementioned customer satisfaction index models are estimated using the Partial Least Square (PLS) method (Fornell and Cha, 1994). PLS is well suited for this particular problem, given that it is a causal modeling method that can handle latent or unobserved variables. PLS is able to combine characteristics of multiple regression and principal components analysis, through an iterative estimation procedure.

The performance of latent variables is operationalized as weighted indices of multiple survey measures, such that the predictive power of the model is maximized. The prediction accuracy is focused on the loyalty variable, which is the most important measure because it is the main survey-based proxy for economic results (Johnson et al., 2001).

Although PLS appears similar to Structural Equation Modeling (SEM), it should be noted that SEM is a path analysis approach with latent variables, focusing on explaining covariance, while the objective of PLS is to explain variance.

However, despite the aforementioned disadvantages, these customer satisfaction barometers constitute basic economic indicators, while the implemented methodologies are quite generic, and thus applicable to very different cases. Usually, these estimated satisfaction indices provide a baseline against which it is possible to track customer satisfaction over time.

Chapter 8
Applications in Business Organizations

8.1 Satisfaction Analysis for a Commercial Bank

8.1.1 Research Background and Survey Details

Service quality can be seen as one of the main determinants of customer satisfaction, which in turn influences purchase intentions (Spreng and Mckoy, 1996; DeRuyter et al., 1997; Bloemer et al., 1998). This is of main interest, particularly in the banking sector, where the highly competitive market has caused the banking system to undergone drastic changes. Institutional changes, creation of extensive product/service portfolios, major changes in the ownership status, heavy use of modern technology and globalization of the banks activities are only some examples of these changes identified in the banking sector (Gortsos, 1998). Due to this heightened competition, bank service quality rises as an important factor that will affect the relevant market shares and profitability in the banking sector (Anderson et al., 1994; Hallowell, 1996; Caruana and Pitt, 1997).

Furthermore, to keep and advance their competitive edge, modern business organizations should better understand and profile their customers. This is more imperative in the banking sector, where the variety of the products and services offered (loans, deposits, credit cards, leasing, factoring, etc.) concern particular groups of customers. Banks need to individualize products and to approach every customer in an individual way. This is usually referred to as "mass customization" (Davids, 1986). Customization requires, however, a profound knowledge of customers and their needs and habits. Such knowledge would help companies to find answers to questions such as:

- Which customers would be interested in certain types of products and services?
- How would a product or service be designed so as to satisfy the needs of an individual, or a group of customers?

E. Grigoroudis and Y. Siskos, *Customer Satisfaction Evaluation*, International Series
in Operations Research & Management Science 139, DOI 10.1007/978-1-4419-1640-2_8,
© Springer Science + Business Media, LLC 2010

- How effective is the marketing on specific customers?
- Which attributes suggest that a certain customer cluster should be (or should not be) targeted with a new product or service?

The presented satisfaction survey concerns one of the leading banking organizations in Greece. The survey took place in two different bank branches in the city of Chania. The survey was conducted within the period July-September 1998 (for more details see Grigoroudis et al., 1999a; Mihelis et al., 2001; Siskos et al., 2001a).

Final input data consist of 303 questionnaires: 122 from store A and 181 from store B. Moreover, 160 private customers and 95 companies have been participated in the survey (the primary relation with the bank has not been identified for the rest of the sample). A more detailed presentation of the general profile of the sample is presented in Figures 8.1 and 8.2: Figure 8.11 presents the profession of the private customers, while Figure 8.2 shows the activity sector for the business segment. The observed distributions show a well-balanced sample.

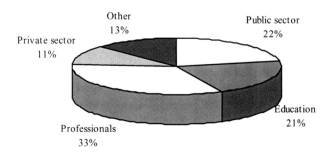

Fig. 8.1 Profession of private customers segment

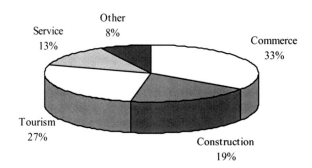

Fig. 8.2 Activity sector for the business segment

The assessment of a consistent family of criteria representing customer satisfaction dimensions is one of most important stages of the MUSA methodology. This assessment can be achieved through an extensive interactive procedure between the analyst and the decision-maker (business organization). In any case, the reliability of the set of criteria/subcriteria has to be tested in a small indicative set of customers.

The hierarchical structure of customers' satisfaction dimensions is presented in Figure 8.3 and it shows the set of criteria and subcriteria used in this survey. The main satisfaction criteria consist of:

- *Personnel of the bank*: This criterion includes all the characteristics concerning personnel (skills and knowledge, responsiveness, communication and collaboration with customers, friendliness, etc.).
- *Products*: This criterion refers mainly to the offered products and services (variety, refund, cost, special services, etc.).
- *Image of the bank*: Credibility of the bank (name, reputation), technological excellence, as well as ability to satisfy future customers' needs are included in this criterion.
- *Service*: This criterion refers to the service offered to the customers; it includes the appearance of the stores, the waiting time (queue, telephone, etc.), the complexity of service processes and the information provided (informing customers in an understandable way, explaining the service and other relevant factors, informing for new products, etc.).
- *Access*: Network expansion of the bank, branches location, as well as observed troubles in the service system (strikes, damaged ATMs, etc.) are included in this criterion.

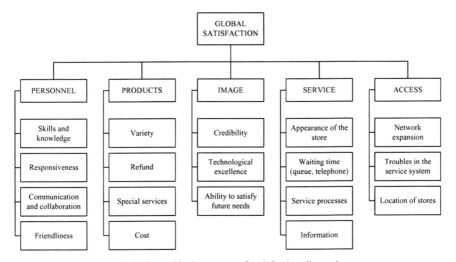

Fig. 8.3 Hierarchical structure of satisfaction dimensions

8.1.2 Overall Satisfaction Analysis

Customers seem to be quite satisfied from the provided service, given that the average global satisfaction index has a very high value (82.1%). Moreover, criteria satisfaction analysis shows that customers are quite satisfied according to the criteria of "Access" and "Personnel", while lower satisfaction indices appear for the rest of the criteria (63.5%-74.7%), as Table 8.1 displays. The most important criterion, with a significant importance level, seems to be "Access". This can justify the high value of the global satisfaction index. Customers are more satisfied according to the most important criterion and less satisfied on the dimensions that seem to play a less important role to their preferences.

Table 8.1 Overall satisfaction results

Criteria	Weight (%)	Average Satisfaction Index (%)	Average Demanding Index
Personnel	15.0	80.6	−0.47
Products	10.3	63.5	−0.23
Image	13.1	74.7	−0.39
Service	11.8	69.3	−0.32
Access	49.8	87.7	−0.68
Overall	-	82.1	−0.42

The added value curve, presented in Figure 8.4, shows that customers do not seem demanding according to their preferences. The majority of customers have an added value greater than 87%. This added value level seems to be the most critical satisfaction index, as shown in Figure 8.5, which presents the percentage of customers having a value lower than or equal to a particular level (this is a form of a cumulative distribution function of customer values based on the satisfaction function of Figure 8.4).

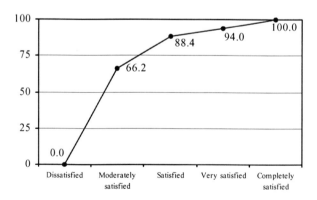

Fig. 8.4 Overall satisfaction function (added value curve)

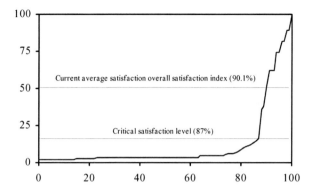

Fig. 8.5 "Fragile" customers curve

The action diagram shows that there are no critical satisfaction dimensions requiring immediate improvement efforts, as presented in Figure 8.6. However, if bank wishes to create additional advantages against competition, the criteria with the lowest satisfaction index should be improved. These improvement efforts should be focused on products, service, and bank's image.

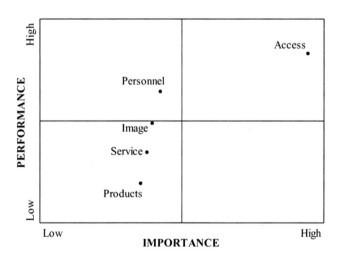

Fig. 8.6 Action diagram for main satisfaction criteria

8.1.3 Criteria Satisfaction Analysis

The analysis of the partial satisfaction dimensions allows for the identification of the criteria characteristics that constitute the strong and the weak points of the bank. The detailed results of Table 8.2 reveal the following:

- Personnel's friendliness constitutes a significant competitive advantage of the bank. This result is considered prospective, since the survey took place in a provincial Greek city.
- Large improvement margins appear for cost and special financial services. This generic result, referring to the low satisfaction level of cost criterion, holds for the total bank sector, since customers have the impression that they are often overcharged. On the other hand, the fact that the satisfaction level with respect to the specialized services is low is particularly worrying. It seems that the bank is not in the position to follow the current evolution of the sector's products.
- The customers are quite satisfied with the ability of the bank to satisfy their future needs. However, it should be noted that the criterion of technological excellence has a quite low satisfaction index. It is worthwhile to mention that the bank has already decided to implement a program for the total technological upgrade of the stores.
- The low satisfaction level with respect to service is mainly due to the subcriteria of the provided information and the waiting time.
- Bank should also pay particular attention to the troubles that are observed in the service system (equipment malfunctions, strikes, etc.), given that there are margins for improvement. Although the satisfaction level is rather high, the importance of this subcriterion is high as well.

Taking also into account the previous remarks, it is possible to determine the improvement priorities of the bank that should focus on the following (see also Grigoroudis et al., 1999a; Mihelis et al., 2000; Siskos et al., 2001a): special services, information provided to the customers, and waiting time.

8.1.4 Concluding Remarks

The presented application highlights the necessity of a permanent customer satisfaction barometer, since customer satisfaction is a dynamic parameter of the business organization. Changes in the current market can affect customer preferences and expectations (e.g. some satisfaction dimensions may become critical in the near future, if customers give more importance to them). The main advantages of a permanent customer satisfaction measurement system in the examined banking organization may be summarized in the following:

Table 8.2 Criteria satisfaction analysis

Criteria	Subcriteria	Weight (%)	Average Satisfaction Index (%)	Average Demanding Index
Personnel	Skills and knowledge	12.2	75.7	−0.34
	Responsiveness	19.6	79.6	−0.59
	Communication-collaboration	12.9	75.1	−0.38
	Friendliness	55.3	87.8	−0.86
Products	Variety	28.0	82.0	−0.57
	Refund	34.8	76.6	−0.77
	Cost	13.2	33.4	0.39
	Special services	24.0	29.9	0.65
Image	Credibility	14.9	78.7	−0.46
	Technological excellence	9.7	74.2	−0.18
	Ability to satisfy future needs	75.3	89.8	−0.89
Service	Appearance of the stores	15.6	76.6	−0.49
	Waiting time	13.2	64.6	−0.39
	Service processes	56.6	86.0	−0.86
	Information	14.6	68.4	−0.45
Access	Network expansion	35.6	85.6	−0.70
	Troubles in the service system	31.1	84.0	−0.74
	Location of stores	33.3	87.5	−0.66

- The bank will have the ability to analyze customer behavior for different regions in the country, taking into account their special characteristics.
- An interior benchmarking system can be established, based on customer satisfaction evaluation in each branch. In this way, the most "weak" stores of the bank may be identified and improved (see application in section 8.5).
- Competition analysis will be performed for different regions of the country.
- The effectiveness of marketing plans will be evaluated through customer satisfaction measurement.
- The establishment of a motivating system for employees may be directly related to customer satisfaction measurement. In this way, productivity may be improved and efficiently measured.

A permanent customer satisfaction barometer can assist Total Quality Management concepts in every business organization (Edosomwan, 1993). Moreover, the focus on total customer satisfaction should be integrated into the accepted management process and the culture of the organization.

8.2 Customer Satisfaction in the Greek Ferry Industry

8.2.1 Preliminary Analysis

The presented application concerns customer satisfaction analysis in the Greek coastal shipping industry in 1998. A key factor for understanding market conditions during the period that satisfaction survey took place is the system of "cabotage", whereby the country's own ships have a protected market position in Greek coastal traffic. This particular characteristic is mainly responsible for the low competition observed during this period.

The implementation of the MUSA method includes a preliminary customer behavioral analysis in which, the assessment of the set of satisfaction criteria follows the principles presented in sections 4.1 and 7.3.2.

In this particular case, the hierarchical structure of customer satisfaction criteria/subcriteria is presented in Figure 8.7, and customers were asked to evaluate/express their satisfaction according to the following criteria:

- *Credibility of the company*: Safety and duration of trip, timetable frequency, delays.
- *Prices*: Ticket, vehicle, bar, restaurant and special discounts.
- *Service*: Personnel's behavior, politeness, service time, etc.
- *Additional service*: Electronic booking system, customer's opinion for mini market, video games, disco, etc.
- *Comfort and service quality*: Cleanliness, ampleness of cabins and common use areas, quality of food.

The satisfaction survey concerns one of the major companies in Greece, and took place in two different ferry links, which represent company's domestic routes. The survey was conducted during winter 1998 and a random sample of passengers was used. Data collection was completed on board, where more than 5,000 questionnaires were distributed to passengers. Final input data consist of 605 questionnaires (the corresponding response rate is approximately 12%). Further information for the details of the survey is given by Grigoroudis et al. (1999b) and Siskos et al. (2001a).

8.2.2 Overall Satisfaction Analysis

The results of the analysis show that there is a significant potential for further improvement, since the average global satisfaction index is less than 80%. It is important to note that the total set of satisfaction criteria, with the exception of company's credibility, have lower satisfaction levels compared to the global index of the total clientele. According to this, the following remarks can be made (Table 8.3):

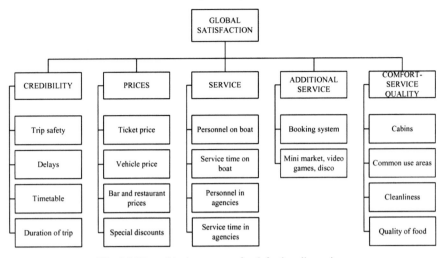

Fig. 8.7 Hierarchical structure of satisfaction dimensions

Table 8.3 Criteria satisfaction results

Criteria	Weight (%)	Average Satisfaction Index (%)	Average Demanding Index
Credibility	62.3	94.4	0.87
Prices	8.6	22.4	0.07
Service	9.9	62.1	−0.19
Additional service	9.3	58.2	−0.14
Comfort-Service quality	9.9	61.3	−0.19
Overall	-	79.7	−0.50

- The global satisfaction index is quite satisfactory due to the high performance of the company according to the credibility criterion (average satisfaction index 94.4%), which is the most important satisfaction dimension (weight 62.3%).
- The customers are not satisfied from company's prices (average satisfaction index 22.4%), although they do not consider important this particular criterion (weight 8.6%).
- The rest of the criteria have a low level of importance for the customers (9-10%), while the performance of the company is rather modest (average satisfaction indices 58-62%).

Regarding the improvement efforts of the company, an inspection of the action diagram (Figure 8.8) reveals that there is no particularly critical satisfaction dimension calling for an immediate improvement. Nevertheless, almost all criteria except credibility could be characterized as potentially critical satisfaction dimensions, given that they are very close to the critical quadrants of the corresponding diagrams. The improvement priorities should be focused on:

- the company prices, given that the average satisfaction index is particularly low, while the customers are not demanding to this criterion, and
- the criteria of the provided services (service, additional service, service quality) where the satisfaction indices allow significant margins for improvement.

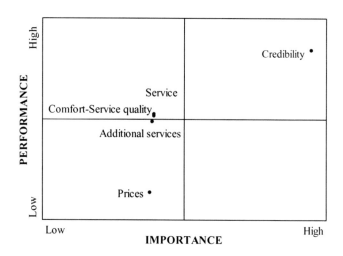

Fig. 8.8 Action diagram for main satisfaction criteria

The criteria satisfaction analysis confirms the previous findings. In general (excluding the subcriteria of prices), the company performance is quite high in these satisfaction dimensions, which are considered important by the customers. This fact justifies the satisfactory level of the distinctive satisfaction indices. On the other hand, however, there are several areas where the company has significant margins for improvement.

The detailed results of Table 8.4 indicate the following points:

- "Trip safety" and "Delays" criteria are the main competitive advantages of the company credibility. Although the customers are not quite satisfied from the duration of trip and company's timetable, they do not seem to consider these particular satisfaction dimensions of high importance.
- Company performance is particularly low in all subcriteria of prices. It is remarkable that the satisfaction dimensions with the higher importance (ticket price, vehicle price, and bar-restaurant prices) have the lower average satisfaction indices.
- The customers are satisfied from the personnel on boat. However, the average service time on boat allows margins for further improvement. On the other hand, the satisfaction level of the provided service in agencies is rather non-

satisfactory although the customers do not give significant importance to the particular subcriteria.

- Both the cleanliness and the booking system constitute competitive advantages of the company, given that they are the most important dimensions holding also the higher levels of importance.

Table 8.4 Subcriteria satisfaction analysis

Criteria	Subcriteria	Weight (%)	Average Satisfaction Index (%)	Average Demanding Index
Credibility	Trip safety	53.9	95.5	−0.85
	Delays	28.0	90.0	−0.57
	Timetable	9.5	58.4	−0.16
	Duration of trip	8.6	32.5	0.07
Prices	Ticket price	25.0	8.8	0.68
	Vehicle price	25.0	4.0	0.68
	Bar and restaurant prices	40.7	6.5	0.80
	Special discounts	9.3	42.7	0.14
Service	Personnel on boat	67.8	90.5	−0.88
	Service time on boat	9.6	59.7	−0.17
	Personnel in agencies	12.6	72.6	−0.36
	Service time in agencies	10.0	64.4	−0.20
Additional service	Booking system	68.8	95.6	−0.85
	Mini market/Games/Disco	31.2	42.5	0.06
Comfort-Service quality	Common use areas	9.7	36.0	0.18
	Cabins	11.1	33.5	0.28
	Cleanliness	66.4	98.2	−0.88
	Quality of food	12.8	43.9	0.22

The improvement efforts of the company should be focused on the following groups of satisfaction dimensions in order of precedence:

- The ticket price (passenger, vehicle), and especially the price of food (bar, restaurant); it should be noticed, however, that the customers are rather high demanding for the particular subcriteria, fact that indicates that the company should make extended efforts in order to increase the satisfaction level.
- The provided comforts (cabins, common use areas), and the quality of food; customers do not consider the particular satisfaction dimensions important, but improvement margins are quite large.
- The frequency of the routes, especially during the peak periods, and the average service time in the ships and the agencies as well; since the customers are not very demanding with respect to the particular subcriteria, the improvement efforts are expected to have an immediate return.

8.2.3 Customer segmentation analysis

In order to identify customers' clusters with distinctive preferences and expectations in relation to the total clientele, the presented analysis is based on variables that can segregate the total clientele, and may refer either to customer's personal characteristics (age, marital status, etc.) or to details of his/her trip (ship, route, etc.).

According to Tables 8.5 and 8.6, the comparative analysis of the customer clusters does not indicate any significant differentiation compared to the results of the analysis of the total clientele presented in the previous section. Nevertheless, the following points raise:

- Young and old customers seem less demanding and more satisfied from the criteria of service, additional service, and comfort-service quality.
- The married customers give higher importance to the comfort-service quality criterion. Note that they are quite satisfied in this particular criterion.
- Medium frequency customers consider of particular importance the criteria of service, additional service, and comfort-service quality.

In general, the total clientele may be divided in two main clusters: married customers with children, 26-50 years old, that do not use often the company's ships and customers of higher or lower age that use to travel with the company's ships.

Regarding the price criterion, which presents a worryingly low satisfaction level, the first customers cluster considers particularly important the prices of vehicle and food, while the second cluster considers the ticket price as the most important subcriterion. This conclusion is very important for the improvement efforts and the determination of the pricing policy of the company.

Table 8.5 Average satisfaction indices per customer segment (%)

Segment		Overall	Credibility	Prices	Service	Additional service	Comfort-Service quality
Age	-25	79.7	93.7	26.5	71.2	65.3	64.9
	26-35	71.9	94.1	19.8	57.8	43.1	32.9
	36-50	78.7	94.4	21.4	61.3	45.9	63.2
	50-	83.0	94.2	21.6	67.3	67.6	76.1
Marital status	Single	77.3	94.6	23.4	61.9	44.6	57.2
	Married	72.3	91.3	13.4	44.5	47.6	78.2
	Married with children	81.5	94.4	21.8	65.4	64.4	65.9
Travel frequency	Low	79.7	95.0	22.8	62.4	57.7	59.2
	Medium	77.2	89.0	18.3	75.5	68.6	73.5
	High	78.6	98.3	23.6	58.8	46.4	55.1

Table 8.6 Criteria weights per customer segment

Segment		Credibility	Prices	Service	Additional service	Comfort-Service quality
Age	-25	55.3	8.7	14.0	11.0	11.0
	26-35	59.8	9.0	9.2	9.3	12.6
	36-50	62.4	8.6	9.6	9.4	10.1
	50-	54.1	8.4	10.1	10.8	16.5
Marital status	Single	61.9	9.0	10.4	9.1	9.6
	Married	51.1	10.6	9.0	9.3	20.0
	Married with children	60.8	8.5	10.1	10.2	10.5
Travel frequency	Low	63.2	8.6	9.7	9.1	9.3
	Medium	40.9	9.3	20.0	13.1	16.7
	High	64.1	8.6	9.1	8.9	9.3

Finally, it should be mentioned that additional analyses with respect to the route, the ship, and the class that the passengers travel at, do not differentiate the basic conclusions of the previous cluster analysis, and do not suggest any other segregation of the clientele (Grigoroudis et al., 1999b).

In general, it seems that the lack of competition and the credibility criterion are responsible for the satisfactory global performance of the company. However, the company should engage itself in the aforementioned particular improvement efforts in order to face the oncoming strong competition.

8.3 Analyzing Satisfaction for a Publishing Company

8.3.1 Introduction

Scientific research in the sector of press readability and specifically magazines is not particularly extensive. However, all relative research indicates that reader satisfaction is a complex, multi-variable experience, which constitutes the resultant of a rich bunch of distinguishable dimensions. Research that was held in 2001 in the USA with the support of the Newspaper Association of America and the American Society of Newspaper Editors indicated the existence of four "cornerstones" of reader satisfaction: content, brand, service excellence and constructive culture. Research in 100 USA magazines attributed a classification of 39 dimensions of reader satisfaction (Calder et al., 2003).

The presented application focuses on planning a reader-oriented strategy for a publishing company using the MUSA methodology (Alexopoulos et al., 2006). The analysis of reader satisfaction concerns RAM, the leading IT monthly magazine in Greece established in 1988. RAM extracted fast the first rank in circulation, with a significant range from the second magazine onwards, among all rival publications. It has kept up this leading role in its entire "circle" as product. During the time of the survey (May 2005), RAM circulation in Greece was 45,000 copies. The importance of developing a new reader-oriented strategy is justified by the increasing intensity of RAM's main competitors. Alexopoulos et al. (2006) present analytically the market conditions as well as RAM's current strategy.

In order to access the reader satisfaction criteria set, the following sources of information were used:

- reader comments through a preliminary satisfaction survey,
- management opinions, collected and ascertained through personal interviews, and
- relevant literature (Carlson, 1985; Katcher, 1995; Calder et al., 2003; Calder and Malthouse, 2004).

The main satisfaction dimensions reflect the following:

- *Culture*: It refers to the magazine's objectivity, its publishing independence, its response to the reader's needs and expectations, the variety and range in content coverage, the effectiveness in the management of change and the degree of participation in notion cultivation.
- *Content*: It concerns the magazine's editorial content disaggregated into editorials, science and technology columns, news reports, user guides, comparative tests, market guide, IT introductory books, special supplements (IT for kids, digital photography, IT for SMEs, games and gadgets), CD-ROM content, internet content and advertising content.
- *Bonus material*: It comprises occasional presents (such as books and movies), and free software applications.
- *Manageability and aesthetics*: This criterion refers to the functionality of the magazine issue as a "package", the manageability of its structure, the aesthetics of pages layout and cover, and also the quality of printing and paper used.
- *Price*: It refers to the reader's satisfaction from issue price and subscription price.
- *Disposition and distribution*: It concerns the extent of the distribution network (area coverage), the efficiency of this network and also the satisfaction from the subscription services.
- *Customer care*: It refers to the reader's satisfaction regarding complaint management, replacement of defective magazine issues or CD-ROM disks, and also telephone reader care/problem-solving services.

The entire customer value hierarchy counts of 7 main criteria and 32 subcriteria (for more details see Alexopoulos et al., 2006).

The questionnaire was included and distributed to readers along with RAM issue of May 2005 (a total of 45,000 questionnaires). The final sample consists of 893 readers (response rate almost 2%) and covers different customer segments according to age, sex, income, education, geographical area, etc.

8.3.2 Main Results

As shown in Table 8.7, the average overall satisfaction index is 94.5%, which is consistent with the high satisfaction indices appearing for the most of the main criteria. However, the readers of RAM magazine appear less satisfied regarding the criteria of "Price", "Bonus material", and "Customer care" (average satisfaction indices of 55%, 74%, and 77%, respectively).

The action diagram of Figure 8.9 shows that there is no significant gap between what readers want (importance) and what readers get (performance). Consequently, it appears that the criteria of "Content", "Manageability and aesthetics", and "Culture" are the relative advantages of the magazine, while the criteria of "Price", "Bonus material", and "Customer care" appear as the most significant weak points. Although readers do not consider these criteria as important (they are located in the "Status quo" quadrant), improvement efforts should be focused on these, mainly due to their relatively low demanding level.

Regarding the satisfaction subcriteria, the results of the MUSA method presented in Table 8.8 reveal the following:

- With respect to the "Content" criterion, a leverage opportunity appears for "News reports", "Consultation and user guides", and "IT introductory books".
- On the other hand, regarding the same criterion, an action opportunity arises for the improvement, firstly of the magazine's website, and secondly, for "Comparative tests", "Digital Photography" supplement, "Knowledge, science and technology columns", and "Editorials".
- Moreover, the expensive "ramkid" (IT for kids) supplement has a relatively high satisfaction index, while generally readers do not consider it important.
- Similarly, regarding the "Bonus Material" criterion, there is a leverage opportunity for "Presents", while unnecessary effort appears to be given to "Software applications".

Table 8.7 Criteria satisfaction results

Criteria	Weight (%)	Average Satisfaction Index (%)
Culture	14.7	94.2
Content	50.1	98.1
Bonus material	4.3	74.0
Manageability and aesthetics	17.1	96.9
Price	4.1	55.0
Disposition and distribution	5.0	87.9
Customer care	4.7	77.0
Overall	-	94.5

- Another interesting finding related to the "Price" criterion: the "Issue price" subcriterion has a weight of 94.6% and an average satisfaction index of 85.8%. Thus, management may consider funding a reader-oriented improvement of the magazine by increasing current issue price (€7.5), since price elasticity appears rather high.

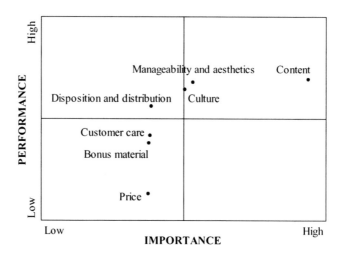

Fig. 8.9 Action diagram for main satisfaction criteria

Using the results of this study, the editor of RAM did decide to proceed to a number of changes in the magazine's editorial strategy. These changes included the following:

- Develop a separate publication issue of "ramkid" specifically focused on kids (it is located in the "Transfer recourses" quadrant, having a relatively high performance and a low importance level according to the previous results).
- Cancel the publication of "Financial RAM" supplement (according to this study, it has one of the smallest weights among the sub-criteria of "Content" and also a moderate average satisfaction index).
- Use the resources savings based on the aforementioned changes to reinforce "Consultation and user guides" and "IT introductory books" supplements (the study indicates them as a leverage opportunity).

As emphasized by Alexopoulos et al. (2006), these changes were very successful in terms of circulation and revenues during a time period of decline for other Greek IT magazines (circulation was boosted nearly 20%, while advertising profits were also significantly increased).

Table 8.8 Criteria satisfaction analysis

Criteria	Subcriteria	Weight (%)	Average Satisfaction Index (%)
Culture	Credibility, objectivity and publishing independence	5.0	85.0
	Response to reader's needs and expectations	20.2	95.3
	Variety, range and completeness in content coverage	6.2	88.6
	Suppleness, change management	64.2	99.8
	Cultivation of participation notion	4.4	67.8
Content	Editorials	5.1	85.4
	Knowledge, science and technology columns	5.8	90.7
	News reports	25.6	97.0
	Consultation and user guides	10.9	92.3
	Comparative tests	6.3	88.9
	Market guide	4.3	74.5
	Ramkid (IT for kids supplement)	4.5	80.3
	Financial RAM (IT for SME supplement)	4.5	70.6
	bit (games and gadgets supplement)	4.6	74.9
	ΨΦ (digital photography supplement)	5.9	86.7
	IT introductory books	9.7	91.1
	CD-ROM content	4.3	74.0
	www.in.gr/RAM	4.1	66.6
	Advertising content	4.4	66.5
Bonus material	Presents	91.0	95.0
	Software applications	9.0	83.7
Manageability and aesthetics	Functionality of the issue package	8.0	92.3
	Manageability of magazine structure (contents-entities)	81.9	99.0
	Content Pages/cover aesthetics	5.3	91.4
	Paper and printing quality	4.8	92.7
Price	Issue price	94.6	85.8
	Subscription price	5.4	58.5
Disposition and distribution	Extend of distribution network (area coverage)	80.0	98.9
	Efficiency of distribution network	12.8	94.2
	Subscription services	7.2	85.8
Customer care	Complaint management-Replacement of defective issues or CD-ROM disks	50.3	93.5
	Telephone reader care-Problem solving	49.7	95.7

8.3.3 Developing New Publishing Strategies

The new reader-oriented strategies presented in this section are based on a segmentation satisfaction analysis applied on different customer groups in order to identify distinguished preferences and expectations.

According to the demographics of the sample, the group of students is rather small in the total population of RAM readers (approximately 18%). This group gives completely different importance to the satisfaction criteria (main criteria and subcriteria) compared to the total sample of readers (see Tables 8.9 and 8.10). Thus, a single strategy that would be able to sufficiently cover both customer groups does not exist.

Table 8.9 Criteria weights and average satisfaction indices (for students)

Criteria	Weight (%)	Average Satisfaction Index (%)
Culture	5.3	85.5
Content	52.3	98.7
Bonus material	4.3	74.5
Manageability and aesthetics	14.3	97.6
Price	4.1	47.7
Disposition and distribution	14.3	96.3
Customer care	5.4	80.8

Table 8.10 Comparison of "Content" subcriteria weights (students vs. all readers)

Criteria	Weight (all readers) (%)	Weight (students only) (%)
Editorials	5.1	41.4
Knowledge and science columns	5.8	4.8
News reports	25.6	4.6
Consultation and user guides	10.9	5.2
Comparative tests	6.3	5.2
Market guide	4.3	4.2
Ramkid (IT for kids)	4.5	4.2
Financial RAM (IT for SME)	4.5	4.3
bit (games and gadgets)	4.6	4.4
ΨΦ (digital photography)	5.9	4.6
IT introductory books	9.7	4.4
CD-ROM content	4.3	4.2
www.in.gr/RAM	4.1	4.1
Advertising content	4.4	4.4

Therefore, a separate edition of an IT magazine focused on students (e.g. "RAM for students") seems like an opportunity for the editor. Students reflect, as leverage opportunity of RAM, the criterion "Content" and would like "RAM for students" to have the lowest possible price, well looked-after "Editorials", "Consultation and user guides", and "Comparative tests". In order to apply this particular strategy, resources could be transferred from actions involved in "Knowledge, science and technology columns", "News reports", "bit", "Digital Photography", and "IT introductory books".

Another important customer segment that seems to have a distinguished preference system refers to women. The participation of this group in the total population of RAM readers is also small (approximately 11%). Tables 8.11 and 8.12 show the estimated weights and average satisfaction indices for women, as well as the comparison of subcriteria weights with the total sample of readers, regarding the magazine's content. These results suggest that "women" is a segment with characteristics that divert significantly from the rest of the population.

Table 8.11 Criteria weights and average satisfaction indices (for women)

Criteria	Weight (%)	Average Satisfaction Index (%)
Culture	50.7	98.5
Content	17.0	95.6
Bonus material	4.2	76.4
Manageability and aesthetics	14.3	96.6
Price	4.2	57.2
Disposition and distribution	4.8	88.3
Customer care	4.8	79.3

Based on the aforementioned findings, a separate edition of an IT magazine focused on women appears as an important market need. Women reflect, as leverage opportunity of RAM, firstly the criterion "Culture" and then the criteria "Content" and "Manageability and aesthetics". Moreover, price elasticity is relatively high for this customer group. According to their preferences, the subcriteria "Editorials", "News reports", "CD-ROM applications", "IT introductory books", and "Consultation and user guides" appear as leverage opportunities of "Content". To effectively financing this separate edition, resources may be transferred from "Knowledge, science and technology columns", "Comparative tests" and "Digital Photography".

Table 8.12 Comparison of "Content" subcriteria weights (women vs. all readers)

Criteria	Weight (all readers) (%)	Weight (women only) (%)
Editorials	5.1	23.0
Knowledge and science columns	5.8	5.1
News reports	25.6	9.6
Consultation and user guides	10.9	7.1
Comparative tests	6.3	5.1
Market guide	4.3	4.7
Ramkid (IT for kids)	4.5	4.7
Financial RAM (IT for SME)	4.5	5.1
bit (games and gadgets)	4.6	4.7
ΨΦ (digital photography)	5.9	4.7
IT introductory books	9.7	7.8
CD-ROM content	4.3	9.6
www.in.gr/RAM	4.1	4.4
Advertising content	4.4	4.4

8.4 Longitudinal Customer Satisfaction Analysis

8.4.1 Introduction

Internet access services are a rapidly growing business sector worldwide, taking advantage of the major technological progress. In most of the cases, this sudden increase has caused a strong price and product competition (Chiou, 2004). This competition is leading some Internet Service Providers (ISPs) to provide free Internet access to attract customers, adopting, at the same time, a "mass customization" strategy, individualizing Internet access services.

Regarding subscription businesses such as ISPs, cable TV operators, and telecommunications network operators, holding onto valuable customers and attracting new ones is a never-ending challenge (Kon et al., 2007). Unlike other cases related with technological products (e.g. personal computers) where consumers face a rather simple purchase decision problem (i.e. buy or not buy), customer behavior in the aforementioned sectors is quite different. For example, ISP customers usually sign a contract and, during this period, if the provided service is not satisfactory, they can discontinue the subscription and switch to competitor providers. This switching behavior is rather complex, and for this reason, conflicting theoretical approaches, addressing it, may be found in the literature (Cai et al., 1998; Madden et al., 1999; Ross, 2002; Kon et al., 2007).

The main aim of the application presented in this section is to discuss a framework for analyzing changes of customer preferences. It should be noted that the principal objective is not to perform long-range comparisons, which will give the ability to evaluate particular customer preferences trends, but rather to analyze short-term changes, given the unstable conditions of the ISP market. Thus, the presented results focus mainly on demonstrating how several tools, like perceptual maps, may be used in order to analyze changes of customer preferences. For the purposes of the presented study, two independent customer satisfaction surveys have been conducted in different time periods on behalf of one of the major ISP in Greece. However, the presented framework may be adopted by the other business organizations operating in similar market conditions (e.g. by subscription business sectors as mentioned before). The analyses are based on non-parametric statistical techniques, as well as on the MUSA method (Grigoroudis et al., 2007b).

8.4.2 Research Background

Internet usage in Greece has been significantly expanded during the last years, although there is a large lag compared to other European countries (ICAP, 2005). The percentage of Internet usage has been doubled between 2001 and 2004 (from 10% in 2001 to almost 20% in 2004). The limited adoption of information technology may justify the previous findings, since only 25% of the population uses a personal computer, while almost 70% uses mobile telephony. Besides, ISPs in Greece are currently paying significant efforts in order to increase broadband Internet usage, although the cost of these services is still relatively high. Apart from limitations by the available technological infrastructure and the government initiatives and incentives to businesses, the behavior of users is one of the most important drivers for this relatively low level of Internet usage. Therefore, it is important to perform an in-depth analysis of current customer preferences and to examine the factors that influence customer loyalty intensions, so that struggling companies might design more effective customer retention strategies (Xanthidis and Nicholas, 2004).

The Greek ISP sector is highly competitive due to the limitations of the market size, as already noted, and the large number of companies offering Internet services. Most of these companies also offer additional telephony services (PSTN: Public Switched Telephone Network, mobile telephony), as well as advanced technology and informatics applications (web hosting, frame relay, VPN: Virtual Private Network, etc.). For these reasons, the ISP market is heavily affected by the market conditions of other related sectors (e.g. telecommunications), as shown by recent mergers and acquisitions (ICAP, 2005). Furthermore, it should be emphasized that market conditions change rapidly due to major technological progress (e.g. ADSL: Asymmetric Digital Subscriber Line broadband Internet access).

However, despite these unstable conditions in the Greek ISP sector, the market size has increased significantly during the last years. The number of Internet subscribers in Greece has increased more than ten times in the last 7 years (from 61,000 subscribers in 1998 to 790,000 in 2004). These findings show an average annual market increase rate of almost 60%. The total value of the ISP market is estimated to be more than 300 million Euros during 2004 (ICAP, 2005).

The structure of the ISP sector in Greece is more complicated, since it includes a large number of non-profit organizations offering Internet services to users (individuals or companies) under special conditions (e.g. scientific or commercial chambers). Also, a national network of research and technology offers free of charge Internet access to more than 85 universities and research institutions in Greece. This particular number of Internet users (professors, researchers, students) is not included in the real size of the market, although it counted more than 300,000 users in 2004.

The ISP sector is also characterized by a highly concentration: the three larger companies have more than 65% of the market, while more than 30 other companies have market shares varying between 0.2% and 1.2%. Furthermore, it should be noted that the market is dominated by the public ISP/PSTN carrier (with market share more than 40%), which creates strong "monopolistic" conditions since the other ISPs should use this public network in order to provide Internet connection to their customers (Xanthidis and Nicholas, 2004).

Conclusively, the aforementioned findings show that the ISP sector is characterized by a highly competitive market of rather limited size, consisting of a large number of operating companies. Competition is focused on price, as well as on product, through "mass customization" strategies, individualizing services and approaching every customer in an individual way.

8.4.3 Customer Survey

The determination of e-service quality measures is a major problem in customer behavior literature, since traditional approaches, like Servqual (Parasuraman et al., 1985; 1988) do not fit well in the case of online services. These traditional approaches are based on interactive processes between customers and service providers through either face to face meeting or traditional communication media (e.g. telephone, fax, etc.). Recently, new approaches, like Esqual (Parasuraman et al., 2005), have been proposed in order to overcome these difficulties. Cai and Jun (2003) present an extensive review and an excellent discussion about customer perceptions and service quality dimensions for the online service environment.

The assessment of the satisfaction criteria used in this survey is mainly based on previous research efforts (Wetzel, 2001; Kyriazopoulos et al., 2006), as well as on an interactive communication process with the managers of the organization. Internet service quality dimensions that are able to affect switching behavior and customer loyalty have also been considered (Kon et al., 2007).

This customer value hierarchy is shown in Figure 8.10, and consists of the following main satisfaction dimensions (Grigoroudis et al., 2007b):

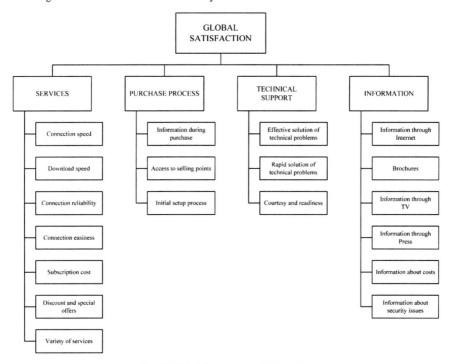

Fig. 8.10 Satisfaction criteria hierarchy

- *Services*: Main technical service characteristics (connection speed, download speed, connection reliability, etc.), cost-related characteristics (subscription cost, discount, special offers), as well as variety of provided services.
- *Purchase process*: Characteristics of the purchase process, like access to selling points, information during purchase, initial setup process, etc.
- *Technical support*: Provided support and solution to technical problems (quickness, effectiveness), as well as employee behavior (courtesy, readiness, etc.).
- *Information*: Main characteristics of the information offered to customers about cost, security, etc., through Internet, brochures, TV, and press.

For the purposes of the analysis, two separate surveys have been conducted on behalf of one of the major ISP in Greece, during summer 2004 and spring 2005. The final sample consists of more than 1,400 questionnaires; 682 subscribers participated in the 2004 survey, while 721 subscribers participated in the 2005 survey.

All necessary information has been collected through personal interviews with the customers, applying a random sampling process. Moreover, an anonymous questionnaire has been used in both of these surveys, having the same structure, in order to collect comparable input data.

The most important descriptive statistical results that seem unvarying during this period and may formulate a customer profile are:

- Despite the fact that a single subscription may be used by several family members, customers are mainly highly educated (45% have a University degree) and males (almost 65% of the sample).
- The most preferred places of Internet connection are home and work. Moreover, more than 60% of the customers prefer to use their Internet subscription in order to find business information and communicate (e.g. email, chat).

Additional analyses have also revealed important changes of customer profile, which are mainly caused by recent technological changes in the Greek ISP market. As a consequence, average customer age and Internet usage have increased. Furthermore, although the percentage of dialup customers is still high (more than 40% during 2005), ADSL subscribers have increased by 240% (from 5% to 17% during the last year). Generally, the 2005 results show that customers increasingly prefer higher connection speed. Additional results and discussion are given by Grigoroudis et al. (2007b) and Kyriazopoulos et al. (2006).

8.4.4 Statistical Analysis

The main objective of the presented statistical analysis is to test changes on customer judgments, rather than to evaluate an overall (or partial) satisfaction level. It should be emphasized that performed analysis should respect the qualitative type of the collected information (i.e. ordinal data).

Overall customer judgments for both years are given in Figure 8.11, where it is shown that almost 80% are "very satisfied" or "satisfied". Furthermore, as shown in Table 8.13, customers appear rather satisfied by the main characteristics of the service offered. However, although the percentage of "very dissatisfied" and "dissatisfied" customers is low, the number of subscribers having a neutral or a high satisfaction level varies among these main criteria.

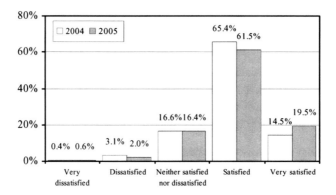

Fig. 8.11 Global satisfaction frequencies

Table 8.13 Main criteria satisfaction frequencies (%)

Year	Satisfaction levels	Services	Purchase process	Technical Support	Information
2004	Very satisfied	8.7	14.4	11.1	4.8
	Satisfied	56.0	56.7	44.4	42.4
	Neither satisfied nor dissatisfied	29.9	26.4	39.7	43.3
	Dissatisfied	4.8	2.1	3.1	7.9
	Very dissatisfied	0.6	0.4	1.6	1.6
2005	Very satisfied	13.2	12.9	11.7	4.2
	Satisfied	55.9	51.1	44.8	40.3
	Neither satisfied nor dissatisfied	26.7	31.7	36.5	44.2
	Dissatisfied	3.8	3.5	6.3	10.3
	Very dissatisfied	0.4	0.7	0.7	1.0

Additional results concerning subcriteria satisfaction may also help to justify previous findings. In particular, customer judgment frequencies for the detailed service dimensions (see satisfaction criteria hierarchy in Figure 8.10) show that 55-75% of the customers are "very satisfied" or "satisfied" regarding almost the whole set of satisfaction subcriteria. Exceptions to this finding may be summarized in the following:

- Customers appear less satisfied regarding the cost-related dimensions. For example, 23% of the customers are "very dissatisfied" or "dissatisfied" and 37% of the customers are "very satisfied" or "satisfied" by the subscription cost in the 2004 survey (18% and 42% respectively for the 2005 survey). Also, while the number of dissatisfied customers concerning the discount criterion appears to have decreased (17% and 15% in the 2004 and 2005 surveys, respectively), the number of satisfied customers regarding this particular subcriterion has also been decreased (46% and 44% in the 2004 and 2005 surveys, respectively).
- Customers appear rather dissatisfied by the technical support of the provider. 11-13% of the customers are "very dissatisfied" or "dissatisfied" by the effective and rapid solution of technical problems during both years. Moreover, while the number of satisfied customers regarding solution effectiveness has decreased (from 51% in 2004 to 49% in 2005), the number of satisfied customers by the speed of technical response has increased (from 46% in 2004 to 47% in 2005).
- The information-related subcriteria appear to have the highest level of dissatisfaction compared to all other satisfaction dimensions. 15-25% of the customers are "very dissatisfied" or "dissatisfied" by the provided information (through Internet, TV, press, brochures, etc.) in both years, while the percentage of satisfied customers varies between 34% and 50%.

Although satisfaction frequencies do not appear very different between these years, there are some notable variations, which, however, are not able to reveal a potential trend. Moreover, these variations are not able to indicate a real change on customer satisfaction regarding each particular service characteristic, because mainly of the ordinal nature of data. Moreover, it is not easy to decide which amount of difference indicates a significant change of customer preferences.

For these reasons, non-parametric statistical analysis has been also used in order to examine potential changes on customer judgments. Particularly, the Kolmogorov-Smirnov test for 2 independent samples has been applied on distribution functions of customer satisfaction judgments (global, criteria, subcriteria). The two-sample Kolmogorov-Smirnov test is used to test whether 2 independent samples of an ordinal variable come from the same sample, or can be considered to be significantly different.

The results of the Kolmogorov-Smirnov test are presented in Tables 8.14 and 8.15, and are focused on the following:

- The overall customer satisfaction and the satisfaction concerning the main criteria of services, technical support and information have not changed during these years. However, there is a difference for satisfaction judgments concerning purchase process (assuming a 10% significance level).
- Almost all of the subcriteria satisfaction frequencies do not appear different in the 2004 and 2005 surveys. Nevertheless, customer satisfaction concerning connection speed and information during process (in a 5% significance level) and download speed, connection reliability, initial setup process, and information about security issues (in a 10% significance level) seems to have changed during last year.

Table 8.14 Kolmogorov-Smirnov test (main criteria)

Criteria	Most extreme differences			K-S z value	Asymp. Sig. (2-tailed)
	Absolute	Positive	Negative		
Services	0.046	0.000	−0.046	0.849	0.466
Purchase process	0.071	0.071	0.000	1.319	0.062
Technical support	0.023	0.023	−0.009	0.435	0.992
Information	0.027	0.027	−0.006	0.502	0.962
Global	0.050	0.001	−0.050	0.934	0.347

The Kolmogorov-Smirnov test may also reveal the direction of potential changes, examining if the most extreme differences are positive or negative. However, it should be noted that this test is a univariate analysis that does not take into account that customer judgments formulate multivariate distribution functions. Furthermore, the problem of ties is very important in this type of analysis, given the 5-level ordinal scale used in the survey. Finally, alternative non-parametric statistical tests concerning hypothesis on cumulative distribution functions of customer judgments may also be used (like Mann-Whitney U test, Wald-Wolfowitz runs, etc.).

Table 8.15 Kolmogorov-Smirnov test (subcriteria)

Criteria	Subcriteria	Most extreme differences			K-S z value	Asymp. Sig. (2-tailed)
		Absolute	Positive	Negative		
Services	Connection speed	0.074	0.000	−0.074	1.389	0.042
	Download speed	0.071	0.000	−0.071	1.323	0.060
	Connection reliability	0.066	0.005	−0.066	1.236	0.094
	Connection easiness	0.051	0.000	−0.051	0.960	0.315
	Subscription cost	0.056	0.000	−0.056	1.048	0.222
	Discount and special offers	0.036	0.017	−0.036	0.671	0.760
	Variety of services	0.048	0.000	−0.048	0.894	0.401
Purchase process	Information during purchase	0.093	0.093	0.000	1.741	0.005
	Access to selling points	0.026	0.026	−0.026	0.494	0.968
	Initial setup process	0.071	0.071	0.000	1.326	0.059
Tech. support	Effective solution of technical problems	0.023	0.020	−0.023	0.424	0.994
	Rapid solution of technical problems	0.036	0.009	−0.036	0.665	0.769
	Courtesy and readiness	0.054	0.054	−0.023	1.013	0.256
Info	Information through Internet	0.056	0.056	−0.021	1.038	0.232
	Brochures	0.033	0.013	−0.033	0.625	0.829
	Information through TV	0.046	0.000	−0.046	0.867	0.440
	Information through Press	0.052	0.000	−0.052	0.969	0.305
	Information about costs	0.064	0.064	0.000	1.188	0.119
	Information about security issues	0.072	0.072	0.000	1.341	0.055

8.4.5 Satisfaction Analysis

The non-parametric statistical analysis shows if there are changes in customer judgments between the 2004 and 2005 surveys. However, the main question in this case remains: Do these changes lead to modification of customer preferences?

The satisfaction analysis presented in this section is based on the results provided by the MUSA method. Table 8.16 displays the most important results for overall and criteria customer satisfaction analysis, which may be summarized as follows:

- "Services" and "Information" are the criteria with the highest weights in both surveys, while customers do not seem to give importance to "Purchase process" and "Technical support".

- "Purchase process" is also the criterion with the highest average satisfaction index, while customers are more dissatisfied from "Information" in both years.
- The average global satisfaction index is not relatively high, which indicates significant improvement margins for the business organization. The same situation appears for particular satisfaction criteria, as well.
- Generally, it seems that there are no changes in customer preferences. This may be justified by applying a Chi-square test for homogeneity in these results (separately for satisfaction criteria weights and average satisfaction indices).

Table 8.16 Criteria weights and average satisfaction indices

Criteria	Weights (%)		Average satisfaction indices (%)	
	2004	2005	2004	2005
Services	36.0	38.0	71.7	74.7
Purchase process	20.0	18.0	82.3	78.5
Technical support	16.0	16.0	71.3	71.6
Information	28.0	29.0	63.4	64.1
Overall satisfaction	-	-	76.3	77.6

The detailed results for the whole set of satisfaction subcriteria are given in Table 8.17 and they show that customer preferences have been affected by the introduction of new services and the improvements on the technological aspects of service quality. A small increase of customer satisfaction may be noticed regarding the subcriteria of "Services", while the importance of these subcriteria appears unvarying. This may be justified by considering a potential increase of customer expectations, although the performance of these characteristics has been improved (e.g. connection speed and reliability, download speed, etc.). On the other hand, the weights of "Information during purchase" and "Initial setup process" have been increased, while customers appear less satisfied in these particular characteristics. The development of new products and the acquisition of new customers may explain these observed changes of subcriteria importance. Finally, all the subcriteria of "Technical support" and "Information" dimensions appear to have an equal importance level, while customer satisfaction varies between the examined years for these specific characteristics.

Action and improvement diagrams may also be very helpful for tracking changes of customer preferences. Figures 8.12 and 8.13 present these relative diagrams for the main satisfaction criteria. The diagrams indicate that there are no significant changes for the strong and the weak points of the ISP. However, "Services" is no more a critical criterion, since it is now located in the leverage opportunity quadrant (action diagram). Although the "Services" criterion is a strong point for the organization in the 2005 survey, it is the quality characteristic with the highest improvement priority (it is close to the 1st priority quadrant in the improvement diagram), mainly because now customers appear less demanding. Moreover, it is important to emphasize that "Information" remains a critical satisfaction dimension in both surveys, since it is located in the action opportunity quadrant (action diagram). On the other hand, as Figure 8.12 shows, the ISP seems to pay unnecessary attention to the "Purchase process" (it is located in the transfer resources quadrant in both surveys).

Table 8.17 Subcriteria weights and average satisfaction indices

Criteria	Subcriteria	Weights (%)		Average satisfaction indices (%)	
		2004	2005	2004	2005
Services	Connection speed	14.58	14.10	74.67	77.58
	Download speed	14.58	14.53	73.04	76.37
	Connection reliability	14.58	14.10	76.49	77.91
	Connection easiness	14.58	14.10	77.72	79.20
	Subscription cost	13.55	14.10	61.31	67.41
	Discount and special offers	13.54	14.10	65.00	68.37
	Variety of services	14.58	14.95	72.29	75.95
Purchase process	Information during purchase	26.13	29.71	76.40	73.70
	Access to selling points	47.74	39.98	87.74	83.75
	Initial setup process	26.13	30.31	78.31	76.33
Tech. support	Effective solution of technical problems	32.54	33.33	68.72	70.41
	Rapid solution of technical problems	33.73	33.33	68.87	69.72
	Courtesy and readiness	33.73	33.33	76.08	74.53
Info	Information through Internet	18.69	18.03	75.04	74.98
	Brochures	16.42	18.03	62.50	67.18
	Information through TV	15.50	16.48	55.87	62.87
	Information through Press	15.49	16.32	55.03	60.19
	Information about costs	17.36	15.85	64.76	59.41
	Information about security issues	16.54	15.28	64.55	58.19

A similar analysis can be also performed for the detailed satisfaction subcriteria. Figures 8.14 and 8.15 show the location of satisfaction subcriteria in action and improvement diagrams in 2004 and 2005 surveys. The most important findings for the ISP may be focused on the following:

- "Access to selling points" remains a strong point for the organization, revealing a good performance regarding the network of retail stores. Furthermore, new strong points of the ISP appear in the 2005 survey, concerning mainly the technological dimensions of the provided services (connection speed, reliability, and easiness, download speed, initial setup process, and variety of services). These satisfaction subcriteria may be used as a competitive advantage by the company.

- The technical support seems improved in the 2005 survey, since "Rapid solution of technical problems" is no more a critical satisfaction dimension, although it is still one of the first improvement priorities (due to significant improvement margins). However, cost-related subcriteria (subscription cost, discount and special offers) appear now in the action opportunity quadrant. These results may indicate a shift from quality to price competition in the ISP market.

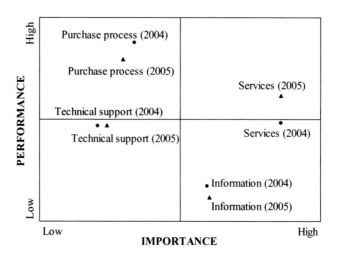

Fig. 8.12 Action diagram (2004-2005)

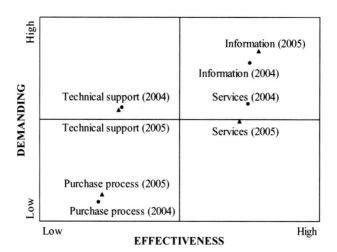

Fig. 8.13 Improvement diagram (2004-2005)

- Particular information-related subcriteria (information during process or though Internet) are still located in the transfer resources quadrant. This means that the ISP continues to pay unnecessary attention to these attributes, although company's resources may be used to improve the critical satisfaction criteria.
- Figure 8.15 reveals also some new critical improvement priorities: "Connection easiness", "Subscription cost", "Effective solution of technical problems", and "Brochures". Customers appear less demanding in these particular satisfaction dimensions, and thus potential improvement efforts may have greater effectiveness.

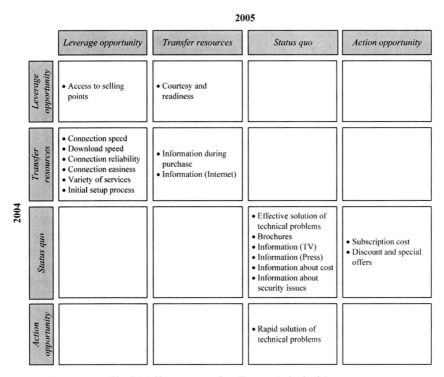

Fig. 8.14 Changes on action diagram (subcriteria)

8.4.6 Concluding Remarks

The analytical results and findings of the presented study confirm the importance of measuring service quality and analyzing customer satisfaction perceptions, and suggest for the ISPs the following:

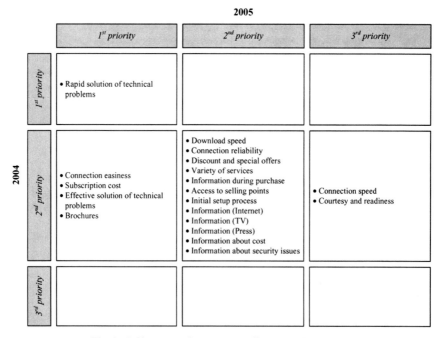

Fig. 8.15 Changes on improvement diagram (subcriteria)

- The performance of ISPs in specific service quality characteristics should be always analyzed by considering also the importance that customers give to these service dimensions. Based on the results of the action diagram (Figure 8.12), a significant gap appears concerning the quality perceived and the quality received (i.e. what customers want and what customers get). Particularly, ISPs should pay much more attention on the information given to customers, instead of using company resources to increase the performance of their purchase process.
- The improvement actions of ISPs for particular service quality characteristics may be based on customer dissatisfaction, but they should take into account the customer demanding level, as well. For example, Figure 8.13 shows that customers appear less demanding on the "Purchase process" compared to the "Technical support" dimension. Thus, although customer satisfaction level is similar to these quality characteristics, ISPs should give priority to the improvement of their purchase process.
- Analyzing changes of customer preferences may show how the strong and weak points of ISPs change over time. For example, as shown in Table 8.14, the importance of quality characteristics related to the technical aspects of provided services (e.g. speed, reliability, and setup process) have been increased, although customer satisfaction has not changed for these subcriteria. Thus,

without changing the performance of an ISP, particular quality characteristics may become competitive advantages (or weak points).

- The relatively low satisfaction level of particular information-related characteristics (information through TV, press, etc.) is an important finding for ISPs. This result may be justified by other studies proposing that information through media plays an important role on customer loyalty and new Internet technologies adoption (Choudrie and Dwivedi, 2006a; 2006b; Kon et al., 2007).
- Customers of Internet services appear to give lower importance to the personal transactions characteristics (e.g. solution of technical problems, courtesy and readiness of personnel), but higher importance to cost-related satisfaction criteria. This is an importance change for the ISP sector that should be further justified and analyzed in future research studies.

Although the presented study concerns the Greek ISP sector, the applied methodological framework may be useful for other business organizations offering e-services or having a subscription type of transactions. Thereby, in order to analyze potential detailed changes of customer perceptions, this study proposes the use of specialized quantitative techniques like multicriteria analysis and non-parametric statistics. Particularly, the additional available results provided by the MUSA method (i.e. action and improvement diagrams) may give managers a clearer view of customer perceptions.

8.5 Satisfaction Benchmarking and Segmentation Analysis

8.5.1 Research Background

The main aim of this application is to present a pilot customer satisfaction survey in the Cypriot private banking sector (Grigoroudis et al., 2002). The satisfaction survey has been conducted in several customer segments and in different branches of the banking organization as well. This approach gives the ability to perform customer segmentation and benchmarking analysis through the assessment of the critical satisfaction dimensions and the determination of customer groups with distinctive preferences and expectations.

It should be noted that the Cyprus domestic banking system can be divided into two groups of credit institutions (commercial banks and specialized credit institutions), while the Central Bank of Cyprus is the competent authority for monetary policy and for the regulation and supervision of banking. Banking in Cyprus has grown almost entirely through private initiatives and, with the exception of a few specialized credit institutions, it continues to be private. More specifically, private banks account for the 96% of banking assets, while only the remaining 4% belongs to government-controlled institutions.

During the last years, banks in Cyprus have been increasingly expanding and diversifying beyond the boundaries of traditional banking. Most of the banks have set up subsidiaries through which they provide a wide range of specialized financial services encompassing underwriting of equities and bonds, brokerage and trading of securities, investment advisory services, portfolio and asset management, venture-capital financing and leasing, etc. These facts verify the highly competitive conditions of the market environment and the need for measuring service quality.

8.5.2 Satisfaction Criteria and Survey Conduct

Based on previous applications of the MUSA method in the banking sector (Grigoroudis et al., 1999a; Mihelis et al., 2001), the set of satisfaction criteria used in the survey consists of:

- *Personnel of the bank*: This criterion includes all the characteristics concerning personnel (skills and knowledge, responsiveness, communication and collaboration with customers, friendliness, etc.).
- *Products*: This criterion refers mainly to the offered products and service (variety, refund, cost, special services, etc.).
- *Image of the bank*: Credibility of the bank (name, reputation), technological excellence, as well as ability to satisfy future customers' needs are included in this criterion.
- *Service*: This criterion refers to the service offered to the customers; it includes the appearance of the stores, the waiting time (queue, telephone, etc.), the complexity of service processes and the information provided (informing customers in an understandable way, explaining the service and other relevant factors, informing for new products, etc.).
- *Access*: Network expansion of the bank, branches location, as well as observed troubles in the service system (strikes, damaged ATMs, etc.) are included in this criterion.

The presented customer satisfaction survey took place in two different branches of a private Bank in Cyprus in the city-area of Nicosia. The survey was conducted during March 2000 and a stratified sampling procedure according to customer types (business/individual) was selected. Data collection was completed in-store using a simple anonymous questionnaire and it was based on a poll-driven process in order to minimize overestimation bias. Final input data consist of 200 questionnaires: 100 from branch A and 100 from branch B. Moreover, 170 individual and 30 business customers have participated in the survey.

8.5.3 Customer Profile

Descriptive statistics analysis is used in order to validate sampling results, as well to formulate a general customer profile for both banking branches (see Grigoroudis et al., 2002 for a detailed presentation).

Customers seem to use all banking products and services almost at the same extent, although savings accounts and credit cards consist more than 60% of the total banking activities. Figure 8.16 shows also that the usage of special services (leasing, factoring, investments, bank assurance, mutual funds, etc.) is quite satisfactory, representing the 18% of banking activities in both branches.

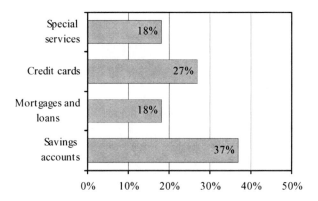

Fig. 8.16 Customer transactions

Comparison of the clientele in the two banking branches reveals that customers prefer branch A, when interested for special banking products and services (Figure 8.17). This fact is very important for customer profiling, given that the size of clientele in branch A is quite larger than in branch B, and that branch A is located in the central area of the city of Nicosia.

Table 8.18 presents the descriptive statistics results concerning global and partial customer satisfaction in both banking branches. It should be noted that the criteria do not use a uniform satisfaction scaling, in order to face the "positive shift" problem appearing in the distribution of customers' answers (Hill, 1996). The detailed results of Table 8.18 indicate the following:

- Generally, customers seem to be quite satisfied with the provided products and services in both banking branches, although potential improvement margins appear in several satisfaction dimensions.
- Customers of branch A seem less satisfied than those of branch B globally and in almost every criterion. The largest differences concern the criteria of personnel, image and access.

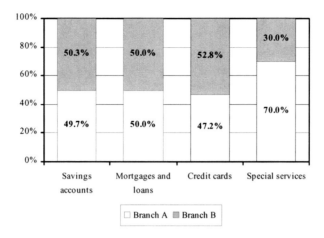

Fig. 8.17 Percentage of customer transactions per branch

Table 8.18 Overall and partial customer satisfaction per branch (% frequencies)

Criteria	Branch A			Branch B		
	Moderately Satisfied	Satisfied	Very Satisfied	Moderately Satisfied	Satisfied	Very Satisfied
Personnel	3	67	30	2	53	45
Products	7	68	25	3	68	29
Image	4	50	46	4	42	54
Service	6	63	31	5	64	31
Access	7	42	51	3	31	66
Overall	5	45	50	2	33	65

8.5.4 Customer Satisfaction Analysis

The results of the MUSA method show that the customers of branch A are less satisfied compared to the clientele of branch B. The average global satisfaction indices for banking branches A and B are 80.9% and 92.5%, respectively. These results can be justified by the criteria satisfaction analysis, from where the following points raise (Table 8.19):

- Branch A has lower partial satisfaction indices compared to branch B in all satisfaction dimensions, with an exception of the criteria of "Access" and "Image".
- The most significant difference appears in the criterion of "Personnel", where the average satisfaction level is more than 20% higher in branch A. The differences concerning the other satisfaction dimensions vary from 2.5% to 5.5% ap-

proximately, and they do not show a significant variation in the performance evaluation of the banking branches.
- Given the high competitive conditions of the market, the performance of particular satisfaction dimensions is not considered relatively high. In this context, the criteria of "Products" and "Service" show a significant potential improvement margin in both branches.
- The importance of the satisfaction criteria does not vary between the banking branches. Therefore, the criterion of "Personnel" is considered as the most important satisfaction dimension, having a weight of approximately 60%.
- The "Access" criterion is also considered important by the customers of both branches (importance level of approximately 20%), while the rest of the criteria do not show a significant importance.

Table 8.19 Weights and average satisfaction indices per branch

Criteria	Branch A		Branch B	
	Weight (%)	Average Satisfaction Index (%)	Weight (%)	Average Satisfaction Index (%)
Personnel	61.6	75.2	59.3	96.2
Products	5.5	68.1	5.8	73.4
Image	7.6	82.6	5.3	80.2
Service	7.8	71.2	6.4	75.1
Access	17.5	94.5	23.2	90.5
Overall	-	80.9	-	92.5

Combining criteria weights and satisfaction indices, the action diagrams presented in Figure 8.18 can be formulated for each banking branch. The detailed results of these diagrams reveal the following:

- The "Personnel" criterion appears as a critical satisfaction dimension for branch A, requiring immediate improvement efforts: it has the lowest average satisfaction index compared to the rest of the criteria, while it is considered as the most important criterion by customers.
- The "Personnel" and the "Access" criteria seem to be the competitive advantages of branch B.
- Although the offered "Products" and "Service" are not located in the critical quadrant of the action diagrams, they can be considered as potential critical factors for both branches: customers are not sufficiently satisfied, and if customers' satisfaction behavior changes in the future and the importance level raises, these criteria will require immediate improvement efforts.

Generally, the criterion of "Personnel' seems to differentiate the performance evaluation between the two branches. Customers prefer to visit branch A more often when interested in advanced banking products and services (see Figure 8.17). In this case, therefore, high skilled personnel is required, while at the same time customers appear rather demanding during their transactions with branch A. This justification indicates that improvement efforts should concern education and training of the personnel in branch A.

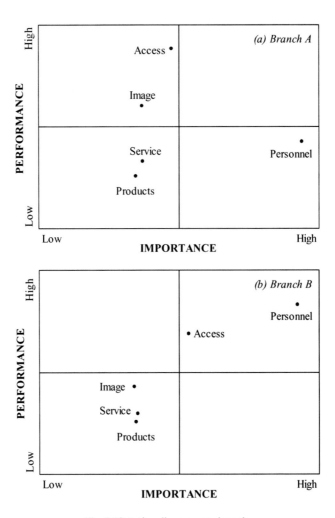

Fig. 8.18 Action diagrams per branch

Provided products and services in both branches should also be examined for improvement efforts. The main reason for the low satisfaction level is focused on the dissatisfaction of clients concerning the cost of provided banking products. All these improvement efforts should be developed taking into account the service quality offered by other banking organizations, though competitors' characteristics may indicate business excellence.

8.5.5 Satisfaction Segmentation Analysis

Identifying particular customer clusters with distinctive perceptions and expectations, in order to classify them according to their satisfaction behavior, is a rather difficult task. The most common approach is an "a priori" classification, in which a set of characteristic factors is assumed to be customers' discriminating variables. The problem is more difficult in the case of banking organizations, considering that classical discriminating variables are not always efficient for the segmentation of the total clientele.

The classification analysis presented in this application is based on a general classification according to the type of collaboration with the bank. So, the groups of individual and business customers are examined. This kind of classification is the most widely accepted, and is also accepted by all banking organizations when developing new products and services.

The global satisfaction analysis shows that the overall satisfaction level does not vary between individual and business customers, given that global average satisfaction index is 91.4% and 91.6%, respectively. However, significant variations are observed with regard to the satisfaction criteria, as shown in Table 8.20. The most important results from criteria comparison analysis are focused on the following points:

- Individual customers seem to be quite satisfied from the criterion of "Access", while the rest of the criteria have relatively low average satisfaction indices varying from 69% to 78%.
- On the other hand, the criteria of "Image" and "Service" have the higher average satisfaction indices for business customers, who, at the same time do not seem to be satisfied from the criteria of "Personnel", "Products" and "Access".
- Partial satisfaction comparison reveals that individual customers are more satisfied with regard to the criterion of "Access", while business customers show higher satisfaction for the "Service" criterion. The performance of the other satisfaction dimensions does not seem to vary between the two customer segments.
- Concerning the criteria weights, individual customers consider the criterion of "Access" as extremely important (importance level of approximately 80%), while the "Image" and "Service" criteria are the most important ones for business customers with significant weights of 60% and 19%, respectively.

The maldistribution of the sample for these particular customer segments (see also 7.3.3) may cause some inconsistency problems in relation to the analysis presented in the previous section. Furthermore, it should be emphasized that the low level of weights appearing for some particular satisfaction dimensions does not necessarily mean that these criteria are not important for the customers (see for example Kano's model).

The action diagrams of Figure 8.19 show that there are no critical satisfaction dimensions requiring immediate improvement for both customer segments. The detailed results from this Importance/Performance analysis are focused on the following points:

- The criterion of "Access" seems to be the most important competitive advantage for individual customers.
- Moreover, the "Products" and "Service" criteria can be considered as potential critical factors for individual customers.
- The "Products" offered and the criterion of "Access" could be potentially critical satisfaction dimensions for the business customers.
- On the other hand, the high global satisfaction level appearing for these customers is mainly due to the criterion of "Image", and more specifically the satisfaction perceived by the ability of the banking organization to satisfy business customers' future needs.

Table 8.20 Weights and average satisfaction indices per customer type

Criteria	Individual		Business	
	Weight (%)	Average Satisfaction Index (%)	Weight (%)	Average Satisfaction Index (%)
Personnel	6.1	77.8	6.7	79.2
Products	5.7	70.9	4.7	66.6
Image	5.3	78.2	59.9	98.3
Service	5.1	68.9	19.2	92.9
Access	77.8	96.4	9.5	68.2
Overall	-	91.4	-	91.6

8.5.6 Concluding Remarks

In this particular application, customer satisfaction evaluation has been applied in different customer segments, given that total banking clientele does not appear homogenous concerning its preferences and expectations. Since the MUSA method is a preference collective methodology, low homogeneity can cause stability problems in satisfaction analysis results.

Moreover, this segmentation analysis may identify particular groups of customers with distinctive preferences and expectations, and so, it may help the development of penetration strategies of the banking organization. Finally, satisfaction analysis in different branches of a bank may be considered as a valid and reliable benchmarking system, in which performance evaluation is not only based on internal organizational measures but also on customer judgments (e.g. financial performance).

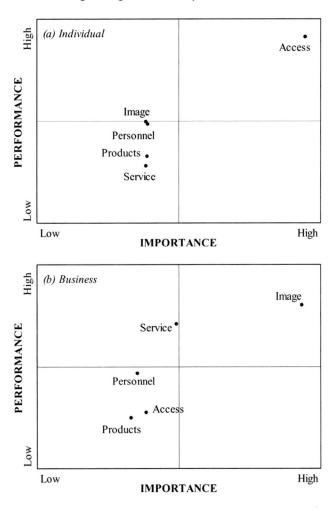

Fig. 8.19 Action diagrams per customer type

The discriminating variables that have been examined during customer satisfaction analysis are the type of customer (individual or business customer), and the visiting branch of the bank. Other discriminating variables that have been examined (age, marital status, income and offered banking products and services) have not shown significant variations (Grigoroudis et al., 2002).

8.6 Other Applications

8.6.1 An industry Satisfaction Barometer

The implementation of the MUSA method for evaluating a customer satisfaction barometer concerns the Greek airline industry. The pilot survey, conducted in the area of Athens during June 2001, was mainly focused on domestic flights. Due to mergers and acquisitions, it is important to mention that only 3 airline companies were operating in domestic flights, during the survey period. Final input data consist of almost 500 questionnaires, collected through personal interviews with customers.

An extensive preliminary consumer behavioral analysis defined 3 main satisfaction dimensions: satisfaction before, during and after flight. As presented in Table 8.21, these main dimensions are defined by a set of analytical quality characteristics/subcriteria.

The results presented in this section are based on a variation of the MUSA method serving as a customer satisfaction barometer model (see section 5.5.1). The results of Table 8.21 show that Greek customers are not satisfied from the provided service, given that the global average satisfaction index has a relatively low value (65.8%). Although the overall average satisfaction index for the quality characteristics during flight has the highest value (78.3%), customers appear very dissatisfied from the service offered before and after flight (average satisfaction indices 56.7% and 51.7%, respectively). Furthermore, satisfaction benchmarking analysis reveals that characteristics related with delays (punctuality, care/info during delays, waiting time on board) may differentiate airline companies. The average satisfaction indices of these quality characteristics show the highest variation within the airline industry (best/worst satisfaction index). Detailed results for the analytical satisfaction subcriteria are presented in Table 8.21 (see also Grigoroudis and Siskos, 2004).

The relative action diagram is shown in Figure 8.20, where all satisfaction subcriteria are presented according to their relative importance and performance (average satisfaction index). This grid can be used in order to identify priorities for improvement and shows that:

- The strong points of the Greek airline industry are focused on the safety standards and the personnel on board.
- The quality characteristics that can be considered as "threats" consist mainly of the price subcriterion and the attributes related with baggage service (handling, delivery time, company's reaction in case of damage/loss, etc.) and delays (punctuality, departure/arrival time, care/info during delays, etc.).

Table 8.21 Satisfaction indices for the Greek airline industry (%)

Service quality criteria		Industry index	Worst/Best index within the industry	
Before flight	Price	45.2	41.0	55.0
	Booking	72.3	68.0	82.2
	Personnel (ground)	73.5	68.0	86.2
	Check-in	69.3	65.0	79.3
	Care/Info during delays	38.0	27.0	63.5
	Departure/arrival times	60.8	58.0	67.4
	Punctuality	42.0	26.0	79.4
During flight	Safety standards	90.3	81.7	94.0
	Snacks and drinks	62.6	57.0	75.7
	Comfort	72.6	71.0	76.2
	Appearance of aircraft	71.6	67.0	82.4
	Personnel (on board)	86.3	83.0	94.0
	Travelling bag closet	71.3	69.5	72.0
	Noise level	65.9	61.0	68.0
After flight	Waiting time (on board)	62.6	58.0	73.4
	Delivery time (baggage)	49.6	44.0	62.6
	Baggage handling	50.3	46.0	60.4

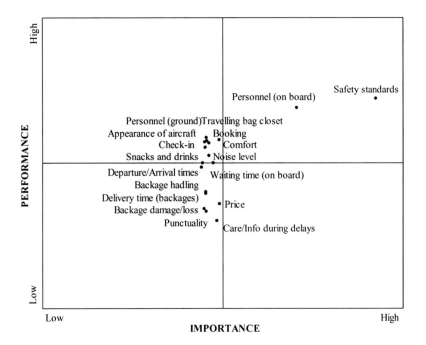

Fig. 8.20 Relative action diagram for the Greek airline industry

The development of a national or industry customer satisfaction barometer constitutes an important effort for determining an overall performance standard of companies and business organizations. The estimated indices usually provide a baseline against which it will be possible to track customer satisfaction over time. These results provide significant information to companies because customer satisfaction ultimately will affect customer retention and, therefore, profitability and competitiveness.

However, as emphasized by Grigoroudis and Siskos (2004), measurement approaches applied in this particular problem may simply provide a comparison standard that organizations have to analyze, considering other performance measures and built their own indicators, taking into account their present situation and strategy.

8.6.2 Application based on Kano's model

The main objective of the application presented in this section is to illustrate the methodology of section 5.4.2 and discuss the modeling of preferences on satisfaction criteria importance.

The applied methodological framework is based on the comparative examination of the relationship between stated and derived importance and consists of two major steps (Figure 8.21):

1. In the first step, stated and derived importance data are collected using a simple questionnaire containing importance and performance judgments (see Figures 4.7 and 5.3). The stated and derived importance of each criterion is estimated through different techniques. Particularly, through performance questions, customers are asked about the level of satisfaction/dissatisfaction from each criterion. Derived importance is then estimated by the original MUSA model. On the other hand, importance questions are used in order to estimate the stated importance on customer satisfaction criteria, using the model of section 4.1.

2. In the second step, stated and derived importance results are comparatively examined through a Dual Importance Diagram that defines different quality levels in agreement with Kano's approach and gives the ability to classify customer requirements (see Figure 5.5). It is possible to identify which attributes the customers rate as important and see how these agree with the truly important and truly unimportant attributes. Thus, it is also possible to determine expected, one-dimensional and attractive characteristics.

The application presented in this section concerns a graphic arts company located in the city of Rethymno (Greece). The survey was conducted during May 2003 and the major satisfaction criteria that were identified and examined are the following: "Quality of the Products", "Pricing", "Customer Service" and "Personnel". Data collection was completed using a simple anonymous questionnaire and final input data consist of 80 questionnaires. Further details of this survey may be found in Grigoroudis and Spyridaki (2003).

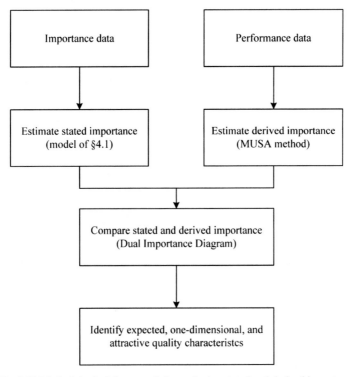

Fig. 8.21 Methodological framework for analyzing stated and derived importance

The final results including stated, as well as derived importance on satisfaction criteria are presented in Table 8.22. It is important to mention that additional analyses have been also performed, using mainly the alternative optimality criteria discussed in section 5.4.1, but no significant variation was found.

Table 8.22 Estimated stated and derived importance

Criteria	Stated importance (%)	Derived importance (%)
Quality	34.67	30.38
Pricing	27.12	18.63
Service	24.68	25.00
Personnel	13.54	26.00

In order to develop the dual importance diagram, these results have been normalized, using the normalization approach of the original MUSA diagrams (see sections 4.3.5-4.3.6). As shown in Figure 8.22, there is an agreement between the stated and the derived importance for the criterion of "Quality" since it is considered of high importance in both cases. On the other hand, it seems to be a disagreement between the stated and the derived importance for the criteria of "Pricing" and "Personnel". The "Pricing" is considered very important when the customers are asked freely and its weight is comparatively low when estimated by the MUSA method. The opposite may be observed for the criterion of "Personnel". The criterion of "Service" should be further examined, since it is rather difficult to ascertain in which quadrant is exactly located.

Based on the previous results, potential management efforts may be focused on "Quality" and "Personnel" since they are the truly important dimensions according to the MUSA model. Additionally, the graphic arts company should focus its marketing efforts mainly on "Quality" and "Pricing". These are the two most important criteria according to the customers' stated judgments.

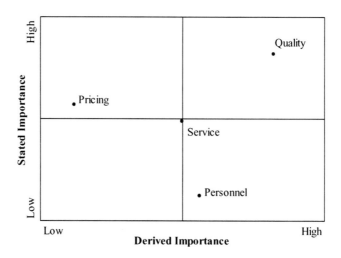

Fig. 8.22 Dual importance diagram for the main satisfaction criteria

Interpreting Figure 8.22 as a dual importance diagram, it is obvious that the criterion of "Quality", which appears in quadrant (i), is one-dimensional (truly important) attribute. This means that an increase in the performance of this criterion will necessarily lead to an increase of customer satisfaction. The criterion of "Personnel" is located in quadrant (ii), which includes the attractive attributes. Thus, a high performance in this particular criterion will lead to high satisfaction, while a low performance will not necessarily imply a low level of customer satisfaction. Finally, the criterion of "Pricing" is located in quadrant (iv), which refers to the attractive attributes. This means that a high performance in this particular criterion will not necessarily imply a high level of customer satisfaction, while a low performance can really cause dissatisfaction.

Chapter 9
Customer Satisfaction and Information Systems

9.1 IT-based Customer Service

Modern technology of information systems offers numerous alternatives for managing relations/transactions between companies and customers. Most of these systems are focused on customer service, while their satisfaction evaluation capabilities are rather limited. This is mainly explained by the lack of methods and techniques purely oriented to customer satisfaction measurement, and the availability of several statistical packages and data analysis applications that solve this particular problem.

The aim of customer service information systems is mainly to satisfy customer requirements or manage customer complaints. In general, the primary requirements expressed by the customers during their transaction with business organizations are (Loris, 1998):

- direct resolution of technical or other problems related to particular product/service,
- on line access to technical or other information provided by the company, and
- ability to provide interactive support.

The type and content of the interaction offered by these information systems depend heavily on the extent and level of the access provided by the business organization. As Figure 9.1 shows, the interaction levels may be as follows (Sterne, 1996):

1. *Product information*: It is the most elementary form of access provided by a business organization with no interaction capabilities.
2. *Problem resolution*: In this particular non continuous form of communication, the customer is able to submit specific questions/requests mainly for technical problems.

3. *Access to people*: This access level refers to the communication ability with specific departments or company employees. However, still no interaction can take place.
4. *Access to process*: This is the most complex form of communication. It supports interaction and provides the customers with the ability to be involved and get information about the service processes of the company (placement and search of orders, monitoring of transactions, etc.).

This progression of giving the customer more and more access to product information, problem resolution information, people and processes may be characterized as customer integration.

Another important feature of modern customer service information systems is their integration/cooperation capability with other software applications installed in business organizations (i.e. office automation systems, accounting applications, electronic filing systems, electronic data interchange systems, etc.), as shown in Figure 9.2. The aim of this approach is to integrate the customer-related information, in order to achieve an optimal coordination of the company's departments and processes.

Furthermore, modern customer service information systems are characterized by the automation of the communication procedures to the maximum possible extent. This automation feature is able to reduce operating costs and increase company's productivity level. Finally, it should be noted that these particular systems ensure, at a satisfactory level, the independency between the communication process with the customers and the medium used.

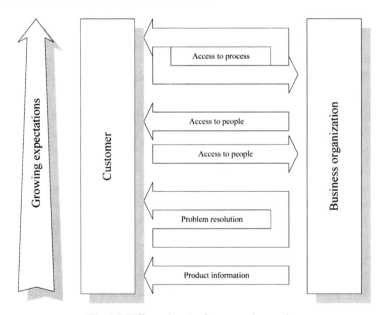

Fig. 9.1 Different levels of customer integration

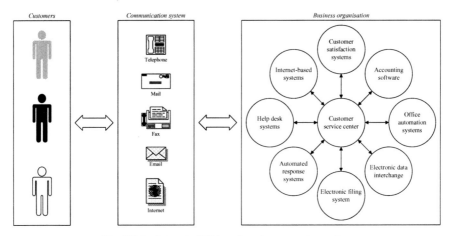

Fig. 9.2 An integrated IT-based customer service system

9.2 Customer Service Systems

9.2.1 Helpline Systems

The majority of these systems refers to the customer service centers (help-desk/helpline systems, call centers). Typical examples of this case are the call centers with free of charge phone lines to the customers, various systems for complaints recording and management, and helpline systems offering forms of continuous communication with customers.

These systems have been significantly developed within the few last years and are broadly used in business organizations, especially in the service sector (Kendall, 1997). It should be noted that it is rather difficult to categorize these systems, since they are based on different platforms, they apply different technologies and they focus on different problems of business organizations.

Helpline systems are combined with other commercial software applications usually installed in organizations such as office automation systems (word processors, spreadsheets, database management systems, etc.), accounting applications, electronic document filing (mail, protocol, etc.), and communications software (fax, Internet, e-mail, etc.) in order to create an integrated communication environment for the management and the analysis of customer-related information (Cogan, 1997). In many cases, this integration process is particularly difficult because there are no widely accepted communications standards, although a large number of such standards are available, like TSAPI, TAPI, JTAPI, CSTA, etc.

Advanced helpdesk information systems make use of technologies that are based on the combination of telephone and computer systems. The process of

Computer Telephony Integration (CTI) is presented in Figure 9.3 and consists of the following steps (Cogan, 1997; Lawrence, 1999; Delgado, 1999):

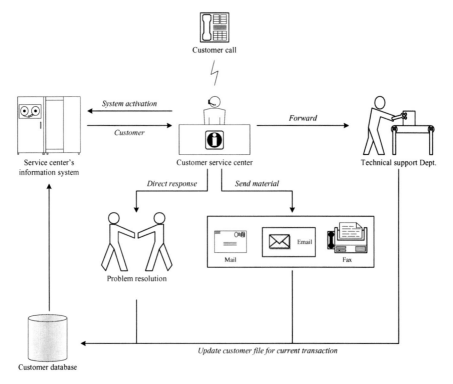

Fig. 9.3 Computer telephony integration

1. The service center of the business organization accepts customer's telephone call.
2. Service center's information system is activated, automatically, by the identification of the telephone call or manually by the employee, in order to search and present customer's info file. The latter usually contains information about customer transactions (products, quantity, transaction dates, etc.), requests and complaints (submission date, procedure, final result, required time, etc.), basic customer information (name, address, phone number, etc.), and other general data (average completion time for orders and requests, open orders or pending requests, etc.).
3. The service center updates the customer's info file with the case at hand (request or complaint submission, query, etc.).
4. The employee prioritize customer's case and either the problem is directly resolved or forwards the case to the appropriate department.

5. In every case, customer's info file is updated, and future actions concerning this particular case are planned, especially if customer's request has not been completed.

9.2.2 Automated Response Systems

Automated Response Systems (ARS) refer to technologies that allow partial or fully automatic provision of services, or satisfaction of customers' requests. According to Yanovsky (1998), the term is used as a general reference for technologies like Automated Response Unit (ARU), Voice Response Unit (VRU), and Interactive Voice Response (IVR).

ARS automate customer service process, by giving the ability of self-service. According to Loris (1998), this may result to the decrease of the service cost, the establishment of a continuous interactive communication with the customers, the depletion of helpline center from simple repeated calls, the development of personalized new products or the cross-selling actions of the business organization, and broadly to the customer relationship strategies.

In general, the operation process of these systems includes the following steps (Figure 9.4):

1. *Contact with the customer*: Customers have the ability to contact the service center using any alternative type of communication method (phone, e-mail, fax, Internet, etc.).
2. *Identification of customer's problem*: Depending on the way the interaction was established, ARS identifies the problem/request of the customer. In general, communication process may include keyed-in requests using telephone devices, voice recognition systems, e-mail or fax messages, and problem recognition wizards using Internet.
3. *Customer's problem resolution*: ARS is able to satisfy simple customers' requests like the direct provision of prescribed information (recorded or written message), the forwarding of the particular request to appropriate department/employee, or the completion of simple business transactions (payments of fixed bills, credit card balance, etc.).

Finally, it should be noted that criticism referring to ARS is mainly focused on the loss of personal contact with the customer and the feeling of "abandonment" that may be created (Yanovsky, 1998). For this reason, using ARS, customers have also the ability to pass over the automated procedures and have a direct communication with the employees.

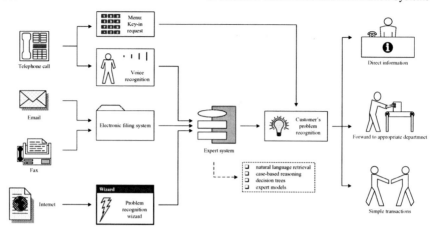

Fig. 9.4 Automated response systems

9.2.3 Electronic Data Interchange

Electronic Data Interchange (EDI) is a business process that allows business organizations to improve their performance by minimizing the bureaucratic procedures. EDI allows the electronic exchange of structured business information among computer systems located in different organizations. Data are handled through internationally accepted standards, so that the messages between the trading sides can be easily sent, received and processed by different computer systems.

EDI is defined as the exchange of electronic documents with predefined format between business trading parties. This exchange permits the unedited transfer of data without any modification or change of codification between business applications located in different business organizations (Hill and Ferguson, 1991). Normally, EDI can be used in order to exchange any type of structured information, since it consists of an automated interactive process between business applications (American National Standards Institute, 1991).

As already stated in the previous sections, customer service information systems allow the handling of simple business transactions. This possibility can be further extended to integrated and automated business actions (order, order tracking, dispatch, payment, etc.) through the installation and cooperation of an EDI system with the company's customer service center. In addition, this leads to the integration of the interaction process between the customers and the company.

The most important advantage of EDI systems is the improvement of customer satisfaction, based on the following points (Canright, 1988; Scala and McGrath, 1993):

- Decreasing necessary time to complete an order.
- Improving the accuracy in the processing of the orders.
- Satisfying customer demands for installation of an EDI system.

The advantages that result from the implementation of EDI systems can only be achieved when this technology is used and/or automated to the greatest possible extent. Major precondition for the installation of automatic customer service systems (EDI or ARS) are the existence of a sizeable clientele and a large number of transactions.

9.3 Customer Satisfaction and Internet

Internet consists one of the most important available media for the interaction between business organizations and customers. Its main feature is the ability to exchange complex information through a user-friendly environment. In addition, its growth and expansion during the last years offers a uniform communication standard.

In general, business organizations use the Internet to provide special services to their customers (products' information, orders, orders' information, bills' tracking, etc.) as well as to conduct satisfaction surveys (Sterne, 1996).

Web-based systems have the ability to record the entire interaction between customers and organizations, maintaining information, such as number of customers (or potential customers) visiting company's web page, software used for browsing and searching, origin of customers (country, type of organization, etc.), duration of communication (average number of visited pages, average time of staying in the company's web page), customer most-wanted information, and number of complaints and requests for technical assistance.

Furthermore, World Wide Web is widely used in conducting customer satisfaction surveys. In fact, several satisfaction survey questionnaires are placed permanently in the web site of business organizations (see Figure 9.5).

The advantages of this approach compared to other classical types of survey conduction (mail, phone, personal interview, etc.) are summarized in the following (Chrisholm, 1998):

- The participation in web-based satisfaction surveys does not consider time or space restrictions.
- This type of satisfaction surveys reduces human interviewer bias.
- Available tools (menus, icons, combo boxes, etc.) are able to provide a user-friendly environment for filling-in the questionnaire.
- Usually, questionnaire information is automatically stored in a database, and this may result to reducing the overall cost of satisfaction survey conduction, and directly accessing survey results, even in real-time.
- Internet provides the ability to automatically validate available collected data.

Tell Us What You Think
Dear Customer:

We want to continually improve the ways we serve you. To help us do this, please tell us how we rate and give us your comments using the quick survey below.

Thank you for taking the time to provide your feedback.

PRIVACY: Your personal privacy is very important to us. Any information you choose to provide will never be given or sold to anyone outside of the organization.

Customer Satisfaction Survey
Please fill out this form and press "Send" to be entered in the drawing:

Name: _____

Title: _____

Company: _____

Country: [Select A Country ▼]

E-mail Address: _____

Telephone: _____

Model(s) Purchased: _____

Product Performance	**Product Quality**
○ Outstanding	○ Outstanding
○ Very Good	○ Very Good
○ Satisfactory	○ Satisfactory
○ Needs Improvement	○ Needs Improvement
○ Unsatisfactory	○ Unsatisfactory
○ No Opinion	○ No Opinion

Sales Support	**After Sales Service**
○ Outstanding	○ Outstanding
○ Very Good	○ Very Good
○ Satisfactory	○ Satisfactory
○ Needs Improvement	○ Needs Improvement
○ Unsatisfactory	○ Unsatisfactory
○ No Opinion	○ No Opinion

If you have any additional comments, please let us know (not required):

_____

What other products, features, or services would you like us to offer (not required)?

_____

[Send] [Reset]

Fig. 9.5 An example of Internet-based customer satisfaction survey

The previous advantages may increase customer participation rate in satisfaction surveys. However, conducting a web-based satisfaction survey should be justified by important conditions, such as Internet access for the total set of customers and a large clientele in order to benefit from the reduction of the related cost (Sterne, 1996, 1998; Chrisholm, 1998).

9.4 Survey-based Systems

A major software category related to customer satisfaction measurement refers to survey-based information systems. The major functions of these systems include the design of the questionnaire, the printing and/or electronic filling of questionnaires, the development of the relevant database, and the statistical analysis and reporting.

An important attribute of these systems is the high level of user-friendliness characterizing the design process of the satisfaction survey questionnaire (Figure 9.6), which is achieved by a set of ready-to-use tools (predefined types of questions, satisfaction scales, etc.) and the implementation of complex information (sounds, images, graphics, etc.). An additional attractive feature of these systems is their ability to validate collected information, which is ensured during the design and development of the structure and the contents of the questionnaire.

Another important feature of these systems refers to the process type of distributing the questionnaire and collecting customer responses. Generally, the following alternatives are provided:

- Print out the questionnaire in order to conduct a mail satisfaction survey.
- Save the questionnaire in electronic format in order to distribute it through the Internet, e-mail, etc. (see Figure 9.7).

The development of the database containing customer responses is to a great extent an automated procedure, which is able to reduce the overall cost of survey conduction. Computerized data entry is achieved either directly by the system when the questionnaire was distributed in electronic format, or using a scanner in case that the questionnaire was printed and distributed by post mail.

Survey-based software packages also provide the ability to perform statistical analyses of the collected data (Figure 9.8), which in general consists of descriptive statistics analysis (frequencies of answers and cross-tabulations). In addition, the user is able to choose predefined templates in order to generate reports with the results of the satisfaction survey.

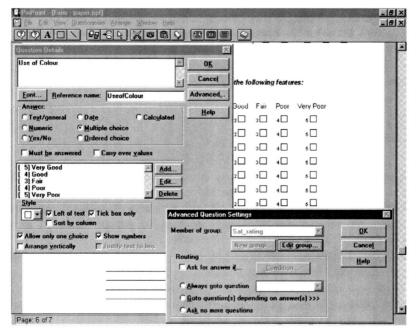

Fig. 9.6 Questionnaire design using a survey-based system

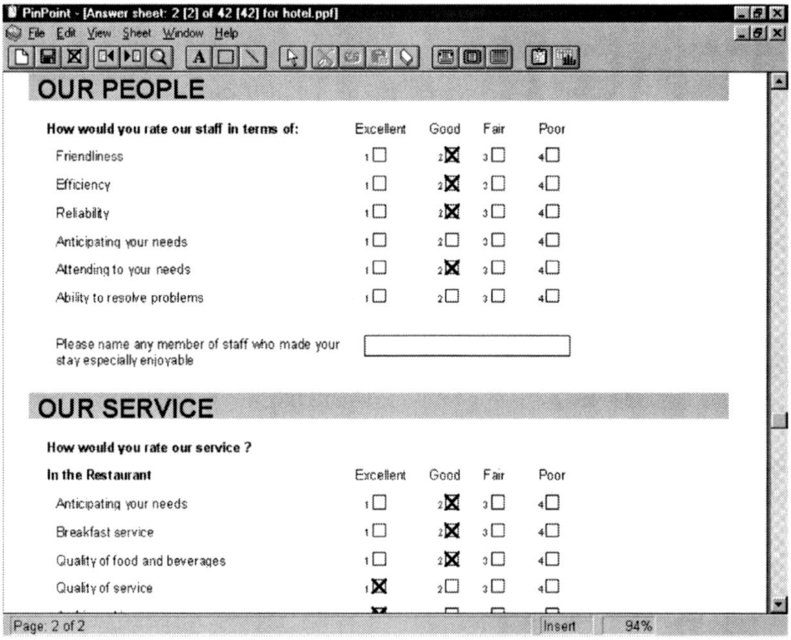

Fig. 9.7 A sample of an electronic customer satisfaction questionnaire

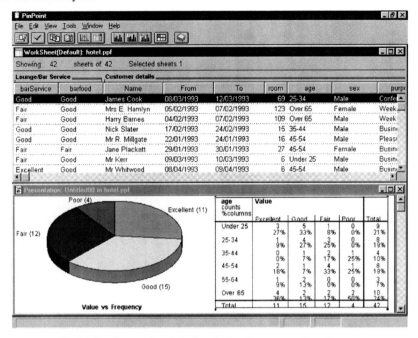

Fig. 9.8 Database and statistical analysis using a survey-based system

9.5 The MUSA System

9.5.1 Overview of the software

The system implements the MUSA methodology in order to assess customer satisfaction. The main features of the system include:

- Simplicity, which is achieved through the use of efficient data management methods.
- Friendliness through the implementation of a graphical user interface.
- Effectiveness, based on the provided analytical results for customer behavior, organization performance, and potential improving actions.

An overview of the system's operation procedure is presented in Figure 9.9 and consists of the following main steps:

1. In the initial step, the user should create or retrieve a file containing customer satisfaction data. The structure of the data file determines also the type of the problem and in particular the number of satisfaction criteria levels (see next section).

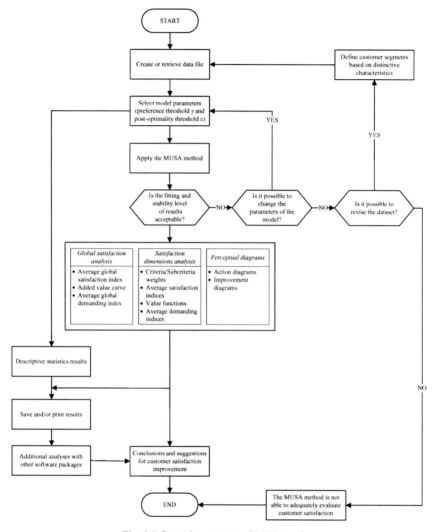

Fig. 9.9 Operation process of MUSA software

2. The next step concerns the implementation of the MUSA method. During this
   step, the customer satisfaction data are transformed in order to formulate and
   solve the appropriate LP. It should be noted that the post-optimality analysis
   phase in also included in this step, since it is considered as an inseparable part
   of the MUSA method.
3. If the user is satisfied by the fitting and stability level of the method, the obtained results are presented. These results refer to the global satisfaction analysis (added value function, average global satisfaction and demanding indices),
   the criteria satisfaction analysis (criteria/subcriteria weights, partial value func-

tions, and average criteria/subcriteria satisfaction and demanding indices), and
the perceptual maps (overall and partial action and improvement diagrams).

4. If the fitting and/or the stability level of the results are not acceptable, the user
   may change the value of the model parameters (see section 6.3.1 and 6.3.2). If
   this is not possible, the segmentation of the customer set into distinct groups
   with more homogenous preferences may be considered (e.g. using demographics or other customer characteristics). If none of the aforementioned options
   work, the MUSA software is not able to adequately analyze this customer satisfaction data set.
5. The final step of this procedure refers to the development of specific customer
   satisfaction improvement suggestions, taking into account the previous MUSA
   results, as well as potential results by other methodological approaches.

It should be noted that during this process, descriptive statistics results are
available separately, in order to give the ability to perform additional analyses
with other software packages (e.g. statistical software).

The main window of the system is displayed in Figure 9.10 and contains the
menu bar with all available commands, the tool bar with selective, commonly
used, commands, and the status bar with useful information for the current satisfaction problem (filename of the current data file, information on the solution of
the linear program, number of levels of satisfaction criteria).

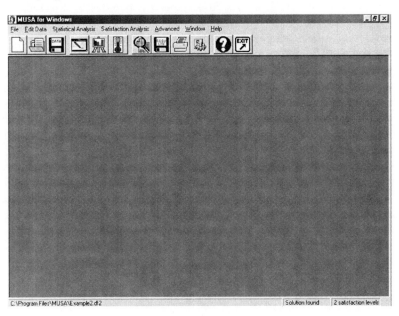

Fig. 9.10 Main window of the MUSA software

9.5.2 Data Management and Selection of Parameters

Input and output data files have a very simple form because they are basically text files (ASCII files). This means that they are fully compatible with almost all application programs, and may be accessed through spreadsheets, database management systems (DBMS), and text editors and word processing packages. This way, MUSA data may be read from an external text file or they may be entered directly to the program. The result data file is also saved in a text format so that the user may use it to perform any kind of complementary analysis with other software packages.

The information required to create data files refers basically to the definition of the variables of the MUSA model and it consists of the title of the problem, the number of customers, the number of criteria, the number of subcriteria per criterion, the global, criteria, and subcriteria satisfaction scaling (number and titles of satisfaction levels), and the main data table (customers' judgements), as shown in Figure 9.11. It should be noted that the main data table consists of ordinal data, and for this reason the appeared numbers represent only the coding for the defined satisfaction levels (see Figure 9.12).

It is very important to mention that the type of information handled by the MUSA system can be either quantitative (price, time, etc.) or qualitative (company's image, personnel's behavior, etc.). Generally, in order to collect input data for the customer satisfaction problem, a predefined qualitative satisfaction scale for the set of criteria/subcriteria should be used. There is no restriction in the number and specification of satisfaction levels in MUSA, which may be different from one criterion/subcriterion to another.

As already mentioned, one of the main characteristic of the system is the ability to insert data created by other commercial applications. An example presented in Figure 9.13 concerns the use of Microsoft Excel for creating a MUSA data file. It should be emphasized that the presented data structure is an important requirement for data compatibility.

Finally, the determination of the model parameters is an important feature of the system, since these parameters play an important role in the customer satisfaction evaluation problem. In particular, the user has the ability to define the number of satisfaction criteria levels (1 or 2 levels) as shown in Figure 9.14, and choose the appropriate values for the preference and the post-optimality thresholds (Figure 9.15). For simplicity reasons, the preference threshold within the MUSA software is chosen equal for both the overall and partial value functions, i.e. $\gamma = \gamma_i \; \forall \; i$.

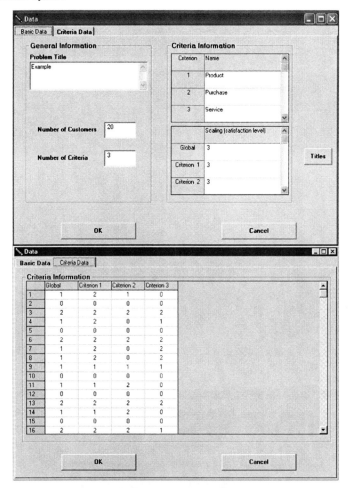

Fig. 9.11 Data files of the MUSA software

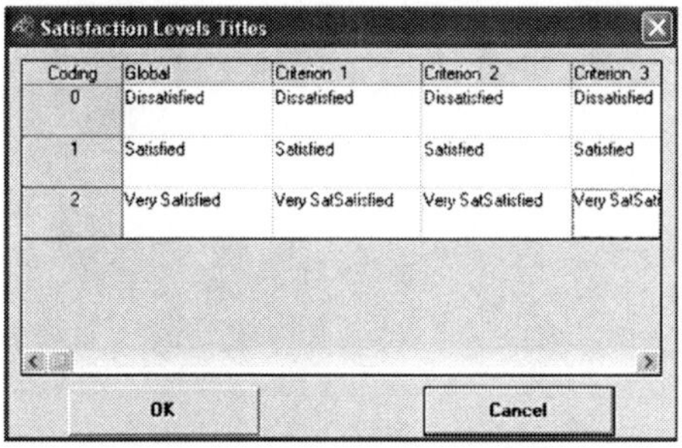

Fig. 9.12 Data files of the MUSA software

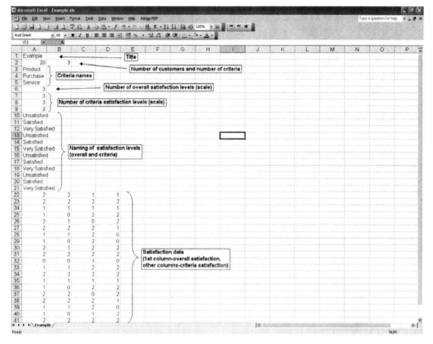

Fig. 9.13 Creating MUSA data file using Excel

Fig. 9.14 Modifying the number of satisfaction criteria levels

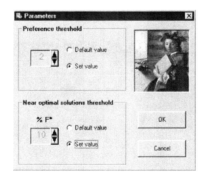

Fig. 9.15 Defining values for the model parameters

9.5.3 Presentation of Results

The MUSA system provides basic descriptive analysis based on the calculated frequencies. Available results consist of global criteria and subcriteria satisfaction frequencies, giving a general view of the customer satisfaction data.

Figure 9.16 presents the results of the descriptive statistical analysis for the numerical example of section 4.4. In this particular data file, customers do not seem globally satisfied (30% of them have responded "Dissatisfied" in the overall satisfaction question), while they present a moderate satisfaction level concerning the "Product" criterion (50% of the customers appear "Very satisfied" by this particular criterion.

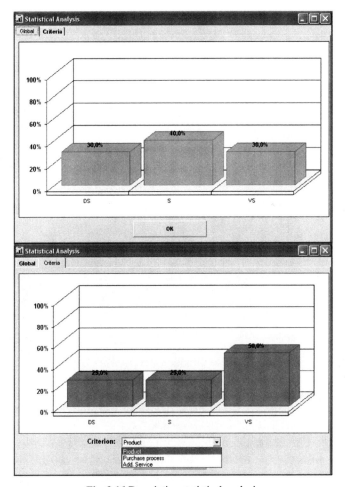

Fig. 9.16 Descriptive statistical analysis

The main results of the method are focused on global and partial explanatory analysis. Global explanatory analysis lays emphasis on customers' global satisfaction and its primary dimensions, while partial explanatory analysis focuses on each criterion and its relevant parameters separately.

In particular, the global explanatory analysis includes the average global satisfaction index, the overall added value curve and the average global demanding index. Figure 9.17 presents the results of the global satisfaction analysis for the selected data file. These results justify the previous findings, since the global satisfaction index is about 50%. Also, the "linear" form of the added value curve indicates a set of customers with a "normal" demanding level. It should be noted that the MUSA system categorizes customers to different demanding groups, according to the following simple rule:

- non-demanding customers if $D \in [-1, -0.333]$,
- "normal" customers if $D \in [-0.333, 0.333]$, and
- demanding customers if $D \in [0.333, 1]$.

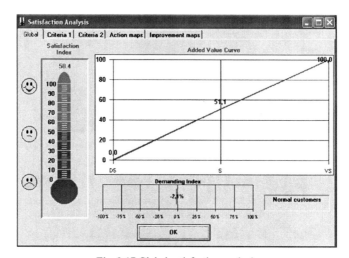

Fig. 9.17 Global satisfaction analysis

It is important to mention that although the data file used in this section concern the numerical example of section 4.4, there are some small differences in the presented results due to different parameter values for the post-optimality analysis stage. In particular, the MUSA software uses a constraint of the form $F \leq (1+\varepsilon)F^*$ in the stability analysis and not the constraint $F \leq F^* + \varepsilon$ that have been proposed in section 4.2.3. This is because it is difficult in several cases to give an appropriate value for ε, since the optimal value of F should be also considered. Thus, it is preferred to assess ε as a percentage of F^* (see also section 6.3.20

Similarly to the previous sets of results, the partial explanatory analysis consists of the following: criteria weights, average satisfaction, demanding, and improvement indices, action and improvement diagrams. As shown in Figure 9.18, customers consider the "purchase process" as the most important criterion (with a weight of almost 49%). In addition, the satisfaction level for the whole set of criteria is relatively low (average satisfaction levels 48-53%). Consequently, these particular results justify the high effectiveness of improving the "purchase process" criterion (relatively high importance and low satisfaction level). Furthermore, the "product" criterion presents the highest demanding level (almost 82%), whereas customers do not appear demanding regarding the "additional services" criterion (average demanding index almost equal to –84%).

Finally, as shown in Figure 9.18, the MUSA software provides a series of additional diagrams, which combine several of the previously presented results. More specifically, the following types of action and improvement diagrams are available:

- Global and partial diagrams (for each set of satisfaction criteria and subcriteria separately).
- Relative and raw diagrams (as they have been assessed in sections 4.3.5 and 4.3.6).

Generally, the findings based on the results of Figure 9.18 do not differ from those presented in section 4.4, regarding the numerical example.

9.5.4 Advanced Results and Reliability Analysis

The MUSA software also provides a series of additional results regarding the post optimality analysis, the partial value functions, and the reliability analysis of the previously presented results.

As shown in Figure 9.19 the system presents the analytical table of post optimality analysis, in order to give a detailed view for the stability of the results estimated by the MUSA method. Additional information concerning the optimization model is also presented (e.g. selected thresholds, optimal value of F in the initial LP problem).

The evaluation of the results is mainly based on the average fitting and stability indices provided by the MUSA software, while other available reliability analysis tools include the variance diagram of the additive value curve, the variation of the global satisfaction index, and the prediction table of global satisfaction.

In particular, the variation of the global satisfaction index is calculated using the variance diagram of the added value curve (maximum and minimum value function during post-optimality analysis) and may be considered as a confidence interval for this particular index.

The screenshots of Figure 9.19 show that the results of the examined data file is very stable, since $AFI = 99.6\%$, $ASI = 99.34\%$, and $OPL = 100\%$. Furthermore, the average global satisfaction index varies in the interval [49%, 51.2%], whereas the final estimation of the method is 50.4%.

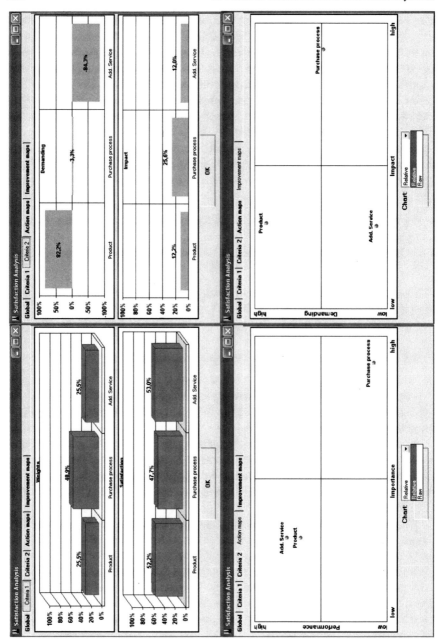

Fig. 9.18 Criteria satisfaction analysis

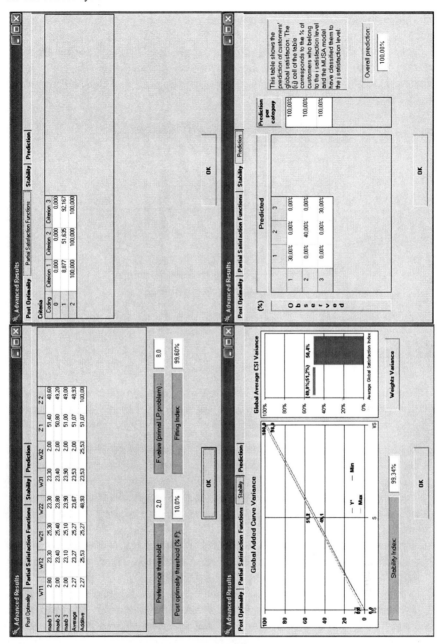

Fig. 9.19 Advanced results and reliability analysis

Another important diagram concerns the variation of weights and summarizes the results of post optimality analysis. This diagram is presented in Figure 9.20

and may provide a confidence interval for the evaluation of the criteria importance.

Concerning the presented illustrative example, this diagram justifies the high stability level of provided results, since the observed variation is very low (for example the weight of the 1st criterion varies between 25.1% and 26.1%, whereas the final estimated value is 25.5%).

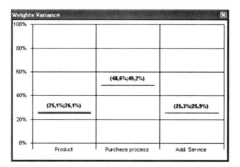

Fig. 9.20 Variation of criteria weights

9.5.5 *Future Extensions*

Several extensions of the MUSA software may be proposed in order to develop an integrated Customer Satisfaction Decision Support System. These extensions may include (Grigoroudis and Siskos, 2003):

- Incorporation of other statistical methods in order to develop an integrated model base subsystem. The system could provide an alternatively and/or complementary implementation of these methods. For example, the MUSA method requires completely and correctly answered questionnaires as input data. In case of missing data, data mining techniques could be used in order to fill in the empty cells in the data table.
- Addition of an expert system in order to fully explain provided results and to recommend the best decision to be taken. Additionally, the expert system may guide users in the value hierarchy development process.
- Development of a database management system, which could assist in the establishment of a permanent customer satisfaction barometer. For example, a history database could record the evolution of customer satisfaction for a particular time period. This way, the effectiveness of business organization's strategies could be evaluated through customer satisfaction measurement.
- Addition of network support in order to perform comparative analysis for a number of different departments/stores within a company. This way, an interior benchmarking system may be established. This system can relate customer sat-

isfaction and company's performance and it may motivate departments and/or employees to perform and achieve higher levels of productivity.

Finally, it should be emphasized that the MUSA system is a decision-aid software, which in addition may serve for the development of a truly customer-focused management and culture.

References

Adams, E.W. and R. Fagot (1959). A model of riskless choice, *Behavioral Science*, 4 (1), 1-10.

Agresti, A. (1984). *Analysis of ordinal categorical data*, John Wiley and Sons, New York.

Agresti, A. (1990). *Categorical data analysis*, John Wiley, New York.

Agresti, A. (1996). *An introduction to categorical data analysis*, John Wiley and Sons, New York.

Aldenderfer, M.S. and R.K. Blashfield (1984). *Cluster analysis*, Sage Publications, Beverly Hills, CA.

Alderfer, C.P. (1972). *Human needs in organizational settings*, Free Press, New York.

Alderfer, C.P., R.E. Kaplan, and K.K. Smith (1974). The effect of variations in relatedness need satisfaction on relatedness desires, *Administrative Service Quarterly*, 19 (4), 507-532.

Alexopoulos, S., Y. Siskos, and N. Tsotsolas (2006). Planning a Reader-oriented Strategy for a Publishing Company: A Case Study, *Journal of Multi-Criteria Decision Analysis*, 14 (1-3), 89-101.

Allen, D.R. and T.R. Rao (2000). *Analysis of customer satisfaction data*, ASQ Quality Press, Milwaukee.

Alreck, P. and R.B. Settle (1995). *The survey research handbook*, Richard D. Irwin, Inc., Burr Ridge, IL.

American National Standards Institute (1990). *X12 standards manual*, New York.

Andersen, E.B. (1990). *The statistical analysis of categorical data*, Springer-Verlag, Berlin.

Anderson, E.W. and C. Fornell (1991). The impact of performance on customer satisfaction and retention: An investigation of industry differences, *National Quality Research Center Working Paper*, University of Michigan, Ann Arbor, MI.

Anderson, E.W. and M.W. Sullivan (1991). Intra-industry differences in the impact of product performance on customer satisfaction and retention, *National Quality Research Center Working Paper*, University of Michigan, Ann Arbor, MI.

Anderson, E.W., C. Fornell, and D.R. Lehmann (1994). Customer satisfaction, market share, and profitability: Findings from Sweden, *Journal of Marketing*, 58 (3), 53-66.

Anderson, E.W. (1994). Cross category variation in customer satisfaction and retention, *Marketing Letters*, 5 (1), 19-30.

Anderson, E.W., C. Fornell, and R. Rust (1997). Customer satisfaction, productivity, and profitability: Differences between good and services, *Marketing Science*, 16 (2), 129-145.

Anderson, E.W. and C. Fornell (2000). Foundations of the American Customer Satisfaction Index, *Total Quality Management*, 11 (7), 869-882.

Anderson, E.W. and V. Mittal (2000). Strengthening the satisfaction-profit chain, *Journal of Service Research*, 3 (2), 107-120.

Anderson, E.W., C. Fornell, and S. Mazvancheryl (2004). Customer satisfaction and shareholder value, *Journal of Marketing*, 68 (4), 172-185.

Anderson, J.C., M. Rungtusanatham, and R. Schroeder (1994). A theory of quality management underlying the Deming management method, *Academy of Management Journal*, 19 (3), 472-509.

Anderson, J.L. and S.U. Bettencourt (1993). A conjoint approach to model product preferences: The New England market for fresh and frozen salmon, *Marine Resource Economics*, 8, 31-49.

Andreassen, T.W. and L.L. Olsen (2004). When the going gets tough: should customer service get going?, Norsk Kundebarometer (http://www.kundebarometer.com/discourse/custserv.pdf).

Arbuckle, J.L. (1997). *AMOS user's guide*, SmallWaters, Chicago.

Arnold, H.J. and D.C. Feldman (1982). A multivariate analysis of the determinants of job turnover, *Journal of Applied Psychology*, 67 (3), 350-360.

Ashford, S.J., C. Lee, and P. Bobko (1989). Content, causes and consequences of job insecurity: a theory-based measure and substantive test, *Academy of Management Journal*, 32 (4), 803-829.

Bagozzi, R.P. and P.R. Warshaw (1990). Trying to consume, *Journal of Consumer Research*, 17 (2), 127-140.

Bagozzi, R.P., H. Baumgartner, and Y. Yi (1992). State versus action orientation and the theory of reasoned action: An application to coupon usage, *Journal of Consumer Research*, 18 (4), 505-518.

Bagozzi, R.P. (1993). On the neglect of volition in consumer research: A critique and proposal, *Psychology and Marketing*, 10 (3), 215-223.

Baourakis, G., N.F. Matsatsinis, and Y. Siskos (1996). Agricultural product development using multidimensional and multicriteria analyses: The case of wine, *European Journal of Operational Research*, 94 (2), 321-334.

Barta, P. and M. Chaker (2001). Consumers voice dissatisfaction with wide variety of companies, *The Wall Street Journal*, May 21 (http://www.cfigroup.com/resources/wsj/WSJ_5_21_01.htm).

Bass, F.M. (1974). The theory of stochastic preference and brand switching, *Journal of Marketing Research*, 11 (1), 1-20.

Bawden, P. (1998). Nortel's practical path to customer loyalty, *Measuring Business Excellence*, 2 (1), 8-13.

Beatty, S.E., L.R. Kahle, and P. Homer (1988). The involvement-commitment model: Theory and implications, *Journal of Business Research*, 16 (2), 149-167.

Beddowes, P., S. Gulliford, M. Knight, and I. Saunders (1987). *Service success! Who is getting there*, Operations Management Association, University of Nottingham.

Belch, G.E. (1981). An examination of comparative and noncomparative television commercials: The effects of claim variation and repetition on cognitive response and message acceptance, *Journal of Marketing Research*, 18 (3), 333-349.

Bell, D.E. (1980). Regret in decision making under uncertainty, *Operations Research*, 30 (5), 961-981.

Bentler, P.M. (1995). *EQS structural equation program manual*, Multivariate Software, Encino, CA.

Berger, C., R. Blauth, D. Boger, C. Bolster, G. Burchill, W. DuMouchel, F. Pouliot, R. Richter, A. Rubinoff, D. Shen, M. Timko, and D. Walden (1993). Kano's methods for understanding customer-defined quality, *The Center for Quality Management Journal*, 2 (4), 2-36.

Bernhardt, K., N. Donthu, and P.A. Kennett (2000). A longitudinal analysis of satisfaction and profitability, *Journal of Business Research*, 47 (2), 161-171.

Bettman, J.R., N. Capon, and R.J. Lutz (1975). Cognitive algebra in multi-attribute attitude models, *Journal of Marketing Research*, 12, 151-164.

Beuthe, M. and G. Scanella (1996). Applications comparées des méthodes d'analyse multicritère UTA, *RAIRO Recherche Opérationnelle*, 30 (3), 293-315.

Beuthe, M., L. Eeckhoudt, and G. Scannella (2000). A practical multicriteria methodology for assessing risky public investments, *Socio-Economic Planning Sciences*, 34 (2), 121-139.

Beuthe, M. and G. Scanella (2001). Comparative analysis of UTA mutlicriteria methods, *European Journal of Operational Research*, 130 (2), 246-262.

Bitner, M.J. and A.R. Hubbert (1994). Encounter satisfaction versus overall satisfaction versus quality: The customer's voice, in: R.T. Rust and R.L. Oliver (eds.), *Service quality: New directions in theory and practice*, Sage, Thousand Oaks, CA, 72-94.

Blau, G.J. (1985). A multiple study investigation of the dimensionality of job involvement, *Journal of Vocational Behavior*, 27 (1), 9-36.

Bloemer, J., J.C. DeRuyter, and P. Peters (1998). Investigating drivers of bank loyalty: The complex relation between image, service quality and satisfaction, *International Journal of Bank Marketing*, 16 (7), 276-286.

Blood, M.R. (1971). The validity of importance, *Journal of Applied Psychology*, 55, 487-488.

Bluedorn, A.C. (1982). The theories of turnover: Causes, effects, and meaning, in: S.B. Bacharach (ed.), *Perspectives in organizational sociology: Theory and research*, 1, JAI Press, Greenwich, CT, 75-128.

Blunch, N.L. (2008). *Introduction to structural equation modelling using SPSS and AMOS*, Sage, Los Angeles.

Bohoris, G.A. (1995). A comparative assessment of some major quality awards, *International Journal of Quality and Reliability Management*, 12 (9), 30-43.

Bollen, K.A. (1989). *Structural equations with latent variables*, Wiley, New York.

Boninger, D.S., F. Gleicher, and A. Strathman (1994). Counterfactual thinking: From what might have been to what may be, *Journal of Personality and Social Psychology*, 67 (2), 297-307.

Bounds, G., G. Dobbins, and O. Fowler (1994). *Management: A total quality perspective*, International Thomson Publishing, Ohio.

Bouyssou, D. (1989). Building criteria: A prerequisite for MCDA, in: C. Bana e Costa, (ed.), *Readings on multiple criteria decision aid*, Springer, Berlin, 58-80.

Brans, J.P. and B. Mareschal (1990). The PROMETHEE methods for MCDM: The PROMCALC, GAIA and BANKADVISER software, in: C.A. Bana e Costa (ed.), *Readings in multiple criteria decision aid*, Springer, Berlin, 216-252.

Brockner, J. and L. Adsit (1986). The moderating impact of sex on the equity-satisfaction relationship: A field study, *Journal of Applied Psychology*, 71 (4), 585-590.

Brogowicz, A.A., L.M. Delene, and D.M. Lyth (1990). A synthesised service quality model with managerial implications, *International Journal of Service Industry Management*, 1 (1), 27-44.

Brooke, P.B., D.W. Russell, and J.L. Price (1988). Discriminant validation of measures of job satisfaction, job involvement, and organizational commitment, *Journal of Applied Psychology*, 73 (2), 139-145.

Brower, M.J. (1994). Implementing TQM with self-directed teams, in: H.I. Costing (ed.), *Readings in total quality management*, Dryden Press, New York, 403-420.

Bryant, B.E. (2003). *ACSI methodology report update*, ASQ Quality Press, Milwaukee.

Buede, D.M. (1986). Structuring value attributes, *Interfaces*, 16 (2), 52-62.

Burns, M.J. and R.B. Woodruff (1991). Value: An integrative perspective, in: C.P. Haugtvedt and D.E. Rosen (eds.), *Proceedings of the Society for Consumer Psychology*, American Psychological Association, Washington, 59-64.

Business Week Guide (1994). *The quality imperative*, McGraw-Hill, New York.

Buttle, F. (1996). SERVQUAL: Review, critique, research agenda, *European Journal of Marketing*, 30 (1), 8-32.

Cadotte, E.R., R.B. Woodruff, and R.L. Jenkins (1987). Expectations and norms in models of consumer satisfaction, *Journal of Marketing Research*, 24 (3), 305-314.

Cadotte, E.R. and N. Turgeon (1988). Dissatisfiers and satisfiers: Suggestions from consumer complaints compliments, *Journal of Satisfaction, Dissatisfaction and Complaining Behavior*, 1, 74-79.

Cai, Y., I. Deilami, and K. Train (1998). Customer retention in a competitive power market: Analysis of a 'double-bounded plus follow-ups' questionnaire, *Energy Journal*, 19 (2), 191-215.

Cai, S. and M. Jun (2003). Internet users' perceptions of online service quality: A comparison of online buyers and information searchers, *Managing Service Quality*, 13 (6), 504-519.

Calder, B.J., E.C. Malthouse, and W. Eadie (2003). Conceptualizing and measuring magazine reader experiences, *Proceedings of the 2003 Worldwide Readership Symposium*, Cambridge, 285-306.

Calder, B.J. and E.C. Malthouse (2004). Qualitative media measures II: magazine experiences, Media Management Center (http://www.mediamanagementcenter.org/research/magazine-measures.pdf).

Camman, C., M. Fichman, D. Jenkins, and J. Klesh (1979). *The Michigan organizational assessment questionnaire*, University of Michigan, Ann Arbor.

Campbell, S.M., J. Braspenning, A. Hutchinson, and M. Marshall (2002). Research methods used in developing and applying quality indicators in primary care, *Quality and Safety in Health Care*, 11 (4), 358-364.

Canright. C. (1988). Seizing the electronic information advantage, *Business Marketing*, 73 (1), 81-88.

Cardozo, R. (1965). An experimental study of consumer effort, expectations and satisfaction, *Journal of Marketing Research*, 2 (3), 244-249.

Carlson, W. (1985). Researching readers' needs, *Folio: The Magazine for Magazine Management* (http://findarticles.com/p/articles/mi_m3065/is_v14/ai_3798125).

Caruana, J. and L. Pitt (1997). INTQUAL: An internal measure of service quality and the link between service quality and business performance, *European Journal of Marketing*, 31 (8), 604-616.

Case, K.E., J.M. Quigley, and R.J. Shiller (2001). Comparing wealth effects: The stock market versus the housing market, Working Paper 8606, National Bureau of Economic Research, Cambridge, MA.

Cauchick, P.A.M. (2001). Comparing the Brazilian national quality award with some of the major prizes, *The TQM Magazine*, 13 (4), 260-272.

Champoux, J.E. (1991). A multivariate test of the job characteristics theory of work motivation, *Journal of Organizational Behavior*, 12 (5), 431-446.

Chandrupatla, T.R. (2009). *Quality and reliability in engineering*, Cambridge University Press, New York.

Charnes, A. and W.W. Cooper (1961). *Management models and industrial applications of linear programming*, Vol I, Wiley, New York.

Cheong, K.J. (1993). Observations: Are cents-off coupons effective?, *Journal of Advertising Research*, 33 (2), 73-78.

Chiou, J.S. (2004). The antecedents of consumers' loyalty toward Internet Service Providers, *Information and Management*, 41 (6), 685-695.

Choudrie, J. and Y.K. Dwivedi (2006a). Investigating factors influencing adoption of broadband in the household, *Journal of Computer Information Systems*, 46 (4), 25-34.

Choudrie, J. and Y.K. Dwivedi (2006b). A comparative study to examine the socio-economic characteristics of broadband adopters and non-adopters, *Electronic Government: An International Journal*, 3 (3), 272-288.

Chrisholm, J. (1998). Using the Internet to measure customer satisfaction and loyalty, in: R. Zemke and J.A. Woods (eds.), *Best practices in customer service*, Amacom, New York, 305-317.

Churchill, G.A. Jr. and C. Surprenant (1982). An investigation into the determinants of customer satisfaction, *Journal of Marketing Research*, 19, 491-504.

Churchill, G.A. Jr. (1991). *Marketing research: Methodological foundations*, The Dryden Press, Hidsdale, IL.

Ciavolino, E. and J.J. Dahlgaard (2007). ECSI-Customer satisfaction modelling and analysis: A case study, *Journal of Total Quality Management and Business Excellence*, 18 (5), 545-554.

Cogan, J. (1997). Technology and call centres, *Customer Service Management*, 16, 48-51.

Cohen, J. (1983). The cost of dichotomization, *Applied Psychological Measurement*, 7 (3), 249-253.

Cohen, J. and P. Cohen (1983). *Applied multiple regression/correlation analysis for the behavioral sciences*, Lawrence Erlbaum, Hillsdale, NJ.

Cohen, J.B., M. Fishbein, and O.T. Ahtola (1972). The nature and uses of expectancy-value models in consumer attitude research, *Journal of Marketing Research*, 9, 456-460.

Converse, J.M. and S. Presser (1986). *Survey questions: Handcrafting and standardized questionnaire*, Sage Publications, Newbury Park, CA.

Cooley, W.W. and P.R. Lohnes (1971). *Multivariate data analysis*, Wiley, New York.

Cooper, L.G. (1994). *Testing the components of customer satisfaction*, Working Paper, Anderson School of Management, University of California, Los Angeles.

Corner, J.L. and C.W. Kirkwood (1991). Decision analysis applications in the operations research literature: 1970-1989, *Operations Research*, 39 (2), 206-219.

Cranny, C.J., P.C. Smith, and E.F.Stone (1992). *Job satisfaction: How people feel about their jobs and how it affects their performance*, Lexington Books, New York.

Cronin, J.J. and S.A. Taylor (1992). Measuring service quality: A reexamination and extension, *Journal of Marketing*, 56 (3), 55-68.

Cronin, J.J. and S.A. Taylor (1994). SERVPERF versus SERVQUAL: Reconciling performance-based and perceptions-minus-expectations measurement of service quality, *Journal of Marketing*, 58 (1), 125-131.

Crosby, L.A. and J.R. Taylor (1983). Psychological commitment and its effects on post-decision evaluation and preference stability among voters, *Journal of Consumer Research*, 9 (4), 413-431.

Crow, S.M. and S.J. Hartman (1995). Can't get no satisfaction, *Leadership and Organization Development Journal*, 16 (4), 34-38.

Czarnecki, M.T. (1999). *Managing by measuring: How to improve your organization's performance through effective benchmarking*, AMACOM, New York.

Czepiel, J.A. and R. Gilmore (1987). Exploring the concept of loyalty in services, in: J.A. Czepiel, C.A. Congram, and J. Shanahan (eds.), *The services challenge: Integrating for competitive advantage*, American Marketing Association, Chicago, 91-94.

Dabholkar, P.A. (1996). Consumer evaluations of new technology-based self-service operations: an investigation of alternative models, *International Journal of Research in Marketing*, 13 (1), 29-51.

Dabholkar, P.A., C.D. Shepherd, D.I. Thorpe (2000). A comprehensive framework for service quality: An investigation of critical conceptual and measurement issues through a longitudinal study, *Journal of Retailing*, 76 (2), 131-169.

Dale, B.G (1999), *Managing quality*, 3rd edition, Blackwell, Oxford.

Daniel, W. and S.F. Wood (1980). *Fitting equations to data*, Wiley, New York.

Davids, S.M. (1986). *Future perfect*, Addison-Wesley, New York.

Dawes, R.M. (1972). *Fundamentals of attitude measurement*, John Wiley and Sons, New York.

Day, R.L. (1977). Toward a process model of customer satisfaction, in: H.K. Hunt (ed.), *Conceptualization and measurement of consumer satisfaction and dissatisfaction*, Marketing Science Institute, Cambridge. MA, 153-186.

Day, R.L. and E.L. Landon (1977). Toward a theory of consumer complaining behavior, in: A.G. Woodside, J.N. Sheth, and P.D. Bennett (eds.), *Consumer and industrial buying behavior*, Elsevier-North Holland, New York, 425-437.

Debreu, G. (1960). Topological methods in cardinal utility theory, in: K.J. Arrow, S. Karlin, and P. Suppes (eds.), *Mathematical methods in the social sciences*, Stanford University Press, Stanford, 16-26.

Delgado, B. (1999). What can Computer Telephony Integration do for you?, *Customer Service Management*, 23, 58-59.

DeMaio, T.J. (1980). Refusals: Who, where and why, *Public Opinion Quarterly*, 44 (2), 223-233.

Deming, W.E. (1981). *Management of statistical techniques for quality and productivity*, New York University Press, New York.

Deming, W.E. (1982). *Quality, productivity, and competitive position*, Center for Advanced Engineering Study, Cambridge.

Deming, W.E. (1986). *Out of the crisis*, Institute of Technology, Center for Advanced Engineering Study, Cambridge, MA.

Deming, W.E. (1993). *The new economics for industry, government, education*, Massachusetts Institute of Technology, Center for Advanced Engineering Study, Cambridge, MA.

Denby, L., R. Gnanadesikan, J.R. Kettenring, and J.W. Suzansky (1990). An analysis of questionnaire data on work design and job satisfaction: A case study in the use of simple graphical displays, in: S. Geisser, J.S. Hodges, S.J. Press and A. Zallner (eds.), *Bayesian and likelihood methods in statistics and econometrics*, Elsevier Science Publishers B.V., North Holland, 121-139.

Denzin, N.K. (1989). *The research act: A theoretical introduction to sociological methods*, Prentice-Hall, Englewood Cliffs, NJ.

DeRuyter, J.C., J. Bloemer, and P. Peters (1997). Merging service quality and service satisfaction: an empirical test of an integrative framework, *Journal of Economic Psychology*, 18 (4), 387-406.

Deschamps, J.P. and P.R. Nayak (1995). *Product juggernauts: How companies mobilize to generate a stream of market winners*, Harvard Business School Press, London

Despotis, D.K., D. Yannacopoulos, and C. Zopounidis (1990). A review of the UTA multicriteria method and some improvements, *Foundation of Computing and Decision Science*, 15 (2), 63-76.

Diakoulaki, D., C. Zopounidis, G. Mavrotas, and M. Doumpos (1999). The use of a preference disaggregation method in energy analysis and policy making, *Energy-The International Journal*, 24 (2), 157-166.

Dick, A. and K. Basu (1994). Customer loyalty: Toward an integrated conceptual framework, *Journal of the Academy of Marketing Science*, 22, (2), 99-113.

Diener, E., R.J. Larsen, S. Levine, and R.A. Emmons (1985). Intensity and frequency: Dimensions underlying positive and negative affect, *Journal of Personality and Social Psychology*, 48 (5), 1253-1265.

Dillman, D.A. (1978). *Mail and telephone surveys: The total design method*, Wiley, New York.

Dolinsky, A.L. (1994). A consumer complaint framework with resulting strategies: An application to higher education, *Journal of Services Marketing*, 8 (3), 27-39.

Doll, W.J. and G. Torkzadeh (1988). The measurement of end-user computing satisfaction, *MIS Quarterly*, 12 (2), 259-274.

Douglas, V. (1995). Questionnaire too long? Try variable clustering, *Marketing News*, 29, 38.

Doumpos, M. and C. Zopounidis (2002). *Multicriteria decision aid classification methods*. Kluwer Academic Publishers, Dordrecht.

Draper, N.R. and H. Smith (1967). *Applied regression analysis*, Wiley, New York.

Dutka, A. (1995). *AMA Handbbok of customer satisfaction: A guide to research, planning, and implementation*, NTC Publishing Group, Illinois.

Dyer, J.S., R.E. Fishburn, J. Steuer, J. Wallenius, and S. Zionts (1992). Multiple criteria decision making, multiattribute utility theory: The next ten years, *Management Science*, 38 (5), 645-654.

Eastman Kodak Company (1989). *Keeping the customer satisfied: A guide to field service*, ASQC Quality Press, Milwaukee.

Edosomwan, J.A. (1993). *Customer and market-driven quality management*, ASQC Quality Press, Milwaukee.

Edwards, A.L. and K.C. Keeney (1946). A comparison of the Thurstone and Likert techniques of attitude scale construction, *Journal of Applied Psychology*, 30, 72-83.

Edwards, D., D.A. Gorrell, J.S. Johnson, and S. Shedroff (1994). Typical definition of satisfaction is too limited, *Marketing News*, 28, 6.

EFQM (2006). *The EFQM excellence model*, European Foundation for Quality Management, Brussels.

Elangovan, A.R. (2001). Causal ordering of stress, satisfaction and commitment, and intention to quit: A structural equations analysis, *Leadership and Organization Development Journal*, 22 (4), 159-165.

Elliott, K. and M. Hall (1994). Organizational commitment and job involvement: Applying Blau and Boal's typology to purchasing professionals, *American Business Review*, 12 (1), 6-14.

Elrod, T. (1988). A management science assessment of a behavioral measure of brand loyalty, in: M.J. Houston (ed.), *Advances in consumer research*, Association for Consumer Research, 15, Provo, UT, 481-486.

Engel, J.F., D. Kollat, and R.D. Blackwell (1978). *Consumer Behavior*, Dryden Press, Illinois.

Engel, J.F. and R.D. Blackwell (1982). *Consumer behavior*, Holt, Rinehart and Winston, New York.

Erdos, P.L. (1983). *Professional mail surveys*, R. E. Krieger Publishing, Huntington, NY.

Erevelles, S. and C. Leavitt (1992). A comparison of current models of customer satisfaction/dissatisfaction, *Journal of Consumer Satisfaction, Dissatisfaction and Complaining Behavior*, 5, 104-114.

Evans, J.P. and R.E. Steuer (1973). A revised simplex method for linear multiple objective programs, *Mathematical Programming*, 5 (1), 54-72.

Federico, S.M., P. Federico, and G.W. Lundquis (1976). Predicting women's turnover as a function of extent of met salary expectations and biodemographic data, *Personnel Psychology*, 29, 559-566.

Festinger, L. (1957). *A theory of cognitive dissonance*, Stanford University Press, Stanford, CA.

Fienberg, S.E. (1980). *The analysis of cross classified categorical data*, MIT Press, Cambridge, MA.

Fishbein, M. (1967). *Readings in attitude theory and measurement*, John Wiley and Sons, New York.

Fishburn, P.C. (1966). A note on recent developments in additive utility theories for multiple factors situations, *Operations Research*, 14, 1143-1148.

Fishburn, P.C. (1967). Methods for estimating additive utilities, *Management Science*, 13 (7), 435-453.

Fishburn, P.C. (1970). *Utility theory for decision making*, Wiley, New York.

Fishburn, P.C. (1972). *Mathematics of decision theory*, UNESCO, The Hague.

Fishburn, P.C. (1982). *The foundation of expected utility*, Reidel, Dordrecht.

Fisk, R.P. and K.A. Coney (1982). Postchoice evaluation: An equity theory analysis of consumer satisfaction/dissatisfaction with service choices, in: H.K. Hunt and R.L. Day (eds.), *Conceptual and empirical contributions to consumer satisfaction and complaining behavior*, Indiana University School of Business, Bloomington, 9-16.

Fisk, R.P. and C.E. Young (1985). Disconfirmation of equity expectations: Effects of consumer satisfaction with services, in: E.C. Hirschman and M.B. Holbrook (eds.), *Advances in Consumer Research Vol. 12*, Association for Consumer Research, Provo, UT, 340-345.

Fletcher, C. and R. Williams (1996). Performance management, job satisfaction and organizational commitment, *British Journal of Management*, 7 (2), 169-179.

Flury, B. and H. Riedwyl (1988). *Multivariate statistics: A practical approach*, Chapman & Hall, London.

Fornell, C. and B. Wernerfelt (1987). Defensive marketing strategy by customer complaint management, *Journal of Marketing Research*, 24 (4), 337-346.

Fornell, C. and B. Wernerfelt (1988). Model for customer complaint management, *Marketing Science*, 7 (3), 271-286.

Fornell, C. (1992). A national satisfaction barometer: The Swedish experience, *Journal of Marketing*, 56 (1), 6-21.

Fornell, C. and J. Cha (1994). Partial least squares, in: R.P. Bagozzi (ed.), *Advanced methods of marketing research*, Blackwell, Cambridge, MA, 52-78.

Fornell, C. (1995). The quality of economic output: Empirical generalizations about its distribution and relationship to market share, *Marketing Science*, 14 (3), 203-211.

Fornell, C., M.D. Johnson, E.W. Anderson, J. Cha, and B.E. Bryant (1996). The American customer satisfaction index: Nature, purpose, and findings, *Journal of Marketing*, 60 (4), 7-18.

Fornell, C. (2001a). Consumer spending depends on customer satisfaction, ACSI press release, August 20 (http://www.theacsi.org/score_commentaries/communtaries/ Q2_01_comm.htm).

Fornell, C. (2001b). *The science of satisfaction. Harvard Business Review*, 79 (3), 120-121.

Fornell, C. (2002). Consumer spending should rebound as customer satisfaction holds steady in manufacturing durables and e-business, ACSI press release, August 19 (http://www.theacsi.org/press_releases/0802q2.pdf).

Fornell, C. and J. Stephan (2002). Consumer spending growth predicted by buyer satisfaction, Working Paper, The National Quality Research Center, University of Michigan Business School, Ann Arbor, Michigan.

Fornell, C. (2003a). Boost stock performance nation's economy, *Quality Progress*, 35 (2), 25-31.

Fornell, C. (2003b). Customer satisfaction gains not enough to sustain recent spending growth, ACSI press release, November 19 (http://www.theacsi.org/press_releases/1103q.pdf).

Fornell, C. (2005). Marginal ACSI improvement - Enough for consumer spending growth? ACSI press release, November 15 (http://www.theacsi.org/score_commentaries/ communtaries/Q3_05_comm.htm).

Fornell, C., S. Mithas, F.V. Morgeson, and M.S. Krishnan (2006). Customer satisfaction and stock prices: High returns, low risk, *Journal of Marketing*, 70 (1), 3-14.

Fowler, F.J. Jr (1993). *Survey research methods*, Sage Publications, Newbury Park, CA.

Fowler, F.J. Jr (1995). *Improving survey questions*, Sage Publications, Thousand Oaks, CA.

French, S. (1993). *Decision theory: An introduction to the mathematics of rationality*, Ellis Horwood, West Sussex.

Frey, J.H. (1983). *Survey research by telephone*, Sage Publications, Beverly Hills, CA.

Fried, Y. and G.R. Ferris (1987). The validity of the job characteristics model: A review and meta-analysis, *Personnel Psychology*, 40 (2), 287-322.

Frost, F.A. and M. Kumar (2000). INTSERVQUAL: An internal adaptation of the GAP model in a large service organization, *Journal of Services Marketing*, 14 (5), 358-377.

Fulford, M.D. and C.A. Enz (1995). The impact of empowerment on service employees, *Journal of Managerial Issues*, 7 (2), 161-175.

Gale, B.T. (1994). *Managing customer value*, The Free Press, New York, NY.

Galloway, L. (1999). Hysteresis: A model of consumer behaviour?, *Managing Service Quality*, 9 (5), 360-370.

Gardial, S.F., S.D. Clemons, R.B. Woodruff, D.W. Schumann, and M.J. Burns (1994). Comparing consumers' recall of prepurchase and postpurchase evaluation experiences, *Journal of Consumer Research*, 20 (2), 548-560.

Garvin, D. (1988). *Managing quality*, The Free Press, New York.

Gattin, P. and D.R. Wittink (1982). Commercial use of conjoint analysis: A survey, *Journal of Marketing*, 46 (3), 44-53.

Gensch, D.H. and W.W. Recker (1979). The multinomial, multiattribute logit choice model, *Journal of Marketing Research*, 16 (1), 124-132.

Gerson, R.F. (1993). *Measuring customer satisfaction: A guide to managing quality service*, Crisp Publications, Menlo Park.

Ghobadian, A., S. Speller, and M. Jones (1994). Service quality: concepts and models, *International Journal of Quality and Reliability Management*, 11 (9), 43-66.

Ginter, J.L. (1974). An experimental investigation of attitude change and choice of a new brand, *Journal of Marketing Research*, 11 (1), 30-40.

Gnanadesikan, R. (1977). *Methods for statistical data analysis of multivariate observations*, Wiley, New York.

Goodstadt, M.S., L. Chung, R. Kronitz, and G. Cook (1977). Mail survey response rates: Their manipulation and impact, *Journal of Marketing Research*, 14 (3), 125-139.

Goodwin, C. and I. Ross (1990). Consumer evaluations of responses to complaints: What's fair and way, *Journal of Service Marketing*, 4 (3), 53-61.

Goris, J.R., B.C. Vaught, and J.D. Pettit (2000). Effects of communication direction on job performance and satisfaction: A moderated regression analysis, *Journal of Business Communication*, 37 (4), 348-368.

Gorman, W.M. (1959). Separable utility and aggregation, *Econometrica*, 27 (3), 469-481.

Gorman, W.M. (1968). The structure of utility functions, *Review of Economic Studies*, 35 (4), 367-390.

Gorsuch, R.L. (1983). *Factor analysis*, Lawrence Erlbaum, Hillsdale, NJ.

Gortsos, C. (1998). *The Greek banking system*, Hellenic Bank Association, Athens.

Graham, W. and J. Balloun (1973). An empirical test of Maslow's need hierarchy theory, *Journal of Human Psychology*, 13 (1), 97-108.

Green, P.E. and V.R. Rao (1971). Conjoint measurement for quantifying judgmental data, *Journal of Marketing Research*, 8 (3), 355-363.

Green, P.E. and J. Wind (1973). *Multi-attribute decisions in marketing: A measurement approach*, The Dryden Press, Hinsdale, Illinois.

Green, P.E. and V. Sprinivasan (1978). Conjoint analysis in consumer research: Issues and outlook, *Journal of Consumer Research*, 5 (2), 101-123.

Green, P.E., S.M. Goldberg, and J.B. Wiley (1983). A cross-validation test of hybrid conjoint models, *Advances in Consumer Research*, 10, 147-150.

Green, P.E. (1984). Hybrid conjoint analysis: An expository review, *Journal of Marketing Research*, 21 (2), 155-159.

Greenbaum, T.L. (1988). *The practical handbook and guide to focus group research*, Lexington Books, Lexington, MA.

Griffin, A. and J.R. Houser (1993). The voice of the customer, *Marketing Science*, 12 (1), 1-27.

Griffin, J. (1995). *Customer loyalty*, Lexington Books, Lexington, MA.

Grigoroudis, E., A. Samaras, N.F. Matsatsinis, and Y. Siskos (1999a). Preference and customer satisfaction analysis: An integrated multicriteria decision aid approach, *Proceedings of the 5th Decision Sciences Institute's International Conference on Integrating Technology & Human Decisions: Global Bridges into the 21st Century*, Athens, Greece, 2, 1350-1352.

Grigoroudis, E., J. Malandrakis, J. Politis, and Y. Siskos (1999b). Customer satisfaction measurement: An application to the Greek shipping sector, *Proceedings of the 5th Decision Sciences Institute's International Conference on Integrating Technology & Human Decisions: Global Bridges into the 21st Century*, Athens, Greece, 2, 1363-1365.

Grigoroudis, E., Y. Siskos, and O. Saurais (2000). TELOS: A customer satisfaction evaluation software, *Computers and Operations Research*, 27 (7-8), 799-817.

Grigoroudis, E. and Y. Siskos (2002). Preference disaggregation for measuring and analysing customer satisfaction: The MUSA method, *European Journal of Operational Research*, 143 (1), 148-170.

Grigoroudis, E., Y. Politis, and Y. Siskos (2002). Satisfaction benchmarking and customer classification: An application to the branches of a banking organization, *International Transactions in Operational Research*, 9 (5), 599-618.

Grigoroudis, E. and O. Spiridaki (2003). Derived vs. stated importance in customer satisfaction surveys, *Operational Research: An International Journal*, 3 (3), 229-247.

Grigoroudis, E. and Y. Siskos (2003). MUSA: A decision support system for evaluating and analysing customer satisfaction, in K. Margaritis and I. Pitas (eds.), *Proceedings of the 9th Panhellenic Conference in Informatics*, TEI of Thessaloniki, 113-127.

Grigoroudis, E. and Y. Siskos (2004). A survey of customer satisfaction barometers: Results from the transportation-communications sector, *European Journal of Operational Research*, 152 (2), 334-353.

Grigoroudis, E., Y. Politis, O. Spiridaki, and Y. Siskos (2004). Modelling importance preferences in customer satisfaction surveys, in: C.H. Antunes, J. Figueira, and J. Climaco (eds.), *Proceedings of the 56th Meeting of the European Working Group "Multiple Criteria Decision Aiding"*, INESC Coimbra, 273-291.

Grigoroudis, E., Ch. Litos, V.A. Moustakis, Y. Politis, and L. Tsironis (2007a). The assessment of user-perceived web quality: Application of a satisfaction benchmarking approach, *European Journal of Operational Research*, 187 (3), 1346-1357.

Grigoroudis, E., P. Kyriazopoulos, Y. Siskos, A. Spyridakos, and D. Yannacopoulos (2007b). Tracking changes of e-customer preferences using multicriteria analysis, *Managing Service Quality*, 17 (5), 538-562.

Grisaffe, D. (1993). Appropriate use of regression in customer satisfaction analyses: A response to William McLauchlan, *Quirk's Marketing Research Review*, February, 10-17.

Grønholdt, L., A. Martensen, and K. Kristensen (2000). The relationship between customer satisfaction and loyalty: Cross-industry differences, *Total Quality Management*, 11 (4), 89-99.

Grönroos, C. (1984). A service quality model and its marketing implications, *European Journal of Marketing*, 18 (4), 36-44.

Gruca, T.S. and L.L. Rego (2005). Customer satisfaction, cash flow and shareholder value, *Journal of Marketing*, 69 (3), 115-130.

Gustafson, D.H., W.L. Cats-Baril, and F. Alemi (1992). *Systems to support health policy analysis: Theory, model and uses*, Health Administration Press, Ann Arbor, Michigan.

Gutman, J. (1982). A means-end chain model based on consumer categorization processes, *Journal of Marketing*, 46 (1), 60-72.

Gutman, J. and S.D. Alden (1985). Adolescents cognitive structures of retail stores and fashion consumption: A means-end chain analysis of quality, in: J. Jacoby and J.C. Olson (eds.), *Perceived quality: How customers view stores and merchandise*, D.C. Health and Company, Lexington, MA, 99-114.

Hackman, J.R. and G.R. Oldham (1975). Development of the job diagnostic survey, *Journal of Applied Psychology*, 60 (2), 159-170.

Hackman, J.R. and G.R. Oldham (1980). *Work redesign*, Addison-Wesley, Reading, MA.

Hallowell, R. (1996). The relationships of customer satisfaction, customer loyalty, and profitability: An empirical study, *International Journal of Service Industry Management*, 7 (4), 27-42.

Hammond, K.R., R.L. Cook, and L. Adelman (1977). POLICY: An aid for decision making and international communication, *Columbia Journal of World Business*, 12, 79-83.

Hanushek, E.A. and J.E. Jackson (1977). *Statistical methods for social scientists*, Academic Press, San Diego, CA.

Harman, H.H. (1976). *Modern factor analysis*, University of Chicago Press, Chicago.

Harrison, J.R. and J.G. March (1984). Decision making and postdecision surprises, *Administrative Science Quarterly*, 29 (1), 26-42.

Hatzinakos, I., D. Yannacopoulos, C. Faltsetas, and C. Ziourkas (1991). Application of the MINORA decision support system to the evaluation of landslide favourability in Greece, *European Journal of Operational Research*, 50 (1), 60-75.

Hauser, J.R. and D. Clausing (1988). The house of quality, *Harvard Business Review*, May-June, 63-73.

Hauser, J.R. (1991). Comparison of importance measurement methodologies and their relationship to consumer satisfaction, *MIT Marketing Center Working Paper*, 91 (1), Massachusetts.

Hausknecht, D. (1988), Emotion measures of satisfaction/dissatisfaction, *Journal of Consumer Satisfaction, Dissatisfaction and Complaining Behavior*, 1 (1), 25-33.

Hausknecht, D. (1990). Measurement scales in customer satisfaction/dissatisfaction, *Journal of Consumer Satisfaction/Dissatisfaction and Complaint Behavior*, 3 (1), 1-11.

Hayes, B. (1992). *Measuring customer satisfaction: Development and use of questionnaires*, ASQC Quality Press, Milwaukee.

Haywood-Farmer, J. (1988). A conceptual model of service quality, *International Journal of Operations and Production Management*, 8 (6), 19-29.

Helson, H. (1964). *Adaptation-level theory*, Harper & Row, New York.

Heneman, H.G. III and D.P. Schwab (1985). Pay satisfaction: Its multidimensional nature and measurement, *International Journal of Psychology*, 20 (2), 129-141.

Heneman, H.G. III and T.A. Judge (2000). Compensation attitudes, in: S.L. Rynes and B. Gerhart (eds.), *Compensation in organizations: Current research and practice*, Jossey-Bass, San Francisco, 61-103.

Hensley, W.E. (1974). Increasing response rate by choice of postage stamps, *Public Opinion Quarterly*, 38, 280-283.

Herzberg, F., B. Mausner, and B.B. Snyderman (1959). *The motivation to work*, Wiley, New York.

Herzberg, F. (1966). *Work and the nature of man*, World Publishing, Cleveland, OH.

Herzberg, F. (1968). One more time: How do you motivate employees?, *Harvard Business Review*, 46, 53-62.

Hill, N. (1996). *Handbook of customer satisfaction measurement*, Gower Publishing, Hampshire.

Hill, N. and J. Alexander (2006). *Handbook of customer satisfaction and loyalty measurement*, Gower, Aldershot.

Hill, N.C. and D.M. Ferguson (1991). Electronic Data Interchange: A definition and perspective, *Principles of EDI*, EDI Group, Oak Park, IL, 12-18.

Hinterhuber, H.H., H. Aichner, and W. Lobenwein (1994). *Unternehmenswert und lean management*, Manz-Verlag, Vienna.

Hirschman, A.O. (1970). *Exit, voice and loyalty: Responses to decline in firms, organizations, and states*, Harvard University Press, Cambridge, MA.

Hoffman, D.L. and G.R. Franke (1986). Correspondence analysis: Graphical representation of categorical data in marketing research, *Journal of Marketing Research*, 23 (3), 454-469.

Holmlund, M. and S. Kock (1995). Buyer perceived service quality in industrial networks, *Industrial Marketing Management*, 24 (2), 109-121.

Hom, P.W. and R.W. Griffeth (1991). Structural equations modeling test of turnover theory: Cross-sectional and longitudinal analyses, *Journal of Applied Psychology*, 76 (3), 350-366.

Hom, P.W. and R.W. Griffeth (1995). *Employee turnover*, South-Western, Cincinnati.

Homans, G.C. (1961). *Social behavior: Its elementary forms*, Harcour, Brace and World, New York.

Horton, R.L. (1974). The Edwards personal preference schedule and consumer personality research, *Journal of Marketing Research*, 11, 335-337.

Howard, J.A. and J. Sheth (1969). *The theory of buyer behavior*, John Wiley and Sons, New York.

Howard, J.A. (1977). *Consumer behavior: Application of theory*, McGraw-Hill, New York.

Huber, G.P. (1974). Multi-attribute utility models: A review of field and field-like studies, *Management Science*, 20 (10), 1393-1402.

Huiskonen, J. and T. Pirttilä (1998). Sharpening logistics customer service strategy planning by applying Kano's quality element classification, *International Journal of Production Economics*, 56-57 (1-3), 253-260.

Hunt, H.K. (1977). Customer satisfaction/dissatisfaction: Overview and future research directions, in: H.K. Hunt (ed.), *Conceptualization and measurement of consumer satisfaction and dissatisfaction*, Marketing Science Institute, Cambridge, MA, 445-488.

Huppertz, J.W., S.J. Arenson and R.H. Evans (1978). An application of equity theory to buyer-seller exchange situations, *Journal of Marketing Research*, 15 (2), 250-260.

Huppertz, J.W. (1979). Measuring components of equity in the marketplace: Perceptions of inputs and outcomes by satisfied and dissatisfied consumers, in: R.L. Day and H.K. Hunt (eds.), *New dimensions of consumer satisfaction and complaining behavior*, Indiana University Scholl of Business, Bloomington, 140-143.

Iacobucci, D., K.A. Grayson, and A.L. Omstrom (1994). The calculus of service quality and customer satisfaction: Theoretical and empirical differentiation and integration, in: T.A. Swartz, D.E. Bowen, and S.W. Brown (eds.), *Advances in services marketing and management*, 3, JAI Press, Greenwich, CT, 1-68.

ICAP (2005). *Internet services sectoral study*, ICAP S.A., Athens.

Ironson, G.H., P.C. Smith, M.T. Brannick, W.M. Gibson, and K.B. Paul (1989). Constitution of a job in general scale: A comparison of global, composite, and specific measures, *Journal of Applied Psychology*, 74 (2), 193-200.

Ittner, C. and D. Larcker (1998). Are non-financial measures leading indicators of financial performance? An analysis of customer satisfaction, *Journal of Accounting Research*, 36 (3), 1-35.

Iverson, R.D. (1996). Employee acceptance of organizational change: The role of organizational commitment, *The International Journal of Human Resource Management*, 7 (1), 122-149.

Jacobson, D. (1991). The conceptual approach to job insecurity, in: J.F. Hartley, D. Jacobson, B. Klandermans, and T. van Vuuren (eds.), *Job Insecurity: Coping with jobs at risk*, Sage, London, 23-39.

Jacoby, J. (1971). A model for multi-brand loyalty, *Journal of Advertising Research*, 11 (3), 25-31.

Jacoby, J. and D.B. Kyner (1973). Brand loyalty versus repeat purchasing behavior, *Journal of Marketing Research*, 10 (1), 1-9.

Jacoby, J. (1975). A brand loyalty concept: Comments on a comment, *Journal of Marketing Research*, 12 (4), 484-487.

Jacoby, J. and R.W. Chestnut (1978). *Brand loyalty: Measurement and management*, Wiley, New York.

Jacquet-Lagrèze, E. and J. Siskos (1982). Assessing a set of additive utility functions for multicriteria decision-making: The UTA method, *European Journal of Operational Research*, 10 (2), 151-164.

Jacquet-Lagrèze, E. (1984). PREFCALC: Evaluation et décision multicritere, *Revue de l'Utilisateur de IBM PC*, 3, 38-55.

Jacquet-Lagrèze, E.R. Meziani, and R. Slowinski (1987). MOLP with an interactive assessment of a piecewise-linear utility function, *European Journal of Operational Research*, 31 (3), 350-357.

Jacquet-Lagrèze, E. (1990). Interactive assessment of preference using holistic judgement: The PREFCALC system, in: C. Bana e Costa, (ed.), *Readings on multiple criteria decision aid*, Springer, Berlin, 335-350.

Jacquet-Lagrèze, E. (1995). An application of the UTA discriminant model for the evaluation of R&D projects, in: P.M. Pardalos, Y. Siskos, and C. Zopounidis (eds.), *Advances in multicriteria analysis*, Kluwer Academic Publishers, Dordrecht, 203-211.

Jacquet-Lagrèze, E. and Y. Siskos (2001). Preference disaggregation: 20 years of MCDA experience, *European Journal of Operational Research*, 130 (2), 233-245.

Jan-Benedict, E. and M. Steenkamp (1990). Conceptual model of the quality perception process, *Journal of Business Research*, 21 (4), 309-333.

Jarvis, L.P. and J.B. Wilcox (1976). Repeat purchasing behavior and attitudinal brand loyalty: Additional evidence, in: K.L. Bernhardt (ed.), *Marketing 1776-1976 and beyond*, American Marketing Association, Chicago, 151-152.

Jaszkiewicz, A. and R. Slowinski (1995). The Light Beam Search: Outranking based interactive procedure for multiple-objective mathematical programming, in P.M. Pardalos, Y. Siskos and C. Zopounidis (eds.), *Advances in multicriteria analysis*, Kluwer Academic Publishers, Dordrecht, 129-146.

Johnson, M.D. (1984). Consumer choice strategies for comparing noncomparable alternatives, *Journal of Consumer Research*, 11 (1), 741-753.

Johnson, M.D. and C. Fornell (1991). A framework for comparing customer satisfaction across individuals and product categories, *Journal of Economic Psychology*, 12 (2), 267-286.

Johnson, M.D., E.W. Anderson, and C. Fornell (1995). Rational and adaptive performance expectations in a customer satisfaction framework, *Journal of Customer Research*, 21 (4), 128-140.

Johnson, M.D., A. Gustafson, T.W. Andreassen, L. Lervik, and J. Cha (2001). The evolution and future of national satisfaction index models, *Journal of Economic Psychology*, 22 (2), 217-245.

Johnson, M.D., A. Herrmann, and A. Gustafsson (2002). Comparing customer satisfaction across industries and countries, *Journal of Economic Psychology*, 23 (6), 749-769.

Johnson, R.M. (1974). Trade-off analysis of consumer values, *Journal of Marketing Research*, 11 (2), 121-127.

Jöreskog, K.G. and D. Sörbom (1993). Testing structural equation models, in: K.A. Bollen and J.S. Land (eds.), *Testing structural equation models*, Sage, Newbury Park, CA, 294-316.

Jöreskog, K.G. and D. Sörbom (1996). *LISREL 8: User's reference guide*, Scientific Software International, Chicago.

Joseph, A.E., B. Smit, and G.P. McIlravey (1989). Consumer preferences for rural residences: A conjoint analysis in Ontario, Canada, *Environment and Planning A*, 21, 47-63.

Juran, J.M. (1988). *Juran on planning for quality*, The Free Press, New York.

Juran, J.M. and F.M. Gryna (1988). *Juran's quality control handbook*, McGraw-Hill, New York.

Juran, J.M. (1993). Made in USA: A renaissance of quality, *Harvard Business Review*, July-August, 42-50.

Kadir, A., M. Abdullah, and A. Agus (2000). On service improvement capacity index: A case study of the public service sector in Malaysia, *Total Quality Management*, 11 (4-6), 134-146.

Kalleberg, A.L. and M.E. van Buren (1996). Is bigger better? Explaining the relationship between organization size and job rewards, *American Sociological Review*, 61 (1), 47-66.

Kanji, G.K. (1998). Measurement of business excellence. *Total Quality Management*, 9 (7), 633-643.

Kanji, G.K. (2001). Forces of excellence in Kanji's business excellence model, *Total Quality Management*, 12 (2), 259-272.

Kano, N., N. Seraku, F. Takahashi, and S. Tsjui (1984). Attractive quality and must-be quality, *Hinshitsu*, 14 (2), 147-56.

Kano, N. (2001). Life cycle and creation of attractive quality, *4th International QMOD (Quality Management and Organisational Development) Conference*, Linköping University, Linköping.

Kanungo, R.N. (1982). *Work alienation*, Preager, New York.

Kasper, H. (1988). On problem perception, dissatisfaction, and brand loyalty, *Journal of Economic Psychology*, 9 (3), 387-397.

Kassarjian, H.H. (1974). Personality and consumer behavior: A review, *Journal of Marketing Research*, 8 (4), 409-418.

Katcher, B.L. (1995). Readership surveys (suggestions for improving effectiveness of magazine reader surveys), *Folio: The Magazine for Magazine Management* (http://findarticles.com/p/articles/mi_m3065/is_n7_v24/ai_16792256).

Katzell, R.A. (1964). Personal values, job satisfaction, and job behavior, in: H. Borow (ed.), *Man in a word of work*, Houghton Mifflin, Boston, 341-363.

Keaveney, S.M. (1995). Customer switching behavior in service industries: An exploratory study, *Journal of Marketing*, 59 (2), 71-82.

Keeney, R.L. and H. Raiffa (1976). *Decisions with multiple objectives: Preferences and value trade-offs*, Wiley, New York.

Keeney, R.L. (1981). Measurement scales for quantifying attributes, *Behavioral Science*, 26 (1), 29-36.

Keeney, R.L. (1988). Structuring objectives for problems of public interest, *Operations Research*, 36 (3), 396-405.

Keeney, R.L. (1992). *Value-focused thinking: A path to creative decision making*, Harvard University Press, London.

Kelly, G.A. (1955). *The psychology of personal constructs*, Norton, New York.

Kendall, H. (1997). Your 10-point guide to choosing helpdesk technology, *Customer Service Management*, 16, 44-46.

Kerlinger, F.N. and E.J. Pedhazur (1973). *Multiple regression in behavioral research*, Holt, Rinehart and Winston, New York.

Kessler, S. (1996). *Measuring and managing customer satisfaction: Going for the gold*, ASQC Quality Press, Milwaukee.

Kirkwood, C.W. (1997). *Strategic decision making: Multiobjective decision analysis with spreadsheets*, Duxbury Press, Belmont.

Klecka, W.R. (1980). *Discriminant analysis*, Sage Publications, Beverly Hills, CA.

Kline, R.B. (1998). *Principles and practice of structural equation modelling*, Guilford, New York.

Knoke, D. and P.J. Burke (1980). *Log-linear models*, Sage Publications, Newbury Park, CA.

Koch, J.L. and R.M. Steers, (1978). Job attachment, satisfaction, and turnover among public sector employees, *Journal of Vocational Behavior*, 12 (2), 119-128.

Kon, M., C. Kunkemueller, and T. Russel (2007). When instinct is not enough: Using the right facts to shape customer experience, *Mercer Management Journal*, 19, 57-63.

Korhonen, E. and J. Wallenius (1990). A multiple objective linear programming decision support system, *Decision Support Systems*, 6 (3), 243-251.

Kotler, P. (1994). *Marketing management: Analysis, planning, implementation and control*, 8th ed., Prentice-Hall, London.

Kovach, K.A. (1978). *Organization size, job satisfaction, absenteeism and turnover*, University Press of America, Washington.

Krantz, D.H., R.L. Luce, P. Suppes, and A. Tversky (1971). *Foundations of measurement*, Academic Press, New York.

Kristensen, K., A. Martensen, and L. Grønholdt (2000). Customer satisfaction measurement at post Denmark: Results of application of the European Customer Satisfaction Index methodology, *Total Quality Management*, 11 (7), S1007-S1015.

Krueger, R.A. (1980). *Focus groups: A practical guide for applied research*, Sage Publications, Beverly Hills, CA.

Kuhl, J. (1985). Volitional mediators of cognition-behavior consistency: Self-regulatory processes and action versus state orientation, in: J. Kuhl and J. Beckman (eds.), *Action control: From cognition to behavior*, Springer-Verlag, Berlin, 101-128.

Kuhl, J. (1986). Motivation and information processing, in: R.M. Sorrentino and E.T. Higgins (eds.), *Handbook of motivation and cognition*, Guilford Press, New York, 404-434.

Kuhnert, K.W., R.R. Sims, and M.A. Lahey (1989). The relationship between job security and employee health, *Group and Organization Studies*, 14 (4), 399-410.

Kuhnert, K.W. and D.R. Palmer (1991). Job security, health and the intrinsic and extrinsic characteristics of work, *Group and Organization Studies*, 16 (2), 178-192.

Kyriazopoulos, P., E. Grigoroudis, Y. Siskos, D. Yannacopoulos, and A. Spyridakos (2006). The quality of e-services: Measuring satisfaction of Internet customers, *Operational Research: An International Journal*, 7(2), 233-254.

Lapidus, R.S. and L. Pinkerton (1995). Customer complaint situations: An equity theory perspective, *Psychology and Marketing*, 12 (2), 105-122.

Lavrakas, P.J. (1987). *Telephone survey methods*, Sage Publications, Beverly Hills, CA.

Lawler, E.E. and D.T. Hall (1970). Relationship of job characteristics to job involvement, satisfaction, and intrinsic motivation, *Journal of Applied Psychology*, 54 (4), 305-312.

Lawrence, A. (1999). What is Computer Telephony Integration?, *Customer Service Management*, 23, 53-55.

Lee, M.C. and J.F. Newcomb (1997). Applying the Kano methodology to meet customer requirements: NASA's Microgravity Science Program, *Quality Management Journal*, 4 (3), 95-110.

Likert, R. (1932). A technique for the measurement of attitudes, *Archives of Psychology*, 140 (22), 1-55.

Lissitz, R.W. and S.B. Green (1975). Effect of the number of scale points on reliability: A Monte Carlo approach, *Journal of Applied Psychology*, 60 (1), 10-13.

Locke, E.A. (1976). The nature and causes of job satisfaction, in: M.D. Dunnette (ed.), *Handbook of industrial and organizational psychology*, Rand McNally, Chicago, 1297-1349.

Locke, E.A. (1984). Job satisfaction, in: M. Gruneberg and T. Wall (eds.), *Social psychology and organizational behavior*, Wiley, New York, 93-117.

Lodge, M. (1981). *Magnitude scaling: Quantitative measurement of opinions*, Sage Publications, Beverly Hills, CA.

Löfgren, M. and L. Witell (2008). Two decades of using Kano's theory of attractive quality: A literature review, *Quality Management Journal*, 15 (1), 59-75.

Loher, B.T., R.A. Noe, N.L. Moeller, and M.P. Fitzgerald (1985). A meta-analysis of the relation of job characteristics to job satisfaction, *Journal of Applied Psychology*, 70, 280-289.

Loomes, G. and R. Sugden (1982). Regret theory: An alternative theory of rational choice under uncertainty, *The Economic Journal*, 92 (368), 805-824.

Loris, K. (1998). Internet self-service support: Beyond search engines to «Smart answers on the Net», in: R. Zemke and J.A. Woods (eds.), *Best practices in customer service*, Amacom, New York, 318-327.

Löthgren, M. and M. Tambour (1999). Productivity and customer satisfaction in Swedish pharmacies: A DEA network model, *European Journal of Operational Research*, 115 (3), 449-458.

Louviere, J.J. (1988). Conjoint analysis modelling of stated preferences, *Journal of Transport Economics and Policy*, 22 (1), 93-113.

Lowenstein, M.W. (1995). Customer retention: An integrated process for keeping your best customers, ASQC Press, Milwaukee.

Madden, G., S.J. Savage, and G. Coble-Neal (1999). Subscriber churn in the Australian ISP market, *Information Economics and Policy*, 11 (2), 195-207.

Maddox, R.N. (1981). Two-factor theory and consumer satisfaction: Replication and extension, *Journal of Consumer Research*, 8 (1), 97-102.

Martensen, A., L. Grønholdt, and K. Kristensen (2000). The drivers of customer satisfaction and loyalty: Cross-industry findings from Denmark, *Total Quality Management*, 11 (4-6), 544-553.

Martins, M. and K.B. Monroe (1994). Perceived price fairness: A new look at an old concept, in: C.T. Allen and D.R. John (eds.), *Advances in Consumer Research Vol. 21*, Association for Consumer Research, Provo, UT, 75-78.

Maslow, A.H. (1943). A theory of human motivation, *Psychological Review*, 50, 370-396.

Maslow, A. H. (1970). *Motivation and personality*, Harper and Row, New York.

Massnick, F. (1997). *The customer is CEO: How to measure what your customers want - and make sure they get it*, AMACOM, New York.

Mathieu, J.E. and S.S. Kohler (1990). A test of the interactive effects of organizational commitment and job involvement on various of absence, *Journal of Vocational Behavior*, 36 (1), 33-44.

Mathieu, J.E. and G.L. Farr (1991). Further evidence for the discriminant validity of measures of organizational commitment, job involvement and job satisfaction, *Journal of Applied Psychology*, 76 (1), 127-133.

Matsatsinis, N.F. and Y. Siskos (1999). MARKEX: An intelligent decision support system for product development decision, *European Journal of Operational Research*, 113 (2), 336-354.

Matsatsinis, N.F., E. Ioannidou, and E. Grigoroudis (1999). Customer satisfaction using data mining techniques, *Proceedings of the European Symposium on Intelligent Techniques - ESIT'99*, Orthodox Academy of Crete, Kolymvari, Greece (http://www.erudit.de/erudit/events/esit99/12753_p.pdf).

Matsatsinis, N.F. and Y. Siskos (2003). *Intelligent support systems for marketing decision*, Kluwer Academic Publishers, Dordrecht.

Matsatsinis, N.F., E. Grigoroudis, and P. Delias (2003). User satisfaction and e-learning systems: Towards a multicriteria evaluation methodology, *Operational Research: An International Journal*, 3 (3), 249-259.

Matzler, K., H.H. Hinterhuber, F. Bailom and E. Sauerwein (1996). How to delight your customers, *Journal of Product and Brand Management*, 5 (2), 6-18.

Mazursky, D., P. LaBarbera, and A. Aiello (1987). When consumers switch brands, *Psychology and Marketing*, 4 (1), 17-30.

Mazursky, D. and A. Geva (1989). Temporal decay in satisfaction: Purchase intention relationship, *Psychology and Marketing*, 6 (3), 211-227.

McAlexander, J., D. Kaldenburg, and H. Koenig (1994). Service quality measurement, *Journal of Health Care Marketing*, 14 (3), 34-44.

McClelland, D.C. (1961). *The achieving society*, Van Nostrand, Princeton, NJ.

McCullagh, P. (1980). Regression models for ordinal data, *Journal of the Royal Statistical Society*, B42, 109-142.

McDonald, W.J. (1993). The roles of demographics, purchase histories, and shopper decision-making styles in predicting consumer catalog loyalty, *Journal of Direct Marketing*, 7 (3), 55-65.

McFarlin, D.B. and R.W. Rice (1992). The role of facet importance as a moderator in job satisfaction processes, *Journal of Organizational Behavior*, 13 (1), 41-54.

McFarlin, D.B., E.A. Coster, R.W. Rice, and A.T. Cooper (1995). Facet importance and job satisfaction: Another look at the range of affect hypothesis, *Basic and Applied Social Psychology*, 16 (2), 489-502.

McLauchlan, W. (1993). Regression-based satisfaction analyses: Proceed with caution, *Quirk's Marketing Research Review*, October, 10-13.

McQuarrie, E.F. (1988). An alternative to purchase intentions: The role of prior behaviour in consumer expenditures on computers, *Journal of the Market Research Society*, 16 (3), 203-226.

Meyer, A. (1994). *Das Deutsche kundenbarometer 1994*, Ludwig-Maximilians Universität, München.

Meyer, A. (1996). *The German customer satisfaction barometer: Quality and satisfaction 1995*, German Marketing Association, Düsseldorf.

Meyer, A. and F. Dornach (1996). *The German Customer Satisfaction Barometer: Quality and satisfaction - Yearbook of customer satisfaction in German 1995*, German Marketing Association e.V. and German Post AG, Düsseldorf.

Mihelis, G., E. Grigoroudis, Y. Siskos, Y. Politis, and Y. Malandrakis (2001). Customer satisfaction measurement in the private bank sector, *European Journal of Operational Research*, 130 (2), 347-360.

Miller, D. and M. Starr (1969). *Executive decisions and operations research*, Prentice-Hall, Englewood Cliffs, NJ.

Mittal, B. and M.S. Lee (1989). A causal model of consumer involvement, *Journal of Economic Psychology*, 10 (3), 363-389.

Mobley, W.H. and E.A. Locke (1970). The relationship of value importance to satisfaction, *Organizational Behavior and Human Performance*, 5 (5), 463-483.

Moore, C.D. (1987). Outclass the competition with service distinction, *Mortgage Banking*, 47 (11).

Morgan, D.L. (1988). *Focus groups as qualitative research*, Sage Publications, Newbury Park, CA.

Morgan, M.S. and C.S. Dev (1994). An empirical study of brand switching for a retail service, *Journal of Retailing*, 70 (3), 267-282.

Morris, M.H. and J.L. Holman (1988). Source loyalty in organizational markets: A dyadic perspective, *Journal of Business Research*, 16 (2), 117-131.

Motorola (1995). *Customer Satisfaction Assessment Guide*, Motorola University Press.

Mowday, R.T., L.W. Porter, and R. Dubin (1974). Unit performance situational factors, and employee attitudes in spatially separated work units, *Organizational Behaviour and Human Performance*, 12 (2), 231-248.

Mowday, R.T., L.W. Porter, and R.M. Steers (1982). *Employee-organization linkages: The psychology of commitment, absenteeism, and turnover*, Academic Press, New York.

Mowen, J.C. and S.J. Grove (1983). Search behavior, price, paid and the "comparison other": An equity theory analysis of post purchase satisfaction, in: R.L. Day and H.K. Hunt (eds.), *International Fare in Customer Satisfaction and Complaining Behavior*, Indiana University, Bloomington, IN, 57-63.

Mueller, C.W., J.E. Wallace, and J.L. Price (1992). Employee commitment: Resolving some issues, *Work and Occupations*, 19 (3), 211-236.

Muffatto, M. and R. Panizzolo (1995). A process-based view for customer satisfaction, *International Journal of Quality & Reliability Management*, 12 (9), 154-169.

Mullet, G.M. (1994). Regression, regression, *Quirk's Marketing Research Review*, October, 12-15.

Murray, H.A. (1938). *Explorations in personality: A clinical and experimental study of fifty men of college age*, Oxford University Press, New York.

Nash, C.A. (1988). A question of service: Action pack, Business Management Programme, Hotel and Catering Industry Training Board, National Consumer Council, London.

National Quality Research Center (1998). *American customer satisfaction index: Methodology report*, University of Michigan Business School, Milwaukee.

National Quality Research Center (2000). *American customer satisfaction index: Federal agencies government-wide customer satisfaction report for the general services administration*, University of Michigan Business School, Milwaukee.

Naumann, E. (1995). *Creating customer value*, Thomson Executive Press, Cincinnati, Ohio.

Naumann, E. and K. Giel (1995). *Customer satisfaction measurement and management: Using the voice of the customer*, Thomson Executive Press, Cincinnati.

Newman, J.W. and R.A. Werbel (1973). Multivariate analysis of brand loyalty for major household appliances, *Journal of Marketing Research*, 10 (4), 404-409.

NIST (2006). *Baldrige national quality program: Criteria for performance excellence*, National Institute of Standards and Technology, US Department of Commerce, Washington, DC.

Noori, H. and R. Radford (1995). *Production and operations management: Total quality and responsiveness*, McGraw-Hill, New York.

Oliva, T. A., P.L. Oliver, and I.C. McMillan (1992). A catastrophe model for developing service satisfaction strategies, *Journal of Marketing*, 56 (2), 83-95.

Oliva, T.A., P.L. Oliver, and W.O. Bearden (1995). The relationships among consumer satisfaction, involvement, and product performance: A catastrophe theory application, *Behavioral Science*, 40, 104-132.

Oliver, R.L. (1977). Effect of expectation and disconfirmation on postexposure product evaluations: An alternative interpretation, *Journal of Applied Psychology*, 62 (4), 480-486.

Oliver, R.L. (1980). A cognitive model of the antecedents and consequences of satisfaction decisions, *Journal of Marketing Research*, 17 (11), 460-469.

Oliver, R.L. (1981). Measurement and evaluation of satisfaction processes in retail settings, *Journal of Retailing*, 57 (3), 25-48.

Oliver, R.L. and W. DeSarbo (1988). Response determinants in satisfaction judgments, *Journal of Consumer Research*, 14 (4), 495-507.

Oliver, R.L. (1997). *Satisfaction: A behavioral perspective on the customer*, McGraw-Hill, New York.

Oral, M., O. Kettani, J.C. Cosset, and M. Daouas (1992). An estimation model for country risk rating, *International Journal of Forecasting*, 8 (4), 583-593.

Organ, D.W. (1988). *Organizational citizenship behavior: The good soldier syndrome*, Lexington Books, Lexington, MA.

Parasuraman, A., V.A. Zeithaml, and L.L. Berry (1985). A conceptual model of service quality and its implications for future research, *Journal of Marketing*, 49 (3), 41-50.

Parasuraman, A., V.A. Zeithaml, and L.L. Berry (1988). SERVQUAL: A multiple item scale for measuring consumer perceptions of service quality, *Journal of Retailing*, 64 (1), 14-40.

Parasuraman, A., V.A. Zeithaml, and L.L. Berry (1991). Refinement and reassessment of the SERVQUAL scale, *Journal of Retailing*, 67 (4), 420-450.

Parasuraman, A., V.A. Zeithaml, and L.L. Berry (1994). Reassessment of expectations as a comparison standard in measuring service quality: Implications for future research, *Journal of Marketing*, 58 (1), 111-124.

Parasuraman, A., V.A. Zeithaml, and A. Malhotra (2005). E-S-QUAL: A multiple-item scale for assessing electronic service quality, *Journal of Service Research*, 7 (3), 213-234.

Payne, S.L. (1951). *The art of asking questions*, Princeton University Press, Princeton, NJ.

Perkins, W.S. and T.J. Reynolds (1988). The explanatory power of values in preference judgements: Validation of the means-end perspective, in: M.J. Houston (ed.), *Advances in consumer research*, Vol. 15, Association for Consumer Research, Provo, UT, 122-126.

Philip, G. and S.A. Hazlett (1997). The measurement of service quality: A new P-C-P attributes model, *International Journal of Quality and Reliability Management*, 14 (3), 260-286.

Pincus, J.D. (1986). Communication satisfaction, job satisfaction, and job performance, *Human Communication Research*, 12 (3), 395-419.

Pindyck, R.S. and D.L. Rubinfeld (1985). *Econometric methods and economic forecasts*, McGraw-Hill, New York.

Ping, R.A. Jr. (1994). Does satisfaction moderate the association between alternative attractiveness and exit intention in a marketing channel?, *Journal of the Academy of Marketing Science*, 22 (4), 364-371.

Porter, L. and S. Tanner (1998). *Assessing business excellence*, Butterworth Heinemann, Oxford.

Price, J.L. (1997). Handbook of organizational measurement, *International Journal of Manpower*, 18 (4-6), 303-558.

Pruden, D.R., R. Sankar, and T.G. Vavra (1996). Customer loyalty: The competitive edge beyond satisfaction, *Quirk's Marketing Research Review*, 24, 49-53.

Pruzan, P.M. and J.T.R. Jackson (1963). On the development of utility spaces for multi-goal systems, *Saertryk af Erhvervsøkonomisk Tidsskrift*, 4, 257-274.

Raju, P.S. (1980). Optimal stimulation level: Its relationship to personality, demographics, and exploratory behavior, *Journal of Consumer Research*, 7 (3), 272-282.

Raykov, T. and G.A. Markoulides (2000). *A first course in structural equation modeling*, Lawrence Erlbaum Associate, Mahwah.

Reckase, M.D. (1990). Scaling techniques, in: G. Goldstein and M. Herson (eds.), *Handbook of psychological assessment*, Pergamon Press, New York, 38-53.

Reeves, C.A. and D.A. Bednar (1994). Defining quality: Alternatives and implications, *Academy of Management Review*, 19 (3), 419-445.

Reichheld, F.F. and W.E. Sasser Jr. (1990). Zero defections: Quality comes to service, *Harvard Business Review*, September-October, 105-111.

Reichheld, F.F. (1993). Loyalty-based management, *Harvard Business Review*, 71 (2), 64-73.

Reynolds, T.J. and J. Gutman (1988). Laddering theory: Method, analysis and interpretation, *Journal of Advertising Research*, 28 (3), 11-31.

Rhodes, S.R. (1983). Age-related differences in work attitude and behaviors: A review and conceptual analysis, *Psychological Bulletin*, 93, 328-367.

Rice, R.W., D.A. Gentile, and D.B. McFarlin (1991). Facet importance and job satisfaction, *Journal of Applied Psychology*, 76 (1), 31-39.

Robbins, S.P., and M. Coulter (1996), *Management*, Prentice-Hall, New Jersey.

Roberts, K.H., G.A. Walter, and R.E. Miles (1971). A factor analytic study of job satisfaction items designed to measure Maslow need categories, *Personnel Psychology*, 24, 205-220.

Roese, N.J. and J.M. Olson (1993). The structure of counterfactual thought, *Personality and Social Psychology Bulletin*, 19 (3), 312-319.

Roese, N.J. (1994). The functional basis of counterfactual thinking, *Journal of Personality and Social Psychology*, 66 (5), 805-818.

Ross, I. (2002). Methods of investigating critical incidents: A comparative review, *Journal of Service Research*, 4 (3), 193-204.

Roy, B. (1976). From optimization to multicriteria decision aid: Three main operational attributes, in: H. Thiriez and S. Zionts (eds.), *Multiple criteria decision making*, Springer, Berlin, 1-32.

Roy, B. and P. Vincke (1981). Multicriteria analysis: Survey and new directions, *European Journal of Operational Research*, 8 (3), 207-218.

Roy, B. (1985). *Méthodologie multicritère d'aide à la Décision*, Economica, Paris.

Roy, B. (1989). The outranking approach and the foundations of Electre methods, in: C. Bana e Costa, (ed.), *Readings on multiple criteria decision aid*, Springer, Berlin, 155-183.

Roy, B. (1990). Decision aid and decision making, *European Journal of Operational Research*, 45 (2-3), 324-331.

Roy, B. and D. Bouyssou (1993). *Aide multicritère à la Décision: Méthodes et cas*, Economica, Paris.

Rummel, R.J. (1970). *Applied factor analysis*, Northwestern University Press, Evanston, IL.

Ryan, M., T. Buzas, and V. Ramaswamy (1995). Making CSM a power tool, *Marketing Science*, 7 (3), 11-16.

Ryan, M.J. and E.H. Bonfield (1975). The Fishbein extended model and consumer behavior, *Journal of Consumer Research*, 2, 118-136.

Scala, S. and R. McGrath Jr. (1993). Advantages and disadvantages of electronic data interchange: An industrial perspective, *Information and Management*, 25 (2), 85-91.

Schlesinger, L.A and J. Heskett (1991). Breaking the cycle of failure in services, *Sloan Management Review*, 32 (3), 17-28.

Schlesinger, L.A and J. Zomitsky (1991). Job Satisfaction, service capability and customer satisfaction: an examination of linkages and management implications, *Human Resource Planning*, 14 (2), 141-149.

Schuman, H. and S. Presser (1996). *Questions and answers in attitude surveys: Experiments on question form, wording and context*, Sage Publications, Thousand Oaks, CA.

Seo, Y., J. Ko, and J.L. Price (2004). The determinants of job satisfaction among hospital nurses: A model estimation in Korea, International *Journal of Nursing Studies*, 41 (4), 437-446.

Shah, R. and S.M. Goldstein (2006). Use of structural equation modeling in operations management research: Looking back and forward, *Journal of Operations Management*, 24 (1), 148-169.

Shen, X.X., K.C. Tan, and M. Xie (2000). An integrated approach to innovative product development using Kano's model and QFD, *European Journal of Innovation Management*, 3 (2), 91-99.

Sheth, J.N., B.I. Newman, and B.L. Gross (1991). *Consumption values and market choices: Theory and applications*, South-Western Publishing Co., Cincinnati, Ohio.

Shikdara, A.A. and B. Das (2003). A strategy for improving worker satisfaction and job attitudes in a repetitive industrial task: application of production standards and performance feedback, *Ergonomics*, 46 (5), 466-481.

Sibbald, B., I. Enzer, C. Cooper, U. Rout, and V. Sutherland (2000). GP job satisfaction in 1989, 1990 and 1998: Lessons for the future?, *Family Practice*, 17, 364-371.

Sirgy, M.J. (1986). A quality-of-life theory derived from Maslow's developmental perspective, *American Journal of Economics and Sociology*, 45 (3), 329-342.

Siskos, J. (1980). Comment modéliser les préférences au moyen de fonctions d'utilité additives, *RAIRO Recherche Opérationelle*, 14, 53-82

Siskos, J. (1984). Le traitement des solutions quasi-optimales en programmation linéaire continue: Une synthèse, *RAIRO Recherche Opérationnelle*, 18, 382-401.

Siskos, J. (1985). Analyses de régression et programmation linéaire, *Révue de Statistique Appliquée*, 23 (2), 41-55.

Siskos, Y. and D. Yannacopoulos (1985). UTASTAR: An ordinal regression method for building additive value functions, *Investigaçao Operacional*, 5 (1), 39-53.

Siskos, J. (1986). Evaluating a system of furniture retail outlets using an interactive ordinal regression method, *European Journal of Operational Research*, 23 (2), 179-193.

Siskos, J. and C. Zopounidis (1987). The evaluation criteria of the venture capital investment activity: An interactive assessment, *European Journal of Operational Research*, 31 (3), 304-313.

Siskos, J. and N. Assimakopoulos (1989). Multicriteria highway planning: A case study, *Mathematical and Computer Modelling*, 12 (10-11), 1401-1410.

Siskos, Y. and D. Despotis (1989). A DSS oriented method for multiobjective linear programming problems, *Decision Support Systems*, 5 (1), 47-55.

Siskos, J. and N.F. Matsatsinis (1993). A DSS for market analysis and new product design, *Journal of Decision Systems*, 2 (1), 35-60.

Siskos, Y., A. Spyridakos, and D. Yannacopoulos (1993). MINORA: A multicriteria decision aiding system for discrete alternatives, *Journal of Information Science and Technology*, 2 (2), 136-149.

Siskos, Y., C. Zopounidis, and A. Pouliezos (1994). An integrated DSS for financing firms by an industrial development bank in Greece, *Decision Support Systems*, 12 (2), 151-168.

Siskos, Y., E. Grigoroudis, N.F. Matsatsinis, and G. Baourakis (1995a). Preference disaggregation analysis in agricultural product consumer behaviour, in: P.M. Pardalos, Y. Siskos, and C. Zopounidis (eds.), *Advances in multicriteria analysis*, Kluwer Academic Publishers, Dordrecht, 185-202.

Siskos, Y., E. Grigoroudis, N.F. Matsatsinis, G. Baourakis and F. Neguez (1995b). Comparative behavioural analysis of European olive oil consumer, in: J. Janssen, C.H. Skiadas and C. Zopounidis (eds.), *Advances in stochastic modelling and data analysis*, Kluwer Academic Publishers, Dordrecht, 293-310.

Siskos, Y., E. Grigoroudis, C. Zopounidis and O. Saurais (1998). Measuring customer satisfaction using a collective preference disaggregation model, *Journal of Global Optimization*, 12 (2), 175-195.

Siskos, Y. and A. Spyridakos (1999). Intelligent multicriteria decision support: Overview and perspectives, *European Journal of Operational Research*, 113 (2), 236-246.

Siskos, Y., A. Spyridakos and D. Yannacopoulos (1999). Using artificial intelligence and visual techniques into the procedures of preference disaggregation: The MIIDAS system, *European Journal of Operational Research*, 113 (2), 281-299.

Siskos Y., E. Grigoroudis, Y. Politis, and Y. Malandrakis (2001a). Customer satisfaction evaluation: Some real experiences, in: A. Colorni, M. Paruccini, and B. Roy (eds.), *A-MCD-A: Multiple Criteria Decision Aiding*, European Commission, Joint Research Center, EUR 19808 EN, 297-314.

Siskos, Y., N.F. Matsatsinis, and G. Baourakis (2001b). Multicriteria analysis in agricultural marketing: The case of French olive oil market, *European Journal of Operational Research*, 130, (2), 315-331.

Siskos, Y., E. Grigoroudis, and N.F. Matsatsinis (2005). UTA methods, in: J. Figueira, S. Greco, and M. Ehrgott (eds.), *Multiple criteria analysis: State of the art surveys*, Springer, New York, 297-344.

Smith, C.A., D.W. Organ, and J.P. Near (1983). Organizational citizenship behavior: Its nature and antecedents, *Journal of Applied Psychology*, 68 (4), 655-663.

Smith, P.C., L.M. Kendall, and C.L. Hulin (1969). *Measurement of satisfaction in work and retirement*. Rand McNally, Chicago.

Smith, R.A. and M.J. Houston (1982). Script-based evaluations of satisfaction with services, in: L.L. Berry, G. Shostack, and G. Upah (eds.), *Emerging perspectives on services marketing*, America Marketing Association, Chicago, IL, 59-62.

Snyder, D.R. (1991). Demographic correlates to loyalty in frequently purchased consumer services, *Journal of Professional Services Marketing*, 8 (1), 45-55.

Spector, P.E. (1985). Measurement of human service staff satisfaction: Development of the Job satisfaction survey, *American Journal of Community Psychology*, 13 (6), 693-713.

Spreng, R.A. and R.D.Mckoy (1996). An empirical examination of a model of perceived service quality and satisfaction, *Journal of Retailing*, 72 (2), 201-214.

Spreng, R.A. and R.W. Olshavsky (1992). A desires-as-standard model of customer satisfaction: Implications for measuring satisfaction, *Journal of Satisfaction, Dissatisfaction and Complaining Behavior*, 5, 53-63.

Sproles, G.B. and E.L. Kendall (1986). A methodology for profiling consumers' decision-making styles, *Journal of Consumer Affairs*, 20 (2), 267-279.

Spyridakos, A., Y. Siskos, D. Yannakopoulos, and A. Skouris (2000). Multicriteria job evaluation for large organisations, *European Journal of Operational Research*, 130 (2), 375-387.

Srinivasan, V. and A.D. Shocker (1973). Linear programming techniques for multidimensional analysis of preferences, *Psychometrika*, 38 (3), 337-396.

Steers, R.M. (1977). Antecedents and outcomes of organizational commitment, *Administrative Science Quarterly*, 22 (1), 46-56.

Stephen, G. and A. Weimerskirch (1994). *Total quality management: Strategies and techniques proven at today's most successful companies*, Wiley, New York.

Sterne, J. (1996). *Customer service on the Internet*, John Wiley and Sons, New York.

Sterne, J. (1998). The World Wide Web was made for customer service, in: R. Zemke and J.A. Woods (eds.), *Best practices in customer service*, Amacom, New York, 297-304.

Stevens, S.S. (1951). Mathematics, measurement, and psychophysics, in: S.S. Stevens (ed.), *Handbook of experimental psychology*, John Wiley, New York, 1-49.

Stewart, M. (1995). *Keep the right customers*, McGraw Hill, New York.

Stum, D.L. and A. Thiry (1991). Building customer loyalty, *Training and Development Journal*, 45 (4), 34-36.

Swan, J.E. and L.J. Combs (1976). Product performance and consumer satisfaction: A new concept, *Journal of Marketing*, 40 (2), 25-33.

Sweeney, J.C., G.N. Soutar, and L.W. Johnson (1997). Retail service quality and perceived value, *Journal of Consumer Services*, 4 (1), 39-48.

Taber, T.D. and G.M. Allinger (1995). A task-level assessment of job satisfaction, *Journal of Organizational Behavior*, 16 (2), 101-121.

Tan, K.C. and T.A. Pawitra (2001). Integrating SERVQUAL and Kano's model into QFD for service excellence development, *Managing Service Quality*, 11 (6), 418-430.

Tarpey, L.X. (1974). A brand loyalty concept: A comment, *Journal of Marketing Research*, 11 (2), 214-217.

Tarpey, L.X. (1975). Brand loyalty revisited: A commentary, *Journal of Marketing Research*, 12 (4), 488-491.

Taylor, S.T. and R. Bogdan (1975). *Introduction to qualitative research: A phenomenological approach to the social sciences*, Wiley, New York.

Teas, R.K. (1993). Expectations, performance evaluation and consumers' perceptions of quality, *Journal of Marketing*, 57 (4), 18-34.

Tellis, G.J. (1988). Advertising exposure, loyalty, and brand purchase: A two-stage model of choice, *Journal of Marketing Research*, 25 (2), 134-144.

Theil, H. (1969). A multinomial extension of the linear logit model, *International Economics Review*, 10 (3), 251-259.

Ting, H.M. (1971). Aggregation of attributes for multiattributed utility assessment, Technical Report, 66, Operations Research Center, MIT, Cambridge, MA.

Tompkins, N.C. (1992). Employee satisfaction leads to customer service, *Human Resources Magazine*, 37 (11), 93-99.

Tornow, W.W. and J.W. Wiley (1991). Service quality and management practices: a look at employee attitudes, customer satisfaction, and bottom-line consequences, *Human Resource Planning*, 14 (2), 105-115.

Tranberg, H. and F. Hansen (1986). Patterns of brand loyalty: Their determinants and their role for leading brands, *European Journal of Marketing*, 20 (3), 81-109.

Tse, D.K. and P.C. Wilton (1988). Models of consumer satisfaction: An extension, *Journal of Marketing Research*, 25 (2), 204-212.

Urban, G. and J. Hauser (1980). *Design and marketing of new products*, Prentice-Hall, Englewood Cliffs, NJ.

Van de Panne, C. (1975). *Methods for linear and quadratic programming*, North-Holland Publishing Company, Amsterdam.

Van Raaij, W.F. (1989). Economic news, expectations, and macro-economic behavior, *Journal of Economic Psychology*, 10 (4), 473-493.

Van Saane, N., J.K. Sluiter, J.H. Verbeek, and M.H.W. Frings-Dresen (2003). Reliability and validity of instruments measuring job satisfaction: A systematic review, *Occupational Medicine*, 53 (3), 191-200.

Vandermerwe, S. (1996). Becoming a customer «owing» corporation, *Long Range Planning*, 23 (6), 770-782.

Vanderpooten, D. (1989). The construction of prescription in outranking methods, in: C. Bana e Costa, (ed.), *Readings on multiple criteria decision aid*, Springer, Berlin, 184-215.

Vavra, T.G. (1995). *Aftermarketing; How to keep customers for life through relationship marketing*, Irwin Professional Publishing, Burr Ridge, IL.

Vavra, T.G. (1997). *Improving your measurement of customer satisfaction: A guide to creating, conducting, analyzing, and reporting customer satisfaction measurement programs*, ASQC Quality Press, Milwaukee.

Vavra, T.G. (2002). *Customer satisfaction measurement simplified: A step-by-step guide for ISO 9001:2000 certification*, ASQ Quality Press, Milwaukee.

Vincke, P. (1992). *Multicriteria decision-aid*, Wiley, West Sussex.

Vinson, D.E., J E. Scott, and L. M. Lamont (1977). The role of personal values in marketing and consumer behavior, *Journal of Marketing*, 41 (2), 44-50.

Vokurka, R., G.L. Stading, and J.A. Brazeal (2000). Comparative analysis of national and regional quality awards, *Quality Progress*, 33 (8), 41-49.

Vollmer, H.M. and J.A. Kinney (1955). Age, education and job satisfaction, *Personnel*, 32 (1), 38-44.

von Neumann, J. and O. Morgenstern (1947). *Theory of games and economic behavior*, Princeton University Press, Princeton.

Von Winterfeldt, E. and W. Edwards (1993). *Decision analysis and behavioral research*, Cambridge University Press, Cambridge.

Vroom, V.H. (1964). *Work and motivation*, Wiley and Sons, New York.

Watson, G.H. (2003). Customer focus and competitiveness, in: K.S. Stephens (ed.), *Six sigma and related studies in the quality disciplines*, ASQ Quality Press, Milwaukee, WI.

Weaver, C.N. (1978). Job satisfaction as a component of happiness among males and females, *Personnel Psychology*, 31 (4), 831-840.

Webb, E.J., D.T. Campbell, R.D. Schwartz, L. Sechrest, and J. Belew (1981). *Nonreactive measures in the social sciences*, Houghton Mifflin, Boston MA.

Weiss, D.J., R.V. Dawis, G.W. England, and L.H. Lofquist (1967). Manual for the Minnesota satisfaction questionnaire, *Minnesota Studies in Vocational Rehabilitation*, 22, University of Minnesota, Minneapolis

Weller, S.C. and A.K. Romney (1990). *Metric scaling*, Sage Publications, Beverly Hills, CA.

Wernefelt, B. (1991). Brand loyalty and market equilibrium, *Marketing Science*, 10 (3), 229-245.

Westbrook, R.A. and M.D. Reilly (1983). Value-percept disparity: An alternative to the disconfirmation of expectations theory of customer satisfaction, in: R.P. Bagozzi and A.M. Tybout (eds.), *Advances in consumer research*, Association for Consumer Research, Ann Arbor, MI, 256-261.

Wetzel, R. (2001). Fifth annual interactive week ISP customer satisfaction survey, Ziff Davis media (http://common.ziffdavisinternet.com/download/0/1212/ isp_attributes.pdf).

Wickens, T.D. (1989). *Multiway contingency tables analysis for the social sciences*, Lawrence, Erlbaum Associates Publishers, Hillsdale, NJ.

Wierzbicki A.P. (1992). Multi-objective modeling and simulation for decision support, *Working Paper of the International Institute for Applied Systems Analysis*, WP92-80, International Institute for Applied Systems Analysis, Laxemburg, Austria.

Wild, R. (1980). *Operations management: A policy framework*, Pergamon Press, New York.

Wilk, M.B. and R. Gnanadesikan (1968). Probability plotting methods for the analysis of data, *Biometrica*, 55 (1), 1-17.

Wilkie, W. and E.A. Pessemier (1973). Issues in marketing's use of multiattribute attitude models, *Journal of Marketing Research*, 10 (4), 428-441.

Winnie, Y.-L.W. and G.K. Kanji (2001). Measure customer satisfaction: Evidence from Hong Kong retail banding industry, *Total Quality Management*, 12 (7-8), 332-346.

Witell, L. and M. Löfgren (2007). Classification of quality attributes, *Managing Service Quality*, 17 (1), 54-73.

Wittink, D. and L. Bayer (1994). The measurement imperative, *Marketing Research*, 6 (2), 14-22.

Woodruff, R.B., D.S. Clemons, D.W. Schuman, S.F. Gardial, and M.J. Burns (1991). The standards issue in customer satisfaction/dissatisfaction research: A historical perspective, *Journal of Satisfaction, Dissatisfaction and Complaining Behavior*, 4, 173-185.

Woodruff, R.B., D.W. Schumann, and S.F. Gardial (1993). Understanding value and satisfaction from the customer's point of view, *Survey of Business*, 29 (1), 33-40.

Woodruff, R.B. and S.F. Gardial (1996). *Know your customer: New approaches to understanding customer value and satisfaction*, Blackwell Publishers, Oxford.

Xanthidis, D. and D. Nicholas (2004). Evaluating Internet usage and E-commerce growth in Greece, *Aslib Proceedings: New Information Perspectives*, 56 (6), 356-366.

Yanovsky, M. (1998). Customer-sensitive automated response systems, in: R. Zemke and J.A. Woods (eds.), *Best practices in customer service*, Amacom, New York, 194-202.

Yi, Y. (1991). A critical review of consumer satisfaction, in: V.A. Zeithaml (ed.), *Review of marketing 1989*, American Marketing Association: Chicago, IL, 68-123.

Yntema, D.B. and W.S. Torgerson (1961). Man-computer cooperation in decisions requiring common sense, *IRE Transactions on Human Factors in Electronics*, HFE-2, 20-26.

Zeithaml, V.A., A. Parasuraman, and L.L. Berry (1990). *Delivering quality services*, The Free Press, New York

Zeleny, M. (1974). *Linear multiobjective programming*, Springer, New York.

Zeleny, M. (1982). *Multiple criteria decision making*, McGraw-Hill, New York.

Zifko-Baliga, G.M. (1998). What customers really want: How that affects what service to deliver in customer service, in: R. Zemke and J.A. Woods (eds.), *Best practices in customer service*, Amacom, New York, 318-327.

Zionts, S. and J. Wallenius (1976). An interactive programming method for solving the multiple criteria problem, *Management Science*, 22 (6), 652-663.

Zionts, S. and J. Wallenius (1983). An interactive multiple objective linear programming method for a class of underlying nonlinear utility functions, *Management Science*, 29 (5), 512-529.

Zopounidis, C. (1987). A multicriteria decision-making methodology for the evaluation of the risk of failure and an application, *Foundations of Control Engineering*, 12 (1), 45-67.

Zopounidis, C., N.F. Matsatsinis, and M. Doumpos (1996). Developing a multicriteria knowledge-based decision support system for the assessment of corporate performance and viability: The FINEVA system, *Fuzzy Economic Review*, 1 (2), 35-53.

Zopounidis, C. and M. Doumpos (1998). Developing a multicriteria decision support system for financial classification problems: The FINCLAS system, *Optimization Methods and Software*, 8 (3-4), 277-304.

Zopounidis, C. and M. Doumpos (1999). Business failure prediction using UTADIS multicriteria analysis, *Journal of the Operational Research Society*, 50 (11), 1138-1148.

Zopounidis, C., M. Doumpos, and S.H. Zanakis (1999). Stock evaluation using a preference disaggregation methodology, *Decision Sciences*, 30 (2), 313-336.

Zopounidis, C. and Doumpos M. (2001). A preference disaggregation decision support system for financial classification problems. *European Journal of Operation Research*, 130 (2), 402-413.

Index

Breinigsville, PA USA
03 March 2010
233496BV00007B/32/P